SpringBoard®
English
Language Arts

STUDENT EDITION   GRADE 7

About The College Board

The College Board is a mission-driven not-for-profit organization that connects students to college success and opportunity. Founded in 1900, the College Board was created to expand access to higher education. Today, the membership association is made up of over 6,000 of the world's leading educational institutions and is dedicated to promoting excellence and equity in education. Each year, the College Board helps more than seven million students prepare for a successful transition to college through programs and services in college readiness and college success—including the SAT® and the Advanced Placement Program®. The organization also serves the education community through research and advocacy on behalf of students, educators, and schools. For further information, visit collegeboard.org.

ISBN: 978-1-4573-1293-9

5 6 7 8   23 24 25 26
Printed in the United States of America

Acknowledgements

The College Board gratefully acknowledges the outstanding work of the classroom teachers who have been integral to the development of this program. The end product is testimony to their expertise, understanding of student learning needs, and dedication to rigorous and accessible English Language Arts instruction.

Lance Balla
Everett School District
Everett, Washington

Christina Bartholet
Goodman Middle
School, Gig Harbor,
Washington

Carisa Barnes
San Diego Unified
School District
San Diego, California

Leia Bell
Hillsborough County
Public Schools
Tampa, Florida

Alysa Broussard
Lafayette Parish
School System
Lafayette, Louisiana

Robert J. Caughey
San Dieguito Union
High School District
San Diego, California

Susie Challancin
Bellevue School District 405
Bellevue, Washington

Amanda Connell
Lisle, Illinois

Paul De Maret
Poudre School District
Fort Collins, Colorado

Michael Gragert
Plano Independent
School District
Plano, Texas

Nancy Gray
Brevard County Schools
Viera, Florida

Charles F. Hall
Peninsula School District
Gig Harbor, Washington

Charise Hallberg
Bellevue School District 405
Bellevue, Washington

T.J. Hanify
Bellevue School District 405
Bellevue, Washington

Cheryl Harris
Hurst-Euless-Bedford
Independent School District
Bedford, Texas

Karen Kampschmidt
Fort Thomas Independent
School District
Fort Thomas, Kentucky

Kerstin Karlsoon
Hillsborough County
Public Schools
Tampa, Florida

LeAnn Klepzig
Bradley County Schools
Cleveland, Tennessee

Michelle Lewis
Spokane Public School
Spokane, Washington

Susie Lowry
Volusia County
School District
Deland, Florida

John Marshall
Mead School District
Mead, Washington

Kristie Messer
Burnet Consolidated
Independent School
District Burnet, Texas

Missy Miles
Carmel Christian School
Charlotte, North Carolina

Glenn Morgan
San Diego Unified
School District
San Diego, California

Amanda Olinger
Harrisburg School District
Harrisburg, South Dakota

Kristin Oliver
Rio Rancho Public
School District
Rio Rancho, New Mexico

Molly Olmstead
Peninsula School District
Gig Harbor, Washington

Julie Pennabaker
Quakertown Community
School District
Quakertown, Pennsylvania

Bryan Sandala
School District of
Palm Beach County
West Palm Beach, Florida

Amanda Shackelford
Lafayette Parish
School System
Lafayette, Louisiana

Angela Shuttles
Hillsborough County Public
Schools Tampa, Florida

Kimberlyn Slagle
Lafayette Parish
School System
Lafayette, Louisiana

Holly Talley
Hillsborough County
Public Schools
Ruskin, Florida

Maria Torres-Crosby
Hillsborough County
Public Schools
Tampa, Florida

Susan Van Doren
Zephyr Cove, Nevada

JoEllen Victoreen
San Jose Unified
School District
San Jose, California

Aimee Welshans
San Diego Unified
School District
San Diego, California

Rebecca Wenrich
Peninsula School District
Gig Harbor, Washington

Research and Planning Advisors

We also wish to thank the members of our SpringBoard Advisory Council and the many educators who gave generously of their time and their ideas as we conducted research for both the print and online programs. Your suggestions and reactions to ideas helped immeasurably as we created this edition. We gratefully acknowledge the teachers and administrators in the following districts.

ABC Unified School District
Cerritos, California

Allen Independent School
District
Allen, Texas

Bellevue, School District 405
Bellevue, Washington

Burnet Consolidated
Independent School District
Burnet, Texas

Community Unit School
District 308
Oswego, Illinois

Fresno Unified
School District
Fresno, California

Frisco Independent
School District
Frisco, Texas

Garland Independent
School District
Garland, Texas

Grapevine-Colleyville
Independent School District
Grapevine, Texas

Hamilton County Schools
Chattanooga, Tennessee

Hesperia Unified
School District
Hesperia, California

Hillsborough County Public
Schools
Tampa, Florida

ICEF Public Schools
Los Angeles, California
IDEA Public Schools
Weslaco, Texas

Irving Independent
School District
Irving, Texas

Keller Independent
School District
Keller, Texas

KIPP Houston
Houston, Texas

Lafayette Parish Schools
Lafayette Parish, Louisiana

Los Angeles Unified
School District
Los Angeles, California

Lubbock Independent
School District
Lubbock, Texas

Mansfield Independent
School District
Mansfield, Texas

Midland Independent
School District
Midland, Texas

Milwaukee Public Schools
Milwaukee, Wisconsin

New Haven School District
New Haven, Connecticut

Ogden School District
Ogden, Utah

Rio Rancho Public Schools
Rio Rancho, New Mexico

San José Unified
School District
San José, California

Scottsdale Unified
School District
Scottsdale, Arizona

Spokane Public Schools
Spokane, Washington

Tacoma Public Schools
Tacoma, Washington

SpringBoard English Language Arts

Lori O'Dea
Executive Director
Content Development

Natasha Vasavada
Executive Director
Pre-AP & SpringBoard

Doug Waugh
Vice President
SpringBoard & Pre-AP
Programs

Sarah Balistreri
Senior Director
ELA Content Development

Florencia Duran Wald
Senior Director
ELA Content Development

Julie Manley
Senior Director
Professional Learning

Joely Negedly
Senior Director
Pre-AP Humanities

Jessica Brockman
Product Manager
English Language Arts

Suzie Doss
Director
SpringBoard Implementation

Jennifer Duva
Director
English Language Arts

Spencer Gonçalves
Director
Digital Content
Development

Rebecca Grudzina
Senior Editor
English Language Arts

Georgia Scurletis
Senior Instructional Writer
Pre-AP English Language
Arts

Abigail Johnson
Editor
English Language Arts

Casseia Lewis
Assistant Editor
English Language Arts

Natalie Hansford
Editorial Assistant
English Language Arts

Table of Contents

ACTIVITY **Unit 2: What Influences My Choices?**

ACTIVITY Unit 3: Choices and Consequences

Resources

Texts not included in these materials.

Introduction to SpringBoard English Language Arts

About SpringBoard ELA

SpringBoard was built around a simple belief: if you give students and teachers the best materials, engaging methods, and ongoing support, then student success will surely follow. Developed by teachers, SpringBoard brings your classroom to life with materials that help you practice the skills and learn the knowledge you need to excel in middle school, high school, and beyond. Read on to find out how SpringBoard will support your learning.

Instructional Materials

SpringBoard English Language Arts supplies a Student Edition and Teacher Edition, in print and digital form, for grades 6–12. In addition to using the English Language Arts curriculum, you can sharpen your reading, writing, and language skills with materials including Language Workshop, Close Reading Workshop, and Writing Workshop.

Design That Begins with the End in Mind

- Based on the Understanding by Design model, SpringBoard teaches the skills and knowledge that matter most to meet AP and college and career readiness standards.

- You will start each unit by unpacking the assessment, so you know where you're heading and why the skills you're developing matter.

- Each activity starts with clear, standards-aligned learning targets.

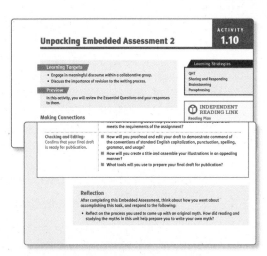

The Practice of Reading Closely

- SpringBoard puts a special focus on close reading, giving you strategies and structure for developing this key skill.

- You will encounter compelling texts—fiction, nonfiction, poetry, drama, visuals, and film.

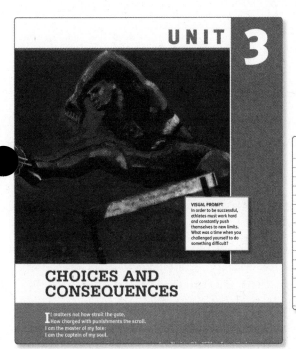

UNIT 3

CHOICES AND CONSEQUENCES

It matters not how strait the gate,
How charged with punishments the scroll.
I am the master of my fate:
I am the captain of my soul.

A Living System of Learning

- SpringBoard puts you and your classmates in charge of your learning to create a more dynamic classroom experience.

- With a flexible design and rich library of tools and resources, SpringBoard helps your teacher personalize instruction for your class.

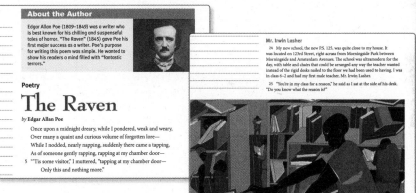

Bringing the Classroom to Life

When you enter a SpringBoard classroom you don't hear a teacher talking in the front of the room. You hear a buzz of excitement, with students working together and taking charge of how they learn. That's what the teachers who designed SpringBoard wanted for their classrooms, so they created a curriculum and materials that are focused on real classroom needs, encouraging teacher and student involvement.

SpringBoard translates the expectations of state standards into engaging daily lessons. We believe that reading, writing, speaking, and listening should all be learned together. You'll see examples of our integrated approach throughout our materials. And we put a special focus on close reading, giving you strategies and structure for developing this key skill.

Our Approach to Reading

In SpringBoard ELA, we move right into compelling texts—fiction, nonfiction, poetry, drama, visuals, and film—and offer the tools, supports, and approaches that will help you get the most out of every reading.

The Practice of Reading Closely

Texts take center stage in the SpringBoard ELA classroom, where you will prepare for close, critical reading of a wide range of materials. With guidance from your teacher, you will develop the habits of close reading that will serve you for a lifetime.

- **Setting a Purpose for Reading:** You ask questions, make predictions, observe genre characteristics and text structures, and prepare to annotate the text.

- **First Reading:** You read on your own, with a partner, in a group, or with the class. You annotate the text as you begin to uncover its meaning.

- **Making Observations:** Your teacher guides you to pause during or right after the first reading to observe the small details within a text in order to arrive at a deeper understanding of the whole.

- **Returning to the Text:** You continue to deepen your understanding of the text by responding to a series of text-dependent questions. You will use text evidence, speak with new vocabulary words, reflect on your classmates' ideas, and make connections among texts, ideas, and experiences.

- **Working from the Text:** You use the text as a source as you move from reading and analysis to productive work, including academic discussion and writing.

Reading Independently

As a SpringBoard student, you'll practice good reading habits in class so that you can read challenging texts in other classes and on your own. Independent reading is an integral part of every SpringBoard English Language Arts unit. At the beginning of the year, you will learn how to make a plan for independent reading. **Independent Reading Lists** for each unit give you a jump-start on selecting texts by offering a list of suggested titles, including a number of Spanish-language titles, that connect to the themes, genres, and concepts of the SpringBoard unit.

While you work your way through each unit, you will respond to **Independent Reading Links** that lead you to make connections between the reading you're doing on your own and the skills and knowledge you're developing in class. Twice per unit, **Independent Reading Checkpoints** give you a chance to reflect on and synthesize your independent reading in an informal writing assignment or discussion.

Reading to Build Knowledge

SpringBoard units are designed so that you can delve deeply into an overarching topic, theme, or idea. Each unit will pose essential questions that relate to the ideas and texts within the unit, and you will return to these questions again and again, each time refining your responses with new understanding and new evidence to support your point of view. You will also deepen your knowledge of key topics by conducting both on-the-spot and extended research, asking and answering questions, evaluating multiple sources, and synthesizing your findings.

Twice a unit you will go on a **Knowledge Quest**. Each Knowledge Quest begins with a Knowledge Question and supporting questions to focus your reading. After reading several texts that explore a topic, theme, or idea, you will get to return to the Knowledge Question and show your growing understanding of the topic by responding to a writing prompt or engaging in a discussion.

At the end of a Knowledge Quest, you will be encouraged to continue building your knowledge of the topic by going to **Zinc Reading Labs** and finding related texts to read. Zinc Reading Labs offers a variety of informational and literary texts that you can choose based on your interests. Vocabulary sets for each text let you learn new words and practice using them.

Your independent reading can also enhance your understanding of the topics you are studying in class if you want it to. SpringBoard's **Independent Reading Lists** include suggested books that relate to the topics and themes from each unit. By choosing those books you can see a different side of the topic, learn new words, and find other topics you want to learn more about.

Reading to Gain Perspectives

Gaining Perspectives features use a text as a jumping off point for examining an issue relevant to you. You will be asked to consider the perspectives of others and to empathize with others who have different points of view. You will also be asked to think about social and ethical norms and to recognize the family, school, and community resources available to you. Each Gaining Perspectives feature concludes with a writing task in which you will summarize the discussion you have with your classmates.

Our Approach to Writing

SpringBoard English Language Arts provides you with the support you need to write in all the major modes, emphasizing argumentative, informational, and narrative. You will write often, and you will learn to become a critical reviewer of your own and your peers' work through frequent opportunities for revision and editing. You will learn to plan with purpose, audience, topic, and context in mind; develop drafts with engaging ideas, examples, facts and commentary; revise for clarity, development, organization, style, and diction; and edit using the conventions of the English language.

The Craft of Writing

As you read texts by skilled authors, you will observe the many choices those authors make. You'll tune in to the ways authors purposefully use words, sentences, and structures to convey meaning. After analyzing and critiquing others' work, you will learn to apply your understanding of author's craft to your own writing. A few SpringBoard features help you do just that:

- **Writing prompts** lead up to the Embedded Assessments and give you practice with writing texts in multiple genres, including personal narratives, argumentative essays, letters, research papers, and more. Writing to Sources writing prompts drive you back to texts you have read or viewed to mine for evidence.

- **Focus on the Sentence** tasks help you process content while also practicing the craft of writing powerful sentences.

- **Grammar & Usage** features highlight interesting grammar or usage concepts that appear in a text, both to improve your reading comprehension and to help you attend to these concepts as you craft your own texts.

- **Language & Writer's Craft** features address topics in writing such as style, word choice, and sentence construction.

- **Language Checkpoints** offer in-depth practice with standard English conventions and guide you to develop an editor's checklist to use as a reference each time you check your own or a peer's written work.

Modes of Writing

SpringBoard helps you become a better academic writer by giving you authentic prompts that require you to use sources, and showing you how to work through the writing process. Over the course of the year you will have the chance to write narratives, arguments, and informational texts, and you will develop a wide range of writing skills:

- Consider task, audience, and purpose when structuring and organizing your writing.

- Incorporate details, reasons, and textual evidence to support your ideas.

- Generate research questions, evaluate sources, gather relevant evidence, and report and cite your findings accurately.

- Use research-based strategies that will guide you through the writing process.

Writing with a Focus on the Sentence

SpringBoard English Language Arts leverages sentence writing strategies that were developed by The Writing Revolution. These evidence-based strategies are part of the Hochman Method, the Writing Revolution's system for helping students learn to write across all content areas and grades. The Writing Revolution emphasizes the importance of embedding writing and grammar instruction into content. That's why SpringBoard's **Focus on the Sentence** tasks integrate sentence-level writing into the curriculum. These tasks not only help you learn and practice important grammar concepts and sentence forms, but they also provide a chance for you to process and demonstrate your understanding of texts, images, class discussions, and other content.

Our Approach to Vocabulary

Vocabulary is threaded throughout each unit and developed over the course of the SpringBoard English Language Arts year. You will have ample opportunities to read and hear new words, explore their meanings, origins, and connotations, and use them in written and oral responses.

- Important academic and literary terms that you will need to actively participate in classroom discussions are called out in your book.

- Challenging vocabulary terms found in reading passages are glossed at the point of use.

- Periodic Word Connections boxes guide you through the process of exploring a word with multiple meanings and nuances, an interesting etymology, a telling root or affix, a helpful Spanish cognate, a relationship to another word, or a connection to another content area.

Zinc Reading Labs

Zinc Reading Labs combines the best features of a typical vocabulary program with those of a typical reading program and makes reading and learning new words a game. Zinc offers a variety of nonfiction and fiction texts that you can choose from based on individual needs and interest. Each article has a corresponding vocabulary set that pre-teaches challenging words through spaced repetition, to help you genuinely learn and internalize the vocabulary. Additional vocabulary games focus on SAT/ACT power words and foundational words for English language learners.

Pre-AP Connections

SpringBoard shares Pre-AP's core principles and encourages you to build skills that you will use in high school and beyond. These principles are evident in every SpringBoard activity.

Close Observation and Analysis
... to notice and consider

When reading, your teacher will guide you to pause to make observations and notice details in the text before analyzing or explaining. Only after you have noticed and enjoyed elements of the text do you then return to the text for deeper analysis and inferential thinking. This close reading sequence helps you interact and engage with the text in increasingly meaningful ways.

Evidence-Based Writing
... with a focus on the sentence

SpringBoard challenges you to write increasingly complex, sophisticated, and precise sentences over the course of the year through regular practice with sentence-level writing. Instead of being isolated from reading, sentence-level grammar and writing exercises are integrated into the curriculum to enhance your comprehension and your ability to compose a variety of texts.

Higher-Order Questioning
... to spark productive lingering

Each unit opens with two essential questions that relate to the topics, themes, and texts within that unit. You return to these questions throughout the unit and refine your answers as new evidence is presented. SpringBoard also encourages you to craft your own questions, and to dig deeply into the texts you read. After each reading passage, you evaluate the meaning of the text and examine the choices that the author made when writing it.

Academic Conversations
... to support peer-to-peer dialogue

SpringBoard classrooms are places where students like you engage in collaborative learning. You will participate in discussion groups, writing groups, debates, Socratic seminars, literature circles, and oral interpretations and performances. These activities create an environment where you can share, compare, critique, debate, and build on others' ideas to advance your learning.

PSAT/SAT Connections

We want students to be rewarded for the hard work you do in your English Language Arts courses, including when you sit down to take important assessments. Therefore, SpringBoard English Language Arts focuses on the same essential knowledge and skills that are the center of the Evidence-Based Reading and Writing sections of the SAT Suite of Assessments (SAT, PSAT/NMSQT, PSAT™ 10, and PSAT™ 8/9). To be sure of our alignment, we conducted a research study, the results of which showed strong to exemplary alignment between the SpringBoard ELA courses and the corresponding SAT Suite tests. This means that you are getting ready for the SAT, PSAT/NMSQT, PSAT™ 10, and PSAT™ 8/9 in the classroom every day.

Tools and Supports

SpringBoard Digital

SpringBoard puts you in charge of what you learn and gives students and teachers the flexibility and support they need. SpringBoard Digital is an interactive program that provides always-available online content that's accessible from any device—desktop computer, laptop, tablet, or interactive whiteboard. The student edition allows you to interact with the text, respond to prompts, take assessments, and engage with a suite of tools, all in the digital space. Teachers get access to a correlations viewer that embeds correlations at point of use, a lesson planner, progress reports, grading, messaging, and more.

Zinc Reading Labs

All SpringBoard users have access to Zinc Reading Labs, where you can find a huge library of reading material chosen specifically to align with the SpringBoard English Language Arts curriculum.

Zinc offers:

- Fresh and engaging nonfiction and fiction content for independent reading.
- Interactive games, quizzes, and tasks that build skills and confidence.
- Freedom of choice: Zinc's massive and ever-growing library means that all students should find texts they want to read.

Turnitin Revision Assistant

When you develop drafts of an available Embedded Assessment through SpringBoard Digital, you can use a tool called Turnitin Revision Assistant. This online tool gives instant feedback to students as they write so they can polish their drafts and practice their revision skills. The feedback model Revision Assistant uses is based on scoring by SpringBoard teachers, and it's trained to assess the same rubric areas that they assess.

Revision Assistant offers:

- A template to help you create an outline.
- Actionable, instant feedback in specific areas such as structure, use of language, and ideas.
- Identification of strengths and weakness in your writing.

A Letter to the Student

Dear Student,

Welcome to the SpringBoard program! We created this program with you in mind: it puts you and your classmates at the center of your learning and equips you with the skills and knowledge you need to excel in middle school, high school, and beyond.

The energy and excitement you bring to class helps you and your classmates learn. You will explore compelling themes through readings, classroom discussions, and projects. You will dive into fascinating texts—some of which you'll choose on your own—from different genres including myths, poems, biographies, plays, and films. You will engage in lively discussions, debates, and performances so that you become confident sharing and presenting your ideas. You will write frequently to sharpen your ability to craft effective sentences, paragraphs, and longer texts. And you'll start each unit with a clear understanding of where you're headed by unpacking the skills and knowledge you'll need to do well on the assessment at the end.

SpringBoard helps you make connections between the concepts you're reading and writing about in class and the real world. Instead of just memorizing how to do things, you'll draw on your own and your classmates' experiences and knowledge to come to new and deeper understandings. When questions arise from the materials you're studying in class, you'll learn how to do both quick and longer-term research to find answers. Plus, you'll have access to tools and resources that are built right into the program, including powerful learning strategies, independent reading lists to help you select texts to read outside of class, and digital tools that you can access any time from any device—desktop computer, laptop, or tablet.

We want students to be rewarded for the hard work they do in their English Language Arts course. That's why the SpringBoard program focuses on the essential knowledge and skills that will prepare you for the challenging work you'll do in your high school classes, in AP courses, and in college.

Students from around the country are talking about how much they like the SpringBoard approach to learning. We hope you enjoy learning with SpringBoard, too.

Sincerely,

The SpringBoard Team

VISUAL PROMPT
What story does this picture tell? Does the image remind you of any situations you have experienced in your own life?

THE CHOICES WE MAKE

Reading a book was not so much like entering a different world—it was like discovering a different language. It was a language clearer than the one I spoke, and clearer than the one I heard around me. What the books said was ... interesting, but the idea that I could enter this world at any time I chose was even more attractive.

—from *Bad Boy* by Walter Dean Myers

The Choices We Make

GOALS

- To use knowledge of genre characteristics and structures to analyze texts
- To examine plot elements in narrative writing
- To apply techniques that create coherence and sentence variety in writing
- To revise and edit drafts before publishing written works

VOCABULARY

ACADEMIC
effect
coherence
internal coherence
external coherence

LITERARY
genre
denotation
connotation
figurative language
narrative
sensory details
folklore
myths
symbol

ACTIVITY	CONTENTS	

My Independent Reading List

Learning Strategies

QHT
Collaborative Groups
Paraphrasing
Marking the Text
Graphic Organizer

My Notes

Learning Targets

- Preview the big ideas and vocabulary for the unit.
- Identify and summarize the knowledge and skills necessary to complete Embedded Assessment 1 successfully.

Preview

In this activity, you will look ahead at the Embedded Assessment coming up in this unit. You will get ready to learn the elements of a narrative.

Making Connections

In this unit, you will learn about personal narratives and write and revise one of your own. By the end of the unit, after studying myths and fables, you will also write and illustrate a myth.

Essential Questions

Based on your current knowledge, how would you answer these questions?

1. How do authors use narrative elements to create a story?
2. What are the elements of effective revision?

Developing Vocabulary

Look again at the Contents page and use a QHT strategy to analyze and evaluate your knowledge of the Academic and Literary Vocabulary for the unit. Think about how well you know each term and then label each word with a letter:

Q: words you have questions about

H: words you've heard before, but aren't sure about the meaning

T: words you could teach

Use print or digital resources to learn more about the terms you sorted into the "Q" and "H" columns. Keep in mind that there is more to knowing a new word than just learning the definition. Truly knowing a word also involves an understanding of its syllabication, pronunciation, word origin, and part of speech.

Unpacking Embedded Assessment 1

Read the assignment for Embedded Assessment 1: Revising a Personal Narrative about Choice.

 Your assignment is to revise the personal narrative with reflection that you previously drafted. Use the revision techniques you have learned in this unit, including meeting in a Writing Group, to improve the beginning, middle, and end of your narrative. You will also write a text explaining the revisions you made to improve your first draft and the effect of the changes on the final piece.

Paraphrase what you will need to know to complete this Embedded Assessment successfully. With your class, create a graphic organizer as a visual reminder of the required skills and tasks.

Exploring the Concept of Choice

Learning Targets

- Paraphrase and analyze quotes related to choices.
- Select a text for your Independent Reading Plan based on texts you have read in the past and prepare a portfolio for your writing throughout the unit.

Preview

In this activity, you will think about the choices you make as a reader and writer, and you will choose a new text to read for your Independent Reading Plan.

Paraphrasing Ideas

1. In the graphic organizer that follows, paraphrase each quote in the first column and write a personal response to the quote in the second column. Remember that to paraphrase means to put information in your own words while maintaining the original meaning of the text.

Read and Paraphrase What is the author saying?	Personal Response To what extent do you agree or disagree with what the author is saying about choice?
"The ultimate measure of a man is not where he stands in moments of comfort and convenience, but where he stands at times of challenge and controversy." –Dr. Martin Luther King Jr., American civil rights leader (1929–1968), from *Strength to Love*	
"While we are free to choose our actions, we are not free to choose the consequences of those actions." –Stephen Covey, American entrepreneur and author (1932–2012), from *The Seven Habits of Highly Effective People*	
"I believe that every single event in life happens in an opportunity to choose love over fear." –Oprah Winfrey, American TV host and entrepreneur (1954–present)	
"We've all got both light and dark inside us. What matters is the part we choose to act on. That's who we really are." –J. K. Rowling, British writer (1965–present), from *Harry Potter and the Order of the Phoenix*	

LITERARY

A literary **genre** is the category or class to which a literary work belongs; poetry, mythology, mysteries, and science fiction are all examples of literary genres. Texts from a particular genre often share common characteristics.

My Notes

Your Choices as a Reader

One choice that you will make is what you will read in your own time. Respond to the following questions in your Reader/Writer Notebook.

2. What have you enjoyed reading in the past? What is your favorite type of text? Who is your favorite author?

3. What is your favorite **genre**? What do you enjoy about texts from that genre?

Select a book to preview.

- What type of visual do you see on the front and back cover?
- What types of fonts and colors are used?
- What do these elements tell you about the book?

Read the first few pages.

- Does this seem interesting?
- Does the text make sense so far?
- Does this seem too hard, too easy, or just right?

🎁 Planning Independent Reading

The first half of this unit will focus on personal narratives. To deepen your understanding of how authors tell personal stories, choose a memoir, biography, or autobiography to read and respond to during this unit. Use the process that was just described to select a book that looks interesting to you and seems manageable. As you read, try to think like a writer; notice the way the author tells his or her own story (in a memoir or autobiography) or the story of the subject (in a biography). Use your Reader/ Writer Notebook to create a reading plan and respond to any questions, comments, or reactions you have to your reading. You can also jot notes in your Independent Reading Log. Refer to those notes as you participate in book discussions with your classmates about how the choices the characters made helped shape the book's theme.

4. Create an independent reading plan for the text you have chosen.

- I have chosen to read _____ by _____

  because _____.

- I will create time to read by _____.

- I should finish this text by _____.

Your Choices as a Writer

5. What types (genres) of texts do you enjoy writing the most?

6. What audience do you enjoy writing for the most? Do you like to compose assignments for school, write things to share with a friend, or create things that you keep to yourself? How do you select a genre that is appropriate for that audience?

7. What sources do you draw from when you plan your writing? When do you use discussions, additional reading, or your own personal interests to guide your choices?

8. Examine the chart that follows.

- In your Reader/Writer Notebook, paraphrase the information in the writing process visual. As you paraphrase, be sure to keep the steps in logical order.
- Which part(s) of the writing process are familiar to you?
- Which part(s) of the writing process are least familiar to you?

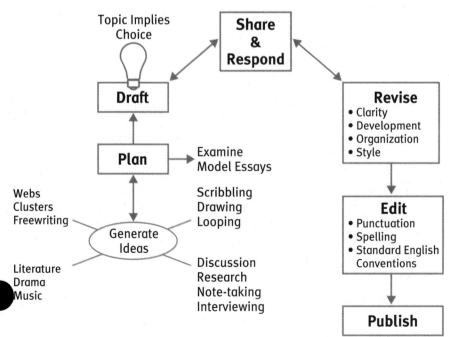

Writing as a Process

My Notes

Sentence Types

9. Different types of sentences can be used for different purposes. Review these four sentence types before completing the Focus on the Sentence that follows.

   A statement tells someone information. A question asks others for a response and ends with a question mark. An exclamation expresses emotion and typically ends with an exclamation point. A command tells another person to do something. A command may not have a stated subject, because it is understood that the subject is the person that you are speaking to. Read these sample sentences about reading:

Statement: It is important to choose books that are manageable.

Question: What genre of books do you like to read?

Exclamation: Shel Silverstein is my favorite poet!

Command: Read for at least 20 minutes a day.

☑ Focus on the Sentence

Write four different sentences about the writing process, each using a different sentence type.

Statement: _____

_____

Question: _____

_____

Exclamation: _____

_____

Command: _____

_____

Preparing Your Portfolio

Your portfolio will be a place for you to collect, review, and revise the work you do during each unit. Create a **portfolio cover** that reflects your brainstorming about choice, the quotes, your response to the quotes, and your thinking, planning, and goal setting as a reader and writer. Creatively express your ideas. The largest thing on your cover should be the word "Choice."

Exploring Your Choices In your Reader/Writer Notebook, create a web titled "My Choices" to brainstorm the choices you have faced and decisions you have made in your life. Think about large and small choices from the past and in the present.

You will return to this web throughout the unit.

Add these ideas to the second section of your portfolio cover. Use words, phrases, or pictures and then label this section "personal choices."

Choices and Consequences:
Paired Poetry

Learning Targets

- Evaluate details in two poems to understand the choices presented and to infer the poems' themes.
- Analyze the effect of poetic conventions, including figurative language, on the mood and tone of two poems.
- Integrate ideas from multiple texts to build knowledge and vocabulary about choices and how they impact our lives.

Preview

In this activity, you will read and compare two poems and an infographic about choices, analyzing how each writer approaches the topic.

Setting a Purpose for Reading

- While you read the poems, use details to help you create a mental image of the sights, sounds, and smells that each narrator describes. Put an asterisk next to any lines that create a vivid image in your mind.
- Circle unknown words and phrases. Try to determine the meaning of the words by using context clues, word parts, or a dictionary.

About the Author

Robert Frost (1874–1963) was one of America's most popular 20th-century poets. For much of his life, he lived on a farm in New Hampshire and wrote poems about farm life and the New England landscape. Frost's poems often appear simple at first, with plain language and traditional rhyme schemes. Upon closer reading, however, they reveal many layers of meaning.

Learning Strategies

Marking the Text
Close Reading
Graphic Organizer

WORD CONNECTIONS

Roots and Affixes
The word *narrator* comes from the Latin word *narrare*, which means "to tell" or "to make known." The root *narr* appears in the English words narrate and narration.

My Notes

GRAMMAR & USAGE

Punctuation
Writers use punctuation in poetry to cluster ideas and communicate meaning. As you read the two poems, look for specific examples of punctuation. Think about how and why the poets used the punctuation as they did.

KNOWLEDGE
QUEST

Knowledge Question:
How do our choices impact our lives?

In Activity 1.3, you will analyze two poems and one infographic about the nature of choices. While you read and build knowledge about the topic, think about your answer to the Knowledge Question.

My Notes

_____

hence: from now

Poetry

The Road Not Taken

by **Robert Frost**

Two roads diverged in a yellow wood,
And sorry I could not travel both
And be one traveler, long I stood
And looked down one as far as I could
5 To where it bent in the undergrowth;

Then took the other, as just as fair,
And having perhaps the better claim
Because it was grassy and wanted wear,
Though as for that the passing there
10 Had worn them really about the same,

And both that morning equally lay
In leaves no step had trodden black.
Oh, I marked the first for another day!
Yet knowing how way leads on to way
15 I doubted if I should ever come back.

I shall be telling this with a sigh
Somewhere ages and ages **hence**:
Two roads diverged in a wood, and I,
I took the one less traveled by,
20 And that has made all the difference.

About the Author

Nikki Giovanni (1943–) is a prominent American poet and writer. Her poetry deals with a wide variety of personal and political themes. In addition to her poetry, Giovanni has published works of nonfiction and children's literature. Her book *The Nikki Giovanni Poetry Collection* was nominated for a Grammy for best spoken-word album.

My Notes

Poetry

Choices

by **Nikki Giovanni**

> if i can't do
> what i want to do
> then my job is to not
> do what i don't want
> 5 to do
> it's not the same thing
> but it's the best i can
> do
>
> if i can't have
> 10 what i want ... then
> my job is to want
> what i've got
> and be satisfied
> that at least there
> 15 is something more
> to want
>
> since i can't go
> where i need
> to go ... then i must ... go
> 20 where the signs point
> though always understanding
> **parallel** movement
> isn't **lateral**
>
> when i can't express
> 25 what i really feel
> i practice feeling

KNOWLEDGE QUEST

Knowledge Question:
How do our choices impact our lives?

parallel: common
lateral: sideways

what i can express
and none of it is equal
i know
30 but that's why mankind
alone among the animals
learns to cry

⊘ Knowledge Quest

- What emotions do you feel after reading each poem?
- What kinds of choices are the narrators making?

Returning to the Text

- Return to the poems as you respond to the following questions. Use text evidence to support your responses.
- Write any additional questions you have about the poems in your Reader/Writer Notebook.

1. What is the choice that the narrator faces in "The Road Not Taken"? Which lines tell you about the factors he considers when making his choice?

   _____

   _____

   _____

2. KQ What does the narrator mean when he says the roads "diverged"? How does this word affect the poem's meaning?

   _____

   _____

   _____

3. In the poem "Choices," which lines indicate that the narrator lacks a real choice?

   _____

   _____

   _____

4. How does the narrator in "Choices" react to each of the things she can't do?

   _____

   _____

   _____

5. KQ How do choices impact the narrators' lives differently in "The Road Not Taken" and in "Choices"?

   _____

   _____

   _____

Working from the Text

6. An author's diction—choice of words—often has an **effect** on the reader. Words may carry a **denotation** and **connotation** as well as **figurative** meanings. Use the graphic organizer to compare and contrast the diction in the two poems and how they contribute to the poems' themes.

"The Road Not Taken"	"Choices"
Examples of connotation:	**Examples of connotation:**
Words and phrases with figurative meanings:	**Words and phrases with figurative meanings:**

7. Look at the words from the poems. Choose words with similar denotations and write them on the lines. Then tell whether the new word has a more positive or negative connotation than the one from the poem.

- trodden _____
- satisfied _____

Setting a Purpose for Reading

- Observe how images and text work together in an infographic to create meaning. Underline key words that tell what to do in each step.
- Circle unknown words and phrases. Try to determine the meaning of the words by using context clues, word parts, or a dictionary.

ACADEMIC

Effect and *effective* are words you will encounter often in academic courses. *Effect* is the way one thing influences or acts upon another. The adjective *effective* describes something that is successful in producing a desired or intended result.

LITERARY

A word's **denotation** is its exact, literal meaning. **Connotation** is the suggested or implied meaning or emotion associated with a word beyond its literal definition.

Figurative language is language used in an imaginative way to express ideas that are not literally true. It is used for effect, such as with personification, simile, metaphor, and hyperbole.

WORD CONNECTIONS

Cognates

A cognate is a word that has the same root meaning as a word in another language. The English word **consequences** comes from the Latin verb *consequi*, which means "following closely." It has the same meaning as a similar word in Spanish. Both the Spanish word *consecuencia* and the English word *consequence* mean "a result or an effect of an action."

Infographic

Decision-Making Made Easy

STEP 1

Get to Know Your Options

- Consider the consequences of each choice. What will happen?
- Consider the risks of each choice. Is it safe? Is it responsible?
- Consider the costs of each choice. Can I afford it? Is it worth it?

Choice 2
Choice 1

STEP 2

Gather Advice

- Talk to someone with experience. What was it like? What did you learn?
- Talk to someone you trust. What would they recommend? Why do you think so?
- Think it over with yourself. What do I want? Which would I prefer?

STEP 3

Make a Choice

- Pay attention to what happens. How does it work out? What will you do next?
- Learn from mistakes. What can you do differently next time? What could you do instead?
- Build on success. What went well? What did you learn?

Goal
Success
Challenges
Start

Knowledge Quest

- What are your first thoughts about this decision-making process?
- Which step of the decision-making process seems the most difficult?

Returning to the Text

- Return to the infographic as you respond to the following questions. Use text evidence to support your responses.
- Write any additional questions you have about the infographic in your Reader/Writer Notebook.

8. KQ What words in Step 1 help you determine the meaning of the word *consequences*?

_____

_____

_____

_____

9. What do the arrows represent in the infographic? How do you know?

_____

_____

_____

_____

10. KQ How does the infographic's approach to the impact of choices compare to the ideas found in the poems "The Road Not Taken" and "Choices"?

_____

_____

_____

_____

11. In Step 1 of the infographic, what is the connotation of the word *cost*? How does that connotation support the overall purpose of the infographic?

_____

_____

_____

_____

12. How could the speaker in "The Road Not Taken" have used the infographic to decide on which path to take? Do you think this would have changed the outcome described in the poem? Explain your response.

_____

_____

_____

_____

INDEPENDENT READING LINK

You can continue to build your knowledge about the impact that choices have on our lives by reading related fiction and poetry at ZINC Reading Labs.

Select the **fiction** and **poetry** filters and type keywords such as *decisions* or *consequences* in the **Search all ZINC articles** field.

 ZINC

 Knowledge Quest

Use your knowledge about the two poems and the infographic to discuss with a partner the impact that choices have on our lives. Be sure to:

- Explain your answer to your partner, be specific, and use as many details as possible.
- Ask for clarification by posing follow-up questions as needed when your partner explains his or her answer.

 Check Your Understanding

Select one word from each selection. In your Reader/Writer Notebook, explain the connotations and denotations of the words you chose. Do they have figurative meanings? What do each poet's word choices tell you about the poems' themes? How do the poets' word choices differ from those of the infographic writer?

 Writing to Sources: Informational Text

Think about the poems and your analysis of their speakers, word choices, and themes along with the infographic. Write a paragraph in which you explain the two narrators' reflections about choices and compare those reflections to the information presented in the infographic. Be sure to:

- Start your paragraph with a topic sentence that clearly communicates the controlling idea.
- Include quotations of words and lines from the poems and infographic that support your ideas about choices.

Choices and Consequences

Many choices have consequences. Go back to your "My Choices" web in your Reader/Writer Notebook and add the consequences for the choices you labeled. Some choices may have several consequences. Add just the most important ones that resulted from your choice.

Exploring the Personal Narrative

Learning Strategies

Activating Prior Knowledge
Graphic Organizer
Note-taking
Metacognitive Markers
Summarize

Learning Targets

- Analyze the use of text structures to effectively recount a personal narrative.
- Summarize a personal narrative by presenting the central incident, response, and reflection in the proper order.

Preview

In this activity, you will read "The Scholarship Jacket," a personal narrative by Marta Salinas. As you read, you will look for the structure and main idea and then write a summary of the story, using your own words.

Introducing the Genre

A personal **narrative** tells a story about something that happened in the writer's life. Unlike an autobiography, which tells about a person's entire life, a personal narrative focuses on a particular event or experience. Because the writer is telling about his or her own life, personal narratives are written with first-person pronouns, such as *I* and *my*. The genre shares many characteristics with short stories, such as setting, dialogue, and **sensory details**.

Introducing the Strategy: Metacognitive Markers

Metacognition refers to the thinking you do about your own learning. Using metacognitive markers involves marking the text with symbols to reflect the thinking you are doing as you read. After reading, you can scan the text and use your metacognitive markers to quickly find evidence when you are talking or writing about a text. Here are the markers:

? Use a question mark for questions you have about the text.

! Use an exclamation point for a reaction to what you are reading.

* Use an asterisk for a comment about the text.

_ Use an underline to identify a key idea or detail in the text.

Setting a Purpose for Reading

- As you read "The Scholarship Jacket," use metacognitive markers to interact with the text and to monitor your comprehension.
- Circle unknown words and phrases. Try to determine the meaning of the words by using context clues, word parts, or a dictionary.

About the Author

Marta Salinas (1949–) was born in Coalinga, California. Her father, like many in the area, worked on farms for low wages. Marta's childhood in Coalinga forms the setting for many of her stories.

VOCABULARY

LITERARY

A **narrative** tells a story or describes a sequence of events in an incident. A personal narrative, like "The Scholarship Jacket," typically describes an incident and includes a personal response to and reflection on the incident.

Authors sometimes use **sensory details**—descriptive words or phrases that appeal to the five senses of sight, hearing, touch, taste, and smell—to help their readers create a vivid mental image of the scenes or events in a story.

My Notes

WORD CONNECTIONS

Roots and Affixes

The word *reflection* comes from the Latin prefix *re-* ("back") and the root *flectere* ("to bend"), so it carries the meaning of "bending or turning back." When you reflect, you turn your thoughts back to think again about a subject.

My Notes

Personal Narrative

The Scholarship Jacket

by **Marta Salinas**

1   The small Texas school that I went to had a tradition carried out every year during the eighth-grade graduation: a beautiful gold and green jacket (the school colors) was awarded to the class valedictorian, the student who had maintained the highest grades for eight years. The **scholarship** jacket had a big gold S on the left front side and your name written in gold letters on the pocket.

2   My oldest sister, Rosie, had won the jacket a few years back, and I fully expected to also. I was fourteen and in the eighth grade. I had been a straight A student since the first grade and this last year had looked forward very much to owning that jacket. My father was a farm laborer who couldn't earn enough money to feed eight children, so when I was six I was given to my grandparents to raise. We couldn't participate in sports at school because there were registration fees, uniform costs, and trips out of town; so, even though our family was quite **agile** and athletic there would never be a school sports jacket for us. This one, the scholarship jacket, was our only chance.

3   In May, close to graduation, spring fever had struck as usual with a vengeance. No one paid any attention in class; instead we stared out the windows and at each other, wanting to speed up the last few weeks of school. I despaired every time I looked in the mirror. Pencil thin, not a curve anywhere. I was called "beanpole" and "string bean," and I knew that's what I looked like. A flat chest, no hips, and a brain; that's what I had. That really wasn't much for a fourteen-year-old to work with, I thought, as I absent-mindedly wandered from my history class to the gym. Another hour of sweating in basketball and displaying my toothpick legs was coming up. Then I remembered my P.E. shorts were still in a bag under my desk where I'd forgotten them. I had to walk all the way back and get them. Coach Thompson was a real bear if someone wasn't dressed for P.E. She had said I was a good forward and even tried to talk Grandma into letting me join the team once. Of course Grandma said no.

4   I was almost back at my classroom door when I heard voices raised in anger as if in some sort of argument. I stopped. I didn't mean to eavesdrop, I just hesitated, not knowing what to do. I needed those shorts and I was going to be late, but I didn't want to interrupt an argument between my teachers. I recognized the voices: Mr. Schmidt, my history teacher, and Mr. Boone, my math teacher. They seemed to be arguing about me. I couldn't believe it. I still remember the feeling of shock that rooted me flat against the wall as if I were trying to blend in with the graffiti written there.

5   "I refuse to do it! I don't care who her father is, her grades don't even begin to compare to Martha's. I won't lie or falsify records. Martha has a straight A-plus average and you know it." That was Mr. Schmidt and he sounded very angry. Mr. Boone's voice sounded calm and quiet.

scholarship: honorable
agile: nimble

My Notes

6 "Look. Joann's father is not only on the Board, he owns the only store in town: we could say it was a close tie and—"

7 The pounding in my ears drowned out the rest of the words, only a word here and there filtered through. " ... Martha is Mexican ... resign ... won't do it ...." Mr. Schmidt came rushing out and luckily for me went down the opposite way toward the auditorium, so he didn't see me. Shaking, I waited a few minutes and then went in and grabbed my bag and fled from the room. Mr. Boone looked up when I came in but didn't say anything. To this day I don't remember if I got in trouble in P.E. for being late or how I made it through the rest of the afternoon. I went home very sad and cried into my pillow that night so Grandmother wouldn't hear me. It seemed a cruel **coincidence** that I had overheard that conversation.

8 The next day when the principal called me into his office I knew what it would be about. He looked uncomfortable and unhappy. I decided I wasn't going to make it any easier for him, so I looked him straight in the eyes. He looked away and fidgeted with the papers on his desk.

9 "Martha," he said, "there's been a change in policy this year regarding the scholarship jacket. As you know, it has always been free." He cleared his throat and continued. "This year the Board has decided to charge fifteen dollars, which still won't cover the complete cost of the jacket."

10 I stared at him in shock, and a small sound of **dismay** escaped my throat. I hadn't expected this. He still avoided looking in my eyes.

11 "So if you are unable to pay the fifteen dollars for the jacket it will be given to the next one in line." I didn't need to ask who that was.

12 Standing with all the dignity I could muster, I said, "I'll speak to my grandfather about it, sir, and let you know tomorrow." I cried on the walk home from the bus stop. The dirt road was a quarter mile from the highway, so by the time I got home, my eyes were red and puffy.

13 "Where's Grandpa?" I asked Grandma, looking down at the floor so she wouldn't ask me why I'd been crying. She was sewing on a quilt as usual and didn't look up.

14 "I think he's out back working in the bean field."

15 I went outside and looked out at the fields. There he was. I could see him walking between the rows, his body bent over the little plants, hoe in hand. I walked slowly out to him, trying to think how I could best ask him for the money. There was a cool breeze blowing and a sweet smell of mesquite fruit in the air, but I didn't appreciate it. I kicked at a dirt clod. I wanted that jacket so much. It was more than just being a valedictorian and giving a little thank you speech for the jacket on graduation night. It represented eight years of hard work and expectation. I knew I had to be honest with Grandpa; it was my only chance. He saw my shadow and looked up.

16 He waited for me to speak. I cleared my throat nervously and clasped my hands behind my back so he wouldn't see them shaking. "Grandpa, I have a big favor to ask you," I said in Spanish, the only language he knew. He still waited silently. I tried again. "Grandpa, this year the principal said the scholarship jacket is not going to be free. It's going to cost fifteen dollars, and I have to take

coincidence: unexpected event
dismay: disappointment

the money in tomorrow, otherwise it'll be given to someone else." The last words came out in an eager rush. Grandpa straightened up tiredly and leaned his chin on the hoe handle. He looked out over the field that was filled with the tiny green bean plants. I waited, desperately hoping he'd say I could have the money.

17 He turned to me and asked quietly, "What does a scholarship jacket mean?"

18 I answered quickly; maybe there was a chance. "It means you've earned it by having the highest grades for eight years and that's why they're giving it to you." Too late I realized the significance of my words. Grandpa knew that I understood it was not a matter of money. It wasn't that. He went back to hoeing the weeds that sprang up between the delicate little bean plants. It was a time-consuming job; sometimes the small shoots were right next to each other. Finally he spoke again as I turned to leave, crying.

19 "Then if you pay for it, Marta, it's not a scholarship jacket, is it? Tell your principal I will not pay the fifteen dollars."

20 I walked back to the house and locked myself in the bathroom for a long time. I was angry with Grandfather even though I knew he was right, and I was angry with the Board, whoever they were. Why did they have to change the rules just when it was my turn to win the jacket? Those were the days of belief and innocence.

21 It was a very sad and withdrawn girl who dragged into the principal's office the next day. This time he did look me in the eyes.

22 "What did your grandfather say?"

23 I sat very straight in my chair.

24 "He said to tell you he won't pay the fifteen dollars."

25 The principal muttered something I couldn't understand under his breath and walked over to the window. He stood looking out at something outside. He looked bigger than usual when he stood up; he was a tall, gaunt man with gray hair, and I watched the back of his head while I waited for him to speak.

26 "Why?" he finally asked. "Your grandfather has the money. He owns a two-hundred acre ranch."

27 I looked at him, forcing my eyes to stay dry. "I know, sir, but he said if I had to pay for it, then it wouldn't be a scholarship jacket." I stood up to leave.

28 "I guess you'll just have to give it to Joann." I hadn't meant to say that, it had just slipped out. I was almost to the door when he stopped me.

29 "Martha—wait."

30 I turned and looked at him, waiting. What did he want now? I could feel my heart pounding loudly in my chest and see my blouse fluttering where my breasts should have been. Something bitter and **vile** tasting was coming up in my mouth; I was afraid I was going to be sick. I didn't need any sympathy speeches. He sighed loudly and went back to his big desk. He watched me, biting his lip.

31 "Okay. We'll make an exception in your case. I'll tell the Board, you'll get your jacket."

32 I could hardly believe my ears. I spoke in a trembling rush. "Oh, thank you, sir!" Suddenly I felt great. I didn't know about adrenalin in those days, but

vile: disgusting

I knew something was pumping through me, making me feel as tall as the sky. I wanted to yell, jump, run the mile, do something. I ran out so I could cry in the hall where there was no one to see me.

33 At the end of the day, Mr. Schmidt winked at me and said, "I hear you're getting the scholarship jacket this year."

34 His face looked as happy and innocent as a baby's, but I knew better. Without answering I gave him a quick hug and ran to the bus. I cried on the walk home again, but this time because I was so happy. I couldn't wait to tell Grandpa and ran straight to the field. I joined him in the row where he was working, and without saying anything I crouched down and started pulling up the weeds with my hands. Grandpa worked alongside me for a few minutes, and he didn't ask what had happened. After I had a little pile of weeds between the rows, I stood up and faced him.

35 "The principal said he's making an exception for me, Grandpa, and I'm getting the jacket after all. That's after I told him what you said."

36 Grandpa didn't say anything; he just gave me a pat on the shoulder and a smile. He pulled out the crumpled red handkerchief that he always carried in his back pocket and wiped the sweat off his forehead.

37 "Better go see if your grandmother needs any help with supper."

38 I gave him a big grin. He didn't fool me. I skipped and ran back to the house whistling some silly tune.

Making Observations
- What details about Martha stand out to you?
- What surprises you about the ending?

☑ Focus on the Sentence
Turn the following fragments into complete sentences, using what you know about the personal narrative "The Scholarship Jacket."

the scholarship jacket is _____

Mr. Schmidt wants _____

Marta's grandfather's actions _____

highest grades _____

Returning to the Text

- Return to the text as you respond to the following questions. Use text evidence to support your responses.
- Be sure to respond with appropriate register, vocabulary, tone, and voice.
- Write any additional questions you have about the personal narrative in your Reader/Writer Notebook.

1. What can be inferred from the conversation Martha overhears between her two teachers? What evidence supports your understanding?

   _____

   _____

   _____

   _____

2. What makes the principal suddenly change his mind in paragraph 30? How do you know?

   _____

   _____

   _____

   _____

3. Martha overhears and then engages in several conversations in this story. How does each conversation move the story forward?

   _____

   _____

   _____

   _____

4. Based on the author's description, what can you tell about her grandfather's personality? Which details from the narrative support your ideas?

   _____

   _____

   _____

   _____

5. What do you think the author learned as a result of this event? Why? Which of your own personal experiences has helped to teach you a similar lesson?

   _____

   _____

   _____

Working from the Text

6. A personal narrative may follow this structure:

- Incident: the central piece of action that is the focus of the narrative
- Response: the immediate emotions and actions associated with the incident
- Reflection: a description that explores the significance of the incident

During class discussion, use the graphic organizer to take notes on the key parts of "The Scholarship Jacket." Use your metacognitive markers to help locate textual evidence that supports your ideas. Evaluate the details you marked to determine the key idea of the story, and include this in the third column. If there are any questions you noted while reading that you have not answered yet, ask your peers if they have an answer.

Incident (what happened)	Response (the narrator's feelings and actions associated with the incident)	Reflection (the lessons the narrator learned from this experience)

My Notes

✍ Writing to Sources: Informational Text

Using the information from your class discussion and the graphic organizer, write a short summary analyzing what the narrator learns from the incident in the story. Be sure to:

• Describe what happens, how the narrator responds, and what she learns from the events in the story.
• Cite specific details from the story.

Learning Targets
- Edit a draft to ensure proper use of possessive nouns.

Preview
In this activity, you will learn how to form both singular and plural possessive nouns as well as identify irregular possessive nouns. You will also review and edit your writing to make sure you have used possessive nouns correctly.

Using Possessive Nouns

Part of being a strong writer is knowing how to follow certain grammatical conventions in your writing and knowing how to check for correct grammar, spelling, and punctuation when revising your work. In this activity, you'll take a close look at how to form possessive nouns.

Possessive nouns show ownership or belonging. For example, in "The Scholarship Jacket," the character Martha lives on her *grandparents'* ranch. The word *grandparents'* is a possessive noun showing that the ranch belongs to or is owned by Martha's grandparents.

1. Read the following excerpt from "The Scholarship Jacket" by Marta Salinas. Mark the words that end in an apostrophe + *s* (for example, *author's*).

   "I refuse to do it! I don't care who her father is, her grades don't even begin to compare to Martha's. I won't lie or falsify records. Martha has a straight A-plus average and you know it." That was Mr. Schmidt and he sounded very angry. Mr. Boone's voice sounded calm and quiet.

   "Look. Joann's father is not only on the Board, he owns the only store in town: we could say it was a close tie and—"

2. Read this excerpt from a student's analysis of "The Scholarship Jacket" and underline words that end in an apostrophe + *s* (for example, *author's*) or an *s* + an apostrophe (for example, *authors'*):

   In Marta Salinas's story, the main character learns to appreciate her grandparents' values about the importance of hard work. The conflict in the story begins when Martha overhears her teachers' argument in the hallway about which student should receive the scholarship jacket.

3. In these excerpts, the words *Martha's, Mr. Boone's, Joann's, Salinas's, grandparents'*, and *teachers'* are possessive nouns. In other words, something belongs to these people. With a partner, try to determine what belongs to each of the possessive nouns in the excerpts.

   Martha's _____

   Mr. Boone's _____

   Joann's _____

   [Marta] Salinas's _____

   grandparents' _____

   teachers' _____

4. What do you notice about the placement of the apostrophe in each of these nouns? With a partner, try to explain the pattern for using apostrophes with possessive nouns.

_____

_____

_____

_____

Forming Possessive Nouns

Even professional writers sometimes make mistakes with punctuation. One of the most common punctuation mishaps is putting an apostrophe in the wrong place in a possessive noun or leaving it out altogether. Mastering the skill of forming possessive nouns will help make your writing clear and polished.

Regular Nouns

With a few exceptions, possessive nouns are formed in English by:

- adding an apostrophe + s to the end of a singular noun, as in *the student's pencil*
- adding an apostrophe to the end of a plural noun, as in *the students' desks*

5. Look at the examples of singular and plural nouns in the following chart. In the blank spaces, write the correct possessive noun. In the last two rows, add your own examples.

Singular Noun	Singular Possessive Noun	Plural Noun	Plural Possessive Noun
student	student's	students	students'
teacher		teachers	
Grandpa		grandparents	
city		cities	
friend		friends	

Irregular Plural Nouns

Sometimes plural nouns are irregular, so they don't end in *s*. For these irregular plural nouns, form the possessive by adding an apostrophe + *s* to the end of the irregular plural, as in *the children's balloons*

6. Look at the examples in the chart that follows. Add the corresponding singular possessive noun, irregular plural noun, and irregular plural possessive noun to each of the blank spaces. Then try to think of one more example to add to the final row.

Singular Noun	Singular Possessive Noun	Irregular Plural Noun	Irregular Plural Possessive Noun
child	child's	children	children's
woman			
man			
person			
goose			

7. Work with a partner to write a story using possessive nouns. Try to use as many nouns as you can from the list that follows. As you use each word from the list, cross it off.

coincidence	argument	toes	scholarship
grades	intelligence	homework	dismay
fruits	tradition	team	coach
eyes	classmate	school	

Editing

Read the following paragraph from a student's analysis essay about "The Scholarship Jacket." Work with a partner to check whether possessive nouns and apostrophes are used correctly. Circle any mistakes you notice and then mark the text to show how you would correct the mistakes.

[1] The main incident in the short story "The Scholarship Jacket" happens when Martha is told she has to pay for this years' scholarship jacket, even though it is supposed to be earned by having good grades. [2] She is angry and upset by her principals request for $15, and then she becomes even more upset by her grandfathers refusal to give her the money. [3] Even though she knows deep down that her grandfather is right and that she should not have to pay for something she earned through hard work, she still feel's frustrated about the situation. [4] When Martha repeats her grandfathers words to the principal, saying " … if I had to pay for it, then it wouldn't be a scholarship jacket," the principal is forced to confront the truth. [5] He changes his mind and decides to "make an exception" for Martha, going against the Board's unethical decision. [6] In the end, Martha learns that scholarship jacket's are less important than doing what is right.

☑ Check Your Understanding

Imagine that you are editing a classmate's writing and you notice the following sentences.

> The character's opinions clash from the beginning of the story. Mr. Boones mild-mannered reaction to the Boards decision makes Mr. Schmidt very upset.

In your own words, write an explanation so that your classmate understands the mistakes and how to correct them. Then add a question to your Editing Checklist to remind yourself to check for possessive nouns and apostrophes.

Practice

Return to the summary you wrote in Activity 1.4 and check it for correct use of possessive nouns. Work with a partner to:

- Circle any possessive nouns.
- Check for correct placement of apostrophes.
- Add two more details using sentences with possessive nouns.

Analyzing Language

Learning Strategies

Marking the Text
Graphic Organizer
Summarizing
Brainstorming
Drafting

Learning Targets

- Analyze the plot elements of a personal narrative, looking for a logical sequence of events.
- Write a personal narrative that includes an incident, a response, and a reflection.

Preview

In this activity, you will read an excerpt from a memoir and look for details and descriptive language to help you understand the author's character.

Setting a Purpose for Reading

- As you read, annotate the text for sensory details and figurative language.
- Circle unknown words and phrases. Try to determine the meaning of the words by using context clues, word parts, or a dictionary.

WORD CONNECTIONS

Etymology
Etymology is the study of the origin of words. Many English words come from other languages, including Latin, German, and Greek. The word *fanatic* comes from the Latin word for "temple." A fanatic was someone "in the temple" or "inspired by divinity." Now the word is used to describe a passionate follower of a performer or a sport.

About the Author

Walter Dean Myers (1937–2014) began writing when he was a child. He published his first book, *Where Does the Day Go?*, in 1969. Over the next four decades, he wrote many books for children and young adults, two of which—*Scorpions* and *Somewhere in the Darkness*—received Newbery Honors. His stories focus on the challenges and triumphs of growing up in a difficult environment. His memoir, *Bad Boy*, reveals how he overcame racial challenges and his own shortcomings to become a successful author.

My Notes

Memoir

from

Bad Boy

by **Walter Dean Myers**

1 By September and the opening of school I was deep into sports and became a baseball fanatic. Along with the pleasure of playing baseball there was the joy of identifying with the ballplayers. I loved the Dodgers. Maybe it was because Mama loved the Dodgers and especially Jackie Robinson. All summer long, kids playing punchball—hitting a pink "Spaldeen" ball with your fist and then running bases drawn in chalk on the streets—had tried to steal home to copy Robinson. We even changed the rules of stoop ball, of which I was the absolute King of the World, to include bases when more than one kid played. You played stoop ball by throwing the ball against the steps of a brownstone.

The ball coming off the steps had to clear the sidewalk and land in the street. If it landed before being caught, you could run the bases. My speed and ability to judge distances made me an excellent fielder. We did occasionally play actual baseball, but not enough kids had gloves to make a good game.

2 My new school was Public School 43 on 128th Street and Amsterdam Avenue, across from the Transit Authority bus terminal. Mrs. Conway was my teacher, and it took me one day to get into trouble with her.

3 In the elementary grades I attended, reading was taught by having kids stand up one at a time and read aloud. Mrs. Conway had us up and reading as soon as the readers had been handed out. When it came to be my turn, I was anxious to show my skills. I read quickly, and there was a chorus of laughter in response. They were laughing at my speech.

4 "Slow down and try it again," Mrs. Conway said.

5 I slowed my speech down and started reading from the top of the page. Johnny Brown started laughing immediately. Johnny always had something to say to make the class laugh. I threw the book sidearm and watched it hit his desk and bounce across the room.

6 "Don't you dare throw a book in my classroom!" Mrs. Conway, red-faced, screamed. "Into the closet! Into the closet!"

7 I had to stand in the closet for the rest of the morning. That afternoon Mrs. Conway divided the class into reading groups. I was put into the slowest group. I stayed there until the next week, when the whole class was given a spelling test and I scored the highest grade. Mrs. Conway asked me to read in front of the class again.

8 I looked at Johnny Brown as I headed for the front of the class. He had this **glint** in his eye, and I knew he was going to laugh. I opened my mouth, and he put his hand across his mouth to hold his laugh in. I went across to where he sat and hit him right on the back of the hand he held over his mouth. I was sent to the principal's office and had to stay after school and wash blackboards. Later in the year it would be Johnny Brown who would be in Mrs. Conway's doghouse for not doing his homework, with her screaming at him that he couldn't be a comedian all his life. He went on to become a television comedian and is still doing well.

9 Being good in class was not easy for me. I had a need to fill up all the spaces in my life, with activity, with talking, sometimes with purely imagined scenarios that would dance through my mind, occupying me while some other student was at the blackboard. I did want to get good marks in school, but they were never of major importance to me, except in the sense of "winning" the best grade in a subject. My filling up the spaces, however, kept me in trouble. I would blurt out answers to Mrs. Conway's questions even when I was told to keep quiet, or I might roll a marble across my desk if she was on the other side of the room.

10 The other thing that got me in trouble was my speech. I couldn't hear that I was speaking badly, and I wasn't sure that the other kids did, but I knew they often laughed when it was my turn to speak. After a while I would tense up

glint: certain look

anytime Mrs. Conway called on me. I threw my books across that classroom enough times for Mrs. Conway to stop my reading once and for all.

11 But when the class was given the assignment to write a poem, she did read mine. She said that she liked it very much.

12 "I don't think he wrote that poem," Sidney Aronofsky volunteered.

13 I gave Sidney Aronofsky the biggest punch he ever had in the back of his big head and was sent to the closet. After the incident with Sidney, Mrs. Conway said that she had had quite enough of me and that I would not be allowed to participate in any class activity until I brought my mother to school. I knew that meant a beating. That evening I thought about telling Mama that the teacher wanted to see her, but I didn't get up the nerve. I didn't get it up the next day, either. In the meantime, I had to sit in the back of the room, and no kid was allowed to sit near me. I brought some comic books to school and read them under my desk.

14 Mrs. Conway was an enormously hippy woman. She moved slowly and always had a scowl on her face. She reminded me of a great white turtle with just a dash of rouge and a touch of eye shadow. It was not a pretty sight. But somehow she made it all the way from the front of the room to the back, where I sat reading a comic, without my hearing her. She snatched the comic from me and tore it up. She dropped all the pieces on my desk, then made me pick them up and take them to the garbage can while the class laughed.

15 Then she went to her closet, snatched out a book, and put it in front of me.

16 "You are," she sputtered, "a bad boy. A very bad boy. You cannot join the rest of the class until your mother comes in." She was furious, and I was embarrassed.

17 "And if you're going to sit back here and read, you might as well read something worthwhile," she snapped.

18 I didn't touch the book in front of me until she had made her way back to the front of the class and was going on about something in long division. The title of the book was *East o' the Sun and the West o' the Moon*. It was a collection of Norwegian fairy tales, and I read the first one. At the end of the day, I asked Mrs. Conway if I could take the book home.

19 She looked at me a long time and then said no, I couldn't. But I could read it every day in class if I behaved myself. I promised I would. For the rest of the week I read that book. It was the best book I had ever read. When I told Mrs. Conway I had finished, she asked me what I liked about the book, and I told her. The stories were full of magic events and interesting people and witches and strange places. It differed from *Mystery Rides the Rails*, the Bobbsey Twins, and a few Honeybunch books I had come across.

20 I realized I liked books, and I liked reading. Reading a book was not so much like entering a different world—it was like discovering a different language. It was a language clearer than the one I spoke, and clearer than the one I heard around me. What the books said was, as in the case of *East o' the Sun*, interesting, but the idea that I could enter this world at any time I chose was even more attractive. The "me" who read the books, who followed the adventures, seemed more the real me than the "me" who played ball in the streets.

My Notes

21 Mrs. Conway gave me another book to read in class and, because it was the weekend, allowed me to take it home to read. From that day on I liked Mrs. Conway.

22 I still didn't get to read aloud in class, but when we had a class assignment to write a poem, she would read mine. At the end of the year I got my best report card ever, including a glorious Needs Improvement in conduct.

23 It was also the golden anniversary of the school, and the school magazine used one of my poems. It was on the first page of the Jubilee Issue, and it was called "My Mother." When I saw it, I ran all the way home to show Mama.

Mr. Irwin Lasher

24 My new school, the new P.S. 125, was quite close to my house. It was located on 123rd Street, right across from Morningside Park between Morningside and Amsterdam Avenues. The school was ultramodern for the day, with table and chairs that could be arranged any way the teacher wanted instead of the rigid desks nailed to the floor we had been used to having. I was in class 6–2 and had my first male teacher, Mr. Irwin Lasher.

25 "You're in my class for a reason," he said as I sat at the side of his desk. "Do you know what the reason is?"

Jacob Lawrence's 1966 painting *The Library* may have been inspired by the hours he spent at libraries conducting research for his paintings depicting historical events.

26 "Because I was promoted to the sixth grade?" I asked.

27 "Because you have a history of fighting your teachers," he said. "And I'm telling you right now, I won't tolerate any fighting in my class for any reason. Do you understand that?"

28 "Yes."

29 "You're a bright boy, and that's what you're going to be in this class."

30 My fight with Mr. Lasher didn't happen until the third day, and in a way it wasn't really my fault. We were going up the stairs, and I decided that, when his back was turned, I would pretend that I was trying to kick him. All right, he paused on the staircase landing before leading us to our floor and the kick that was supposed to delight my classmates by just missing the teacher hit him squarely in the backside. He turned quickly and started toward me. Before I realized it, I was swinging at him wildly.

31 Mr. Lasher had been in World War II and had fought in the Battle of the Bulge. He didn't have much trouble handling me. He sat me in a corner of the classroom and said that he would see me after class. I imagined he would send a note home, and that my mother would have to come to school. I was already practicing what I would say to her when I gave her the note. But instead of sending a note home, he came home with me! Down the street we came, my white teacher and me, with all my friends looking at me and a few asking if it meant I was going to get a beating. I thought it probably would, but I didn't give them the satisfaction of an answer. Mama was sitting on the park bench across from our house when I came down the street with Mr. Lasher firmly holding my hand.

32 "Mrs. Myers, I had a little problem with Walter today that I think you should know about," he said, sitting next to her on the bench.

33 He called Mama by my last name, not knowing that I was an informal adoptee. Her last name was Dean, of course, but she didn't go into it. Mr. Lasher quietly explained to my mother that all the tests I had taken **indicated** that I was quite smart, but that I was going to throw it all away because of my behavior.

34 "We need more smart Negro boys," he said. "We don't need tough Negro boys."

35 Mr. Lasher did two important things that year. The first was that he took me out of class one day per week and put me in speech therapy for the entire day. The second thing he did was to convince me that my good reading ability and good test scores made me special.

36 He put me in charge of anything that needed a leader and made me coach the slower kids in reading. At the end of the year I was the one student in his class whom he recommended for placement in a rapid advancement class in junior high school.

37 With Mr. Lasher my grades improved significantly. I was either first or second in every subject, and he even gave me a Satisfactory in conduct. As the tallest boy in the sixth grade, I was on the honor guard and was scheduled to carry the flag at the graduation exercises, an honor I almost missed because of God's revenge. ...

indicated: showed

Making Observations

- Whom do we meet in the excerpt?
- Which detail about the narrator do you find most interesting? Why?

Returning to the Text

- Return to the text as you respond to the following questions. Use text evidence to support your responses.
- Write any additional questions you have about the memoir in your Reader/Writer Notebook.

1. Reread paragraphs 9–10. What were the main causes of the narrator's bad behavior?

2. What is the metaphor in paragraph 14, and how does it help characterize Mrs. Conway?

3. Reread paragraph 20. Based on what the narrator says and what you know about his character, why might books and reading be so important to him?

4. How does Mrs. Conway's opinion of Walter change during the school year? Use text evidence to support your answer.

5. In paragraph 22, what word does the narrator use to describe his "Needs Improvement" mark on his report card? What does that word choice convey to the reader?

Working from the Text

6. Complete the graphic organizer to summarize the central incidents, response, reflection, and characterization in the story.

Organization	Sequence of Events Using Transitions of Time	Character Traits Revealed	Textual Evidence for Character Traits
Incident: Summarize the central incidents that take place in the first part of the story.	In the beginning of the story,		
Response: In the second part of the story, what is the main result of the incidents from the beginning of the story?	Then,		
Reflection: How does the narrator change or grow by the end of the story?	Finally,		

7. Review the text and locate examples of sensory details and figurative language. How does this language help you visualize the characters and events in the story?

☑ Check Your Understanding

With a partner, share your text evidence as well as your explanation of how this evidence helps you understand the characters and their actions in the story. Note how your partner's responses are similar to or different from yours.

INDEPENDENT READING LINK

Read and Connect

In your Reader/Writer Notebook, note the incidents, responses, and reflections you've noticed in your independent reading text. Also, look for examples of sensory details and figurative language. Make connections between your independent reading and the excerpt from *Bad Boy*. Compare and contrast the texts' use of sensory details and figurative language. Write a paragraph in your Independent Reading Log about how the authors' use of language helps develop the plots, characters, and themes.

My Notes

LANGUAGE & WRITER'S CRAFT: Sentence Variety

One way to vary sentence types is to add transitions. **Transitions** help the reader understand a change in time or place. Transitions for a narrative may include words and phrases such as *in the beginning, then, next, after, later, in the end,* and *finally*.

> **Example:** <u>At first</u>, Mrs. Conway does not allow Walter to take a book home. <u>Later</u>, she does when she sees how much Walter enjoys reading.

In addition to using transitions to create sentence variety, consider using **parallel sentence structure**. Parallel sentence structure uses the same pattern of words to show that two or more ideas have equal importance.

> **Example:** Walter <u>throws a book</u>, <u>hits another student</u>, and <u>blurts out answers</u>. [The underlined word groups are parallel because each starts with an action verb and ends with a direct object that is a noun.]

PRACTICE Rewrite the following sentences by adding a transition to the beginning of the second sentence and using parallel structure to finish the third sentence.

At the beginning of the story, Walter is impulsive and does not think before he acts. _____, his teachers help him. They _____, _____, and _____.

Then return to your short summary from Activity 1.4 and check for places where you could vary sentence types by adding transitions or using parallel sentence structure.

📝 Narrative Writing Prompt

Think about all of the choices you can make in a school day. Brainstorm some of the choices you make at school and the consequences you face as a result.

Using your brainstorm, think of a specific time you had to make a choice at school. Write a short personal narrative with an incident, response, and reflection. Be sure to:

- Use transitions to organize the incident, response, and reflection.
- Use sensory details and/or figurative language.
- Incorporate parallel sentence structure.
- Check to make sure you have correctly spelled and punctuated possessive nouns and pronouns.

Timed Writing: Choosing a Topic and Drafting a Personal Narrative

Learning Targets

- Plan a first draft response to a writing prompt.
- Develop and revise a writing plan within a writing group.
- Correctly use and punctuate transitions.

Preview

In this activity, you will prepare and write a response to a writing prompt while working with a writing group.

Writing Groups

During the writing process, you can get feedback for revision in a writing group. All members of a writing group work collaboratively to respond to one another's writing and to help each other through the revision process by asking clarifying questions. Writing groups use sharing and responding as a revision strategy to communicate with another person or a small group of peers about suggestions in order to improve writing. It is the responsibility of the members of the writing group to help each other develop quality writing.

Writing Group Roles		
Role	**Guidelines**	**Response Starters**
The reader: Reads the text silently, then aloud. Begins the conversation after reading.	The reader's purpose is to share an understanding of the writer's words. The reader sees the physical structure of the draft and may comment on that as well. The reader follows all listeners' guidelines as well.	Reader's and listeners' compliments: • I liked the words you used, such as … • I like the way you described … • This piece made me feel … • This piece reminded me of …
The listeners: Take notes and prepare open-ended questions for the writer or make constructive statements.	The listeners begin with positive statements. The listeners use "I" statements and talk about the writing, not the writer. The listeners make statements and must provide reasons.	Reader's and listeners' comments and suggestions: • I really enjoyed the part where … • What parts are you having trouble with? • What do you plan to do next? • I was confused when …
The writer: Listens to the draft, takes notes, responds to questions, and asks questions of the writing group.	As the work is being read aloud by another, the writer gets an overall impression of the piece. The writer takes notes on what might need to be changed. The writer asks questions to get feedback that will lead to effective revision.	Writer's questions: • What do you want to know more about? • What part doesn't make sense? • Which section of the text doesn't work?

My Notes

Rules for Discussion

Along with group roles, each writing group member is responsible for helping make the group as effective as possible. Group members do this by agreeing to follow rules for discussion such as these.

- Be prepared. Each group member should be prepared to carry out his or her role by having the necessary materials, such as their drafts and a notebook and pen to take notes.
- Listen attentively. Pay close attention as drafts are read, noting questions or comments for discussion.
- Take turns. Allow all group members the chance to speak during the discussion.
- Respond thoughtfully. Ask questions and make comments that invite participation from other group members.
- Stay on topic. Keep comments and discussion focused on the writing drafts.
- Keep an open mind. Allow your views and opinions to be changed by new ideas and information from other group members.

Think about the list of rules. How will following these rules improve your writing? What other rules might your writing group follow?

Preparing for Responding to a Writing Prompt

Tip 1: Address all aspects of the prompt. Make sure you understand what the prompt is asking you to do.

- Circle the key verbs in the prompt. The verbs identify what you will do.
- Underline the nouns. The nouns identify what you will write about and may give you a clue about what genre would be appropriate.
- List the verbs next to the nouns. This list prioritizes what you have to do when you write in response to this prompt. You can use this list as a checklist to ensure that you have addressed all aspects of the prompt.

Tip 2: Pace yourself. You will have _____ minutes to write your essay. How many minutes will you use for each phase?

_____ Prewrite: Plan my essay and generate ideas.

_____ Draft: Put my plan into action and get my writing on paper.

_____ Revise/Edit: Make sure my writing is as clear as possible for my readers.

Tip 3: Plan your essay. Look back at your portfolio cover and at your choices/consequences/reflection web. Select one incident in which you made a choice.

Use a prewriting strategy to create a plan for your draft. Consider creating a web, a plot diagram, or an outline.

📝 Drafting the Embedded Assessment

Write a multiparagraph narrative about an incident on your "choices" graphic organizer. Include information about the choice you made and the consequences of your action. Be sure to:

- Include the elements of incident, response, and reflection.
- Use transitions to connect ideas for your reader.
- Include insights about the effects and consequences of the choice.

LANGUAGE & WRITER'S CRAFT: Coherence

When responding to a writing prompt, it is important to consider the **coherence** of your writing. Transitions within a paragraph create **internal coherence**, and transitions between paragraphs create **external coherence**, as shown in the paragraphs below.

> <u>In the beginning of the year</u>, I wasn't a good basketball player. I had to prove myself to the coach and the other players. <u>In fact</u>, I struggled to keep up, but I continued to practice, and my game improved.

> <u>Toward the end of the year</u>, I was asked to start in an important game. <u>At first</u>, I was nervous. <u>After</u> I made a couple of goals, I began to enjoy myself.

> <u>Now</u>, I can see how my hard work has paid off. I am a good basketball player after all.

In the paragraphs above, notice how the transitions within paragraphs improve the flow of the writing and help readers understand the sequence of events. Then notice how the transitions between paragraphs help readers track the passage of time from the beginning of the year to the end. These transitions signal the shift from one time frame to another. Transitions can also signal a shift from one setting to another in a narrative.

PRACTICE Exchange your narrative with a partner. Highlight one transition used to create internal coherence and one used to create external coherence. If you and your partner are unable to highlight transitions, work together to locate places where transitions could be added.

My Notes

Revising Your Narrative

Review your notes from your writing group. Based on the feedback you received, create a revision plan by responding thoughtfully to the following:

• After rereading your draft and meeting with your writing group, what do you like best about your personal narrative? Why?

• At this point, what do you think could be improved? Why?

• What do you plan to change, and how will those changes improve the draft?

• After reading my draft, I realize that in the next draft I should revise

_____ because _____.

You will revisit this draft for Embedded Assessment 1.

☑ Check Your Understanding

Describe the main steps to responding to a writing prompt. Explain how a writing group can help you improve writing.

Once Upon a Time: Revising the Beginning

Learning Strategies

Summarizing
Close Reading
Graphic Organizer
Rereading
Revisiting Prior Work

Learning Targets

- Examine the effectiveness of narrative introductions.
- Revise an introduction, focusing on clarity, word choice, and organization.

Preview

In this activity, you will practice writing a hook for your personal narrative.

Writing and Revision

1. Read this quotation about revision: "If a teacher told me to revise, I thought that meant my writing was a broken-down car that needed to go to the repair shop. I felt insulted. I didn't realize the teacher was saying, 'Make it shine. It's worth it.' Now I see revision as a beautiful word of hope. It's a new vision of something. It means you don't have to be perfect the first time. What a relief!" –Naomi Shihab Nye

   Summarize what Naomi Shihab Nye means about revision. What does this quote make you think about writing and revision?

What Is a Lead?

2. A lead, or hook, comes at the beginning of a piece of writing. Its purpose is to encourage your readers to keep reading. A lead may use dialogue, action, or a surprising statement to draw readers in and make them want to find out more.

In the Beginning

3. Many writers struggle with how to begin their writing with an interesting lead. Review these types of leads, or hooks. Mark the important words in the definitions of the "Type of Lead" column.

Type of Lead	Examples from Published Authors
Reaction: Some writers choose to open a narrative with a character thinking about or reflecting on the event.	"The Treasure of Lemon Brown," by Walter Dean Myers The dark sky, filled with angry, swirling clouds, reflected Greg Ridley's mood as he sat on the stoop of his building. His father's voice came to him again, first reading the letter the principal had sent to the house, then lecturing endlessly about his poor efforts in math. "I had to leave school when I was thirteen," his father had said, "that's a year younger than you are now. If I'd had half the chances you have, I'd ... "
Dialogue: Some writers choose to show the reader a key event, using dialogue between characters.	*Charlotte's Web,* by E. B. White "Where's papa going with that ax?" said Fern to her mother as they were setting the table for breakfast. "Out to the hoghouse," replied Mrs. Arable. "Some pigs were born last night." "I don't see why he needs an ax," continued Fern, who was only eight.
Action: Some writers choose to open a narrative with the main character doing something; this type of lead puts the reader right in the middle of the action.	"The Gold Cadillac," by Mildred D. Taylor My sister and I were playing out on the front lawn when the gold Cadillac rolled up and my father stepped from behind the wheel. We ran to him, our eyes filled with wonder. "Daddy, whose Cadillac?" I asked. And Wilma demanded, "Where's our Mercury?" My father grinned. "Go get your mother and I'll tell you all about it."

4. Revisit the openings from the texts you have read in this unit to examine how authors hook readers.

Text	Kind of Lead	Why is this lead effective? How does it "hook" readers and leave them wanting to read more?
Bad Boy, by Walter Dean Myers (Activity 1.5)		
"The Scholarship Jacket," by Marta Salinas (Activity 1.4)		
My own selection from Independent Reading		

Revision of Narrative Lead

5. Review the graphic organizer about the hooks used by the authors of the texts you have read. Use the leads of those texts as models as you revise your own lead technique—reaction and reflection, dialogue, and action. Remember that your goal is to open with a strong lead that engages readers, encouraging them to continue reading your personal narrative. A strong lead will also set up your narrative to be well-organized. In the next two activities, you will revise the middle and the end of your narrative. As you revise your lead, think about the middle and ending you drafted and how the beginning should work with the rest of your narrative.

6. Effective writers reflect upon the changes they make in order to become more aware of specific techniques they use during the writing process. Describe how you have changed your opening. How did your change make your opening more engaging for your reader?

Learning Strategies

Marking the Text
Discussion Groups
Paraphrasing
Adding
Looping

GRAMMAR & USAGE

Compound-Complex Sentences

A compound-complex sentence is one that has two or more independent clauses and one or more dependent clauses. Compound-complex sentences are often used when a writer wants to explain something in detail.

Achilike creates a compound-complex sentence when she writes: "I was my parents' first joy, and in their joy, they gave me the name that would haunt me for the rest of my life, Immaculeta Uzoma Achilike."

What is Achilike explaining in this sentence? What details does she provide?

Learning Targets

- Identify and use sensory language and details to convey deeper meaning.
- Revise a draft for word choice.

Preview

In this activity, you will read a personal narrative, noting the author's use of sensory and figurative language. Then you will use sensory and figurative language in writing.

Setting a Purpose for Reading

- While you read the narrative, note sensory details and use them to create a mental image of the action and characters in the narrative.
- Circle unknown words and phrases. Try to determine the meaning of the words by using context clues, word parts, or a dictionary.

About the Author

Imma Achilike studied medicine at the University of Texas, San Antonio. She is now a doctor practicing anesthesiology. She wrote this story when she was a student at Naaman Forest High School in Garland, Texas.

Personal Narrative

Why Couldn't I Have Been Named Ashley?

by **Imma Achilike**

1 "Ashley!" exclaimed Mrs. Renfro, and simultaneously three heads whipped around at attention towards the **perturbed** teacher. At the same time, all three Ashleys proudly replied, "Yes, ma'am?"

2 When I was a fourth grader, I remember sitting in class that day just before the bell rang for dismissal. I remember thinking of all the names in the world, how I could have possibly been stuck with such an alien one. I thought about all the popular kids in the class. I figured that I wasn't popular because of my weird name. I put some things together in my mind and came up with a **plausible** equation: COOL NAME = POPULARITY. The dismissal bell rang. As I mechanically walked out to catch my ride, I thought to myself, "Why couldn't I have been named Ashley?"

3 I was the first American-born Nigerian in both of my parents' families. I was my parents' first joy, and in their joy, they gave me the name that would haunt me for the rest of my life, Immaculeta Uzoma Achilike.

perturbed: troubled
plausible: believable

4   The first time I actually became aware of my name was on the first day of first grade. I went to school loaded with all my school supplies and excited to see all of my old kindergarten friends. I couldn't wait to see who my new teacher was. As I walked into the classroom, all my friends pushed up to me, cooing my name: "Imma, Imma I missed you so much." The teacher walked in with the attendance sheet. She told everyone to quiet down so she could call roll. Before she started, she said something I thought would have never applied to me. She said, "Before I call roll, I apologize if I mispronounce anyone's name" with a very apologetic look on her face. She looked down at the attendance sheet, paused for a minute, and then looked up with an extremely puzzled look on her face. I remember thinking that there was probably some weird name before mine; although, my name was always the first name to be called in kindergarten. Suddenly, my palms started sweating and then she began to hopelessly stutter my name, "Im-Immaculet Arch-liki, I mean, Achei. ..." Here, I interrupted. My ears burned with embarrassment and droplets of perspiration formed on my nose. "Did I say it right?" she said with the same apologetic look on her face. Before I responded, the laughs that the other kids in class had been holding back suddenly exploded, like a **volatile** vial of nitroglycerin, into peals of laughter. One kid thought it was so funny his chubby face started turning red and I could see a tear gradually making its way down his face. I found myself wishing I could sink into the ground and never come back. I hated being the laughing stock.

5   I never really recovered from the shock of that day. From that day forward, the first day of school was always my most feared day. I didn't know what to do; all I could do was to tell my teachers, "I go by Imma."

6   I felt so alone when all the other girls in my class had sparkly, pink pencils with their names printed on them. You know, the ones they sell in the stores along with name-**embossed** sharpeners, rulers and pencil pouches. Every year I searched through and rummaged around that rack at the store, but I could never find a pencil with my name on it.

7   The summer of my seventh-grade year, my family and I took a vacation to our "home" in Nigeria, where my parents were born. My cousin and I were playing cards, talking girl talk, and relating our most embarrassing moments. Each tried to see whose story could top whose. I told one story of how I wet the bed at a sleepover, and she told me how she had farted in class during a test. That was a hoot. Then, I told her the story of how I was laughed at because of my weird name. I thought it was pretty funny, but she didn't laugh. She had the most serious look on her face, then she asked me, "Immaculeta Uzoma Achilike, do you know what your name means?" I shook my head at her and that's when she started laughing. I thought she was making fun of me, and as I started to leave she said: "Immaculeta means 'purity', 'Uzoma' means 'the good road' and ... " Having heard her words, I stopped walking away and turned around in amazement. "What does Achilike mean?" I asked. After a long pause she calmly said, "Achilike means 'to rule without force.'" I was astonished and pleased. I never knew what my name meant.

My Notes

volatile: explosive
embossed: adorned

My Notes

8 My name is Immaculeta Uzoma Achilike. I am the daughter of first-generation Nigerian immigrants. I am the daughter of hardworking and brave parents. My name means "to rule without force." My grandfather was a wealthy man of generous character. When I say my name in Nigeria, people know me as the granddaughter of a wealthy man of generous character. They know me by my name. There my name is not embossed on any pencil or vanity plate. It is etched in the minds of the people.

9 My name is Immaculeta Uzoma Achilike.

Making Observations

- What are your first thoughts about the personal narrative?
- When have you experienced the narrator's desire to fit in with others?

☑ Focus on the Sentence

Use your knowledge about conjunctions and your understanding of this personal narrative to write three sentences.

Imma used to be embarrassed by her name because _____

_____

Imma used to be embarrassed by her name, but _____

_____

Imma used to be embarrassed by her name, so _____

_____

Returning to the Text

- Return to the text as you respond to the following questions. Use text evidence to support your responses.
- Write any additional questions you have about the personal narrative in your Reader/ Writer Notebook.

1. Over the course of the text, the narrator has two distinctly different reactions to her name. How are they different? Which details in the story tell you how the author feels?

_____

_____

_____

_____

2. Find an example of visual sensory language used in paragraph 4. How does this language make the incident more vivid?

_____

_____

_____

_____

3. How does the author choose to begin the narrative? What is the author's purpose in beginning the narrative this way?

_____

_____

_____

_____

My Notes

Working from the Text

4. Complete the graphic organizer to analyze the organization and use of language, including sensory details, in "Why Couldn't I Have Been Named Ashley?"

	Incident	Response	Reflection
Paraphrase each part of the narrative and mark the text for specific textual evidence.			
Record textual evidence of language use in each part of the narrative (sensory details, figurative language, precise words or phrases).			

5. Practice writing descriptive sentences with the photographs in the next part of this activity. First, write a literal description of what is in the photograph. Then, write a sentence that uses sensory details and figurative language to describe the photograph. When finished, circle any sensory details and underline examples of figurative language. Evaluate the language in each sentence, and revise as necessary to make the description even more vivid.

Example:

Literal description: *A woman skates on a frozen pond.*

_____

Descriptive Sentence: *The young woman, bundled in warm layers of wool, makes a rhythmic scraping sound as she glides across the glassy frozen pond.*

_____

Picture 1

Literal description: _____

_____

_____

Descriptive Sentence: _____

_____

_____

_____

Picture 2

Literal description: _____

_____

_____

Descriptive Sentence: _____

_____

_____

_____

Picture 3

Literal description: _____

_____

_____

Descriptive Sentence: _____

_____

_____

_____

INDEPENDENT READING LINK

Read and Recommend

Reread the notes you have been taking in your Reader/Writer Notebook about your independent reading. Then choose one of the books to recommend to your classmates. Write a one-paragraph review of the book that explains why you like it. Be specific. For example, you might focus on character development, the author's use of language, or the book's vivid descriptions of time or place.

My Notes

Introducing the Strategy: Looping

Looping is a revision strategy in which you underline an important sentence and then add two sentences of additional elaboration. Use looping to add additional information to images, using sensory details or figurative language.

6. Practice looping with the following sentences.

   - I could not imagine a more beautiful fall day.
   - Just then the professor turned and, with an odd smile on his face, threw open the door to his laboratory.

7. Review your narrative draft and use looping to add sensory details and figurative language. Look for opportunities to replace nondescript words with more descriptive language.

8. Review the organization of your narrative draft. Do the events in the middle of your draft flow in a logical sequence? Are there any ideas that you need to move?

LANGUAGE & WRITER'S CRAFT: Commas

Commas can be used to set off words, phrases, or clauses in sentences. By using commas, writers create more elaborate sentences.

A **complex sentence** includes one independent clause and one or more dependent clauses. An **independent clause** contains a subject and verb and is a complete thought. An independent clause can stand alone as a sentence. A **dependent clause** contains a subject and verb but does not express a complete thought. When a dependent clause modifying a verb begins a complex sentence, it is followed by a comma.

   Example: *When I was a fourth grader*, I remember sitting in class that day just before the bell rang for dismissal.

"When I was a fourth grader" is a dependent clause that tells the reader when the action in the independent clause occurred.

Transition words help connect the ideas in one sentence to those in the next, often indicating the order in which things happen. You should usually use a comma to set off the transition word from the rest of the sentence.

   Example: I told one story of how I wet the bed at a sleepover, and she told me how she had farted in class during a test. That was a hoot. *Then*, I told her the story of how I was laughed at because of my weird name.

In this example, "Then" tells the reader what happened and in what order. It connects the action in one sentence to the action in the one before it.

PRACTICE Review your narrative draft to ensure that you have used commas correctly in complex sentences and with transitions.

☑ Check Your Understanding

Describe how you have changed the middle of your draft. Reflect on your use of looping to improve your draft.

Tie It Together: Revising the Ending

ACTIVITY
1.9

Learning Targets

- Understand how the narrative ending contributes to the author's purpose.
- Revise the narrative ending to ensure clarity of story and message.

Preview

In this activity, you will recognize effective narrative endings and then use that knowledge to review and revise your own narrative ending.

Learning Strategies

Discussion Groups
Graphic Organizer
Summarizing
Adding

Narrative Endings

1. Read this quote by Henry Wadsworth Longfellow: "Great is the art of beginning, but greater is the art of ending." What makes a great ending to a narrative?

2. Revisit the endings of these texts to examine how the authors provide effective endings. What was each author's purpose in structuring the text with this ending?

Text	Length of Ending	Summarize the Ending	Author's Purpose in Using This Ending
"The Scholarship Jacket," by Marta Salinas (Activity 1.4)			
Bad Boy, by Walter Dean Myers (Activity 1.5)			
"Why Couldn't I Have Been Named Ashley?" by Imma Achilike (Activity 1.8)			

Revising Your Narrative Ending

3. Review the graphic organizer you just completed about the endings of the texts you read. Go back and scan the endings of those texts before you revise the reflection at the end of your own narrative. Think about how each writer incorporated a reflection in order to bring the narrative to a meaningful and satisfying close. Then use the following questions to help generate ideas for the reflective ending for your narrative:

   • What did I learn from the experience?

   • Why does this matter?

   • Can I revisit a concept or idea from my lead or an image in the middle to create coherence?

4. Once you have revised your narrative ending, share your work with your writing group. After sharing, ask your group to provide feedback on your ending. To make sure you receive clear feedback, you might ask the members of your group to answer questions about your writing, such as:

   • Was my ending clear?

   • Did it accurately reflect the point of my narrative?

   • What details are missing?

   • What information should I add?

You will also have to provide feedback for the other members of your writing group. When it is your turn to share feedback, be sure to clearly give instructions to the writer that can help them improve their draft.

☑ Check Your Understanding

Describe how you have changed your ending. How did this change make your ending more effective for your reader?

⊕ Independent Reading Checkpoint

Write a summary about how the theme of choice is presented in your independent reading book. Explain the significance of these choices and use text evidence to support the explanations. Tell how the theme of choice in your book compares to the theme of choice in at least one of the assigned texts you read.

Revising a Personal Narrative about Choice

 ASSIGNMENT

Your assignment is to revise the personal narrative with reflection that you drafted earlier in the unit. Use the revision techniques you have learned in this unit to improve the beginning, middle, and end of your narrative. You will also write a text explaining the revisions you made to improve your first draft and the effect of the changes on the final piece.

Planning and Prewriting: Meet with your writing group to share and refine your revision ideas.	■ How will you present and discuss your draft and revision plan (Activities 1.7, 1.9) with your writing group? ■ How will you apply the revision strategies in Activities 1.8–1.9 to your draft to revise organization, coherence, and narrative elements? ■ How will reading and discussing your group members' drafts and revision plans help your efforts to revise?
Revising: Review your plan and revise your narrative.	■ How will you incorporate your group's suggestions and ideas into your revision plan? ■ How can the Scoring Guide help you evaluate how well your draft meets the requirements of the assignment? ■ How can you give feedback to your peers that will help them to revise their own narratives?
Checking and Editing: Confirm that your final draft is ready for publication.	■ How will you check for correct spelling and grammatical accuracy? ■ How can your writing group assist you with the editing and proofreading? ■ How will you prepare a final draft for publication?
Reflecting on Writing: Write an explanation of your revision process.	■ What were the most significant changes that you made to your original draft? ■ Why did you make these changes, and what was your intended effect on the reader? ■ How did your peers help you with the writing process?

Reflection

After completing this Embedded Assessment, think about how you went about accomplishing this task, and respond to the following:

- Explain how the activities in this unit helped prepare you for success on the Embedded Assessment.
- Which activities were especially helpful, and why?

SCORING GUIDE

Scoring Criteria	Exemplary	Proficient	Emerging	Incomplete
Ideas	The narrative • skillfully describes an incident and a choice made, and thoroughly reflects on the lesson learned • shows clear evidence of skillful revision to improve meaning, clarity, and adherence to narrative style • includes thoughtful reflection with explanations for changes.	The narrative • describes a choice, explains the consequences of the decision made, and reflects on the lesson learned • outlines and implements an appropriate revision plan that brings clarity to the narrative • includes reasons for the changes made.	The narrative • is missing one or more elements of an effective personal narrative (the incident, the choice, the consequences, and/or the reflection) • includes no clear outline or implementation of a plan for revision • is minimal and/or unclear.	The narrative • does not describe or develop a personal incident • shows little or no evidence of revision to improve writing, communication of ideas, or transitions to aid the reader.
Structure	The narrative • has an engaging beginning that hooks the reader and reveals all aspects of the incident • has a middle that vividly describes the series of events leading to the incident as well as the narrator's feelings, thoughts, and actions • has a reflective ending that examines the consequences of the choice.	The narrative • includes a beginning that introduces the incident • includes a middle that adequately describes the narrator's feelings, thoughts, and actions • provides an ending that examines the consequences of the choice.	The narrative • reflects very little revision to the first draft's organizational structure • may not include a beginning, a middle, or a reflective conclusion • may include an unfocused lead, a middle that merely retells a series of events, and/or an ending with minimal reflection and closure.	The narrative • begins unevenly with no clear introduction or lead • may be missing one or more paragraphs describing the incident and the narrator's feelings about it • has an inconclusive ending that does not follow from the incident or the narrator's choices.
Use of Language	The narrative • effectively uses sensory details and figurative language to vividly "show" the incident • contains few or no errors in spelling, punctuation, or capitalization.	The narrative • uses sensory images and details to make the incident clear • contains spelling, punctuation, and capitalization mistakes that do not detract.	The narrative • does not use sensory images and details to make the incident clear • contains mistakes that detract from meaning and/or readability.	The narrative • does not clearly describe the incident or provide details • contains mistakes that detract from meaning and/or readability.

Unpacking Embedded Assessment 2

Learning Targets
- Engage in meaningful discourse within a collaborative group.
- Discuss the importance of revision to the writing process.

Preview

In this activity, you will review the Essential Questions and your responses to them.

Making Connections

In the first part of this unit, you learned how to create a personal narrative to relate an incident, a response to the incident, and a reflection about the impact of the incident. In this half of the unit, you will expand on your narrative writing skills by creating an original myth.

Developing Vocabulary

1. Do a new QHT sort with the academic vocabulary and literary terms from this unit. You can find these terms listed on the Contents page.

Essential Questions

2. How has your understanding of the Essential Questions changed? How would you respond to these ideas now?

    - How do authors use narrative elements to create a story?
    - What are the elements of effective revision?

3. Share your latest responses to the Essential Questions in a collaborative group. Discuss how your latest responses have changed from your first thinking.

    - What questions can you ask your classmates about their responses?
    - What connections can you make between their responses and your responses?

Unpacking Embedded Assessment 2

Read the assignment for Embedded Assessment 2: Creating an Illustrated Myth:

 Your assignment is to work with a partner to create an original myth that explains a belief, custom, or natural phenomenon through the actions of gods or heroes. Be sure that your myth teaches a lesson or a moral and includes illustrations that complement the myth as it unfolds.

In your own words, paraphrase what you will need to know to complete Embedded Assessment 2 successfully.

INDEPENDENT READING LINK

Reading Plan

Find mythology from a culture you are interested in learning more about for your new Independent Reading text. As you read the myths, consider what you learn about the culture they come from. Consider what the myths tell you about what was important to the culture. For example, what roles do gods and goddesses play? How powerful are the human beings in the stories? What do the myths tell you about the beginning of the world? Write down your discoveries in your Independent Reading Log.

My Notes

Expanding Narrative Writing: Myths and Folklore

Learning Strategies

Marking the Text
Graphic Organizer
Activate Prior Knowledge
Sharing and Responding
Brainstorming

VOCABULARY

LITERARY

Folklore includes the stories, traditions, sayings, and customs of a culture or a society. **Myths** are traditional stories that explain beliefs, customs, or natural phenomena through the actions of gods or heroes.

WORD CONNECTIONS

Roots and Affixes

The word **fable** comes from the Latin word *fabula*, meaning "tale." Other English words derived from this word are *fabulous*, *affable*, and *confabulate*.

Learning Targets

- Identify the structure and purpose of myths as well as demonstrate knowledge of the literary genre of myths.
- Analyze how plot elements and plot structure advance the narrative of a story.
- Understand and describe how authors use figurative language to achieve a specific purpose.

Preview

In this activity, you will learn how authors use symbolism and plot structure in myths.

The Stories and Folklore of Myth

Folklore and **myth** are genres that begin with the oral tradition of telling stories to share them with people. They were often stories meant to make meaning of the world and to teach important lessons about life. You are probably familiar with many types of folklore, such as fairy tales, fables, or legends. These stories often have morals, or lessons, to teach us about human weaknesses such as greed, pride, recklessness, and thoughtlessness.

The characters of myth and folklore often are ordinary people in extraordinary situations. Usually, the actions of the characters in folklore have consequences that change the life of an entire culture or help explain what seems unexplainable.

Human beings have told stories throughout the ages to entertain, to teach, and to explain the mysteries of the world.

Review the Elements of a Short Story

1. What do you remember about the elements of a short story? Match the element to the definition.

Element	Definition
1. Plot	a. the time and place in which a story takes place
2. Character	b. a struggle, problem, or obstacle in a story
3. Conflict	c. the sequence of events that make up a story
4. Setting	d. a writer's central idea or main message about life
5. Theme	e. people, animals, or imaginary creatures that take part in a story

2. Review the elements of the **plot structure** of most narratives:

- **Exposition:** Background information or events necessary to understand a story; often includes an introduction to characters and setting (place and time story takes place)
- **Rising Action:** The conflicts and complications that develop a story
- **Climax:** The peak of the action; the most intense or suspenseful moment, often represents a turning point in the story

- **Falling Action:** The events after the climax (often the consequences of the climax) that lead to the resolution of the story
- **Resolution:** The end result or conclusion; "tying up any loose ends"; in a personal narrative, the resolution may include a reflection

☑ Check Your Understanding

With a partner or small group, discuss the elements of plot structure and place them on the plot diagram.

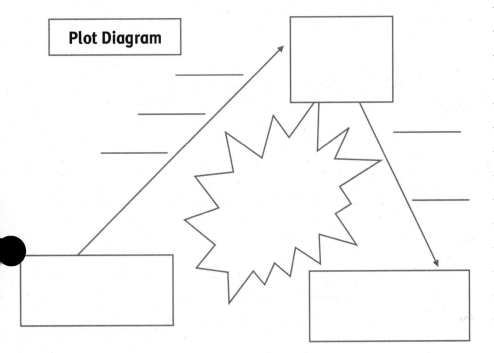

Plot Diagram

The Meanings of Words

The *literal* meaning of a word or phrase is expected to be understood exactly as it is stated, while a *figurative* meaning is one that suggests some idea beyond the literal level.

A **symbol** is a figurative use of an object or image so that it represents something beyond itself. You might think of a symbol as having two meanings: one meaning is literal, and the other is figurative. A flag is literally a piece of cloth with a design; it is symbolic of a nation, clan, or state. Writers commonly use symbolism in literary works to add depth of meaning.

3. Colors can sometimes be used symbolically in texts. Think about what these colors represent, and brainstorm each color's symbolic meaning.

Color	Symbolic Representation
Blue	sadness, water, cold, sky, heaven, peace, purity
Green	
Gold	
Red	

VOCABULARY

LITERARY
A **symbol** is an object, a person, or a place that stands for something else. *Symbolism* is the use of symbols in a literary work.

Poor Choices: "Phaethon"

Learning Targets

- Analyze how characters' motivations and behaviors influence the events of a story.
- Identify how plot elements, such as conflict and climax, advance the narrative of a story.
- Analyze how a story's theme and setting influence character development.

Preview

In this activity, you will read a myth and analyze its plot and characters.

My Notes

Phaethon
Apollo

Introducing the Strategy: Diffusing

With this strategy, you use context clues to help find the meaning of unknown words. When **diffusing**, circle words that are unfamiliar. Think of two possible substitutions (synonyms) and confirm your definition. You can confirm your definition by checking reference sources such as a dictionary or a thesaurus.

Setting a Purpose for Reading

- As you read, mark the text as you learn or infer details about Phaethon.
- Circle unknown words and phrases. Try to determine the meaning of the words by using context clues, word parts, or a dictionary.

About the Author

Bernard Evslin (1922–1993) wrote many books for young people and is best known for his adaptations of tales from Greek mythology. *Heroes, Gods and Monsters of the Greek Myths,* his best-known work, has sold more than 10 million copies worldwide and has been translated into 10 different languages. Evslin's work has won a number of awards, and his book *The Green Hero* was nominated for a National Book Award.

Myth *Feelings   Actions   Sayings   Thoughts*

Phaethon

by **Bernard Evslin**

Apollo
He was proble
filled Jelesy

Chunk 1

1   Long ago, when the world was very new, two boys were racing along the edge of a cliff that hung over a deep blue sea. They were the same size; one boy had black hair, the other had yellow hair. The race was very close. Then the yellow-haired one **spurted** ahead and won the race. The loser was very angry.

2   "You think you're pretty good," he said. "But you're not so much. My father is Zeus."[1]

3   "My father is Apollo," said the yellow-haired boy, whose name was Phaethon.[2]

4   "My father is the chief god, king of the mountain, lord of the sky."

5   "My father is lord of the sun."

6   "My father is called the thunderer. When he is angry, the sky grows black and the sun hides. His spear is a lightning bolt, and that's what he kills people with. He hurls it a thousand miles and it never misses."

Chunk 2

7   "Without my father there would be no day. It would always be night. Each morning he hitches up his horses and drives the golden chariot of the sun across the sky. And that is day time. Then he dives into the ocean stream and boards a golden ferryboat and sails back to his eastern palace. That time is called night."

8   "Sometimes I visit my father," said Epaphus,[3] the other boy. "I sit on Olympus[4] with him, and he teaches me things and gives me presents. Know what he gave me last time? A little thunderbolt just like his—and he taught me how to throw it. I killed three vultures, scared a fishing boat, started a forest fire. Next time I go, I'll throw it at more things. Do you visit your father?"

9   Phaethon never had. But he could not bear to tell Epaphus, "Certainly," he said, "very often. I go to the eastern palace, and he teaches me things too."

10   "What kind of things? Has he taught you to drive the horses of the sun?"

11   "Oh, yes. He taught me to handle their reins and how to make them go and how to make them stop. And they're huge horses. Tall as this mountain. They breathe fire."

12   "I think you're making it all up," said Epaphus. "I can tell. I don't even believe there is a sun chariot. There's the sun, look at it. It's not a chariot."

13   "Oh, what you see is just one of the wheels," said Phaethon. "There's another wheel on the other side. The body of the chariot is slung between

---

[1] **Zeus** [züs]: King of the gods in Greek mythology
[2] **Phaethon** [fā´ə thon]
[3] **Epaphus** [ə pā´ fəs]
[4] **Olympus** [ō lim´ pəs]: A mountain in Greece where ancient gods were said to live

spurted: ran quickly

My Notes

15 action feelings

14 to 21 Saying

them. That is where the driver stands and whips his horses. You cannot see it because your eyes are too small, and the glare is too bright."

14 "Well," said Epaphus, "Maybe it is a chariot, but I still don't believe your father lets you drive it. In fact, I don't believe you've been to the palace of the sun. I doubt that Apollo would know you if he saw you. Maybe he isn't even your father. People like to say they're **descended** from the gods, of course. But how many of us are there, really?"

15 "I'll prove it to you," cried Phaethon, stamping his foot. "I'll go to the palace of the sun right now and hold my father to his promise. I'll show you."

16 "What promise?"

17 "He said I was getting to be so good a charioteer that next time he would let me drive the sun chariot *alone*. All by myself. From dawn to night. Right across the sky. And this time is next time."

18 "Proof—words are cheap," said Epaphus. "How will I know it's you driving the sun? I won't be able to see you from down here."

19 "You'll know me," said Phaethon. "When I pass the village I will come down close and drive in circles around your roof. You'll see me all right. Farewell."

20 "Are you starting now?"

21 "Now. At once. Just watch the sky tomorrow, son of Zeus."

Chunk 3

22 And he went off. He was so stung by the words of his friend, and the **boasting** and lying he had been forced to do, that he traveled night and day, not stopping for food or rest, guiding himself by the morning star and the evening star, heading always east. Nor did he know the way. For, indeed, he had never once seen his father Apollo. He knew him only through his mother's stories. But he did know that the palace must lie in the east, because that is where he saw the sun start each morning. He walked on and on until finally he lost his way completely, and weakened by hunger and exhaustion, fell swooning in a great meadow by the edge of a wood.

23 Now, while Phaethon was making his journey, Apollo sat in his great throne room on a huge throne made of gold and rubies. This was the quiet hour before dawn when night left its last coolness upon the Earth. And it was then, at this hour, that Apollo sat on his throne, wearing a purple cloak embroidered with the golden sign of the zodiac.[5] On his head was a crown given him by the dawn goddess, made of silver and pearls. A bird flew in the window and perched on his shoulder and spoke to him. This bird had sky-blue feathers, golden beak, golden claws, and golden eyes. It was one of Apollo's sun hawks. It was this bird's job to fly here and there gathering gossip. Sometimes she was called the spy bird.

24 Now she said, "Apollo, I have seen your son!"

25 "Which son?"

26 "Phaethon. He's coming to see you. But he has lost his way and lies exhausted at the edge of the wood. The wolves will surely eat him. Do you care?"

descended: relatives who came
boasting: prideful talking

[5] **zodiac** [zō´ dē ak]: An imaginary belt of the heavens, divided into 12 parts, called signs, and named after 12 constellations

27 "I will have to see him before I know whether I care. You had better get back to him before the wolves do. Bring him here in comfort. Round up some of your companions and bring him here as befits the son of a god."

28 The sun hawk seized the softly glowing rug at the foot of the throne and flew away with it. She summoned three of her companions, and they each took a corner of the rug. They flew over a desert and a mountain and a wood and came to the field where Phaethon lay. They flew down among the howling of wolves, among burning eyes set in a circle about the unconscious boy. They pushed him onto the rug, and each took a corner in her beak, and flew away.

29 Phaethon felt himself being lifted into the air. The cold wind of his going revived him, and he sat up. People below saw a boy sitting with folded arms on a carpet rushing through the cold, bright moonlight far above their heads. It was too dark, though, to see the birds, and that is why we hear tales of flying carpets even to this day.

30 Phaethon was not particularly surprised to find himself in the air. The last thing he remembered was lying down on the grass. Now he knew he was dreaming. A good dream—floating and flying—his favorite kind. And when he saw the great cloud castle on top of the mountain, all made of snow, rise in the early light, he was more sure than ever that he was dreaming. He saw sentries in flashing golden armor, carrying golden spears. In the courtyard he saw enormous woolly dogs with fleece like clouddrift guarding the gate. These were Apollo's great sun hounds.

31 Over the wall flew the carpet, over the courtyard, through the tall portals. And it wasn't until the sun hawks gently let down the carpet in front of the throne that he began to think that this dream might be very real. He raised his eyes shyly and saw a tall figure sitting on the throne. Taller than any man, and **appallingly** beautiful to the boy—with his golden hair and stormy blue eyes and strong laughing face. Phaethon fell on his knees.

Chunk 4

32 "Father," he cried. "I am Phaethon, your son!"

33 "Rise, Phaethon. Let me look at you."

34 He stood up, his legs trembling.

35 "Yes, you may well be my son. I seem to see a resemblance. Which one did you say?"

36 "Phaethon."

37 "Oh, Clymene's[6] boy. I remember your mother well. How is she?"

38 "In health, sire."

39 "And did I not leave some daughters with her as well? Yellow-haired girls—quite pretty?"

40 "My sisters, sire. The Heliads."

41 "Yes, of course. Must get over that way and visit them all one of these seasons. And you, lad—what brings you to me? Do you not know that it is courteous to await an invitation before visiting a god—even if he is in the family?"

---

[6] **Clymene** [klī men ē´]

appallingly: amazingly

My Notes

30 Dreaming

42 "I know, Father. But I had no choice. I was taunted by a son of Zeus, Epaphus. And I would have flung him over the cliff and myself after him if I had not **resolved** to make my lies come true."

Chunk 5

43 "Well, you're my son, all right. Proud, rash, accepting no **affront**, refusing no adventure. I know the breed. Speak up, then. What is it you wish? I will do anything in my power to help you."

44 "Anything, Father?"

45 "Anything I can. I swear by the river Styx,[7] an oath sacred to the gods."

46 "I wish to drive the sun across the sky. All by myself. From dawn till night."

47 Apollo's roar of anger shattered every crystal goblet in the great castle.

48 "Impossible!" he cried. "No one drives those horses but me. They are tall as mountains. Their breath is fire. They are stronger than the tides, stronger than the wind. It is all that *I* can do to hold them in check. How can your puny grip restrain them? They will race away with the chariot, scorching the poor Earth to a cinder."

49 "You promised, Father."

50 "Yes, I promised, foolish lad. And that promise is the death warrant. A poor charred cinder floating in space—well, that is what the **oracle** predicted for the earth—but I did not know it would be so soon ... so soon."

Chunk 6

51 "It is almost dawn, Father. Should we not saddle the horses?"

52 "Will you not withdraw your request—allow me to preserve my honor without destroying the earth? Ask me anything else and I will grant it. Do not ask me this."

53 "I have asked, sire, and you have promised. And the hour for dawn comes, and the horses are unharnessed. The sun will rise late today, confusing the wise."

54 "They will be more than confused when this day is done," said Apollo. "Come."

55 Apollo took Phaethon to the stable of the sun, and there the boy saw the giant fire-white horses being harnessed to the golden chariot. Huge they were. Fire-white with golden manes and golden hooves and hot yellow eyes. When they neighed, the trumpet call of it rolled across the sky—and their breath was flame. They were being harnessed by a Titan, a cousin of the gods, tall as the tree, dressed in asbestos[8] armor with a helmet of tinted crystal against the glare. The sun chariot was an open shell of gold. Each wheel was the flat round disk of the sun as it is seen in the sky. And Phaethon looked very tiny as he stood in the chariot. The reins were thick as bridge cables, much too large for him to hold, so Apollo tied them around his waist. Then Apollo stood at the head of the team gentling the horses speaking softly to them, calling them by name—Pyrocis,[9] Eous,[10] Aethon,[11] Phlegon.[12]

---

[7] **Styx** [stiks]: In Greek myths, a river that led to Hades or Hell

[8] **asbestos** [as bes' təs]: A mineral that does not burn or conduct heat

[9] **Pyrocis** [pï rō' chis]

[10] **Eous** [e' us]

[11] **Aethon** [a' thon]

[12] **Phlegon** [fle' gon]

resolved: decided
affront: insult
oracle: holy advisor

56 "Good lads, good horses, go easy today, my swift ones. Go at a slow trot and do not leave the path. You have a new driver today."

57 The great horses dropped their heads to his shoulder and whinnied softly, for they loved him. Phaethon saw the flame of their breath play about his head, saw Apollo's face shining out of the flame. But he was not harmed, for he was a god and could not be hurt by physical things.

Chunk 7

58 He came to Phaethon and said, "Listen to me, son. You are about to start a terrible journey. Now, by the obedience you owe me as a son, by the faith you owe a god, by my oath that cannot be broken, and your pride that will not bend, I put this rule upon you: Keep the middle way. Too high and the earth will freeze, too low and it will burn. Keep the middle way. Give the horses their heads; they know the path, the blue middle course of day. Drive them not too high nor too low, but above all, do not stop. Or you will fire the air about you where you stand, charring the earth and blistering the sky. Do you heed me?"

59 "I do, I do!" cried Phaethon. "Stand away, sire! The dawn grows old and day must begin! Go, horses, go!"

60 And Apollo stood watching as the horses of the sun went into a swinging trot, pulling behind them the golden chariot, climbing the first eastern steep of the sky.

61 At first things went well. The great steeds trotted easily along their path across the high blue meadow of the sky. And Phaethon thought to himself, "I can't understand why my father was making such a fuss. This is easy. For me, anyway. Perhaps I'm a natural-born coachman though ... "

62 He looked over the edge of the chariot. He saw tiny houses down below and specks of trees. And the dark blue puddle of the sea. The coach was trundling across the sky. The great sun wheels were turning, casting light, warming and brightening the earth, chasing all the shadows of night.

63 "Just imagine," Phaethon thought, "how many people now are looking up at the sky, praising the sun, hoping the weather stays fair. How many people are watching me, me, me ... ?" Then he thought, "But I'm too small to see. They can't even see the coach or the horses—only the great wheel. We are too far and the light is too bright. For all they know, it is Apollo making his usual run. How can they know it's me, me, me? How will my mother know, and my sisters? They would be so proud. And Epaphus—above all, Epaphus—how will he know? I'll come home tomorrow after this glorious journey and tell him what I did and he will laugh at me and tell me I'm lying, as he did before. And how shall I prove it to him? No, this must not be. I must show him that it is I driving the chariot of the sun—I alone. Apollo said not to come too close to earth, but how will he know? And I won't stay too long—just dip down toward our own village and circle his roof three times—which is the signal we agreed upon. After he recognizes me, I'll whip up the horses and resume the path of the day.

Chunk 8

64 He jerked on the reins, pulled the horses' heads down. They whinnied angrily and tossed their heads. He jerked the reins again.

My Notes

My Notes

65 "Down," he cried. "Down! Down!"

66 The horses plunged through the bright air, golden hooves twinkling, golden manes flying, dragging the great glittering chariot after them in a long flaming swoop. When they reached his village, he was horrified to see the roofs bursting into fire. The trees burned. People rushed about screaming. Their loose clothing caught fire, and they burned like torches as they ran.

67 Was it his village? He could not tell because of the smoke. Had he destroyed his own home? Burned his mother and his sisters?

68 He threw himself backward in the chariot, pulling at the reins with all his might, shouting, "Up! Up!"

69 And the horses, made furious by the smoke, reared on their hind legs in the air. They leaped upward, galloping through the smoke, pulling the chariot up, up.

70 Swiftly the earth fell away beneath them. The village was just a smudge of smoke. Again he saw the pencil-stroke of mountains, the inkblot of seas. "Whoa!" he cried. "Turn now! Forward on your path!" But he could no longer handle them. They were galloping, not trotting. They had taken the bit in their teeth. They did not turn toward the path of the day across the meadow of the sky, but galloped up, up. And the people on earth saw the sun shooting away until it was no larger than a star.

71 Darkness came. And cold. The earth froze hard. Rivers froze, and oceans. Boats were caught fast in the ice in every sea. It snowed in the jungle. Marble buildings cracked. It was impossible for anyone to speak; breath froze on the speakers' lips. And in village and city, in the field and in the wood, people died of the cold. And the bodies piled up where they fell, like firewood.

Simile 72 Still Phaethon could not hold his horses, and still they galloped upward dragging light and warmth away from the earth. Finally they went so high that the air was too thin to breathe. Phaethon saw the flame of their breath, which had been red and yellow, burn blue in the thin air. He himself was gasping for breath; he felt the marrow of his bones freezing.

73 Now the horses, wild with change, maddened by the feeble hand on the reins, swung around and dived toward earth again. Now all the ice melted, making great floods. Villages were swept away by a solid wall of water. Trees were uprooted and whole forests were torn away. The fields were covered by water. Lower swooped the horses, and lower yet. Now the water began to steam — great billowing clouds of steam as the water boiled. Dead fish floated on the surface. Naiads moaned in dry riverbeds.

74 Phaethon could not see; the steam was too thick. He had unbound the reins from his waist, or they would have cut him in two. He had no control over the horses at all. They galloped upward again—out of the steam—taking at last the middle road, but racing wildly, using all their tremendous speed. Circling the earth in a matter of minutes, smashing across the sky from horizon to horizon, making the day flash on and off like a child playing with a lamp. And the people who were left alive were bewildered by the light and darkness following each other so swiftly.

Chunk 9

75 Up high on Olympus, the gods in their cool garden heard a **clamor** of grief from below. Zeus looked upon earth. He saw the runaway horses of the sun and the hurtling chariot. He saw the dead and the dying, the burning forests, the floods, the weird frost. Then he looked again at the chariot and saw that it was not Apollo driving, but someone he did not know. He stood up, drew back his arm, and hurled a thunderbolt.

76 It stabbed through the air, striking Phaethon, killing him instantly, knocking him out of the chariot. His body, flaming, fell like a star. And the horses of the sun, knowing themselves driverless, galloped homeward toward their stables at the eastern edge of the sky.

77 Phaethon's yellow-haired sisters grieved for the beautiful boy. They could not stop weeping. They stood on the bank of the river where he had fallen until Apollo, unable to comfort them, changed them into poplar trees. Here they still stand on the shore of the river, weeping tears of amber sap.

78 And since that day no one has been allowed to drive the chariot of the sun except the sun god himself. But there are still traces of Phaethon's ride. The ends of the earth are still covered with icecaps. Mountains still rumble, trying to spit out the fire started in their bellies by the diving sun.

Making Observations
- What surprises you about this myth?
- What image from the myth did you picture clearly?

clamor: noisy shouting

☑ Focus on the Sentence

Use your knowledge about conjunctions and your understanding of "Phaethon" to write three sentences.

Phaethon wants to drive his father's chariot across the sky because _____

_____

Phaethon wants to drive his father's chariot across the sky, but _____

_____

Phaethon wants to drive his father's chariot across the sky, so _____

_____

Returning to the Text

- Return to the text as you respond to the following questions. Use text evidence to support your responses.
- Write any additional questions you have about the myth in your Reader/Writer Notebook.

1. In chunk 2, how does Phaethon respond to Epaphus's taunting? What might this tell you about his character?

_____

_____

_____

_____

2. Look at paragraphs 22–23. How does the argument between the friends set the plot in motion? Cite details from the story to support your answers.

_____

_____

_____

_____

3. Read paragraph 27. How does Apollo feel about his son Phaethon? What dialogue shows his attitude toward his son?

_____

_____

_____

_____

4. In paragraph 41, what is a synonym for the word *courteous*? Why do you think the author chose this word?

_____

_____

_____

5. Reread chunk 6. Why does Apollo want Phaethon to change his request? How do you know?

_____

_____

_____

_____

6. At the end of paragraph 58, Apollo asks, "Do you heed me?" Using context to clarify meaning, what does this phrase mean?

_____

_____

_____

_____

7. Reread chunk 7. What details reveal Phaethon's character and qualities through his thoughts? Use text evidence to support your ideas.

_____

_____

_____

_____

8. Reread chunk 8. What relationship do the words *feeble* and *tremendous* have? What does this relationship highlight?

_____

_____

_____

_____

9. Reread paragraph 63. How does Phaethon 's character influence the climax of the story and the resolution of the conflict? Which lines in the following paragraphs describe the story's climax?

_____

_____

_____

_____

10. Make an inference about what consequences might happen because of Phaethon's disobedience. What evidence from the text supports your answer?

_____

_____

_____

_____

11. Briefly summarize the myth "Phaethon" in your own words, making sure your summary maintains logical order and is true to the story.

_____

_____

_____

_____

Working from the Text

12. Using the plot diagram from Activity 1.11, determine the major conflict of the story and where the climax and falling action of the story occur.

13. Indicate whether you agree or disagree with the following statements about Phaethon and Apollo. Then find and record the textual evidence that supports your position. Go back to the text and highlight your textual evidence.

Agree	Disagree	
		Phaethon is a thoughtless, headstrong boy. Textual Evidence:
		Phaethon is an adventurous, courageous boy. Textual Evidence:
		Phaethon is _____. (Insert your description.) Textual Evidence:
		Apollo is a disinterested, ineffective parent. Textual Evidence:
		Apollo is deeply concerned for his son's well-being. Textual Evidence:
		Apollo is _____. (Insert your description.) Textual Evidence:

14. Reflect on how diffusing vocabulary helped you to understand the myth Phaethon more deeply. Are there any words that you still need to clarify? If so, use a reference to determine meaning, part of speech, and word origin.

 Writing to Sources: Informational Text

How do the character traits of Apollo or Phaethon drive the story to its tragic conclusion? Write a paragraph about either Phaethon or Apollo. Be sure to:

- Include a controlling idea that states the character's qualities and how those qualities drive the plot of the story.
- Use precise language to express your ideas clearly; avoid wordiness and unnecessary repetition.
- Use appropriate register, tone, and voice in your response.
- Support your ideas about the character's tragic traits. Include at least two examples of textual evidence in your paragraph, such as the character's actions, thoughts, and dialogue.

A Matter of Pride

Learning Targets

- Compare and contrast character traits across multiple myths.
- Analyze the relationship between character and plot and between conflict and resolution.

Preview

In this activity, you will read a myth whose main character's traits bring about surprising events.

Setting a Purpose for Reading

- As you read, underline details you learn about Arachne's qualities.
- Circle unknown words and phrases. Try to determine the meaning of the words by using context clues, word parts, or a dictionary.

About the Author

Olivia Coolidge (1908–2006) grew up in England in the early 1900s. She became a teacher of Latin, Greek, and mythology, and taught in England, Germany, and the United States. Coolidge wrote numerous histories and biographies for children and young adults. Her work is noted for high interest and vivid descriptions. Coolidge published 27 books, including many titles for young adults.

My Notes

Exposition:
Character
Setting
Time
Place

Myth

Arachne

by **Olivia E. Coolidge**

1   Arachne was a maiden who became famous throughout Greece, though she was neither wellborn nor beautiful and came from no great city. She lived in an **obscure** little village, and her father was a humble dyer of wool. In this he was very skillful, producing many varied shades, while above all he was famous for the clear, bright scarlet which is made from shellfish, and which was the most glorious of all the colors used in ancient Greece. Even more skillful than her father was Arachne. It was her task to spin the fleecy wool into a fine, soft thread and to weave it into cloth on the high, standing loom within the cottage. Arachne was small and pale from much working. Her eyes were light and her hair was a dusty brown, yet she was quick and graceful, and her fingers, roughened as they were, went so fast that it was hard to follow their flickering movements. So soft and even was her thread, so fine her cloth, so gorgeous her embroidery, that soon her products were known all over Greece. No one had ever seen the like of them before.

> obscure: not well known

My Notes

2   At last Arachne's fame became so great that people used to come from far and wide to watch her working. Even the graceful nymphs would steal in from stream or forest and peep shyly through the dark doorway, watching in wonder the white arms of Arachne as she stood at the loom and threw the shuttle from hand to hand between the hanging threads, or drew out the long wool, fine as a hair, from the distaff as she sat spinning. "Surely Athene herself must have taught her," people would murmur to one another. "Who else could know the secret of such marvelous skill?"

3   Arachne was used to being wondered at, and she was immensely proud of the skill that had brought so many to look on her. Praise was all she lived for, and it displeased her greatly that people should think anyone, even a goddess, could teach her anything. Therefore when she heard them murmur, she would stop her work and turn round **indignantly** to say, "With my own ten fingers I gained this skill, and by hard practice from early morning till night. I never had time to stand looking as you people do while another maiden worked. Nor if I had, would I give Athene credit because the girl was more skillful than I. As for Athene's weaving, how could there be finer cloth or more beautiful embroidery than mine? If Athene herself were to come down and compete with me, she could do no better than I."

4   One day when Arachne turned round with such words, an old woman answered her, a grey old woman, bent and very poor, who stood leaning on a staff and peering at Arachne amid the crowd of onlookers.

5   "Reckless girl," she said, "how dare you claim to be equal to the immortal gods themselves? I am an old woman and have seen much. Take my advice and ask pardon of Athene for your words. Rest content with your fame of being the best spinner and weaver that mortal eyes have ever beheld."

6   "Stupid old woman," said Arachne indignantly, "who gave you the right to speak in this way to me? It is easy to see that you were never good for anything in your day, or you would not come here in poverty and rags to gaze at my skill. If Athene resents my words, let her answer them herself. I have challenged her to a contest, but she, of course, will not come. It is easy for the gods to avoid matching their skill with that of men."

7   At these words the old woman threw down her staff and stood erect. The wondering onlookers saw her grow tall and fair and stand clad in long robes of dazzling white. They were terribly afraid as they realized that they stood in the presence of Athene. Arachne herself flushed red for a moment, for she had never really believed that the goddess would hear her. Before the group that was gathered there she would not give in; so pressing her pale lips together in **obstinacy** and pride, she led the goddess to one of the great looms and set herself before the other. Without a word both began to thread the long woolen strands that hang from the rollers, and between which the shuttle moves back and forth. Many skeins lay heaped beside them to use, bleached white, and gold, and scarlet, and other shades, varied as the rainbow. Arachne had never thought of giving credit for her success to her father's skill in dyeing, though in actual truth the colors were as remarkable as the cloth itself.

indignantly: angrily
obstinacy: stubbornness

8   Soon there was no sound in the room but the breathing of the onlookers, the whirring of the shuttles, and the creaking of the wooden frames as each pressed the thread up into place or tightened the pegs by which the whole was held straight. The excited crowd in the doorway began to see that the skill of both in truth was very nearly equal, but that, however the cloth might turn out, the goddess was the quicker of the two. A pattern of many pictures was growing on her loom. There was a border of twined branches of the olive, Athene's favorite tree, while in the middle, figures began to appear. As they looked at the glowing colors, the spectators realized that Athene was weaving into her pattern a last warning to Arachne. The central figure was the goddess herself competing with Poseidon for possession of the city of Athens; but in the four corners were mortals who had tried to **strive** with gods and pictures of the awful fate that had overtaken them. The goddess ended a little before Arachne and stood back from her marvelous work to see what the maiden was doing.

9   Never before had Arachne been matched against anyone whose skill was equal, or even nearly equal to her own. As she stole glances from time to time at Athene and saw the goddess working swiftly, calmly, and always a little faster than herself, she became angry instead of frightened, and an evil thought came into her head. Thus as Athene stepped back a pace to watch Arachne finishing her work, she saw that the maiden had taken for her design a pattern of scenes which showed evil or unworthy actions of the gods, how they had deceived fair maidens, resorted to trickery, and appeared on earth from time to time in the form of poor and humble people. When the goddess saw this insult glowing in bright colors on Arachne's loom, she did not wait while the cloth was judged, but stepped forward, her grey eyes blazing with anger, and tore Arachne's work across. Then she struck Arachne across the face. Arachne stood there a moment, struggling with anger, fear, and pride. "I will not live under this insult," she cried, and seizing a rope from the wall, she made a noose and would have hanged herself. The goddess touched the rope and touched the maiden. "Live on, wicked girl," she said. "Live on and spin, both you and your descendants. When men look at you they may remember that it is not wise to strive with Athene." At that the body of Arachne shriveled up, and her legs grew tiny, spindly, and distorted. There before the eyes of the spectators hung a little dusty brown spider on a slender thread.

10   All spiders descend from Arachne, and as the Greeks watched them spinning their thread wonderfully fine, they remembered the contest with Athene and thought that it was not right for even the best of men to claim equality with the gods.

Making Observations

- What happens in this myth?
- What is a detail you noticed about Arachne that someone else might miss?

strive: compete

Returning to the Text

- Return to the text as you respond to the following questions. Use text evidence to support your responses.
- Write any additional questions you have about the myth in your Reader/Writer Notebook.

1. In the first three paragraphs of the story, what do Arachne's words and actions tell you about the kind of person she is?

2. Find one quote from Arachne that demonstrates how her qualities influenced the plot. Explain your choice.

3. Read the details about the images that Athene and Arachne weave. How might these images relate to the theme of the story? Use details from the text to support your answer.

4. How do Arachne's character traits determine how the conflict is resolved?

5. What message does the author convey in the ending of the myth?

Working from the Text

6. Both Arachne and Phaethon possess traits that contribute to their demise. Use the graphic organizer to compare and contrast the two characters' attitudes and character traits and how these traits lead to self-destruction. Cite evidence from the text. Then, below the graphic organizer, write how the two myths together teach a lesson.

	Character Traits	How do these traits lead to self-destruction?
Arachne		
Phaethon		

Lesson:

7. Myths like "Arachne" have been used for generations to explain natural phenomena such as lightning, tsunamis, and volcanic eruptions. Use your knowledge of myths to identify the element of nature the myth explains, Arachne's choices, and the lessons this myth teaches (themes).

Element of Nature	Choices	Lesson

My Notes

_____
_____
_____
_____
_____
_____
_____
_____
_____
_____
_____
_____
_____
_____
_____
_____
_____
_____
_____
_____
_____
_____
_____
_____
_____
_____
_____
_____
_____
_____
_____
_____
_____
_____
_____
_____
_____
_____

☑ Focus on the Sentence

Use your notes and discussions about "Arachne" and "Phaethon" to write sentences that synthesize your understanding about the characters, events, and themes in the two myths.

Write one statement about the two characters: _____
_____

Write a question you would like to ask Arachne and Phaethon: _____
_____

Write a command or piece of advice for each character: _____
_____

8. Working with a partner, select a god or goddess. Conduct further research in order to create a "Missing" or "Wanted" poster for him or her. Be sure to:

   • Include all the relevant information identified from your research.
   • Include symbolism through your use of colors or images.
   • Include a visual (you can sketch or use another visual) of the god or goddess.
   • Prepare to present this poster to a group and display it in the classroom.
      Name: _____ Age: _____

      Also known as: _____

      Role:

      Last known location:

      Physical description:

      Significant actions/crimes:

      Presumed dangerous? Why?

      Known associates:

      Additional information/distinguishing features:

Animals as Symbols

Learning Targets

- Engage in a productive discussion within a collaborative group.
- Describe how figurative language and symbolism are used to convey a specific meaning

Preview

In this activity, you will read a fable and analyze its message and its use of animals as symbols.

Setting a Purpose for Reading

- As you read, underline choices the characters make.
- Circle unknown words and phrases. Try to determine the meaning of the words by using context clues, word parts, or a dictionary.

About the Author

Angel Vigil is an author, performer, storyteller, theatrical director, and educator. He grew up in New Mexico, and stories have been a part of his life since childhood. Some of his fondest memories are of family gatherings where he would sit in a circle, listening to exciting conversations filled with stories and tales. His many books and storytelling performances explore the traditional stories of the Hispanic Southwest and Mexico.

My Notes

Fable

The Burro
and The Fox

by **Angel Vigil**

1   Like many other animals in the animal kingdom, the burro is a beast of burden, spending his life toiling in the hot sun in order to make his master's life a little easier. The burro knows no other existence and is destined to a life of service and loyalty to his master.

2   The worst fate for a burro, however, is to have a cruel master. Some masters love and care for their burro, respecting that their own life is dependent on this creature. Others take the burro for granted and just expect the burro to always be there to carry their heavy load. Others, the worst ones,

WORD CONNECTIONS

Roots and Affixes

The word *dependent* comes from the Latin root *pend*, which means "to hang," and the affix *de-*, which means "down." When someone is dependent, he or she hangs on to another for support. You can find the root *pend* in other words, such as *independent*, *pending*, and *pendant*.

My Notes

take their own mean temperament out on the poor, defenseless burro by whipping, beating, and starving their burro. They have little or no concern for the burro's well-being, and if the burro dies, no remorse or sense of loss is felt by the master.

3 It just so happens that in this story, our burro has one of these mean masters. This master would beat the burro if it walked too fast, walked too slowly, stopped too abruptly, or started too suddenly. He would beat the burro if it tripped on the steep, rocky mountain path or if it stopped for water by a mountain stream. Some days, he would beat the burro just for being in the way.

4 Finally, the burro had had enough of his master's beatings and decided to run away. Late one night, while the master was sleeping, the burro broke out of the corral and took off down the road with a quick trot. He was free—free at last!

5 The burro loved his new freedom. He strolled along a shady mountain path, eating the new spring grasses. He lounged by a mountain stream, sipping its cool, fresh waters. He paused and rested when he wanted, and he walked along when he wanted. Most of all, he did not pass his days in fear of a beating.

6 One day, as he walked along a forest path, the burro ran into a fox. The fox asked the burro, "Why are you walking alone so far in the forest? Where is your master?"

7 The burro replied, "I have run away from my master, because he beats me all of the time. I am a free burro, and I will walk wherever my spirit leads me."

8 The fox then told the burro, "I am a servant of the lion, the king of the forest. Perhaps you should come to meet the lion and see if you could join our band of free animals. The lion is a strong and wise ruler, and perhaps he could help you find a new life. Come with me, and I will announce you to the lion. You will be well received by him."

9 The burro followed the fox. He was thankful that he had at last met up with other free animals and was hopeful that the lion could help him find a new life. He had been enjoying his free wanderings, but he did not want to be a nomad and never have a home again.

10 The fox and burro arrived at the home of the lion. The fox went to the lion and announced the burro's arrival, "I have run into an old burro who has run away from his master. I have brought him here so that you may meet him and have told him that he will be well received by you."

11 The lion told the fox, "Bring this burro to me right away. I do want to meet him."

12 The fox brought the burro to the lion. He introduced the burro to the lion and then left so the lion could question the burro by himself.

13 While the lion addressed the burro, he paced around and around the burro. The burro began to get nervous, because lions usually only pace when they are hungry. As the lion circled the burro, he got closer and closer, making the circle around the burro tighter and tighter with each pass.

14 Finally, the lion suddenly jumped toward the burro and nipped at his flanks. He continued to circle and nip at the burro with such strength that he almost knocked the burro over with his attacks.

15 The burro finally got the idea that the lion was trying to bite him— probably even eat him. The burro turned and struck out at the lion with his hooves. The lion was old and had already spent many years as a fierce hunter, but those years were behind him. He did not have the speed or reflexes he once had.

16 The burro's hooves slammed into the lion and knocked him to the ground. As the lion hit the ground, the burro bolted away from the lion and raced away down the forest path.

17 On his way from the lion, the burro again ran into the fox. As he whizzed by the fox, the fox called out, "Why are you in such a hurry?! Did your meeting with the lion not go well? The lion is always anxious to meet new animals. I was sure you would be well received."

18 Without even stopping, the burro called back, "That was the trouble. I was too well received by the lion. He liked me so much that he wanted to eat me! He even tried to bite me and start his evening meal early."

19 The fox yelled back, "No! No! The lion was only trying to give you a good welcome!"

20 The burro did not believe the fox. He told the fox, "Thank you for your good welcome. But now I am running away from the lion too."

21 As the burro disappeared into the distance, the fox yelled, "Don't run that way! That way leads back to your master!"

22 The burro answered, "I am going back to my master. I'd rather be with a master who beats me than a lion who wants to eat me!"

Making Observations
- What happens in this story?
- Which details stand out to you after reading?

My Notes

Returning to the Text

- Return to the text as you respond to the following questions. Use text evidence to support your responses.
- Write any additional questions you have about the fable in your Reader/Writer Notebook.

1. Use context to clarify the meaning of the word *nomad* in paragraph 9.

_____

_____

_____

_____

2. In paragraph 8, the fox says the burro will be "well received" by the lion. Knowing what happens later in the story, make an inference about what the fox means by "well received."

_____

_____

_____

_____

3. Reread paragraph 19. Is the fox being honest when he says, "The lion was only trying to give you a good welcome"? Use evidence from the text to support your inference.

_____

_____

_____

_____

4. Paraphrase the moral of this fable in your own words, making sure you maintain its meaning.

_____

_____

_____

_____

Working from the Text

5. Identify a choice the burro makes in the story. What lesson could be taught by this choice?

Choice	Lesson

6. Animals are often used symbolically. Earlier, you found that the Greek gods and goddesses have animals associated with them. Think about the animals in "The Burro and the Fox" and other animals that are featured in well-known fairy tales or stories. What do these animals symbolize? Use the graphic organizer to explore their symbolic meanings.

Animal	Figurative (symbolic) Meaning
Snake	
Bear	
Rat	
Ant	
Burro	
Fox	
Lion	
One of Your Choice:	

☑ Check Your Understanding

Think back to your wanted poster. What animal(s) could you incorporate to symbolize certain characteristics? Justify your choice by explaining each animal's symbolic meaning in connection to the story or character.

 Gaining Perspectives

Imagine your friend was in a similar situation as the burro. What steps would you take to help your friend? To help you create a thoughtful decision-making process, brainstorm answers to the following questions:

- What are the problems your friend is facing?
- What does your friend need?
- What do you need to consider before you can meet your friend's needs?

Write clear, detailed responses to the questions in your Reader/Writer Notebook. Then work together with a partner to share problems and solutions. Create a thoughtful decision-making process that applies to both your and your partner's scenarios.

Learning Targets

- Engage in a productive discussion within a collaborative group.
- Use text evidence to analyze and compare different creation myths.
- Write an original myth, using genre characteristics.
- Integrate ideas from multiple texts to build knowledge and vocabulary about myths.

Preview

In this activity, you will learn about creation myths and compare three different creation myths from around the world.

Setting a Purpose for Reading

- As you read the informational text, underline words that help you understand what a creation myth is.
- Circle unknown words and phrases. Try to determine the meaning of the words by using context clues, word parts, or a dictionary.

Informational Text

✏ KNOWLEDGE QUEST

Knowledge Question:
What do myths reveal about the connection between the natural world and humans?

In Activity 1.15, you will read an informational text about creation myths and three creation myths. While you read and build knowledge about the topic, think about your answer to the Knowledge Question.

from In the Beginning:
Creation Stories from Around the World

by **Virginia Hamilton**

1   Myth stories about creation are different. In a **prophetic** voice, they relate events that seem outside of time and even beyond time itself. Creation myths ... go back beyond anything that ever was and begin before anything has happened.

2   The classic opening, although not the only opening, of a creation myth is "In the beginning ... " The most striking purpose of a creation myth is to explain something. Yet it also asks questions and gives reasons why groups of people perform certain rituals and live in a particular way. Creation myths describe a place and time impossible for us to see for ourselves. People everywhere have creation myths, revealing how they view themselves to themselves in ways that are movingly personal.

3   Creation, then, means the act of bringing into existence—something. These myths from around the world were created by people who sensed the wonder and glory of the universe. Lonely as they were, by themselves, early people looked inside themselves and expressed a longing to discover, to explain who they were, why they were, and from what and where they came.

prophetic: divine

Working from the Text

1. What are the purposes of a creation myth according to the text?

2. Summarize the central ideas from each of the three paragraphs in the informational text you just read.

Setting a Purpose for Reading

- As you read the myths, underline text that explains an aspect of nature.
- Circle unknown words and phrases. Try to determine the meaning of the words by using context clues, word parts, or a dictionary.

About the Culture

Africa is a continent consisting of more than 50 countries and thousands of different ethnic and cultural groups. By some estimates, there are 1,500–2,000 languages spoken throughout Africa. The Bapedi and Bavenda people come from the northern part of South Africa. The Kuba people traditionally live in the southeastern part of the Democratic Republic of the Congo. All three cultures speak a dialect of the Bantu family of languages.

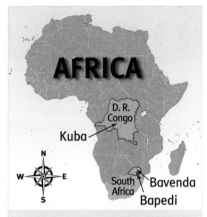

Look at the map above. Where are the Kuba people located in relation to the Bapedi and Bavenda peoples?

Creation Myths

from Voices of the Ancestors: African Myth

by **Tony Allan, Fergus Fleming, and Charles Phillips**

> ### KNOWLEDGE QUEST
> Knowledge Question:
> What do myths reveal about the connection between the natural world and humans?

Huveane and Clay People

1   The Bapedi and Bavenda, Bantu tribes from Transvaal in South Africa, recount that the first human, Huveane the shepherd, was a lawless trickster who loved to make mischief.

2   Huveane cared for his father's goats and sheep—for although he was the first man, he had parents. One day he set about making a being of his own: he took some clay, formed a baby with it and then breathed life into it. Then he hid the baby near his parents' house. He cared for it lovingly, creeping out each dawn to feed it, but his parents noticed the dwindling supply of milk. Curious, Huveane's father followed him one day and saw the child. Taking it in his arms, he hid it beneath the house with the firewood. That evening Huveane discovered that his precious creation was missing; distraught, he slumped glumly with his parents at the fire. Distressed by his low spirits, his mother asked him to fetch some logs, whereupon he discovered the unharmed baby and capered with joy. His parents were so pleased to see him happy again that they allowed him to keep it.

Read and Connect

As you come to the conclusion of your independent reading, think about the myths or folktales you have read on your own. Is there an overarching theme that covers all of them? Are there multiple themes within the genre? What about the myths you have read in the unit, such as "Arachne" and "The Burro and the Fox"? In your Independent Reading Log, explain your response in a short paragraph that uses evidence from several texts.

KNOWLEDGE QUEST

Knowledge Question:

What do myths reveal about the connection between the natural world and humans?

lithe: graceful

Mbombo

3 The Kuba, who live in the abundant rainforest of Central Africa, call their creator god Mbombo and picture creation as a sudden eruption from his mouth. Once, according to their account, nothing existed but restless water lost in darkness—and Mbombo, a spirit who moved over the water. Then in the deep, dark hours of the first day, Mbombo was stricken by a sharp stomach pain and vomited, producing the sun, moon, and a stream of bright stars. Light fell all around him. As the sun shone, the ocean became clouds and the water level fell, revealing hills and plains. Again Mbombo's stomach convulsed, this time sending forth a wonderful and various stream of life: the tall sky, the sharp-forked lightning, deep-rooted trees, animals in all their **lithe** power and the first man and woman.

About the Culture

Apache is the collective name for several Native American tribes in the United States. The Jicarilla Apache people were nomadic until just before European contact in the 18th century. They lived and traded throughout the southwestern United States and across the Great Plains. Today, the Jicarilla Apache nation is located in northern New Mexico.

Creation Story

The Creation of Earth, Sky, Animals, and Man

by **Edward Morris Opler** *from Myths and Tales of the Jicarilla Apache Indians*

1 In the beginning nothing was here where the world now stands; there was no ground, no earth,—nothing but Darkness, Water, and Cyclone. There were no people living. Only the Hactcin[1] existed. It was a lonely place. There were no fishes, no living things.

2 All the Hactcin were here from the beginning. They had the material out of which everything was created. They made the world first, the earth, the underworld, and then they made the sky. They made Earth in the form of a living woman and called her Mother. They made Sky in the form of a man and called him Father. He faces downward, and the woman faces up. He is our father and the woman is our mother.

3 In the beginning there were all kinds of Hactcin living in the underworld, in the place from which the emergence started. The mountains had a Hactcin, the different kinds of fruit each had one, everything had a Hactcin.

---

[1] Hactin: Supernaturals, personifications of the power of objects and natural forces

4 It was then that the Jicarilla Apache dwelt under the earth. Where they were there was no light, nothing but darkness. Everything was perfectly spiritual and holy, just like a Hactcin.

5 Everything there was as in a dream. The people were not real; they were not flesh and blood. They were like the shadows of things at first.

6 The most powerful Hactcin down there was a Black Hactcin. The Hactcin were all there already but in the darkness Black Hactcin was the leader. It was there, before anything else was made, that Black Hactcin made all the animals.

...

7 This is how animals and men first came to be made. Black Hactcin first tried to make an animal. He made it with four legs of clay and put a tail on it. He looked at it. He said, "It looks rather peculiar." Then he spoke to the mud image. "Let me see how you are going to walk with those four feet." That is why little children always like to play with clay images. Then it began to walk.

8 "That's pretty good," said Black Hactcin. "I think I can use you in a beneficial way."

9 He spoke to the image. "You have no help; you are all alone. I think I will make it so that you will have others from your body."

10 Then all sorts of animals came out from that same body. Black Hactcin had the power; he could do anything.

11 Now there were all kinds of animals. Black Hactcin stood and looked. He laughed to see all those different kinds of animals; he just couldn't help it when he saw those animals with all their different habits. That is why people laugh today at the habits of animals. They see a hog and laugh at it, saying, "See that dirty animal lying in the mud." All animals were there, some with horns, like the deer and elk, some with big horns like the mountain sheep. All were present. But at the time all those animals could speak, and they spoke the Jicarilla Apache language.

12 And those animals spoke to Black Hactcin. Each one came to speak to him. They asked him many questions. Each asked him what he should eat and where he should go to live, and questions of that order.

13 The Hactcin spoke to them. He divided all foods among them. To the horse, sheep, and cow he gave grass. "That is what you shall eat," he said. To some he gave brush, to some pine needles. Some he told to eat certain kinds of leaves but no grass.

14 "Now you can spread over the country," he told them. "Go to your appointed places and then come back and tell me where you want to stay all your lives."

15 He sent some to the mountains, some to the desert, and some to the plains. That is why you find the animals in different places now. The animals went out and chose their places then. So you find the bear in the mountains and other animals in different kinds of country.

16 Hactin said, "It is well. It looks well to see you in the places you have chosen."

17 So all the animals were set apart.

...

18 Black Hactcin started to make more images of animals and birds. The ones who were already made called a council and came together. The birds and animals were together at this council, for they all spoke the same language in those days.

19 "Now what are we going to do?" they asked Black Hactcin. "We need a companion, we need man."

20 "What do you mean?" asked Black Hactcin. "Why do you need another companion?"

21 The birds and animals said, "You are not going to be with us all the time; you will go elsewhere some of the time."

22 "I guess that's true. Perhaps some day I'll go away to a place where no one will see me."

23 So all the birds and animals gathered all different objects: pollen, specular iron ore, water scum, all kinds of pollen, from corn, tule and the trees. They put these all together. They added red ochre, white clay, white stone, jet, turquoise, red stone, Mexican opal, abalone, and assorted valuable stones. They put all these before Black Hactcin.

24 He told them, "You must stay a little distance from me. I don't want you to see what I make."

25 He stood to the east, then to the south, then to the west, then to the north. He traced an outline of a figure on the ground, making it just like his own body, for the Hactcin was shaped just as we are today. He traced the outline with pollen. The other objects and the precious stones he placed around on the inside, and they became the flesh and bones. The veins were of turquoise, the blood of red ochre, the skin of coral, the bones of white rock, the fingernails were of Mexican opal, the pupil of the eye of jet, the whites of the eyes of abalone, the marrow in the bones of white clay, and the teeth, too, were of Mexican opal. He took a dark cloud and out of it fashioned the hair. It becomes a white cloud when you are old.

26 This was a man which Black Hactcin was making. And now the man came to life.

⊘ Knowledge Quest
- What does this myth explain about the world?
- What images from the myths can you picture vividly?

Returning to the Text

- Return to the text as you respond to the following questions. Use text evidence to support your responses.
- Write any additional questions you have about the creation myths in your Reader/Writer Notebook.

3. Look at the first paragraph of "Huveane and Clay People." What are some synonyms for the word *recount*? Why might the authors have chosen this word specifically?

_____

_____

_____

_____

4. KQ Use context to explain what the phrase "breathed life into" means in the second paragraph of "Huveane and Clay People." Which phrases from the other myths signal a similar event?

_____

_____

_____

_____

5. What qualities are important to the Bapedi and Bavenda in "Huveane and Clay People"? How can you tell? Provide text evidence to support your thinking.

_____

_____

_____

_____

6. Use context to clarify meaning of the word *convulsed* in "Mbombo."

_____

_____

_____

_____

7. What text evidence in "Mbombo" supports the inference that the creation of the earth was a violent or volatile occurrence?

_____

_____

_____

_____

8. Use context to clarify the meaning of "flesh and blood" in paragraph 5 of "The Creation of Earth, Sky, Animals, and Man."

9. What text evidence points to Black Hactcin's great power and influence?

10. Why did Black Hactcin laugh when he saw all of the animals he had made? Use text evidence to support your response.

11. Make an inference about why Black Hactcin didn't want the animals to see what he was making.

12. KQ What explanation does each story give about the natural world and people? Use text evidence to compare the stories and support your ideas.

Knowledge Quest

Use your knowledge about the three creation myths to discuss with a partner the value of creation myths and the ways they explain the natural world and humans. Be sure to:

- Explain your answer to your partner, be specific, and use as many details as possible.
- Ask for clarification by posing follow-up questions as needed when your partner explains his or her answer.

INDEPENDENT READING LINK

You can continue to build your knowledge about creation myths and ancient civilizations by reading related fiction and articles at ZINC Reading Labs. Search for keywords such as *mythology*, *ancient civilizations*, and *origins*.

ZINC

Working from the Text

13. What messages do these authors explain within each text? What do these three myths have in common?

14. Return to the informational text by Virginia Hamilton from the beginning of this activity. How do the three stories you read exemplify the qualities of creation myths described in the informational text?

15. Look over the following elements of nature. Brainstorm how people in the distant past might have explained the origins of these natural phenomena.

Element	Explanation
The Sun	
The Stars	
The Earth	
The Moon	
Rainbows	
Thunder	
Snow	

☑ Check Your Understanding

What are some of the elements or qualities of the myths you read in this activity that you plan on using as inspiration for the illustrated myth you will create at the end of the unit?

ⓘ Independent Reading Checkpoint

With a partner, discuss the different explanations for natural phenomena you have discovered through your independent reading. Consider these questions: *Was one natural phenomenon explained different ways in different myths or folktales you read? What might each explanation tell you about the culture from which it came? Which explanation surprised you?* Take notes during your discussion in your Independent Reading Log.

Brainstorming an Original Myth

Work in a collaborative group to generate ideas for an original myth to explain a natural phenomenon. Create a poster that demonstrates those ideas. You may choose one of the natural phenomenon you explained in the Check Your Understanding section of this activity or a natural phenomenon of your choice.

Be creative. Try to fill up as much of the poster (sample format follows) as possible, using individual words, phrases, symbols, and visuals. Be sure to incorporate the following elements into your poster:

- the name of your natural phenomenon
- the characters (animals/gods/heroes)
- the setting of the myth
- the main conflict and character choices
- the lesson or conclusion

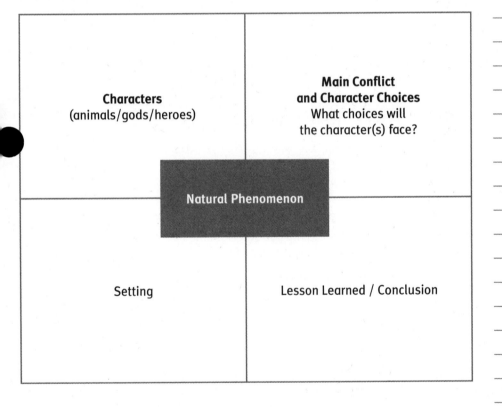

Creating an Illustrated Myth

 ASSIGNMENT

Your assignment is to work with a partner to create an original myth that explains a belief, custom, or natural phenomenon through the actions of gods or heroes. Be sure that your myth teaches a lesson or a moral and includes illustrations that complement the myth as it unfolds.

Planning and Prewriting: Take time to make a plan for your illustrated myth.	▪ How can you use the stories from the unit as models for your own myth? ▪ How will you choose possible natural phenomena that you could explain in your myth? ▪ Which prewriting strategy (such as the plot diagram or outline) will you use to plan the organization?
Drafting: Create a draft that includes the elements of an effective narrative.	▪ How will you hook the reader with an engaging opening or lead? ▪ How will you apply your knowledge of sensory and figurative language and purposeful dialogue to vividly tell a story? ▪ How will you show the characters' responses to the event, including their thoughts and feelings? ▪ How will you express the lesson learned or the significance of the experience? ▪ How will you find or create illustrations to capture key parts of your myth?
Evaluating and Revising the Draft: Create opportunities to review and revise your work.	▪ During the process of writing, when will you share your work with your writing group? ▪ What is your plan to include suggestions and revision ideas into your draft? ▪ How can the Scoring Guide help you self-evaluate how well your draft meets the requirements of the assignment?
Checking and Editing: Confirm that your final draft is ready for publication.	▪ How will you proofread and edit your draft to demonstrate command of the conventions of standard English capitalization, punctuation, spelling, grammar, and usage? ▪ How will you create a title and assemble your illustrations in an appealing manner? ▪ What tools will you use to prepare your final draft for publication?

Reflection

After completing this Embedded Assessment, think about how you went about accomplishing this task, and respond to the following:

• Reflect on the process you used to come up with an original myth. How did reading and studying the myths in this unit help prepare you to write your own myth?

SCORING GUIDE

Scoring Criteria	Exemplary	Proficient	Emerging	Incomplete
Ideas	The myth • describes a natural phenomenon and includes the idea of choice while cleverly teaching a lesson • skillfully uses story elements to engage the reader and lead to a satisfying resolution • includes vivid visuals that use effective symbolism for the ideas in the myth.	The myth • explains a natural phenomenon and teaches a lesson • uses story elements to hook the reader and create a satisfying resolution • includes visuals that connect the ideas in the myth.	The myth • does not explain a natural phenomenon or teach a lesson • is hard to follow and does not include sufficient narrative elements to aid the reader • includes few if any visuals to demonstrate the ideas in the myth.	The myth • does not tell about a natural phenomenon or teach a lesson • does not use narrative elements • has no visuals to support the myth or demonstrate ideas.
Structure	The myth • is well organized and clearly follows the plot structure of a story • uses transitions to skillfully guide the reader.	The myth • uses essential story elements and follows a plot structure • uses some transitions to move between ideas.	The myth • is not well organized and includes only some elements of plot structure • includes few, if any, transitions.	The myth • is disorganized and difficult to follow • does not follow plot structure • includes no transitions.
Use of Language	The myth • effectively uses figurative language and sensory details to vividly "show" the incident • has few or no errors in grammar, spelling, punctuation, or capitalization.	The myth • includes details to enhance the descriptions of characters and setting • contains few errors in grammar, spelling, punctuation, or capitalization, and they do not detract from meaning.	The myth • includes details that do not fit the story or descriptions that are not complete • contains mistakes in grammar, spelling, punctuation, and capitalization that detract from meaning.	The myth • describes details in confusing language • contains errors in grammar, spelling, punctuation, and capitalization that interfere with meaning.

VISUAL PROMPT
How do you use different sources of information to help you make decisions about what to buy or to do?

WHAT INFLUENCES MY CHOICES?

Are people forgetting to be present in the moment, scattering their focus by looking at life through a screen? Should you be living your life or living it for others to see it?

—from "Should We Live Life, Or Capture It?" by Marcelo Gleiser

What Influences My Choices?

ACTIVITY	CONTENTS	

My Independent Reading List

My Notes

_____
_____
_____
_____
_____
_____
_____
_____
_____
_____
_____
_____

Learning Targets

- Preview the big ideas and vocabulary for the unit and collaborate with a group.
- Begin to plan a piece of writing by discussing sources and background knowledge of the topic.

Preview

In this activity, you will consider the issue of marketing to young people and unpack the skills and knowledge needed to write an informational essay on this topic.

Making Connections

You see some form of advertising around you every day. What catches your attention? Is it television? Internet ads? Print ads? Radio? Advertising influences the choices that you make. You might also be influenced by other things, such as what people are saying on social media or what people are wearing or doing on television. In this unit, you will examine various types of media and the techniques advertisers use to convince you to buy their products.

Essential Questions

Based on your current knowledge, how would you answer these questions?

1. What role does advertising play in the lives of youth?

2. What makes an effective argument?

As you read the texts in this unit, think about these two questions. How does each text help you to answer them?

Developing Vocabulary

Mark the Academic Vocabulary and Literary Terms on the Contents page using the QHT strategy.

INDEPENDENT READING LINK

Reading Plan

In the first part of this unit, you will be reading informational texts about marketing to young people. For outside reading, find articles about advertising or choose one of your favorite brands and read about how that company markets its products. Use your Reader/ Writer Notebook to create an independent reading plan and respond to any questions, comments, or reactions you have to your reading. You can also record notes in your Independent Reading Log.

Unpacking Embedded Assessment 1

Read the assignment for Embedded Assessment 1: Writing an Informational Essay and Participating in a Collaborative Discussion.

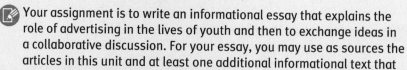 Your assignment is to write an informational essay that explains the role of advertising in the lives of youth and then to exchange ideas in a collaborative discussion. For your essay, you may use as sources the articles in this unit and at least one additional informational text that you have researched.

With your classmates, identify what you will need to do for the assessment. Create a graphic organizer to list the skills and knowledge you will need to accomplish these tasks. To help you complete the graphic organizer, be sure to review the criteria in the Scoring Guide for Embedded Assessment 1.

What Is the Issue?

Setting a Purpose for Reading

- As you read, underline the reasons the author gives for being concerned about advertising to young people.
- Circle unknown words and phrases. Try to determine the meaning of the words by using context clues, word parts, or a dictionary.

Informational Text

How Kids Can Resist Advertising and Be Smart Consumers

by **Caroline Knorr**

The best defense against sneaky advertiser tricks? Teaching kids to decode the real messages.

1   Commercials are nothing new. We all grew up with them and can probably sing a dozen or more jingles. What is new is how advertisers have adapted to digital media—especially apps, websites, and social media. Many of today's ads—from product placements in movies and on TV to online contests, viral videos, and chatbots (robots that send instant messages)—don't look like ads. And that's by design. Adapting to ever more **jaded** and **fickle** viewers, marketers have developed ways to integrate ads into entertainment, so it's hard to tell where the real content ends and the ads begin. These techniques also encourage us to interact (click, swipe, play, chat), which gives marketers data about our habits, likes, and preferences.

2   A few important advertising tricks of the trade have not changed, though. Companies still practice these successful marketing techniques:

- Expanding a product's target age to get younger and older kids to buy it (think Dora the Explorer becoming a miniskirted tween).

WORD CONNECTIONS

Multiple-Meaning Words
Market (noun) refers not only to a place to buy goods but also generally to the world of business and commerce.
Market (verb) means "to offer for sale." *Marketers* plan how products will be sold and advertised to customers.

 KNOWLEDGE QUEST

Knowledge Question:
What role does advertising play in the choices young consumers make?
Across Activities 2.2 and 2.3, you will read two texts about kids and advertising. While you read and build knowledge about the topic, think about your answer to the Knowledge Question.

jaded: bored, unimpressed
fickle: frequently changing

My Notes

- Using a multi-platform approach (web, TV, toys, movies) because the more a kid sees a product, the more likely she will be to buy it later.
- Building brand loyalty—again, the younger the better—to get kids hooked on certain brands as early as possible.

3 Obviously, commercials aren't going anywhere. In fact, they're becoming ever **stealthier** and more sophisticated to take advantage of new technologies. But kids—especially young kids—are vulnerable to marketing messages. Children are so impressionable that a number of organizations, including the American Psychological Association, the American Academy of Pediatrics, and the Campaign for a Commercial-Free Childhood, have called for heavy restrictions on advertising to children. Wanting more and more material things can cause anxiety, depression, and anger. It can make kids judge their self-worth by what they own. Helping kids understand how advertising works can help protect them from being exploited.

Tips for Middle and High School Kids

- **Demystify brands.** Brands sell images to kids as much as they sell products. Companies are smart about making brands seem so cool that every kid will want the products. Know that you are much more than what you own.

- **Discuss smartphone and app ads.** Some advertisers get kids to trade personal information for freebies—soda, candy, and the like. Marketers also are able to get information on kids through messaging apps such as Kik and Snapchat and send them text ads.

- **Understand how location-based ads work.** Using your phone's GPS (and other data), companies send targeted texts advertising nearby products and services. You can turn off your phone's GPS and turn off notifications like this in your apps.

- **Resist peer pressure.** Many ads will count on the fact that kids are especially sensitive to peer pressure. Remember that advertisers are counting on this vulnerability to sell things.

- **Strengthen media-literacy skills.** Question everything you see online and in apps, as those platforms are not subjected to the same advertising rules as TV. Why was this ad created? What features does it have, and what messages does it send? What information does it include, and what does it leave out?

⦸ Knowledge Quest

- What details from the article stand out to you about advertising and kids?
- What is your initial reaction to the information in the article?

stealthier: sneakier

Returning to the Text

- Return to the text as you respond to the following questions. Use text evidence to support your responses.
- Write any additional questions you have about the informational text in your Reader/ Writer Notebook.

1. In the first paragraph, the author states that many of today's ads don't look like ads. Why does the author think this is a problem? Use text evidence in your response.

_____

_____

_____

_____

2. In the first paragraph, the author focuses on advertising in digital media. How does that focus change in paragraph 2? According to the author, why is this information important?

_____

_____

_____

_____

3. The author uses a list to organize information in two places in the article. What information is presented in the bulleted lists? How are the lists different?

_____

_____

_____

_____

4. KQ In paragraph 3, the author says that when kids understand advertising techniques, they are less likely to be exploited. What does *exploited* mean in this context? What context clues help you to identify the meaning?

_____

_____

_____

5. Paraphrase the main idea of the article.

_____

_____

_____

6. **KQ** How does understanding how mobile marketing works help people use smartphones safely and responsibly? What evidence from the text supports your answer?

_____

_____

_____

_____

Working from the Text

Collaborative Discussion: For this activity, you will participate in a discussion of the text and video "How Kids Can Resist Advertising and Be Smart Consumers." Before you and your partner discuss the text, review the guidelines for effective collaborative discussions. Listen actively and ask clarifying questions as you and your partner discuss the article and your responses to the ideas in the text. If you have the opportunity, use a vocabulary word from the text. To review the elements of collaborative discussion, read the following table.

Collaborative Discussions
All group members should:
• Be prepared for the discussion by reading the text and watching the video ahead of time.
• Be alert; use appropriate eye contact and engage with your partner.
• Speak up so that the other group members can hear.
• Take turns speaking and listening; everyone should have an opportunity to share ideas.
• Keep the goals of the discussion in mind; stay on topic and watch the time.
• Ask clarifying questions that build on other students' ideas and help guide the discussion.
• Paraphrase comments from other group members to ensure understanding.

Paraphrase the points in the preceding table by writing the actions you will take in group discussions, as both a speaker and a listener.

As a speaker, I will ...	As a listener, I will ...

Discussion Questions

7. What advertising technique mentioned in the article and video did you find most surprising or interesting? Explain why and cite specific information.

8. What techniques has the writer used to organize information in this article? Why do you think the author used this technique?

9. What do you think is the writer's purpose in writing this text? What was the purpose of the video? Compare the two sources, and cite evidence from the text to support your answer.

Generating Questions

Generating questions after reading can help you to deepen your understanding of the text. You might ask a question that is easy to answer through research. For example, you might ask: *How many advertisements does the average thirteen-year old see per day?* You might also ask a question that is harder to answer, that spurs you to think more deeply about the topic. For example: *How do advertisements reflect the society that creates them?*

10. How are the article and video the same? How are they different? Do you think one is more persuasive than the other? Why or why not?

11. Based on the article, the video, and your discussion, what are some questions you have about the issue of advertising, media, and youth? Record the questions in your Reader/Writer Notebook.

☑ Focus on the Sentence

Use information from the article you read, the video you viewed, and your collaborative discussion to write one of each of the following types of sentences.

Statement (.)

_____

Question (?)

_____

Exclamation (!)

_____

Command (. or !)

_____

Analyzing Informational Text

Learning Strategies

Skimming/Scanning
Marking the Text
Graphic Organizer

VOCABULARY

ACADEMIC

Text features are aspects of a text designed to help you locate, understand, and organize information. Different text features are used to convey different types of information.

KNOWLEDGE QUEST

Knowledge Question:
What role does advertising play in the choices young consumers make?

Learning Targets

- Recognize text features and graphics in an informational text and use them to better comprehend ideas and information.
- Generate and refine a question for formal research.
- Integrate ideas from multiple texts to build knowledge and vocabulary about the role advertising plays in the choices of young consumers.

Preview

In this activity, you will read an article about marketing to children and begin to think about your own research on the topic.

Text Features

In this part of the unit, you will be reading informational texts. Informational texts usually follow a different structure than short stories or other genres of fiction. For example, you might find the following **text features** in an informational text:

- **Organizing features** such as a table of contents, glossary, index, and references
- **Text divisions** such as introductions, summaries, sections with headings, footnotes or endnotes, and information about the author
- **Graphics** that present information in a visual format, such as diagrams, charts, tables, graphs, maps, timelines, and so on. Graphics support the information and ideas presented in the text.
- **Special formatting** such as boldface, italics, numbered or bulleted text, or the use of different typefaces and sizes. For example, in this list, the types of text features are placed in boldface to draw attention to them.

Setting a Purpose for Reading

- As you read, underline examples of survey results and put a star next to informational graphics.
- Circle unknown words and phrases. Try to determine the meaning of the words by using context clues, word parts, or a dictionary.

Informational Text

Mobile Kids

from **Nielsen**

1   These days, a kid with a smartphone in their hand is as common as seeing a kid playing with a yo-yo in the years before the digital age.

2   But today's kids aren't just carrying smartphones—they're mastering them. In fact, many are just as skilled as their parents—or even more so in some cases. So whether today's youth are texting, playing a game, or engaging

in the plethora of other activities that smartphones offer, there's no doubt that this digital **demo** is one that marketers are keen to reach.

3   As the saying goes, with kid comes a parent. So what are parents' motivations and concerns when it comes to subscribing to a wireless service? To find out, Nielsen's fourth-quarter 2016 Mobile Kids Report delved into the subject and shares the insights from respondents of parents of kids' ages 6–12 who answered on behalf of their children.

4   To start, the report looked at the age that kids get a smartphone. Slightly less than half (45 percent) of mobile kids got a service plan at 10–12 years old. The most predominant age when kids got a service plan was age 10 (22 percent), followed by 8 years old (16 percent) and ages 9 and 11 were tied at 15 percent. The mobile child also skews more male (56 percent) than female (44 percent), with at least one in five being Hispanic. Among 10–12-year-olds, the highest percentage of age represented was age 10 at 34 percent. The vast majority (93 percent) are on the same plan as their parents, and 72 percent have all mobile wireless services including voice, messaging and data.

5   Among parents likely to get their kids wireless service before they turn 13, being able to get hold of their child easily and that their child can reach out to them easily (90 percent) were their top primary reasons for getting their child wireless service. 80 percent said so they could track their child's location, and 66 percent said that their child has been asking for wireless service for a while.

Why are parents getting their kids wireless service before their child turns 13?

Agree/strongly agree, among those likely to get their child wireless service

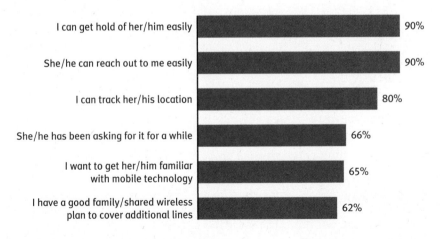

I can get hold of her/him easily	90%
She/he can reach out to me easily	90%
I can track her/his location	80%
She/he has been asking for it for a while	66%
I want to get her/him familiar with mobile technology	65%
I have a good family/shared wireless plan to cover additional lines	62%

Read as: Among parents likely to get their child wireless service, 90% said getting hold of their child easily was a reason for getting their child wireless service before they turn 13.

Source: Nielsen

6   And with parenting comes concern for the welfare of their child, as well as questions about their children's level of responsibility. Seventy-seven percent said that they are concerned that the phone could be lost easily. Seventy-two

---

My Notes

GRAMMAR & USAGE

Introductory Words and Phrases

A comma should be used after an introductory word or phrase at the beginning of a sentence. For example, look at the first sentence in paragraphs one, three, and four of "Mobile Kids." They each begin with an introductory phrase: "These days," "As the saying goes," and "To start." Each is also followed by a comma.

It's important to recognize this writing convention while reading and writing informational texts. As you read, look for introductory words and phrases. As you write and edit your own writing, remember that introductory words and phrases are separated from the rest of the sentence with a comma.

---

demo (demographic): group

---

percent of parents were concerned that smartphones pose too much distraction, and 71 percent worried that their children would spend too much time with their devices. The lack of control of what content their kids would see online was also a concern (68 percent), and 67 percent expressed concern that their children might not know how to use their phones responsibly.

7　According to parents, the antidote to these concerns include better safety controls and features to block inappropriate content (55 percent), better usage controls to limit access (48 percent) and better service plan options for children (34 percent).

8　So once a child has a phone, how are they spending time on their device? The top mobile activities include text messaging (81 percent), downloading apps (59 percent) and playing preinstalled games and mobile internet/accessing websites (tied at 53 percent).

Top Mobile Activities

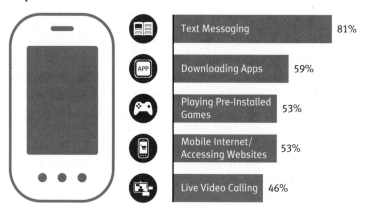

Read as: In Q4 2016 among kids 6–12, 81% of kids sent text messages which was their top mobile activity

Source: Nielsen

Methodology

9　Nielsen's Fourth-Quarter 2016 Mobile Kids Report gathered a sample of 4,646 parents aged 18+ years with kids between the ages of 6–12 years old. Parents of children aged 6–12 were identified through Nielsen's Mobile Insights Survey. Parent respondents answered on behalf of their 6–12 year olds.

⌀ Knowledge Quest
- What text features do you notice in this text?
- What is one detail from the graphs or charts you noticed that someone else might have missed?

Returning to the Text

- Return to the text as you respond to the following questions. Use text evidence to support your responses.
- Write any additional questions you have about the informational text in your Reader/ Writer Notebook.

1. What was the goal of Nielsen's "Mobile Kids" survey? Explain using details from the article.

_____

_____

_____

_____

2. KQ Use context to clarify the meaning of the word *marketers* in paragraph 2. Explain how you determined the word's meaning using context clues.

_____

_____

_____

_____

3. Based on paragraph 2, what inference can you make about the intended audience? What details in the article support your inference?

_____

_____

_____

_____

4. How does the author's use of text features add to your understanding of the article? How might the article be different if the graphics were not included?

_____

_____

_____

_____

5. KQ How do advertising and technology affect young people? Use evidence from both texts in your response.

_____

_____

_____

_____

INDEPENDENT READING LINK

You can continue to build your knowledge about advertising by reading other articles at ZINC Reading Labs.

Search for keywords such as *consumerism* or *advertising*.

 ZINC

 Knowledge Quest

Use your knowledge about "How Kids Can Resist Advertising and Be Smart Consumers" and "Mobile Kids" to discuss with a partner how your understanding of advertising has changed. What steps would you recommend kids like you take to reduce the influence advertising has on your choices? Be sure to:

- Explain your answer to your partner, be specific and use as many details as possible.
- When your partner explains their answer, ask for clarification by posing follow-up questions as needed.
- After the discussion, write down the ideas you talked about.

Working from the Text

6. The author presents a lot of information and statistics about how and why kids under 13 use mobile devices. Some of this information is presented in the text of the article, and some is presented in the two graphs. How does the format of the information affect your understanding? Why do you think the author chose to use both formats?

7. What do you notice about the orange heading that comes before the last paragraph? Why do you think the author included this section?

☑ Check Your Understanding

Turn back to "How Kids Can Resist Advertising and Be Smart Consumers," in the previous activity. Find one text feature the author used in this text. Why do you think the author chose to use this feature?

Develop Your Research Plan

In this unit, you will be researching the influence of advertising on young people. Before you begin your research, it's important to create a plan. How familiar are you with the research process? Read and paraphrase each step in the graphic organizer that follows. Then try to think of any resources (Internet, library, your teacher, a computer, and so on) that you might use during each step.

Research Process Steps	Paraphrase	Resources You Might Use
1. Identify the topic, issue, or problem to be researched.		
2. Write questions that can be answered through research.		
3. Gather evidence; revise plan as needed by writing additional questions to narrow or broaden research.		
4. Evaluate sources for reliability and relevance.		
5. Draw conclusions about findings.		
6. Communicate findings.		

Choosing a Research Topic

When choosing your own topic for research, you might consider several approaches:

- Brainstorm ideas with a partner.
- Write down any ideas that come to mind about topics that interest you.
- Choose an interesting general topic about which you would like to know more. An example of a general topic might be the toy industry in America or films of the 1950s.
- Do some preliminary research on your general topic to see what's already been done and to help you narrow your focus. What questions does this early research raise?

Writing a Research Question

A research question is a clear, focused, concise, and complex question that drives your research. Research questions help you focus your research by providing a path through the research process. Creating research questions will help you work toward supporting a clear thesis.

> **WORD CONNECTIONS**
>
> **Roots and Affixes**
> Hypothesis comes from the Greek words *hypo* ("under") and *thesis* ("a proposition"). A hypothesis is a guess or theory that an argument is based on. Notice the relationship between *hypothesis* and the word *thesis*, which is the purpose statement of an essay.

To write a research question:

> **Think about your general topic.** What do you want to know?

↓

> **Consider your audience.** Keep your audience in mind when developing your question. Would that particular audience be interested in this question?

↓

> **Start asking questions.** Ask open-ended "how" and "why" questions about your general topic to help you think of different areas of your topic.

↓

> **Evaluate your possible questions.** Research questions should not be answerable with a simple "yes" or "no" or by easily found facts. They should, instead, require both research and analysis on the part of the researcher.

↓

> **Hypothesize possible answers.** After you have written your research question, use what you already know to think of possible answers or explanations. This will help guide your research.

8. Which of these questions can be considered effective research questions?

   - How did Abraham Lincoln get the 13th Amendment to the Constitution passed?
   - When was slavery abolished in the United States?
   - What book did Frederick Douglass write during the abolitionist movement?
   - Why were slave narratives effective tools in working to abolish slavery?

9. Practice writing research questions about the influence of advertising on young people. Write at least five possible questions. Then share your ideas with a partner and use the flowchart from earlier in this activity to evaluate your questions.

Research Topic: The influence of advertising in the lives of youth
Research Questions:

ACTIVITY
2.4

How Do They Do It? Analyzing Ads

Learning Targets

- Identify techniques used in advertisements.
- Determine the purpose of persuasive advertisements and analyze how they use language to achieve that purpose.
- Write a thesis statement for a paragraph describing the effectiveness of advertising techniques.

Preview

In this activity, you will look at ads to analyze the techniques advertisers use to sell products.

Learning Strategies

Paraphrasing
Visualizing
Graphic Organizer

WORD CONNECTIONS

Etymology
The word **bandwagon** comes from the wagon that carried the band in political victory parades. People who joined the cause once it became successful were described as having jumped on the bandwagon.

Advertising Techniques

1. To understand how advertisers market to teens, it is important to understand the many persuasive advertising techniques they use. Read the descriptions of advertising techniques that follow. Then paraphrase and create a visual representation of each technique. Your visualization may include both words and symbols.

2. As you read about the techniques, think about the cause-and-effect relationship in advertising. For example, with bandwagon, the persuasion may be that "Everyone is buying this product (*cause*), so you should buy this product, too (*effect*)." With the avant-garde appeal, it might be, "This product is the newest on the market (*cause*), and you should be one of the first to have it (*effect*)."

Technique	Paraphrase	Visualize
Bandwagon: Advertisers make it seem that everyone is buying this product, so you feel you should buy it, too. For example, an ad for a new video game may claim: "The ultimate online game is sweeping the nation! Everyone is playing! Join the fun!" This statement is intended to make you feel left out if you are not playing.		
Avant-Garde: This technique is the opposite of bandwagon. Advertisers make it seem that the product is so new that you will be the first on the block to have it. The idea is that only supercool people like you will even know about this product.		
Testimonials: Advertisers use both celebrities and regular people to endorse products. For example, a famous actor might urge consumers to buy a certain car. Pay close attention: sometimes the celebrity does not actually say that he or she uses the product.		

Technique	Paraphrase	Visualize
Facts and Figures: Statistics, percentages, and numbers are used to convince you that this product is better or more effective than another product. However, be aware of what the numbers are actually saying. What does "30 percent more effective than the leading brand" really mean?		
Transfer: To recognize this technique, pay attention to the background of the ad or to the story of the commercial. The transfer technique wants you to associate the good feelings created in the ad with the product. For example, a commercial showing a happy family eating soup may want you to associate a feeling of comfort and security with the company's soup products.		

My Notes

3. What advertising techniques might you see together in one ad? Why would they work well together to influence an audience?

4. As you look at print, online, or television advertisements, analyze the use of advertising techniques. Circle the technique(s) used in the ads and provide evidence for each technique used in the graphic organizer that follows.

Advertisement	Persuasive Techniques + Evidence from Ad
Source: Product: Target Audience:	Bandwagon: Avant-Garde: Testimonials: Facts and Figures: Transfer:
Source: Product: Target Audience:	Bandwagon: Avant-Garde: Testimonials: Facts and Figures: Transfer:
Source: Product: Target Audience:	Bandwagon: Avant-Garde: Testimonials: Facts and Figures: Transfer:

VOCABULARY

LITERARY

Informational writing is a form of writing whose purpose is to explain or inform.

A **thesis statement** is a sentence, usually in the introduction of an essay, that states the writer's position or opinion on the topic of the essay. A thesis statement should go beyond telling the reader the topic of the essay. It should tell the reader what the writer thinks about the topic.

5. **Quickwrite:** Think about an advertisement that you consider interesting and effective. You might consider if you or someone you know would buy this product based on the advertisement. Which persuasive technique does the advertiser use successfully? What is the cause-and-effect relationship being suggested? Why do you think that particular technique was selected for the advertisement?

Informational Writing

In contrast to narrative, whose purpose is to tell a story, the primary purpose of **informational writing** is to provide information or an explanation. The introduction of an informational essay typically includes the **thesis statement**.

6. Look at the following thesis statement for an informational essay about the bandwagon advertising technique. Is this a strong thesis statement? Why or why not?

   Some advertisers use the bandwagon technique.

My Notes

7. A strong thesis statement goes beyond stating a topic. It also tells the reader about your opinion or commentary on the topic. Brainstorm ways to improve the bandwagon thesis statement by responding to the following questions.

   Advertisers use the bandwagon technique. Why?

   Advertisers use the bandwagon technique. How?

   Advertisers use the bandwagon technique. Who is their audience?

8. Use the ideas you brainstormed to create a strong thesis statement.

☑ Check Your Understanding

Select one of the advertisements you identified in Step 4. Write a thesis statement that explains how the advertisement tries to influence its target audience. Be sure to:

• State the topic of the essay.
• Express a point of view or commentary on the topic.

Advertising for All

Learning Targets

- Analyze and discuss advertising for commonly used products and how it affects consumers.
- Analyze the claims and techniques used in an ad.
- Write an informational paragraph about the effect of advertisements and celebrity endorsements.

Preview

In this activity, you will analyze and discuss advertisements, the techniques advertisers use, and how ads affect consumers.

My Notes

The Effect of Advertising on Consumers

Just about every type of media is supported by advertising. Advertising refers to any form of communication—print, video, sound—that businesses and organizations use to try to convince people to buy their products. Commercials appear throughout TV shows, and ads fill many pages of a magazine. Both commercials and ads are common online.

When you go to your favorite website, you may see ads for several products. Advertising dollars support companies that use the Internet, making many of their services free to users. Advertisers hope that their advertising dollars will draw Internet users to buy their products.

1. Respond to the questions that follow:

   - Where else do you see ads?

   - Do you ever see ads in your school? If so, where and when?

2. With your group, engage in a collaborative discussion about advertisements. Are they necessary, annoying, interesting, or funny? Are they effective? Before you discuss, review the guidelines for effective discussions. Be sure to:

   - Listen actively and ask questions as you discuss your impressions, feelings, and reactions to advertisements.
   - Respond appropriately when your partner asks questions of you.
   - Build on others' ideas by using the following sentence starters when you ask clarifying questions.

Are you saying that . . .	I see your point, but what about . . .
Can you please clarify?	Another way of looking at it is . . .
To share an idea, . . .	I'm still not convinced that . . .
Another idea is to . . .	How did you reach your conclusion?
What if we tried . . .	What makes you think that?
I have an idea, . . .	

Consumer Choices

3. Think about some of the things you have recently wanted to buy. Next to each category in the following chart, list at least one specific item that you wanted to buy or wanted someone else to buy for you within the past year. You may leave some categories blank. In the last column, note whether or not you saw an advertisement for the product.

Category	Brand, Name, or Title of Product	Saw Ad?
Personal Item (e.g., clothing, shoes, sports equipment, makeup, hobby supplies)		
Entertainment (e.g., music, movies, video games)		
Technology (e.g., computer, phone, mobile devices, accessories, apps)		
Food/Beverage (e.g., fast food, snacks, sports drinks, bottled water)		
Other		

4. Choose one of the items for which you saw an ad. What was the central message of the ad? Who was the target consumer? How do you know? What techniques were used?

5. Are you influenced by advertisements? Explain.

Celebrities and Marketing

6. With a partner or a small group, identify famous singers, musicians, actors, or sports figures who have influenced how people dress or behave.

Gaining Perspectives

You've been learning about messages and persuasion in advertising. Think about advertisements that are designed to create a negative opinion of something or someone, like ads about political candidates or certain health topics. Imagine you are helping someone create a political ad or an anti-smoking ad. What strategies would you suggest to get information across? What strategies would you recommend avoiding? Share your ideas with a partner. Then role play the conversation you would have. When you are done, summarize the outcome of the discussion in your Reader/Writer Notebook.

☑ Focus on the Sentence

Complete the following sentences by drawing on information from your discussion about celebrities and marketing.

Celebrity marketing is effective because _____

_____

Celebrity marketing is effective, but _____

_____

Celebrity marketing is effective, so _____

_____

Writing Informational Paragraphs

7. Earlier you learned about writing strong thesis statements. Informational paragraphs support the thesis statement and follow a specific structure:

- **Topic sentence:** A sentence that presents a topic and the writer's claim about or position on the topic

- **Transitions:** Words and phrases used to connect ideas (*for example, however, on the other hand*)

- **Supporting information:** Specific and relevant facts and details that are appropriate for the topic

- **Commentary:** Sentences that explain how the detail is relevant to the topic sentence

- **Concluding Statement:** A final piece of commentary (*as a result, overall, in conclusion*) that supports the explanation. The concluding sentence brings a sense of closure to the paragraph.

Read the following prompt and then use the outline that follows to plan your paragraph.

✍ Writing to Sources: Informational Text

Using evidence from the advertisements you have analyzed so far, write a well-developed paragraph about celebrities and marketing. Be sure to:

- Introduce your topic clearly and organize your ideas with coherence.
- Develop your topic with supporting evidence, including relevant details and examples from the advertisements you have analyzed.
- Express your ideas with precise, clear language and avoid wordiness.

⬛ INDEPENDENT READING LINK

Read and Discuss

In class, you are reading about marketing to kids. What is another issue that interests you or affects your daily life? For outside reading, read and respond to an article or book about an issue that interests you. How does your existing background knowledge about this topic help you understand the text? Use your Reader/ Writer Notebook to respond to any questions, comments, or reactions you might have to your reading. You can also record notes on this page. Refer to those notes as you participate in discussions with classmates.

Creating an Outline

(Topic Sentence) Celebrities can have significant influence on consumer choices because ...

(Example/Detail) For example, ...

(Commentary) This example shows ...

(Example/Detail) Another example ...

(Commentary) This example shows ...

(Example/Detail) One last example, or Finally ...

(Commentary) This example shows ...

Writing Research Questions

Write at least two more research questions on the topic of marketing to children.

Evaluating Sources: How Credible Are They?

Learning Targets

- Identify and gather relevant information from a variety of research sources.
- Differentiate between primary and secondary sources.
- Examine research sources for reliability and credibility.

Preview

In this activity, you will evaluate research sources for reliability, accuracy, credibility, timeliness, and purpose/audience.

Learning Strategies

Predicting
Note-taking
Graphic Organizer
Questioning the Text
RAFT

ACADEMIC

Credibility comes from the word *credible*, which means "believable or trustworthy." A source that is credible should be free from bias, and present the facts fairly.

VOCABULARY

Research Sources

After choosing a topic and writing research questions, the next step is to find sources of information. Sources might be books, magazines, documentary films, or online information. Not all sources are equal, however. Some are better than others. Learning how to tell the difference is a skill you need for both your academic success and your life.

Evaluating Sources

1. You can evaluate both print and online resources using five separate criteria, including authority, accuracy, **credibility**, timeliness, and purpose/audience. Use a dictionary or work with your classmates and teacher to define each term in the graphic organizer that follows. Then add questions that you can ask yourself when evaluating sources based on this criterion.

Source Criteria	Definition	Questions to Consider
1. Authority		
2. Accuracy		
3. Credibility		
4. Timeliness		
5. Purpose/ Audience		

Reading for Credibility

In this part of the activity, you will read a letter to a kids' magazine publisher. You will practice evaluating the text and another text provided to you by your teacher using the criteria you learned earlier in the activity.

Setting a Purpose for Reading

- As you read, underline the reasons and evidence that are mentioned in the text.
- Circle unknown words and phrases. Try to determine the meaning of the words by using context clues, word parts, or a dictionary.

Informational Text

Re: Advertising in the New York Times For Kids

December 20, 2017
Arthur O. Sulzberger, Jr., Chairman
The New York Times Company
620 Eighth Avenue
New York, NY, 10018

Re: Advertising in the New York Times For Kids
from Campaign for a Commercial-Free Childhood website

Dear Mr. Sulzberger:

1   We are writing to urge the New York Times ("the Times") to make future editions of the New York Times For Kids ("the Times For Kids") advertising-free.

2   We applaud the concept of a children's **supplement** of the Times to **foster** an interest in reading the newspaper. But when we reviewed the November 19, 2017 edition of the Times For Kids, we were **dismayed** to find that five of its 16 pages—31% of the supplement—were full-page ads for the Google Home Mini.

3   Parents who trust the Times for its well-deserved reputation for journalism likely had no idea the supplement was merely a Trojan horse for Google advertising, particularly if they followed the supplement's "Editor's Note" which said, "This section should not be read by grown-ups." And since the advertisements were unfairly disguised as content, children probably didn't know they were being targeted with marketing.

4   Marketing directed at children is always unfair. Children are considerably more vulnerable to the effects of advertising than adults. Research has found that most children do not understand the persuasive intent of advertising until they reach the age of 11 or 12.[1] That research is based on children's

supplement: additional publication
foster: develop
dismayed: upset

---

[1] Owen B.J. Carter, et al., Children's understanding of the selling versus persuasive intent of junk food advertising: Implications for regulation, Science Direct, http://www.sciencedirect.com/science/article/pii/S027795361100061X ("Highlights" section on webpage) (last visited Nov. 29, 2017).

My Notes

understanding of television advertising, where regulations dictate clear separation between ads and programming. When such separation doesn't exist, it's even harder for children to recognize and understand advertising.[2]

5   Such is the case with the November 19 edition of the Times For Kids. The ads were brightly colorful cartoon drawings, with interwoven questions in bubbles meant to engage children—a visual style quite similar to much of the editorial content of the supplement. Each ad was disguised as a puzzle for kids, with this question at the bottom referring to Google characters **embedded** in the ads: "Can you find the donut, G, and Android in each drawing?" These advertisements were **deceptive** to children and **violated** the guidelines of the Children's Advertising Review Unit, an industry self-regulatory program, which state: "Advertising should not be presented in a manner that blurs the distinction between advertising and program/editorial content in ways that would be misleading to children."

6   We believe the advertisements also violated the Times' own Advertising Acceptability Manual, which says "Advertisements that, in our opinion, **simulate** New York Times news or editorial matter or that may be confused with our news or editorial matter are unacceptable." If such advertisements are unacceptable for all Times readers, they are especially unfair when directed at children.…

7   …The Times has announced it will publish the Times For Kids monthly, beginning in January 2018. Getting kids in the habit of reading your newspaper will undoubtedly pay long-term benefits for The New York Times Company. Rather than trying to squeeze out additional profits at the expense of families who have already paid for the Sunday newspaper, the Times should make future editions of the Times For Kids completely free of advertising. We welcome the opportunity to meet with you to discuss our concerns.

Sincerely,
Campaign for a Commercial-Free Childhood
Center for Digital Democracy
Consumer Action
Consumer Federation of America
Consumer Watchdog
Corporate Accountability
New Dream Parent Coalition for Student Privacy
Public Citizen's Commercial Alert
The Story of Stuff Project

cc: Arthur Gregg Sulzberger, Deputy Publisher, NY Times Sundar Pichai, CEO, Google, Inc. Children's Advertising Review Unit

> **embedded:** that were placed
> **deceptive:** misleading
> **violated:** ignored
> **simulate:** look like

---

[2] Dr. Barbie Clarke & Siv Svanaes, Digital marketing and advertising to children: a literature review, Advertising Education Forum 45 (2012) (citing Mallinckrodt and Mizerski 2007; Ali, Blades et al. 2009).

VOCABULARY

ACADEMIC

A **primary source** is an original account or record created at the time of an event by someone who witnessed or was involved in it. Autobiographies, letters, and government records are types of primary sources. **Secondary sources** analyze, interpret, or critique primary sources. Textbooks, books about historical events, and works of criticism, such as movie and book reviews, are secondary sources.

Working from the Text

2. What effect does the advertising most likely have on young readers? How do you know?

3. What evidence does the text provide to support the statement that "These advertisements were deceptive to children and violated the guidelines of the Children's Advertising Review Unit…"?

4. According to the text, what action does the text attempt to persuade the New York Times Company to take for future editions of their kids' magazine? What next step is provided in the letter?

5. Your teacher will provide you with an outside source to read. Read the text closely. Then use the graphic organizer that follows to evaluate "Re: Advertising in the New York Times For Kids" and the text provided to you by your teacher based on the five criteria to determine reliability.

Re: Advertising in the New York Times For Kids	Outside Source
Authority:	Authority:
Accuracy:	Accuracy:
Credibility:	Credibility:
Timeliness:	Timeliness:
Purpose/Audience:	Purpose/Audience:

Primary and Secondary Sources

When choosing credible and reliable sources, you will find **primary** and **secondary** **sources**. Primary sources are original documents; they are often used in historical research. For example, if you are researching the era of the Civil War, you might use the primary resource of Lincoln's Gettysburg Address. You might find that speech in a secondary source written about the Civil War or on the Internet.

6. Revisit the texts you have read so far in the unit, including the advertisements you have analyzed. Are they primary or secondary sources? How do you know?

Evaluating Online Resources

Anyone can publish writing on the Internet. This openness is both one of the strengths and one of the weaknesses of the Internet. Being aware of the differences in quality among websites is an important step toward becoming an effective researcher.

A good place to start evaluating a website's credibility and reliability is by looking at its domain suffix. The domain suffix, the letters that follow the dot, can help you determine who created the website. The most commonly used domain suffixes are described in the following graphic organizer.

Domain Suffix	Definition/Description
.com	Stands for "commercial." Usually, websites with this suffix intend to make some sort of profit from their Internet services. Typically, these are the websites that sell goods or services.
.org	Stands for "organization." Primarily used by not-for-profit groups such as charities and professional organizations.
.net	Stands for "network." Often used by Internet service providers or web-hosting companies.
.edu	Stands for "education." Used by colleges, universities, educational organizations, or other institutions.
.gov	Stands for "government." Used by federal, state, and local government sites.

7. Which of the domain suffixes do you associate with more credible information? Why?

Searching for Sources

When using the Internet for research, your first step might be to use a search engine to find sources. Depending on the term you enter into the search a search For example, if you enter the search term "advertising," you will get many sites because the term is so broad. If you are just looking for information about celebrity endorsements, narrowing your search to that term would give you better results.

8. To research the effect of marketing and advertising to young people, what search terms might you use? Refine your terms to narrow your results as you go.

9. Using your search term(s), find information on the topic of marketing and advertising aimed at young people. Choose one or two sites to explore further. Record the URLs in the graphic organizer that follows. As you look through each site, use the criteria and questions in the graphic organizer to help you decide whether the website provides reliable information without bias.

Search Term	Number of Results	Sites to Explore Further

Criteria	Question	Notes
Authority	• Is it clear who is sponsoring this page? • Is there information available describing the purpose of the sponsoring organization? • Is there a way to verify the credibility of the page's sponsor? (For instance, is a phone number or address available to contact for more information?) • Is it clear who developed and wrote the material? Are his or her qualifications for writing on this topic clearly stated? Is there contact information for the author of the material?	
Accuracy	• Are the sources for factual information given so they can be verified? • If information is presented in graphs or charts, is it labeled clearly? • Does the information appear to have errors?	
Credibility	• Is the page and the information from a reliable source? • Is it free of advertising? • If there is advertising on the page, is it clearly separated from the informational content? • Are there any signs of bias?	
Timeliness	• Do dates on the page indicate when the page was written or last revised? • Are there any other indications that the material is updated frequently to ensure timely information? • If the information is published in print in different editions, is it clear what edition the page is from?	

Criteria	Question	Notes
Purpose/ Audience	• Does the site indicate who the intended audience is? • Is there any evidence of why the information is provided?	

Reliability

A source is considered reliable if you can find a pattern of true facts from that source. In order to determine if a source is reliable, you can select facts from that source and look them up in another source. You can also research the source to see if they have been caught presenting wrong information before. Review your sources to determine if they can be considered reliable.

☑ Focus on the Sentence

Think about your analysis of the two websites' credibility. Write two sentences about the websites using the words that follow.

although/credible_____

_____

since/domain suffix_____

_____

Faulty Reasoning

Sometimes, you can determine the credibility of a source by examining where it came from. Other times, the way that the author uses language can indicate how reliable the text is. When you read sources for your research project, look for faulty reasoning that can reveal an unreliable source.

10. Read the graphic organizer that follows. Then revisit the websites you analyzed and look for examples of faulty reasoning to add to the graphic organizer.

Term	Definition	Sample	Examples from Sources
emotional appeal	statements that create an emotional response in order to persuade the audience	Our children depend on us to protect them from harmful advertising!	
stereotype	a widely held belief about a person or thing that is often an oversimplified idea or opinion	Teenagers want to fit in, so they are especially vulnerable to bandwagon advertisements.	
hyperbole	an exaggerated claim that is not meant to be taken literally	My brother is on social media 24/7. He must see a million ads a week!	

ACTIVITY 2.6
continued

☑ Check Your Understanding

Describe how you will check your research sources for faulty reasoning.

LANGUAGE & WRITER'S CRAFT:
Revising for Precise Language and Formal Style

When writing for an academic audience, you should use precise and domain-specific language and a formal writing style. Domain-specific language is language related to the topic. When you revise your writing, pay close attention to your word choice: consider how choosing one word instead of another improves your clarity and message. Remember to keep your audience in mind as you revise and publish your writing.

Domain-specific language: Your choice of words (diction) should include the domain-specific terms that you are learning, as they apply to the topic. For example:

Original: The advertisement used a celebrity to help sell its product.

Revised: The advertisement used the advertising technique of a testimonial to sell its product by using the professional athlete Derek Jeter.

Precise language: Another way to strengthen your writing is to provide detailed information about a text or resource you are citing.

Original: In the news story it says that ...

Revised: In the news story from the *New York Times* on Sunday, March 18, the author claims that ...

Formal language: Formal language avoids slang, and it generally does not use contractions. Most slang that you might use in everyday language is too casual for academic writing. Words or phrases you use with your peers may not be understood by different audiences or appropriate for an academic topic.

Original: I'm a teenager, and, like, most of us look at famous people as cool and in the know.

Revised: Teenagers generally believe that famous people are models for their own thoughts and behavior.

PRACTICE In your Reader/Writer Notebook, revise the examples that follow to include precise and domain-specific language as well as a formal writing style. Work to eliminate wordiness and redundancy, or unnecessarily repeated ideas. Then, look back at the paragraph you wrote in Activity 2.5. Look for sentences that you can revise for formal language and precise writing.

> There was this ad I saw for a video game and it made it seem like everyone wanted one when I watched the video game ad. It's not cool when advertisers use famous people to sell things and convince people something is so great when people might not have wanted it in the first place.

✏️ Writing to Sources: Informational Text

Using information from one of your searches, write a paragraph summarizing the information you found about marketing to young people. Be sure to:

- Use precise and formal language to present information.
- Use transitions that create coherence.
- Include a concluding statement that explains why the source is credible, and if the source is also reliable.

Gathering Evidence from a Film

Learning Targets

- Analyze a film to establish its purpose and assess its credibility.
- Identify and gather relevant research information about a film.
- Engage in a collaborative discussion about research findings.

Preview

In this activity, you will watch a film about marketing food to kids and assess its purpose and credibility.

My Notes

Film Study

1. To help you understand the genre and purpose of the film *The Myth of Choice: How Junk-Food Marketers Target Our Kids*, record details using the following graphic organizer as you listen to your teacher read information about the film.

Role Who created this film?	Response: Evidence:
Audience Who do you think it was created for?	Response: Evidence:
Format What type of film is it? How will the information be presented? Is the film a primary or secondary source?	Response: Evidence:
Topic What will this film be about? What is its purpose?	Response: Evidence:

2. Use the graphic organizer that follows or some other form to take notes about the film that might help you answer the research question you have selected. Write your research question(s) at the top of the graphic organizer.

Research question(s) I hope to answer:

Evidence from the Film	Personal Response	What evidence answers your research questions? What new questions do you have?
Food companies tell us they're just doing their job.	I have experienced ... I have read about ... I have heard about ... This reminds me of ... I think ... I feel ...	
"Still, I can just say no, right?"		
"The food industry has spent millions"		

Collaborative Discussion

In preparation for a group discussion, answer the following questions.

3. How did this resource help you answer your research question? Provide specific details from the film as support.

4. What additional information did you find interesting?

5. What is one other question the film prompted you to think about?

6. Respond to the essential question: What role does advertising play in the lives of youth? Think about how advertisers attempt to influence consumers.

7. From what you can tell, how reliable is this source?

8. Look back at the informational writing you did in Activities 2.5 and 2.6. What new understandings did you gain from this film that might affect how you would respond to those prompts today?

In collaborative discussion groups, share your responses. Remember to:

- Explicitly refer to facts and examples from note-taking.
- Ask open-ended questions that bring about further discussion.
- Paraphrase others' comments and respond to others' questions.
- Revise your own ideas as you gain information from others.

Learning Targets

- Make connections between information presented in the text and information presented in a film.
- Write a paragraph comparing and contrasting information presented in different texts across genres.

Preview

In this activity, you will read an article about marketing to children. Then you will compare and contrast information from the article with information from a film on the same topic.

Setting a Purpose for Reading

- As you read the article, pause after each chunk and write one question you have about what you just read.
- Circle unknown words and phrases. Try to determine the meaning of the words by using context clues, word parts, or a dictionary.

About the Author

Michele Norris (1961–) is an award-winning journalist and the first African American woman to host NPR, where she interviewed world leaders, American presidents, and Nobel laureates. In an NPR interview, Norris said, "People think the most important thing I do is talk...when in fact, the single most important thing I do is listen."

Learning Strategies

Skimming/Scanning
Marking the Text
Close Reading

My Notes

News Article

More Companies Market Directly to Kids

by **Michele Norris, ABC News**

Chunk 1

1 At first glance it looks like a pizza party—a circle of pre-teens munching on thick slices slathered with melted cheese and pepperoni. But between bites, these Stamford, Conn., youngsters are enthusiastically engaged in a conversation about corporate logos.

2 "Tell me all the car brands you know," says Wynne Tyree, the adult leading the discussion, and hands shoot up all over the room. She points to

a young boy with a paper plate on his lap and he begins rattling off names. "Miata, Fiat, Mitsubishi …."

3   This informal gathering is actually a focus group organized by the Just Kid Inc. market research group. It's designed to help companies **gauge** how much children know about their products. Based on their responses, these children know what they like.

4   Some concerns are practical. They look for cleanliness in hotel rooms, fast service in restaurants and perks to keep them entertained when traveling. "Jet Blue has like leather seats that are nice and each person has their own individual TV with 25 channels," says a blond boy, waving his hands around for emphasis. Other concerns are more highbrow, such as chocolate on the pillow in the hotel at night.

Chunk 2

Courting the Kids

5   The children in this group are a decade away from buying their own cars or planning their own vacations, yet these youngsters are aggressively courted by a growing number of companies whose services have little or nothing to do with childhood.

6   "Security companies are targeting kids, airline companies are targeting kids, gasoline companies are targeting; those things that we traditionally think of as adult products are targeting kids," said James McNeal, author of the Kids Market, a book that examines children and their spending habits.

7   Brand awareness is keen among the pre-teens in the Connecticut focus group. Tyree asks the group to "think of a logo that has a red ball and a yellow ball. And they kind of go together." Before she even finishes the sentence, the kids shout out, "MasterCard!!!"

Chunk 3

'More Market Potential' in Kids

8   Markets are motivated by research conducted by McNeal and others, showing that children begin to recognize corporate labels as early as 18 months. About a year later they are able to **associate** the items in their world with a particular brand name. For example, when they think about juice, they don't just think about the beverage, they think about the brand name associated with the beverage.

9   "By the age of 2 or 3 years old, when you ask kids to draw things, they tend to draw brands, … they will not draw a generic doll, they will draw a Barbie; they won't draw a computer, they will draw a Dell Computer," said George Carey, president of Just Kid Inc.

10   By first grade, most American children have learned 200 logos, and research shows they are much more likely to stick with those brands throughout their lifetime. That's why companies are eager to expose their logos

gauge: find out
associate: connect

to as many youngsters as possible, stamping corporate logos all over children's toys and hanging their banners at children's events like the circus or ice-skating programs.

11   And if you think commercials for cell phones or cars that run during the cartoon hour are there to **entice** parents, you're wrong. Little kids are the big catch. "Kids have more market potential than any other demographic group," McNeal said.

12   In addition to being consumers of the future, children already spend $30 billion on everything from clothing to video games. On top of that, they influence how their parents spend their money. That accounts for another $600 billion in sales.

13   So companies are crafting ad campaigns with kids in mind. The Embassy Suites hotel chain (a division of Hilton Hotels Corp.) runs a commercial featuring smiling happy children running through the halls and playing in-room video games. The ad is based on the assumption that youngsters tip the scales when choosing a vacation spot.

Chunk 4

Field Trips to Companies

14   A growing number of businesses, including several large retail chains, have hired a Chicago firm called the Field Trip Factory to deliver schoolchildren to their sites for real-world lessons on everything from nutrition to health care.

15   "It's a really easy, viable way to reinforce classroom lessons in a real-life environment," said Susan Singer, president of the Field Trip Factory.

16   The program has been **phenomenally** successful, growing from eight to 43 states in just two years, in large part because the programs are free. Because of budget cuts, many schools now charge a small fee for traditional field trips to the zoo or museums.

17   Educators and kids give the field trips high marks because they allow children to learn in a hands-on environment, and they turn the local community into an extension of the classroom. At a recent trip to a Saturn Dealership in Dundee, Ill., children learned about car safety by learning how to change dirty car oil or how to correctly buckle a seat belt. The highlight of the visit was an unusual exercise where children were asked to jump up and down on top of a car door to test the strength of steel.

18   The field trips give **retailers** a chance to invest in education, but it's also an opportunity to invest in future earnings, recognizing that today's school children could well be tomorrow's customers.

19   "We get to market to local areas, to local schools," said Mary McHugh, from the Dundee Saturn dealership. "We are reaching teachers, we are reaching parents, we're reaching the children. This becomes dinner conversation: 'What did you do today?' 'Well we went to Saturn, we got to see this.'"

GRAMMAR & USAGE

Compound Sentences

Compound sentences are formed by combining two independent clauses with a coordinating conjunction such as *but*, *and*, *for*, *yet*, *or*, or *so*.
Example: Advertisers market to children, and children in turn pressure their parents to buy.

A **complex sentence** contains one independent clause and at least one dependent clause. Dependent clauses often begin with markers such as *after*, *since*, *because*, *although*, *even though*, or *when*.

Example: When I turn on the television, I always see advertisements with kids my age in them.

Look for compound and complex sentences in the passage. Think about how they make the relationships between ideas clearer.

My Notes

---

entice: attract
phenomenally: extremely
retailers: businesses

INDEPENDENT READING LINK

Read and Research

In class, you are reading about food marketing to kids and how to gather credible evidence from a text. What is another topic that could be the subject of a news article? For outside reading, read and respond to a recent news article about a topic that interests you. How does your background knowledge about this topic help you understand the text? Discuss your ideas with a partner.

My Notes

Making Observations

- Which sections of the article stand out to you as particularly memorable?
- How did the chunks of text help you understand the information better?
- What did you notice about the text's organizational pattern?

Returning to the Text

- Return to the text as you respond to the following questions. Use text evidence to support your responses.
- Write any additional questions you have about the news article in your Reader/ Writer Notebook.

1. What are some of the factors that make it attractive for companies to market to children? Cite text evidence that helps you answer the question.

2. What is meant by the phrase "tip the scale"? Use context to clarify the meaning.

3. What benefits do educators and companies hope to gain from corporate field trips? How are those benefits the same? How are they different?

Working from the Text

4. Revisit the text and mark it by stopping, thinking, and writing a response for each chunk of the text in the margin. Your annotations should include:

- Connecting (text to self/text/world)
- Questioning ("I wonder …" "Why did …")
- Visualizing (draw a picture or symbol)

- Paying attention to new learning ("Wow," "Cool," "No way," etc.)
- Analyzing how the text's organizational pattern helps readers learn about multiple topics (what topics are discussed in each section)

5. Join another pair or small group and share your understandings and summaries. Then discuss by making connections to your own or others' ideas. As a listener, remember to make eye contact with the speaker, take notes, and actively respond with questions or comments.

6. In informational texts, authors use citations when they use a direct quote from another author or source. When you include a quote in your writing, it's important to give credit to the original writer. Identify places in the text where the author cites information from a specific source.

☑ Check Your Understanding

With your group, discuss one way information from *The Myth of Choice* is like information from the article you just read. Then discuss one way it is different. Be sure to give details from both texts in your discussion.

LANGUAGE & WRITER'S CRAFT: Sentence Variety

Using a variety of sentence structures helps emphasize and connect ideas as well as create reader interest. Writing that contains many sentences of the same pattern bores both the writer and the reader.

Add variety and clarity by experimenting with different sentence structures. Choose a structure that best relates the ideas.

Simple sentence: contains one independent clause (a word group that has a subject and a verb and expresses a complete thought)

> Advertisers are concerned about kids. Advertisers want kids to buy their products.

Compound sentence: contains two independent clauses combined with a comma and a coordinating conjunction or with a semicolon; compares or contrasts ideas

> Advertisers care about kids, but they are more concerned that kids buy their products.

Complex sentence: contains one independent clause and one or more subordinate, or dependent, clauses; can show cause-and-effect relationships, compare and contrast, identify sequence

> Even though advertisers say they care about kids, they are more concerned about selling their products to kids.

PRACTICE Combine the following simple sentences into compound or complex sentences that either show a cause-and-effect relationship between ideas or compare or contrast ideas. Write the new sentences in your Reader/Writer Notebook.

- Children often influence what their parents buy. Children are the targets of advertisers.
- Parents try to protect their children from marketers. Watchdog agencies also try to keep advertisers honest.

Writing to Compare and Contrast

To make comparisons between two things, mention both in your topic sentence(s). **Sample topic sentence:** Both *The Myth of Choice* and "More Companies Market Directly to Kids" emphasize the importance of children as targets for advertisers, but "More Companies Market Directly to Kids" includes more personal examples.

Transitions:

To compare and contrast the texts, use transitions between the ideas from each text.

For comparison and contrast:

similarly, on the other hand, in contrast, although, like, unlike, same as, in the same way, nevertheless, likewise, by contrast, conversely, however

For conclusion:

as a result, therefore, finally, last, in conclusion, in summary, all in all

Examples:

On the other hand, some parents have started to limit the amount of television their toddlers watch each day.

All in all, most parents of toddlers agree that they will start regulating the number of hours their children spend in front of a screen.

 Writing to Sources: Informational Text

Using evidence from the film and article, write a paragraph in which you compare and contrast information in both sources. What information is similar? What is different? Be sure to:

- Introduce your topic clearly and provide a strong topic sentence.
- Use transitional words and phrases to show comparison and contrast.
- Use headings to structure your ideas.
- Include a chart or table as necessary to present information clearly.
- Use formal style and precise language.
- Provide a concluding statement that follows and supports the explanation.
- Use specific facts from both sources.

Gathering Evidence: Bringing It All Together

Learning Targets
- Identify and gather relevant information from a variety of sources.
- Organize an informational essay.

Preview
In this activity, you will review some of the characteristics and structures of informational text, and you will write a conclusion for an informational essay.

Characteristics of Informational Writing

You learned about the structure of an informational paragraph in Activities 2.4 and 2.5. The characteristics of this writing mode must be expanded to create an informational essay so that each paragraph contains the following:

- **Topic sentence** that presents a topic and the writer's claim or position about the topic in relation to the thesis statement
- **Transitions** to connect ideas (*for example, however, on the other hand*)
- **Supporting information** from a variety of sources that includes specific facts and details that are relevant to the topic
- **Commentary** that explains how the detail is relevant to the topic sentence
- **Concluding statement**, a final piece of commentary (*as a result, overall, in conclusion*) that supports the explanation. The concluding sentence brings a sense of closure to the paragraph and essay.

Outlining Ideas

Many writers find it helpful to create an outline of their ideas prior to drafting an essay. You might use the following format to outline your ideas to share the information from your research question(s).

Marketing to Youth

I. Introduction/Thesis Statement That Answers the Prompt

II. Body Paragraphs (with examples and information to support the main ideas of the thesis) that include the following:

   A. Evidence and Commentary in Each Paragraph that synthesizes information from multiple sources

III. Concluding Statement

1. In this part of the unit, you have read several texts on marketing to young people, viewed a documentary film, and had numerous group discussions about the topic. In addition, you have collected information from websites. Using the information from these sources, create an outline for an informational essay about this topic.

My Notes

2. Remember that when you use sources in your writing, it's important to use them ethically and responsibly. This means that you must present the information accurately, use quotation marks when including someone's exact words, and cite the source. When you present information from a source in your own words, or by paraphrasing, you must still cite the source that it came from. If you don't follow these rules, you are presenting someone else's work as your own, which is called plagiarism. What sources will you need to cite in your informational essay?

Drawing Conclusions

3. Based on your reading about this topic and the notes you have taken, what are the top 10 opinions or conclusions presented in your reading and research? Paraphrase or quote from the information you have gathered.

 Writing to Sources: Informational Text

Using evidence from the advertisements you have analyzed so far, write a well-developed paragraph about celebrities and marketing. Be sure to:

- Introduce your topic clearly and organize your ideas with coherence.
- Develop your topic with supporting evidence, including relevant details and examples from the advertisements you have analyzed.
- Express your ideas with precise, clear language and avoid wordiness.

🎲 Independent Reading Checkpoint

With a partner, discuss the information and approaches to marketing you have learned about in your independent reading. Take notes on your discussion in your Reader/Writer Notebook or Independent Reading Log.

Writing an Informational Essay and Participating in a Collaborative Discussion

 ASSIGNMENT

Your assignment is to write an informational essay that explains the role of advertising in the lives of youth and then to exchange ideas in a collaborative discussion. For your essay, you may use as sources the articles in this unit and at least one additional informational text that you have researched.

Planning and Prewriting: Take time to make a plan for your essay.	■ How will you review the ideas you have generated to select the most relevant examples and information? ■ How can you work with a peer to revise your plan to be sure you have a clear topic?
Drafting: Create an organized draft to identify and explain your topic.	■ How will you use what you have learned about beginning an essay as you write your draft? ■ Have you reviewed and evaluated your sources and facts to be sure they are clear and relevant? Have you synthesized information from your research in a logical way? ■ How will you finish your draft with a conclusion that supports the information in your essay? ■ How will you be sure you are not plagiarizing any sources?
Revising and Editing: Strengthen your writing with attention to task, purpose, and audience.	■ How can you use strategies such as **adding** and **replacing** to revise your draft for organization, cohesion, clarity, diction, and language? ■ How can the Scoring Guide help you evaluate how well your draft meets the requirements of the assignment? ■ How will you proofread and edit your draft to demonstrate formal style and a command of the conventions of standard English capitalization, punctuation, spelling, grammar, and usage?
Preparing for Discussion: Take time to make a plan for your collaborative discussion.	■ What personal speaking and listening goals will you set for participation in the collaborative discussion? ■ How can you use an outline or a copy of your essay to plan your talking points? ■ How will you take notes in order to actively engage as an audience participant as you listen to your peers?

Reflection

After completing this Embedded Assessment, think about how you went about accomplishing this task, and respond to the following:

• How did writing, speaking, and listening help you engage with your topic on a deeper level?

• Did you meet the speaking and listening goals that you set for yourself? How could you improve for next time?

SCORING GUIDE

Scoring Criteria	Exemplary	Proficient	Emerging	Incomplete
Ideas	The essay • presents a topic with a clearly stated and insightful controlling idea • supports the topic with specific and relevant facts, evidence, details, and examples to guide understanding of main ideas • skillfully combines ideas from several sources.	The essay • presents a topic with a controlling idea • supports the topic with facts, evidence, details, and examples that guide the reader's understanding of the main ideas • combines ideas accurately from several sources.	The essay • presents a topic with an unfocused controlling idea • contains insufficient or vague facts, evidence, details, and examples that confuse the reader's understanding of the main ideas • uses ideas from limited sources.	The essay • presents an unclear or vague topic with no controlling idea • contains few facts, evidence, details, or examples • cites few or no sources or misstates ideas from sources.
Structure	The essay • leads with an effective, engaging introduction • effectively sequences ideas and uses meaningful transitions to create cohesion and clarify relationships • provides an insightful conclusion that follows from and supports the explanation presented.	The essay • presents a clear and focused introduction • sequences ideas and uses transitions to create coherence • provides a conclusion that connects the larger ideas presented in the essay.	The essay • contains an underdeveloped and/or unfocused introduction • presents disconnected ideas and limited use of transitions • contains an underdeveloped or unfocused conclusion.	The essay • contains a vague, unfocused introduction • presents little, if any, commentary and no use of transitions • contains a vague or no conclusion.
Use of Language	The essay • uses precise diction deliberately chosen to inform or explain the topic • uses a variety of sentence structures to enhance the explanation • demonstrates technical command of the conventions of standard English.	The essay • uses appropriate diction to inform or explain • uses a variety of sentence structures • demonstrates general command of conventions; minor errors do not interfere with meaning.	The essay • uses informal diction that is not appropriate to inform or explain • shows little or no variety in sentence structure • demonstrates limited command of conventions; errors interfere with meaning.	The essay • uses informal diction that is inappropriate for the purpose • shows no variety in sentence structure • demonstrates limited command of conventions; errors interfere with meaning.

Unpacking Embedded Assessment 2

Skimming/Scanning
Graphic Organizer
Quickwrite
Summarizing
Marking the Text

Learning Targets

- Identify the skills needed to complete Embedded Assessment 2 and draw on your background knowledge to understand the text.
- Recognize the characteristics and structures of argumentative text.

Preview

In this activity, you will preview and unpack the knowledge and skills required to complete Embedded Assessment 2.

Making Connections

In the first part of this unit, you learned how to conduct research and to write an informational essay explaining a topic. In this part of the unit, you will expand on your writing skills by writing an argumentative essay to persuade an audience to agree with your position on an issue.

Essential Questions

Now that you have analyzed how advertising affects young people, would you change your answer to the first Essential Question on the role that advertising plays in young people's lives? If so, how would you change it?

Developing Vocabulary

Look at your Reader/Writer Notebook and review the new vocabulary you learned as you studied the research process and informational writing. Which words do you know in depth, and which words do you need to learn more about?

Unpacking Embedded Assessment 2

Read the assignment for Embedded Assessment 2: Writing an Argumentative Essay.

 Your assignment is to write an argumentative essay that states and supports a claim about an issue of importance to you.

In your own words, summarize what you will need to know to complete this assessment successfully. With your class, create a graphic organizer to represent the skills and knowledge you will need to complete the tasks identified in the Embedded Assessment.

INDEPENDENT READING LINK

Reading Plan

In this part of the unit, you will be reading informational texts as well as some well-known speeches. Speeches are often made to persuade an audience on a topic. You might consider reading famous speeches or informational texts about issues on which you have a definite position. Use your Reader/Writer Notebook to create a reading plan and respond to any questions, comments, or reactions you might have to your reading. You can also jot notes in your Independent Reading Log. Refer to those notes as you participate in discussions with your classmates about how the speeches or information affects the choices people make.

Preparing for Argumentative Writing

Learning Strategies

Brainstorming
Quickwrite
Writing Groups

WORD CONNECTIONS

Roots and Affixes

Persuade comes from a Latin word meaning "to advise or urge." The root *suad* is also related to "sweet." To persuade, then, is to present an argument in a pleasing manner.

My Notes

Learning Targets

- Recognize the characteristics and structures of argumentative text.
- Begin to write a multi-paragraph argumentative text.

Preview

In this activity, you will learn about the characteristics of argumentative text and prepare to write your own.

Writing to Persuade

Writers and speakers use persuasive arguments to convince others to support their positions on a topic.

1. Brainstorm a list of times you tried to convince someone of something. What did you say to achieve the result you wanted?

2. **Quickwrite:** Choose an argument in which you were successful. On a separate sheet of paper, write about the situation and how you convinced your audience. Share your ideas in a small group.

Writing Process: Generating a Topic for an Argument

In this part of the unit, your class will write a model argumentative text to learn about the elements of an argument. Following are 20 issues you might consider. Feel free to add your own. As a class, choose a topic on which to write your class-constructed essay and write it on the following line:

Class topic: _____

Possible argumentative essay topics:

1. Kids should be able to watch unlimited television.

2. Kids should get paid for good grades.

3. Kids should have less homework.

4. Magazine advertisements send unhealthy signals to young women.

5. Standardized tests are important.

6. The voting age should be lowered to 16.

7. I'm old enough to babysit.

8. Class sizes are too big.

9. Social media is dangerous.

10. Internet access should be free.

11. Cell phones should be allowed in school.

12. People become adults at age 21.

13. Sports should be required for graduation.

14. Parents of bullies should have to pay a fine.

15. The school year should be longer.

16. School days should start later.

17. All students should wear uniforms.

18. Schools should teach students how to eat healthy foods.

19. Pets should be allowed in school.

20. Students should attend school year-round, four days a week.

Writing with a Group

You have worked a lot in collaborative groups. As you begin writing a model argumentative text, it is important to have meaningful discussions with your group. Remember to give and accept constructive feedback as you discuss. Consider the following writing group norms.

WORD CONNECTIONS

Roots and Affixes
The word **norm** comes from the Latin *norma*, "carpenter's square, rule, pattern." Other words from the same root include *normal*, *paranormal*, and *enormous*.

Writing Group Norms
1. A writing group is a safe place to try out new ideas and present work in progress. Use it to take intellectual risks.

Paraphrase or example:

2. As a thinker and contributor, don't apologize for your ideas or work. Don't be embarrassed to share your thoughts or work.

Paraphrase or example:

3. As a peer, be thoughtful and specific in your feedback.

Paraphrase or example:

4. As a group, celebrate together.

Paraphrase or example:

My Notes

My Notes

Learning Targets

• Recognize the characteristics and structures of argumentative text and analyze a claim.
• Identify the thesis, or controlling idea, of a text.
• Identify the intended audience of an argumentative text.

Preview

In this activity, you will read and analyze a humorous argumentative text about pollution and waste. Then you will begin crafting your own argumentative text on the issue your class has chosen.

Setting a Purpose for Reading

• Interact with the text as you read, taking notes and underlining examples of loaded language.
• Circle unknown words and phrases. Try to determine the meaning of the words by using context clues, word parts, or a dictionary.

About the Author

Andrew Rooney (1911–2011) was a popular commentator on the TV news program *60 Minutes* for more than 30 years. In that time, he wrote more than 800 essays, which he presented either on television or in the newspaper. He earned many awards for his writing, which was often humorous and sometimes controversial.

Essay

America the Not-So-Beautiful

by **Andrew A. Rooney**

1   Next to saving stuff I don't need, the thing I like to do best is throw it away. My idea of a good time is to load up the back of the car with junk on a Saturday morning and take it to the dump. There's something satisfying about discarding almost anything.

2   Throwing things out is the American way. We don't know how to fix anything, and anyone who does know how is too busy to come, so we throw it

away and buy a new one. Our economy depends on us doing that. The trouble with throwing things away is, there is no "away" left.

3   Sometime around the year 500 B.C., the Greeks in Athens passed a law prohibiting people from throwing their garbage in the street. This Greek law was the first recognition by civilized people that throwing things away was a problem. Now, as the population explodes and people take up more room on Earth, there's less room for everything else.

4   The more civilized a country is, the worse the trash problem is. Poor countries don't have the same problem because they don't have much to discard. Prosperity in the United States is based on using things up as fast as we can, throwing away what's left, and buying new ones.

5   We've been doing that for so many years that (1) we've run out of places to throw things because houses have been built where the dump was and (2) some of the things we're throwing away are poisoning the Earth and will eventually poison all of us and all living things.

6   Ten years ago most people thought nothing of dumping an old bottle of weed or insect killer in a pile of dirt in the back yard or down the drain in the street, just to get rid of it. The big companies in America had the same feeling, on a bigger scale. For years the chemical companies dumped their poisonous wastes in the rivers behind the mills, or they put it in fifty-gallon drums in the vacant lots, with all the old, rusting machinery in it, up behind the plants. The drums rusted out in ten years and dumped their poison into the ground. It rained, the poisons seeped into the underground streams and poisoned everything for miles around. Some of the manufacturers who did this weren't even evil. They were dumb and irresponsible. Others were evil because they knew how dangerous it was but didn't want to spend the money to do it right.

WORD CONNECTIONS

Roots and Affixes
Prosperity comes from the Latin word meaning "to cause to succeed" or "fortunate." The root *sper-*, meaning "hope," is also found in *desperate*. The suffix *-ity* forms a noun.

7   The problem is **staggering**. I often think of it when I go in the hardware store or a Sears Roebuck and see shelves full of poison. You know that, one way or another, it's all going to end up in the Earth or in our rivers and lakes.

8   I have two pint bottles of insecticide with 3 percent DDT in them in my own garage that I don't know what to do with. I bought them years ago when I didn't realize how bad they were. Now I'm stuck with them.

9   The people of the city of New York throw away nine times their weight in garbage and junk every year. Assuming other cities come close to that, how long will it be before we trash the whole Earth?

10   Of all household waste, 30 percent of the weight and 50 percent of the volume is the packaging that stuff comes in.

11   Not only that, but Americans spend more for the packaging of food than all our farmers together make in income growing it. That's some statistic.

12   Trash collectors are a lot more independent than they used to be because we've got more trash than they've got places to put it. They have their own schedules and their own holidays. Some cities try to get in good with their trash collectors or garbage men by calling them "sanitation engineers." Anything just so long as they pick it up and take it away.

13   We often call the dump "the landfill" now, too. I never understood why land has to be filled, but that's what it's called. If you're a little valley just outside town, you have to be careful or first thing you know you'll be getting "filled."

14   If 5 billion people had been living on Earth for the past thousand years as they have been in the past year, the planet would be nothing but one giant landfill, and we'd have turned America the beautiful into one huge landfill.

15 The best solution may be for all of us to pack up, board a spaceship, and move out. If Mars is **habitable**, everyone on Earth can abandon this planet we've trashed, move to Mars, and start trashing that. It'll buy us some time.

habitable: a place where people could survive

Making Observations
- What captures your attention the most in this essay?
- What emotions did you feel while reading this essay?

Returning to the Text
- Return to the text as you respond to the following questions. Use text evidence to support your responses.
- Write any additional questions you have about the essay in your Reader/Writer Notebook.

1. How does the author use loaded language to convey his point of view about throwing things away? Cite examples from the text.

2. How does the author connect the idea of prosperity to the amount of trash people throw away?

3. In paragraph 4, the author says, "The more civilized a country is, the worse the trash problem." What does he mean by "civilized" in this sentence?

4. What are two central ideas of the text? What details support these ideas throughout the essay?

5. How does Rooney's use of humor in the last paragraph affect the tone of the essay? What is the effect?

Working from the Text

Introducing the Strategy: SOAPSTone

The letters in **SOAPSTone** stand for *subject*, *occasion*, *audience*, *purpose*, *speaker*, and *tone*. This acronym gives you a helpful tool for analyzing text by breaking it down into separate parts.

6. Use the SOAPSTone strategy to analyze Andrew A. Rooney's argumentative essay. Think about how the idea that "throwing things out is the American way" influences individuals to act as if Earth were a huge trash dump.

SOAPSTone	Analysis	Textual Support
Subject: What is the topic?		
Occasion: What are the circumstances surrounding this text?		
Audience: Who is the target audience?		
Purpose: Why did the author write this text?		
Speaker: What does the reader know about the writer?		
Tone: What is the writer's attitude toward the subject?		

7. While a thesis in an informational text most often explains the writer's main idea, a thesis or **claim** in an argumentative text is the writer's position or point of view on an issue. Read the example of a claim that follows. Mark the claim by <u>underlining</u> its subject (usually nouns), circling its opinion (words with strong connotations), and highlighting the reasons to be developed.

   Claim: There are numerous downsides to year-round schooling; it has no positive effects on education, it adds to the cost, and it disturbs the long-awaited summer vacation.

8. Write a clear and concise claim for Andrew Rooney's essay. Use information from your SOAPSTone analysis. Reread the text as needed to write the claim.

Writing Process: Writing a Claim for an Argumentative Essay

9. **Quickwrite:** Write your ideas about both sides of the issue your class chose to write about. Share your position with your writing group. As a group, come to a consensus about your position and make a claim. Present your writing group's position and claim to the class.

10. As a class, select a position and claim.

   Class position/claim about the issue:

ACADEMIC

A **claim** in this usage is a statement that can be argued, such as whether a fact is true or not, a situation is good or bad, or one action is better than another. In an argumentative text, the claim is supported by reasons and evidence.

WORD CONNECTIONS

Cognates
The English word **consensus** means "general agreement." It has the same meaning as the Spanish word *consenso*. Both words come from the Latin word *consentı̄re*, which means *agree*.

 INDEPENDENT READING LINK

Reading Plan
In class, you just read an argumentative text about trash and pollution. What is another issue that interests you or affects your daily life? For outside reading, read an article or book about another controversial issue. You may want to refer back to the list in Activity 2.11 for ideas. Compare and contrast that text to the one in this activity. Use your Reader/Writer Notebook to record your ideas.

11. Use a SOAPSTone graphic organizer to generate your initial ideas about the class position/claim.

12. Draft your claim.

☑ Check Your Understanding

Review the draft of your claim. Does it clearly state the issue and your position? If not, revise your draft to achieve a clear and concise claim.

Language Checkpoint: Writing Parallel Lists

- Understand how to create parallel lists of words, phrases, and clauses.
- Correctly use commas and semicolons to separate parallel items in a series.

Preview

In this activity, you will practice writing parallel lists and punctuating them correctly.

Writing Parallel Lists

Strong writers use various techniques to make their writing clear and engaging. One such technique is using parallel structure when writing lists. When a list is parallel, all the items in the list share a similar structure.

1. Look at the example that follows from the article "America the Not-So-Beautiful" by Andrew A. Rooney. Notice the words in bold. How many items does Rooney list? What is similar about them?

    The best solution may be for all of us to **pack** up, **board** a spaceship, and **move** out.

2. Look at this sample student sentence from an essay about "America the Not-So-Beautiful." What do you notice about the items in the list? Discuss with a partner how you might change the sentence to make it clearer.

    Rooney is worried that poisonous wastes are seeping into rivers, make people sick, and damaging the environment.

Parallel Lists with Words and Phrases

Sometimes lists contain a series of words or phrases. In these cases, the words or phrases should have a similar form. In other words, they should be parallel. Look at the following examples.

Not Parallel: My mom likes to recycle, reusing, and refurbishes old things.

Parallel: My mom likes recycling, reusing, and refurbishing things around our house.

Notice how the words take the same form in the correct sentence. The consistent use of the *-ing* ending clarifies the meaning and draws attention to the action.

Not Parallel: The recycling truck comes down the street, around the block, and then he would come by our house.

Parallel: The recycling truck comes down the street, around the block, and by our house.

In the parallel sentence, the items in the list are all short prepositional phrases. The meaning is clear, and the sentence flows nicely.

3. Complete each sentence by filling in the blank with the word group in brackets that will make the structure parallel.

   a. Collecting recyclable trash and _____ the water bottles are included in Simon's jobs as waste management leader. [also to refill / refilling / refill]

   b. Sweat poured off her face, ran down her neck, and _____ as Cheyenne focused intently on picking up trash in her neighborhood. [soaked her shirt / was soaking her shirt / did soak her shirt]

   c. "My idea of a good time is to _____ up the back of the car with junk on a Saturday morning and _____ it to the dump" (Rooney). [load; taking / load; take / then load; taking]

4. Choose one of your answers and explain to a partner how you knew which answer was correct.

Parallel Lists with Clauses

A clause is a word group that contains both a subject and a verb. Clauses can stand alone when they express a complete thought (independent clause), or they can need another clause to help them make sense (dependent clause). Sometimes a sentence can contain a series of clauses. In these cases, the clauses should be written in parallel form.

Not Parallel: The sanitation workers were told that **long sleeves would protect their skin, goggles would protect their eyes, and to use dust masks to protect their throat and lungs.**

Parallel: The sanitation workers were told that **long sleeves would protect their skin, goggles would protect their eyes, and dust masks would protect their throat and lungs.**

Because clauses are typically longer, it is important to use parallel structure when writing them, or your reader may become confused.

5. Read the following sentences related to the article "America the Not-So-Beautiful." Mark the words, phrases, and clauses that are parallel.

   • Hazardous chemicals dumped in the street will pollute rivers, streams, and oceans.

   • Larger human populations mean increased pollution, diminished animal habitats, and reduced landfill space.

   • Our family tries to buy products that use natural substances, include recycled materials, and break down quickly.

6. Read the sentences and decide whether or not they contain parallel structure. If the sentence is correct, write "correct" in the correction column. If it is incorrect, mark the part or parts that are not parallel and rewrite the sentence to demonstrate how it could be fixed.

Sentence	Correction (if needed)
In 1031, the Japanese began to recycle and then repulped their paper.	
When the Black Death struck Europe in 1348, the illness spread because of the garbage people threw in the streets and the lack of sanitary living.	
One of the early purposes of the Salvation Army was to collect, sorting, and recycling used or unwanted items.	
Today, neighborhoods are filled with dark green cans for trash and bright blue cans in order for people to be able to recycle.	

7. Choose a sentence and explain your revision to your partner.

Punctuating Parallel Lists

Now that you understand how to create parallel lists of words, phrases, and clauses, the next step is to make sure you correctly punctuate these structures.

Punctuation Rules:

- Use a comma to separate items in a series. For logic and consistency, it is helpful to include a final comma (called a serial, or Oxford, comma) before the conjunction; however, it is usually not incorrect to omit it.
- Use a semicolon to join items in a series when the items themselves include commas.

8. Underline the parallel phrases in the following sentence and circle the commas that separate them.

Andrew A. Rooney also says, "Prosperity in the United States is based on using things up as fast as we can, throwing away what's left, and buying new ones" ("America the Not-So-Beautiful").

9. Underline the parallel items in the following sentence and circle the semicolons that divide them.

My parents had their first meeting on April 3, 1992; their first conversation on April 27, 1992; and their first date on April 30, 1992.

Revising

Read the sample student response and make corrections to create parallel structure.

[1] Sometimes it's hard to think about the results of recycling or not to recycle because we only see the immediate effects of our choices. [2] However, this should be a reason to care about recycling. [3] We are preparing the world where our grandkids will live and hope that it will be better. [4] My mom won't let me keep food in my room because she knows that it will cause a bug infestation. [5] It's the same with recycling. [6] Since we know what will happen if we don't start taking care of our trash, we should do all we can to stop our own "infestation."

☑ Check Your Understanding

In Activity 2.12, you were asked to write a "clear and concise claim for Andrew Rooney's essay" using information from the SOAPSTone analysis. The following is a sample response. Correct any mistakes in parallel structure, using correct punctuation, and then write an explanation for how you knew that something was wrong and what you did to fix it.

In his article "America the Not-So-Beautiful," Andrew Rooney addresses the trash problems of our country in order to get people's attention and then he wants to present the problem and after that to inspire change.

_____

_____

_____

_____

Now add an item to your Editor's Checklist to help you remember to check for parallel structure in your writing.

Practice

Using the information you collected in your SOAPSTone from Activity 2.12, write a short paragraph (4–5 sentences) about what you believe would be the best way to address the problem of too much waste. Be sure to:

- Use at least one example of parallel structure.
- Keep your verb tenses consistent.
- Punctuate any listing.

Exploring and Evaluating Reasons and Evidence

Learning Targets

- Explain how evidence is used to support an author's purpose and message.
- Identify the claim of an argumentative text.

Preview

In this activity, you will review the characteristics of argumentative text and conduct research to identify valid reasons and evidence to support a claim.

Learning Strategies

Skimming/Scanning
Brainstorming
Graphic Organizer
Marking the Text
Discussion Groups

ACADEMIC

Facts and details in a text are **valid** when they support the claim a writer is making and are credible and true.

Supporting a Claim

1. In a successful argument, the claim must be backed up with support, such as **valid** facts, details, and examples. A writer can support his or her viewpoint with both reasons and evidence. Brainstorm what you already know about these concepts.

   Reasons are:

   Evidence is:

   Types of evidence include:

2. In the space that follows, write the claim you wrote for Andrew Rooney's essay "America the Not-So-Beautiful." Scan the essay for examples of reasons and evidence to support the claim.

Claim:	
Reasons	**Evidence**

Setting a Purpose for Reading

- Interact with the text as you read by underlining the statistics the author uses as evidence.
- Circle unknown words and phrases. Try to determine the meaning of the words by using context clues, word parts, or a dictionary.

GRAMMAR & USAGE

Easily Confused Words
Learn to use *affect* and *effect* correctly. *Affect* is generally used as a verb and means "to influence."

Example: Marketers ... are aware of new calls for federal action—including voluntary marketing guidelines that would affect food marketers.

Effect is generally used as a noun and means "a result."

Example: But the net effect on kids' diets was not good.

News Article

Another Study Highlights the Insanity of Selling Junk Food in School Vending Machines

by **Karen Kaplan/Los Angeles Times**

1   For many students, "back to school" means back to a vending machine diet. As you might guess, this isn't necessarily a good thing for student health.

2   Vending machines are found in 16% of U.S. elementary schools, 52% of middle schools and 88% of high schools. About 22% of students in grades 1 through 12 buy food in vending machines each day—and those purchases added an average of 253 calories to their diets, according to a new study in the September issue of the *Journal of School Health*.

3   Just to be clear, those were not 253 calories' worth of tofu, yogurt or carrot sticks. The most popular vending machine items included soft drinks, candy, chips, crackers, cookies, cakes and ice cream. On the plus side, kids also bought low-fat milk, fruit juice and even fruit, the study found.

4   But the **net effect** on kids' diets was not good. Those who bought from vending machines ate an average of 156 grams of sugar per day, compared with 146 grams for those who abstained. They also consumed less dietary fiber, iron and B vitamins like thiamine, riboflavin, niacin and folate.

5   One silver lining: Vending machine customers ate 4% less sodium than other students—an average of 3,287 milligrams per day compared with 3,436 mg for those who didn't buy from vending machines. That's probably because the extra snacks made kids too full to eat as much at mealtime, when dishes are especially salty. In any event, kids should eat no more than 1,200 to 1,500 mg of sodium each day, according to the Mayo Clinic. (Even for adults, the government recommends a daily limit of 2,300 mg.)

6   Overall, vending machines in school appear to be taking a toll on public health. The researchers—from the University of Michigan, Michigan State University and Food & Nutrition Database Research Inc. of Okemos, Mich.— calculated that all that snacking adds up to about 14 extra pounds per child per school year.

7   "For some students this might be a serious contributor to weight issues," they wrote. Other public health problems include Type 2 diabetes and cavities.

8   The study was based on data collected from 2,309 children nationwide for the third School Nutrition Dietary Assessment Study, which was conducted by the U.S. Department of Agriculture's Food and Nutrition Service.

net effect: overall result

Making Observations

- What do you notice in the article that someone skimming it might miss?
- Which statistics are most surprising? Why?

Returning to the Text

- Return to the text as you respond to the following questions. Use text evidence to support your responses.
- Write any additional questions you have about the news article in your Reader/Writer Notebook.

3. Which sentences in the text introduce the author's purpose and message?

_____

_____

_____

_____

4. In paragraph 4, what context clues help you understand the likely meaning of the word *abstained*?

_____

_____

_____

_____

5. What evidence supports the notion that selling junk food in school vending machines is "insanity"? Why might the author have chosen such a strong word?

_____

_____

_____

_____

6. Notice the emphasis on facts and statistics. What inference can you make about how the writer is trying to convince the audience?

_____

_____

_____

_____

Working from the Text

Complete a SOAPSTone analysis of the text to help you prepare for your collaborative discussion.

SOAPSTone	Analysis
Subject: What is the issue?	
Occasion: What circumstances surrounding the issue make it important or relevant?	
Audience: Who would care about or be affected by this issue?	
Purpose: What do you want the audience to do?	
Speaker/writer: How do you show authority in presenting this issue?	
Tone: What attitude do you want to show about this issue (serious, humorous, passionate, indignant)?	

7. Meet in a collaborative discussion group to share your analysis. In order to come to the discussion prepared, use a graphic organizer similar to the following to complete your portion of the analysis.

Text	Claim (Directly Stated or Implied)	Most Logical Reason(s) and Relevant Evidence	Credibility of Reasons/ Evidence (Explain)
"Another Study Highlights the Insanity of Selling Junk Food in School Vending Machines"			

Gaining Perspectives

Over the course of the unit, you have read several texts about public and current issues. With a partner, select one of the topics that you read about. Do some quick research online to find other perspectives on your topic. Discuss the different perspectives with your partner and decide whether these perspectives seem valid. Identify the claims, evidence, and appeals each perspective includes. Then summarize the perspectives in your Reader/ Writer Notebook.

Conducting Research for the Class-Constructed Argument

8. In this part of the activity, you will begin researching the topic of your class claim in preparation for writing a paragraph with reasons and evidence supporting the claim. Review the class claim and brainstorm a list of questions you have about your position.

9. Brainstorm possible reasons and evidence in support of the claim.

10. You will need to conduct research to gather reasons and evidence to support your claim. What sources should you consider? Make a list of the resources that might be most reliable for helping you learn about the topic and position.

11. You will need a plan for your research. With the guidance of your teacher, use the graphic organizer that follows these steps to create a research plan.

12. As you conduct research, record information for each source in a Research Log like the one that follows. Be prepared to share your top pieces of evidence and reasoning in your writing group. Be sure to select reasons that are logical and evidence that is relevant and accurate. Both should clearly support your position. If you prefer, you can create a note card for each resource and record information on that card.

Argumentative Essay Research Log

Topic/Issue: _____

Claim (position on the issue): _____

_____

Source Plus Citation	Notes/Examples/Quotes	Comments

Research Plan for an Argumentative Essay

Steps of Research Process	Plan
1. Identify the issue or problem.	**K:** What do you already **know** about your topic?
2. Write questions that can be answered through research.	**W:** What do you **want** to know? What are you are curious about?
3. Gather evidence and examples.	**H: How** will you research your topic? What primary and secondary sources will be most helpful to learn about the issue? **L:** Use a research log to record what you have **learned**.
4. Evaluate sources.	

Steps of Research Process	Plan
5. Draw conclusions.	
6. Communicate findings.	

13. **Evaluate your reasoning and evidence:** During the class discussion, are you hearing repeated reasons and evidence? Think about how this evidence may signal support that will resonate with your audience.

14. This is a good moment to revise your research plan. Do you need to conduct further research about your issue or change your research questions? Do you need more evidence from accurate and credible sources? What other sources could you use?

LANGUAGE & WRITER'S CRAFT: Sentence Structure

When citing evidence to support a claim, writers use phrases at the beginning, in the middle, or at the end of sentences to show readers how that evidence connects to its source. Citations that connect evidence with its source are often phrases that begin with words such as *in*, *from*, *by*, and *according to*. These phrases are set off from the rest of the sentence by punctuation (such as a comma or dash), as shown in the following examples.

Phrase at the beginning: In the *Journal of School Health*, a recent study showed that 22% of students in Grades 1 through 12 buy food from a vending machine.

Phrase in the middle: The researchers—from the University of Michigan, Michigan State University, and Food & Nutrition Database Research Inc. of Okemos, Mich.—calculated that all that snacking adds up to about 14 extra pounds per child per school year.

Phrase at the end: In any event, kids should eat no more than 1,200 to 1,500 mg of sodium each day, according to the Mayo Clinic.

PRACTICE In your Reader/Writer Notebook, write a sentence in which you use a phrase to cite the following evidence to its source. Use proper punctuation to set off the citation.

Evidence: The most popular vending machine items are soft drinks, candy, chips, crackers, cookies, cakes, and ice cream.

Source: a study in the *Journal of School Health*

15. As a class, outline a body paragraph for the class argumentative essay. You might plan the essay as follows:

I. Claim: The claim is part of the introductory paragraph.

II. Supporting Paragraph

    a. Main reason of support for the claim; this reason or evidence will become a topic sentence for a paragraph.

    b. Evidence and examples to support the reasoning

    c. Commentary that includes an explanation of the significance of the evidence or the connection to the claim

My Notes

Argumentative Writing Prompt

Draft a paragraph or paragraphs with your writing group, following your teacher's directions. Be sure to:

- Introduce a clear claim.
- Cite examples from your research and readings to support your claim with valid reasons and relevant evidence.
- Use phrases at the beginning, in the middle, or at the end of sentences to show how evidence connects to its source.

If you need a reminder about transitional words and phrases, skim and scan the texts you have read so far in this part of the unit. Add what transitional words you find and others to a transitions word bank. You might also keep a transitions word bank in your Reader/Writer Notebook.

Transitions Word Bank

Copy the draft of the class-created body paragraph to your Reader/Writer Notebook.

Just the Right Rhetoric: Logical Appeals

Learning Targets

- Analyze the effectiveness of counterclaims and alternatives to an author's argument.
- Compare and contrast a speech in different media.
- Integrate ideas from multiple texts to build knowledge and vocabulary about how women influence changes in society.

Preview

In this activity, you will read two speeches by well-known women and analyze the speeches for their use of rhetorical appeals and their effectiveness.

Learning Strategies

Close Reading
Marking the Text
Paraphrasing
Note-taking

LITERARY

Rhetoric is the language a writer or speaker uses to persuade an audience. One characteristic of speeches is that they often include powerful rhetoric.

Rhetorical Appeals

You have learned about claims, reasons, and evidence as important elements of effective arguments.

Rhetoric is the art of using words to persuade in writing or speaking. Writers find interesting ways to use just the right words that appeal to their audience in order to convince them.

Rhetorical appeals can strengthen an argument by appealing to logic (*logos*), emotions (*pathos*), or a sense of right and wrong (*ethos*).

Let's look more closely at the appeal of logos, or logic, as a way to build and strengthen an argument. Logos is one of the most important appeals in an effective argument because of its use of facts and logic to build relevant and valid reasoning.

Paraphrase the definition of *logos*:

WORD CONNECTIONS

Roots and Affixes

The word **logic** comes from the Greek word *logos*, which means "reason." Based on this, what do you think an appeal to logic would be most concerned with?

Direct Address

Direct address is when a writer or speaker mentions their audience, either by name or with another term. In persuasive writing or persuasive speeches, direct address can be used to connect with the audience. For example, a speaker may say, "My fellow citizens, please act now!" in order to get their audience's attention.

Setting a Purpose for Reading

- As you read the speeches, mark the text with "L" for *logos* when you notice a statistic, fact, or example. Underline any examples of direct address you notice in the speech.
- Circle unknown words and phrases. Try to determine the meaning of the words by using context clues, word parts, or a dictionary.

About the Author

Born into slavery in New York State, Sojourner Truth (1797–1883) became a well-known antislavery speaker sometime after she gained her freedom in 1827. "Ain't I a Woman" is the name given to an extemporaneous speech she delivered at the Women's Convention in Akron, Ohio, on May 29, 1851. The speech received wide publicity in 1863 during the American Civil War when Frances Dana Barker Gage published a new version that became known as "Ain't I a Woman?"

KNOWLEDGE QUEST

Knowledge Question:

How do women influence changes in society?

In Activity 2.14, you will read two speeches about women's rights. These speeches were given more than 160 years apart. While you read and build knowledge about the topic, think about your answer to the Knowledge Question.

Speech

Ain't I a Woman?

by **Sojourner Truth**

1   Well, children, where there is so much racket there must be something out of kilter. I think that 'twixt the negroes of the South and the women at the North, all talking about rights, the white men will be in a fix pretty soon. But what's all this here talking about?

2   That man over there says that women need to be helped into carriages, and lifted over ditches, and to have the best place everywhere. Nobody ever helps me into carriages, or over mud-puddles, or gives me any best place! And ain't I a woman? Look at me! Look at my arm! I have ploughed and planted, and gathered into barns, and no man could head me! And ain't I a woman? I could work as much and eat as much as a man—when I could get it—and bear the lash as well! And ain't I a woman? I have borne thirteen children, and seen most all sold off to slavery, and when I cried out with my mother's grief, none but Jesus heard me! And ain't I a woman?

3   Then they talk about this thing in the head; what's this they call it? [member of audience whispers, "intellect"] That's it, honey. What's that got to do with women's rights or negroes' rights? If my cup won't hold but a pint, and yours holds a quart, wouldn't you be mean not to let me have my little half measure full?

4   Then that little man in black there, he says women can't have as much rights as men, 'cause Christ wasn't a woman! Where did your Christ come from? Where did your Christ come from? From God and a woman! Man had nothing to do with Him.

5   If the first woman God ever made was strong enough to turn the world upside down all alone, these women together ought to be able to turn it back, and get it right side up again! And now they is asking to do it, the men better let them.

6   Obliged to you for hearing me, and now old Sojourner ain't got nothing more to say.

Write your own caption for this painting:

About the Author

Malala Yousafzai (1997–) received international recognition after surviving an assassination attempt by the Taliban when she was only 15. Her story spread beyond the borders of her home country of Pakistan, increasing awareness, especially in the West, about her activism for education rights and garnering both praise and criticism. On December 10, 2014, she gave her Nobel acceptance speech in Oslo, Norway, as the youngest-ever Nobel laureate.

KNOWLEDGE QUEST

Knowledge Question:
How do women influence changes in society?

My Notes

Speech

Nobel Lecture

by **Malala Yousafzai**

Speech given in Oslo, 10 December 2014

1   Dear sisters and brothers, today is a day of great happiness for me. I am humbled that the Nobel Committee has selected me for this precious award.

2   Thank you to everyone for your continued support and love. Thank you for the letters and cards that I still receive from all around the world. Your kind and encouraging words strengthen and inspire me.

3   I am proud, well in fact, I am very proud to be the first Pashtun, the first Pakistani, and the youngest person to receive this award. Along with that, I am pretty certain that I am also the first recipient of the Nobel Peace Prize who still fights with her younger brothers. I want there to be peace everywhere, but my brothers and I are still working on that.

4   This award is not just for me. It is for those forgotten children who want an education. It is for those frightened children who want peace. It is for those voiceless children who want change.

5   I am here to stand up for their rights, to raise their voice … it is not time to pity them. It is time to take action so it becomes the last time that we see a child deprived of education.

6   I have found that people describe me in many different ways.

7   Some people call me the girl who was shot by the Taliban.

8   And some, the girl who fought for her rights.

9   Some people call me a "Nobel Laureate" now.

10   However, my brothers still call me that annoying bossy sister. As far as I know, I am just a committed and even stubborn person who wants to see every child getting quality education, who wants to see women having equal rights and who wants peace in every corner of the world.

11 Education is one of the blessings of life—and one of its necessities. That has been my experience during the 17 years of my life. In my paradise home, Swat[1], I always loved learning and discovering new things. I remember when my friends and I would decorate our hands with henna[2] on special occasions. And instead of drawing flowers and patterns we would paint our hands with mathematical formulas and equations.

12 We had a thirst for education, because our future was right there in that classroom. We would sit and learn and read together. We loved to wear neat and tidy school uniforms and we would sit there with big dreams in our eyes. We wanted to make our parents proud and prove that we could also excel in our studies and achieve those goals, which some people think only boys can.

13 But things did not remain the same. When I was in Swat, which was a place of tourism and beauty, it suddenly changed… I was just ten when more than 400 schools were destroyed.

14 Education went from being a right to being a crime.

15 Girls were stopped from going to school.

16 When my world suddenly changed, my priorities changed too.

17 I had two options. One was to remain silent and wait to be killed. And the second was to speak up and then be killed.

18 I chose the second one. I decided to speak up.

19 We could not just stand by and see those injustices of the terrorists denying our rights, ruthlessly killing people and misusing the name of Islam. We decided to raise our voice and tell them: Have you not learnt, have you not learnt that in the Holy Quran Allah says: if you kill one person it is as if you kill all of humanity?

20 The terrorists tried to stop us and attacked me and my friends who are here today, on our school bus in 2012, but neither their ideas nor their bullets could win.

21 We survived. And since that day, our voices have grown louder and louder.

22 I tell my story, not because it is unique, but because it is not.

23 It is the story of many girls.

24 Sometimes people like to ask me why should girls go to school, why is it important for them. But I think the more important question is why shouldn't they? Why shouldn't they have this right to go to school?

25 In my own village, there is still no secondary school for girls. And it is my wish and my commitment, and now my challenge to build one so that my friends and my sisters can go to school there and get a quality education and get this opportunity to fulfil their dreams.

26 This is where I will begin, but it is not where I will stop. I will continue this fight until I see every child in school.

27 My great hope is that this will be the last time we must fight for education. Let's solve this once and for all.

---

[1] Swat Valley is located in Northern Pakistan.
[2] Henna is a dye that can be used to create temporary body art.

GRAMMAR & USAGE

Phrases and Clauses

Writers use phrases and clauses to provide readers with detailed information.

Phrases are groups of words that together function as a single part of speech—usually a noun, a verb, an adverb, or an adjective. Yousafzai uses a prepositional phrase when she says, "Along with that."

A **clause** is a group of words that contains a subject and a verb. If a clause can stand alone as a complete sentence, it is an independent clause. If the clause does not express a complete idea, it is a dependent clause. In this sentence from Yousafzai's speech, the bold part is a dependent clause: *It is for those forgotten children who want an education.*

As you read Yousafzai's speech, notice how she uses phrases and clauses to fully explain her ideas.

My Notes

28 We have already taken many steps. Now it is time to take a leap.

29 It is not time to tell the world leaders to realise how important education is—they already know it and their own children are in good schools. Now it is time to call them to take action for the rest of the world's children.

30 We ask the world leaders to unite and make education their top priority.

31 The world can no longer accept that basic education is enough. Why do leaders accept that for children in developing countries, only basic literacy is sufficient, when their own children do homework in Algebra, Mathematics, Science and Physics?

32 Leaders must seize this opportunity to guarantee a free, quality, primary and secondary education for every child.

33 Dear sisters and brothers, dear fellow children, we must work ... not wait. Not just the politicians and the world leaders, we all need to contribute. Me. You. We. It is our duty.

34 Let us become the first generation that decides to be the last that sees empty classrooms, lost childhoods and wasted potentials.

35 Let this be the last time that a girl or a boy spends their childhood in a factory.

36 Let this be the last time that a child loses life in war.

37 Let this be the last time that we see a child out of school.

38 Let this end with us.

39 Let's begin this ending ... together ... today ... right here, right now. Let's begin this ending now.

40 Thank you so much.

⌀ Knowledge Quest

- What emotions do you feel while reading these speeches?
- Which words or phrases stand out to you as they relate to women's rights?

☑ Focus on the Sentence

Before analyzing the speeches more closely, use what you have observed so far to change the following fragments into complete sentences. Add correct punctuation and capitalization.

Sojourner Truth thinks that _____

_____

wants girls to be able to _____

_____

both of the speeches _____

_____

⬡ INDEPENDENT READING LINK

Read and Research

In class, you just read two speeches by well-known speakers. Extend your understanding of these speeches by doing some outside research about one of the speakers, the historical context of the speech, or the social issues discussed. Use your Reader/Writer Notebook to record your findings.

Returning to the Text

- Return to the text as you respond to the following questions. Use text evidence to support your responses.
- Write any additional questions you have about the speeches in your Reader/Writer Notebook.

1. What is Sojourner Truth's response to the argument that women are weak and need to be taken care of? Find details in the text that help you answer the question.

_____

_____

_____

_____

2. Throughout the speech, Truth mentions what other people are saying about equal rights. How does she respond to each of these statements? Cite examples from the text.

_____

_____

_____

_____

3. What does Yousafzai mean when she says, "This award is not just for me"? Find sentences in her speech that support your answer.

_____

_____

_____

_____

4. What is the purpose and effect of Yousafzai's use of the word "we" throughout her speech?

_____

_____

_____

_____

5. KQ What does "Nobel Laureate" mean in paragraph 9 of Yousafzai's speech? Use context clues to infer the meaning of the phrase.

_____

_____

_____

_____

My Notes

6. **KQ** How have Sojourner Truth and Malala Yousafzai worked to create change in society?

_____

_____

_____

_____

7. Find examples of cause-and-effect relationships in Yousafzai's speech. How do they contribute to the overall tone of the text?

_____

_____

_____

_____

INDEPENDENT READING LINK

You can continue to build your knowledge about women's rights by reading other articles at ZINC Reading Labs.

Search for keywords such as *feminism*.

ZINC

VOCABULARY

LITERARY

A **counterclaim**, also called a counterargument, is a claim made by someone with an opposing opinion on a given issue. When creating an argument, you must be able to argue against counterclaims.

⊘ Knowledge Quest

Use your knowledge about "Ain't I a Woman?" and "Nobel Lecture" to discuss with a partner how your understanding of the continuing movement for women's rights has changed. Be sure to:

- Explain your answer to your partner, be specific and use as many details as possible.
- When your partner responds, ask for clarification by posing follow-up questions as needed.
- After the discussion, write down the ideas you talked about.

Working from the Text

8. Revisit the speeches to identify the elements of argumentation: claim, reasons, evidence, and opposing arguments or **counterclaims**.

9. The use of logos is critical in presenting an argument that contains relevant and valid evidence. Scan your annotations for both speeches to find examples of logos. Discuss the effectiveness of each example for the purpose and audience of the speech.

10. Search the Internet for a recording of Sojourner Truth's speech "Ain't I a Woman" or for a video of Malala Yousafzai's speech and listen carefully for the speaker's delivery. How does the speaker emphasize certain words or phrases to strengthen the argument? How effective is the delivery of the speech?

LANGUAGE & WRITER'S CRAFT: Using Rhetorical Devices

Writers of argumentative texts often use rhetorical devices to create their appeals. Three rhetorical devices used in argumentation are the rhetorical question, parallel structure, and repetition.

- A **rhetorical question** is one for which the writer expects no reply or clearly directs the reader to one desired reply. Writers use rhetorical devices to emphasize an idea or to draw a conclusion from facts.

    Example: "And ain't I a woman?" (Sojourner Truth)

- **Parallel structure** is using the same pattern of words to show that two or more ideas have the same level of importance.

    Example: "I have ploughed and planted, and gathered into barns, and no man could head me!" (Sojourner Truth)

- **Repetition** is when key words or phrases are repeated for emphasis or deliberate effect.

    Example: "Some people call me the girl who was shot by the Taliban. And some, the girl who fought for her rights. Some people call me a 'Nobel Laureate' now. However, my brothers still call me that annoying bossy sister." (Malala Yousafzai)

PRACTICE Find another example of a rhetorical question, parallel structure, or repetition in one of the speeches in this activity. Write a sentence in your Reader/Writer Notebook to describe how the rhetorical device strengthens the speaker's argument.

11. Where in her speech does Malala Yousafzai use direct address, and who is her audience? What effect does this create?

12. Reread the two speeches, noting their use of rhetorical devices. Record your findings in the graphic organizer. What rhetorical device stands out to you the most? Why?

Title: Malala Yousafzai, "Nobel Lecture"	
Rhetorical Devices	**Effect**

Title: Malala Yousafzai, "Nobel Lecture"	
Rhetorical Devices	**Effect**

Title: Sojourner Truth, "Ain't I a Woman?"	
Rhetorical Devices	**Effect**

Logical Fallacies

A logical fallacy is when an author uses reasoning that is not logical. Loaded language is a type of logical fallacy where an author uses words that are charged with emotion. The words may have a strong positive or negative connotation, which works to persuade the reader. Sweeping generalizations are another type of logical fallacy. A sweeping generalization is when an author makes a statement about a large group that isn't true for every member of that group.

13. Yousafzai also uses some examples of logical fallacies in her speech. While logical fallacies can sometimes be a sign that a source is not credible, other times an author may use them intentionally to create a certain effect. Locate examples of loaded language and sweeping generalizations in Yousafzai's speech, and complete the graphic organizer that follows.

Example	Effect on reader	Why Yousafzai uses this logical fallacy
loaded language:		
sweeping generalizations:		

📝 Argumentative Writing Prompt

Return to the body paragraph you drafted in Activity 2.13. Work collaboratively in your writing group to add counterclaims, rhetorical devices, and appeals to logic to strengthen your argument. Be sure to:

- Incorporate logical reasoning to strengthen your argument.
- Make use of at least one rhetorical device and at least one counterclaim.

After drafting, exchange your text with a peer or a different writing group. Mark the text you receive to identify the use of logos and rhetorical devices. Provide feedback by celebrating successes and by suggesting ideas for improvement.

Differing Opinions: Acknowledging Opposing Claims

My Notes

Learning Targets

- Analyze the logic in the development of different points of view and the consideration of alternatives.
- Create a claim and argue a position in a debate, using an appropriate mode of delivery.

Preview

In this activity, you will read and analyze two articles with different points of view about the value of capturing daily life on social media. Then you will present arguments about the issue in a debate with your classmates.

Setting a Purpose for Reading

- As you read, take notes in the My Notes space on the author's feelings about social media.
- Circle unknown words and phrases. Try to determine the meaning of the words by using context clues, word parts, or a dictionary.

About the Author

Marcelo Gleiser (1959–) is a professor of physics and astronomy. His research covers both the very big (the universe as a whole) and the very small (particle physics, or the smallest material constituents in the universe). He's also very interested in the origin of life on Earth and the possibility of life elsewhere in the universe.

Essay

Should We Live Life, Or Capture It?

by **Marcelo Gleiser**

1   Everyone is, or wants to be, the star of their own life, and the rage is on to capture every moment deemed meaningful. … There is a side of it that makes sense; we all matter, our lives matter, and we want them to be seen, shared, appreciated. But there is another side that leads to a disengagement with the moment.

2   Are people forgetting to be present in the moment, scattering their focus by looking at life through a screen? Should you be living your life or living it for others to see it?

3   It is telling, however, that this all started before the cellphone revolution. Something happened between the private journal we kept locked in our drawer and the portable video camera. For example, in June 2001 I led a group … on a cruise to see a total solar eclipse in Africa. On board were a crowd of "eclipse groupies," people who go around the world chasing eclipses. Once you see one you can understand why. A total solar eclipse is a deeply moving experience that awakens a primal connection with nature, linking us to something bigger and truly awesome about the world. It needs total commitment and focus of all senses. Yet, as **totality** approached, the ship's deck was a sea of cameras and tripods, as dozens of people prepared to photograph and videotape the four-minute-long event.

4   Instead of fully engaging with this most spectacular natural phenomenon, people chose to look at it from behind their cameras. I was shocked. There were professional photographers onboard and they were going to sell/give pictures away. But people wanted to take their pictures and videos anyway, even if they weren't going to be half as good. I went to two other eclipses, and it's always the same thing. No full personal engagement. The gadget is the eye through which they choose to see reality.

5   What cellphones plus social media have done is to make the archiving and the sharing of images amazingly easy and efficient. The reach is much wider and the gratification (how many "likes" a photo or video gets) is **quantitative**. Lives become a shared social event.

6   Now, there is a side of this that is fine, of course. We celebrate meaningful moments and want to share with those we care about. The problem starts when we stop fully participating in the moment because we have this urge to record it. … Without trying to sound too nostalgic (but sounding), there is nothing like eye-to-eye contact or the sharing of an experience through the real act of engaging in a conversation with friends and family. The gadgets are awesome, of course. But they should not define the way we live—only complement it.

Making Observations
- What image from the article sticks in your mind?
- Who is the author's intended audience?

---

totality: the moment when the sun was completely covered
quantitative: measurable

Returning to the Text

- Return to the text as you respond to the following questions. Use text evidence to support your responses.
- Write any additional questions you have about the essay in your Reader/Writer Notebook.

1. What is the author's main claim in the text?

_____

_____

_____

_____

2. What evidence does the author use to support his argument?

_____

_____

_____

_____

3. What might *totality* mean in the second paragraph? Use context clues to infer its meaning.

_____

_____

_____

_____

4. What rhetorical device does the author use in the text? What is the effect of this question on the reader?

_____

_____

_____

_____

Setting a Purpose for Reading

- As you read, underline the author's claims or opinions. Put a star next to any sources used to support the claims.
- Circle unknown words and phrases. Try to determine the meaning of the words by using context clues, word parts, or a dictionary.

About the Author

Megan Garber is a staff writer at *The Atlantic*, where she writes about technology and culture. She is a founding editor for the innovation section of *Columbia Journalism Review'* s website. In recognition of excellence in media reporting, Garber earned the Mirror Award. She attended Columbia, where she earned a master's degree in journalism.

Essay

The Joy of Instagram

by **Megan Garber**

1   Is there any genre of image that better captures the current technological moment than the sea of screens, at a concert or a rally or a show, thrust upward to document a shared experience? The layering of the lights—reflecting an event in the moment, and capturing it for later—neatly conveys the frenetic beauty of life as it's lived at the dawn of the Internet age. And the anxieties, too, because, you know: Does documenting something cheapen it? Does that sea of screens take something meaningful away from the stage they are aimed at? Does our impulse to snap and Insta and tweet and otherwise capture the events of our lives denude those events, and by extension those lives?

2   According to a new paper: Nope. Kristin Diehl, an associate professor of marketing at the University of Southern California Marshall School of Business, and a team of colleagues wanted to put those ideas to the test. … Capturing experiences through photos, the team found, far from compromising people's enjoyment of those experiences, actually seemed to amplify that enjoyment. A photographic mindset doesn't seem to prevent people from "living in the moment," as the old accusation goes; it might actually help them to do that living.

   …

3   It's not the act of photo-taking itself, to be clear, that leads to that enjoyment; it's the kind of mental curation that is required when you're thinking about what is worth documenting in the first place. Instagram makes us the editors of the texts of our own lives; it demands choices about what is significant—and therefore worth saving, and savoring, and remembering—and what is less so. … Diehl and her colleagues tested the idea on a sightseeing bus, with nearly 200 participants—and found that the people who photographed the sights in question enjoyed the experience much more than those who simply sat and watched and absorbed. They tested it in museums, too: People reported enjoying exhibits more when they photographed them. And, yep, the findings held when it came to that most clichéd of activities: the Instagramming of food. The study participants who were encouraged to take photos while they ate lunch … ended up being more immersed in the dining experience than the people who weren't.

2.15

My Notes

4 It may come down to the difference between "dining" and merely "eating"—the notion that even something as simple as lunch can be, if you allow it to, An Experience: something worth savoring in the present, sure, but also worth preserving for the future.

Making Observations

- What are your first thoughts about the article?
- Which details stand out the most to you?

Returning to the Text

- Return to the text as you respond to the following questions. Use text evidence to support your responses.
- Write any additional questions you have about the essay in your Reader/Writer Notebook.

5. What is this author's claim? Identify text that helps you answer the question.

_____

_____

_____

_____

6. What does *denude* mean in the first paragraph? Use context clues to infer the meaning of the word.

_____

_____

_____

_____

7. What is the purpose of including the rhetorical questions in the first paragraph?

_____

_____

_____

_____

8. How does the author add credibility to her argument?

_____

_____

_____

_____

Working from the Text

9. Reread and mark the texts for logical reasoning and devices. Annotate by analyzing or commenting on the effect of the reasoning and devices in the My Notes section.

10. Complete the graphic organizer to evaluate the arguments.

Reasons + Evidence FOR Documenting Life through Social Media	Is the argument effective?	Reasons + Evidence AGAINST Documenting Life through Social Media	Is the argument effective?

GRAMMAR & USAGE

Complex Sentences

Notice that a complex sentence with a dependent marker is a structure that helps the writer to acknowledge and refute a counterclaim. Example: *Yes, you worry about me, but I need to learn independence.*

Keep an eye out for complex sentences that serve this purpose in arguments that you read.

Acknowledging Counterclaims

Part of arguing effectively is considering alternatives and acknowledging opposing claims, also known as counterclaims—the "other side" of the issue. Recognizing counterclaims adds to a writer's credibility (ethos) because it shows that he or she is knowledgeable about the issue. To acknowledge a counterclaim, a writer or speaker recognizes an opposing viewpoint and then argues against it, perhaps by finding weaknesses within the opposing reasons and evidence and thereby supporting his or her own argument. In other words, it is the "yes, but" part of the argument. "Yes" is recognizing the counterclaim; "but" is the writer's response to it.

Example:

Issue: A teenager wants parental permission to go to a concert.

Claim: I should be allowed to go to a concert without an adult.

- **Of course you are worried about me going without you;** *however, I have a cell phone with me, and we can check in throughout the concert.*

- **Certainly I can see why you might be concerned because you don't know all my friends,** *but I'll be glad to ask their parents to call and reassure you.*

- **Admittedly, it is a good point that I do have homework;** *on the other hand, the concert is only a few hours long, and I plan to get most of my homework completed before I go.*

Practice Scenario

Issue: Mobile devices (e.g., cell phones, tablets)

Claim: Mobile devices should be banned at school.

The Principal's Argument	The Student's Argument

Plan and Present an Argument: Class Debate

To plan and prepare for a debate on the use of social media, consider the claim, reasons, and evidence you will use to present your assigned side of the argument. Also take into consideration the possible counterclaims and be prepared to respond to them logically. Use the graphic organizer to plan your argument. During the debate, present your argument clearly, emphasize important points, and include relevant facts, details, and examples. Speak clearly at an understandable volume and use appropriate eye contact.

We should focus on enjoying moments, not documenting them.

Assigned Position (circle one): FOR   AGAINST

Claim:

Reasons:	**Evidence (Logos):**

Recognizing counterclaim:

Rhetorical appeals I can use for effect:
Pathos:

Ethos:

Rhetorical devices I can use for effect:

☑ Focus on the Sentence

After the debate, reflect on your own claim as well as the ideas your classmates shared. Write two sentences starting with the subordinating conjunctions that follow.

While _____

_____

Even though _____

_____

After the Debate

Reflect: How well did each speaker deliver his or her argument? How clear was each speaker's claim? Did each speaker incorporate adequate evidence (logos) and address the counterclaim?

LANGUAGE & WRITER'S CRAFT:
Complex Sentences with Subject-Verb Agreement

Writers construct sentences so that phrases and clauses convey meaning clearly. Different types of sentences show different relationships between ideas. A clause is a group of words that includes a subject and a verb. An **independent clause** has a subject and a verb, and it can stand alone as a sentence. A **dependent clause** has a subject and a verb, but it cannot stand alone as a sentence. A **complex sentence** is composed of one independent clause and at least one dependent clause. The dependent clause provides more information about the independent clause.

Example:

Although they could engage fully with this most spectacular natural phenomenon, people chose to look at it from behind their cameras.

Dependent clause: Although they could engage fully with this most spectacular natural phenomenon

Independent clause: people chose to look at it from behind their cameras.

In any clause, the **subject** and the **verb** must agree. A singular subject takes a singular verb, and a plural subject takes a plural verb. In a complex sentence, a dependent clause might appear between the subject and verb of the independent clause. Even when the main subject and verb are separated in this way, they must still agree.

Example:

The **speaker**, who is a professor of media studies, **offers** a fascinating perspective on the effects of social media.

PRACTICE With a partner, add dependent clauses to some of your sentences to provide more information about an idea. Then work together to check for and correct subject-verb agreement in your argument.

Argumentative Writing Prompt

In your writing group, revise your text to incorporate an acknowledgment of a counterclaim. Draw on information from your classmates' claims and evidence from the debate. Use adding or replacing in your draft. Be sure to:

- Clearly describe and acknowledge the counterclaim.
- Use transitions and complex sentences with phrases and clauses to make your point.
- Use correct spelling, grammar, and punctuation.
- Check to make sure you have used parallel structure in lists or series of words, infinitives, prepositional phrases, or clauses.
- Establish and maintain a formal style.

To Introduce and Conclude

Learning Strategies

Note-taking
Writing Groups
Think-Pair-Share
Quickwrite
Self-Editing/Peer Editing

Learning Targets

- Recognize the structure of argumentative text, including an introductory and concluding paragraph.

Preview

You will study how the student introduces and concludes the essay.

Setting a Purpose for Reading

- As you read, underline any claims that the author makes and put a star next to sources that the author cites. Circle words that signal a transition.
- Circle unknown words and phrases. Try to determine the meaning of the words by using context clues, word parts, or a dictionary.

Student Essay

Screen Time?

1   How does screen time really affect you and others you know? Does the new technology make life better? The answer is no, screen time affects youth in a negative way. Imagine a future world without teenagers, instead, as people in the United Kingdom like to call it, screenagers—kids that have a variety of mental and physical illnesses and are no longer capable of doing some of the jobs that are most important to our society. Because spending too many hours in front of any kind of screen, even a phone, can become addicting, spark psychological difficulties, and cause lower grades in school, screen time for youth should be limited to two hours a day or less.

2   Screen addiction is a serious problem in our society. A study conducted by the "Kaiser Family Foundation" states that nearly every kid in the U.S. uses an electronic device almost every second outside of school. Kids ages eight to eighteen spend an average time of seven and one half hours a day. That's over 53 hours a week which is way too much considering that the recommended time per day is two hours. An experiment on kids who got all their screens withdrawn had positive outcomes. The kids seemed calmer, fought less often, and slept better. A lot of kids feel like the overuse of screens has no effect on them, but it actually does, they just don't notice it at all. In addition, in a survey of youth ages eight to eighteen, nearly one in four kids felt addicted to screens. Preventing the over-use of screens could prevent addiction and the failure of a whole society.

3   Something else the overuse of screens causes is psychological difficulties such as hyperactivity, emotional and conduct problems, as well as difficulties with peers. A survey by the Chiba University says that 25,000 people that spend most of their time in front of a screen feel depressed. The cause of this is not necessarily looking at the screen, but much rather the addiction, not knowing when to stop, and being isolated from others. Depression is a severe illness which causes lots of deaths. In addition, the hyperactivity caused by the screen

GRAMMAR & USAGE

Misplaced Modifiers
A word or phrase that modifies the wrong word is called a **misplaced modifier**. Look at this example:

Misplaced: The two students talked quietly in the **corner with cell phones.** (It sounds like the corner has the cell phones.)

Correct: The two **students with cell phones** talked quietly in the corner. (The students have the cell phones.)

My Notes

My Notes

addiction causes an unhealthy diet and might lead to other dangerous diseases. All these psychological and physical problems caused by one screen, it's really not worth it.

4   Finally, using screens too much may cause a decrease in grades at school. It is proven that adolescents who watch three or more hours of television a day are at especially high risk for poor homework completion, negative attitudes toward school, poor grades, and long-term academic failure. This might result in a bad future with a bad job or no job at all. This mainly happens because of the lack of enthusiasm towards school and the time spent using a screen instead of studying. In addition, the content of some TV shows out there doesn't necessarily make you smarter, in fact, some of them make you dumber. Considering this, you should think about how every hour you watch TV instead of studying makes it harder to have a promising future.

5   In conclusion, decreasing screen time below two hours a day could prevent youth from having a bad life. Reduced screen time helps you in school, helps you have a healthier diet, be more physical, and tends to get you more engaged in activities. The end of our world will most likely not be caused by a bunch of earthquakes and tsunamis as shown in the movie "2012"; it is going to be our young generation wasting away in front of screens. So, go home, unplug your screen, and save our future society. The results will be much better than some TV Show.

Making Observations
• Which ideas from the article stand out to you the most? Why?

Returning to the Text

- Return to the text as you respond to the following questions. Use text evidence to support your responses.
- Write any additional questions you have about the essay in your Reader/Writer Notebook.

1. Which sentence in the introduction presents the student's central claim?

2. What evidence does the writer provide to support her claim?

3. Look again at the main claim and the main ideas in each paragraph. How does the student structure her ideas?

4. Analyze the author's word choices. Is the style consistently formal? Identify text that helps you answer the question.

Working from the Text

5. Look again at the introduction and conclusion of the essay.

- What does the speaker do to introduce the argument?

- What does the speaker do to conclude the argument?

- How effective are the introduction and conclusion to this essay? Explain your answer.

LANGUAGE & WRITER'S CRAFT: Revising for Cohesion and Clarity

Cohesion and **clarity** in writing refer to how ideas flow together. A way to write with cohesion and clarity is to use the **TLQ** format when writing a detail sentence. The **TLQ** format includes:

T — Transition word or phrase, such as:

For example,

To illustrate,

In this case,

In addition,

Most important,

Likewise,

Finally,

L — Lead-in: The lead-in is usually a phrase that sets the context for the specific information that follows; it often answers the question *Where?* or *When?*

Q — Quote: A quote may be used to support the topic. The "quote" portion of the detail sentence does not always need to be a direct quote in quotation marks; it can be paraphrased material explaining the fact, detail, or example.

> **EXAMPLE:** For instance [**transition**], in the magazine advertisement for Gatorade sports drink [**lead-in**], the ad uses the technique of testimonial by showing a picture of Major League Baseball player Derek Jeter holding up his fist to the fans and by including text under the picture stating, "Gatorade has always been a part of Derek Jeter's team." [**quote**]

PRACTICE Use TLQ to evaluate the writing you did for the Argumentative Writing Prompt. Revise to improve the lead-in, add quotations, or change or add transitions.

Argumentative Writing Prompt

Create an outline and then generate ideas for a potential introduction and conclusion to your class-constructed body paragraph. Use the sample essay as a model for beginning and ending your essay. Be sure to:

- Introduce your claim in an introduction.
- Include a hook, a connection between the hook and the claim, and the claim.
- Provide a conclusion that supports your argument. (Why does the claim that you made matter? What should the audience do, based on your claim?)

Independent Reading Checkpoint

You have read a variety of sources relating to your topic. Which information supports your claim? Which information counters your claim? How can you use this information to strengthen your argument? Record your ideas in your Independent Reading Log.

Language Checkpoint: Placing Modifiers

Learning Targets

- Identify phrases within a sentence, recognizing and correcting misplaced and dangling modifiers.
- Understand how to place modifiers for clarity and meaning when writing.

Preview

In this activity, you will learn about the importance of placing and using modifiers correctly in your writing.

Placing Modifiers

A modifier is a word, phrase, or clause that makes the meaning of another word or word group more specific. Modifiers can function as adjectives (describing a noun) or adverbs (describing a verb, an adjective, or another adverb).

Example: Eva played the game that had been given to her by her mother.

The underlined words are a clause that makes the meaning of *game* more specific. Notice that the modifier is placed right after the noun it is describing. Placing a modifier close to the word it is describing helps make the meaning clear.

Example: During the band concert, the flute player was on her phone with the pink hair.

In this sentence it sounds as if the phone has pink hair, so *with the pink hair* should be moved next to the word it modifies, *player*.

Improved: During the band concert, the flute player with the pink hair was on her phone.

Before you can move modifiers to appropriate positions within sentences, you must be able to identify modifiers.

1. Underline any phrase or clause that is used as a modifier in the following sentences.

   A. Shannon showed us a phone case that is purple.

   B. Jogging by, Felix spotted a phone.

   C. After setting her laptop down, Marie left the room.

   D. "I can't hear you," said the customer wearing headphones.

2. Now highlight the word(s) each phrase or clause is modifying.

Misplaced Modifiers

Positioning modifiers near the words they modify helps make writing clear. A misplaced modifier is a modifier that is not near the word it modifies.

Example: Stephon took off his jacket, sat on the couch, and started the movie, which was soggy from the rain.

In this sentence, Stephon's movie wasn't soggy from the rain. His jacket was. Because this is not essential information, the clause should also be surrounded by commas. **Stephon took off his jacket, which was soggy from the rain, sat on the couch, and started the movie.**

3. Read the following sentences and underline the misplaced modifiers.

4. Revise the sentences so the modifiers are correctly placed.

Before Revision	After Revision
My sister tracks my TV time and lets me watch only one hour a day <u>in charge while Mom's at work.</u>	My sister, in charge while Mom's at work, tracks my TV time and lets me watch only one hour a day.
The Key Club had a phone drive to collect old phones and recycle them at school.	
Flora played a song that Taylor Swift wrote for her recital.	
During his job interview, the alarm would not stop beeping on Dionte's phone.	

5. Choose one sentence from the preceding exercise and explain how you knew where the misplaced modifier was and why you revised it the way you did.

Dangling Modifiers

Another common error writers make is the dangling modifier. A dangling modifier occurs when a word, phrase, or clause does not logically modify any word or word group in the sentence. To fix a dangling modifier, you will have to add or replace words to give the modifier something to describe.

Example: While watching a movie, our pipes broke.

This wording says that *pipes* were watching a movie. The words "While watching a movie" have nothing to connect with because the "who" is left out. Who is watching? To revise the sentence, just add what is missing.

Improved: While **we** were watching a movie, our pipes broke.

The word "we" explains who is watching a movie.

6. **Quickwrite:** Why do you think some writers make the mistake of using dangling modifiers?

7. Revise the following sentences to correct the dangling modifiers. You may add words to the sentences.

Before Revision	After Revision
After apologizing to her friends, the plans were moved back to Saturday evening.	
Before moving to college, the computer was replaced.	
Angry, the foot smashed through the TV while playing the video game.	
With a desperate groan, the phone was heaved into the air after receiving the bad news.	

Revising

Read the following personal narrative. Work with a partner to correct the four misplaced or dangling modifiers in the paragraph. First, find and underline the misplaced or dangling modifiers. Then, rewrite unclear sentences, moving misplaced modifiers to better locations or adding missing information to correct dangling modifiers.

When my mom first gave me my cell phone, I thought it would be a fun distraction for playing games when I was bored and keeping in touch with my friends when I wasn't at school. Carried around like a piece of treasure from King Tut's tomb, I found myself often checking for text messages and posts from my friends. But what began as a fun way to keep connected quickly escalated until I found myself in need of a full-blown "technology intervention." Sleek and shiny, I slept with my phone, ate with my phone, and went to the bathroom with my phone. It was like the best friend I'd never had. Inseparable, every minute was spent together. Eventually, I found myself having to check my phone every two minutes throughout my day. I didn't realize this, of course. That was one of the things I learned later. I began hearing my phone ring when it hadn't, and I would often think I had felt it vibrate with a message when there was no message there. This didn't worry me though, because all my friends were doing the very same thing. One day, I forgot to charge the battery the night before. Breaking down emotionally, my phone was about to die. I actually had a panic attack over a phone—not because my dog died or my mom was in an accident or anything else you could think of that would cause a kid to freak out. It was a phone—a piece of plastic.

☑ Check Your Understanding

Imagine that you are a teacher and you have to explain to your class what is wrong with the following sentence: **Seeing the sun come out, the TV was turned off.**

What is the problem? _____

How can you fix it? _____

Write the revised sentence. _____

_____

Share with a partner what you would say about the problem and how to fix it.

Practice

Write three sentences according to the instructions given. Make sure not to create any misplaced or dangling modifiers.

[1] Write a sentence about what happened when you got home from school yesterday. Begin your sentence with the word *when*.

[2] Write a sentence about what happened after someone surprised you. Begin your sentence with the word *after*.

[3] Write a sentence that includes the phrase *at the store*.

Writing an Argumentative Essay

 ASSIGNMENT

Your assignment is to write an argumentative essay that states and supports a claim about an issue of importance to you.

Planning and Prewriting: Take time to make a plan for generating ideas and research questions.	■ What prewriting strategies (such as freewriting or webbing) can you use to select and explore a timely and relevant issue that interests you? ■ How will you draft a claim that states your position? ■ What questions will guide your research?
Researching: Gather information from a variety of credible sources.	■ What strategies can you use (such as KWHL or SOAPSTone) to guide your research and evaluate sources? ■ How will you take notes by summarizing, paraphrasing, quoting, responding, and recording bibliographic information? ■ Will you use a research log (see Activity 2.13) to record your research and sources?
Drafting: Write an argumentative essay that is appropriate for your task, purpose, and audience.	■ How will you select the best reasons and evidence from your research? ■ What strategies can you use (such as outlining) to organize your draft? ■ Who is the audience, and what would be an appropriate tone and style for this audience? ■ How will you be sure you are not plagiarizing any sources?
Evaluating and Revising the Draft: Create opportunities to review and revise your work.	■ During the process of writing, when can you pause to share and respond with others? ■ What is your plan to include suggestions and revision ideas into your draft? ■ How can the Scoring Guide help you evaluate how well your draft meets the requirements of the assignment?
Checking and Editing for Publication: Confirm your final draft is ready for publication.	■ How will you proofread and edit your draft to demonstrate command of the conventions of standard English capitalization, punctuation, spelling, grammar, and usage?

Reflection

You have used and been introduced to a number of strategies for constructing a well-reasoned and researched argumentative essay. Which strategies were most effective in helping you to write an effective argument and how did you use them?

SCORING GUIDE

Scoring Criteria	Exemplary	Proficient	Emerging	Incomplete
Ideas	The argument • skillfully presents a claim and provides appropriate background and a clear explanation of the issue • effectively supports claims with logical, convincing reasoning and evidence, as well as skillful use of rhetorical devices • summarizes and refutes counterclaims with relevant reasoning and clear evidence.	The argument • supports a claim that is clearly presented with appropriate background details • develops claims and counterclaims fairly and uses valid reasoning, relevant and sufficient evidence, and a variety of rhetorical devices • concludes by revisiting the main points and reinforcing the claim.	The argument • presents a claim that is vague or unclear and does not adequately explain the issue or provide background details • presents reasons and evidence that may not logically support the claim or come from credible sources • concludes by listing the main points of the thesis.	The argument • states an unclear claim and does not explain the issue or provide background details • presents few if any relevant reasons and evidence to support the claim • includes reasons that are not relevant or sufficient for the evidence • concludes without restating the claim.
Structure	The argument • follows a clear structure with a logical progression of ideas that establishes relationships between the essential elements of an argument • links main points with effective transitions that establish coherence.	The argument • establishes clear relationships between the essential elements of an argument • uses transitions to link the major sections of the essay and create coherence.	The argument • demonstrates an awkward progression of ideas, but the reader can understand them • uses some elements of hook, claim, evidence, and conclusion • spends too much time on some irrelevant details and uses few transitions.	The argument • does not follow a logical organization • includes some details and elements of an argument, but the writing lacks clear direction and uses no transitions to help readers follow the line of thought.
Use of Language	The essay • uses precise diction deliberately chosen to inform or to explain the topic • uses a variety of sentence structures to enhance the explanation • demonstrates technical command of conventions of standard English.	The essay • uses appropriate diction for the information or explanation • uses a variety of sentence structures • demonstrates general command of conventions; minor errors do not interfere with meaning.	The essay • uses informal diction that is inappropriate at times for the information or explanation • shows little or no variety in sentence structure • demonstrates limited command of conventions; errors interfere with meaning.	The essay • uses informal diction that is inappropriate for the purpose • shows no variety in sentence structure • demonstrates limited command of conventions; errors interfere with meaning.

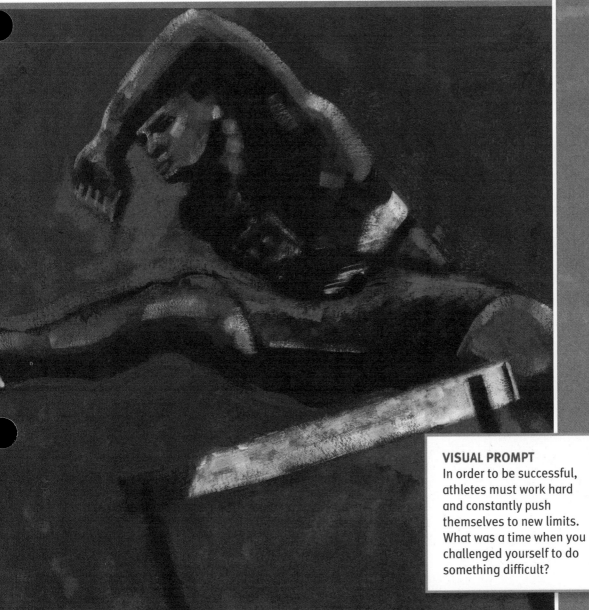

VISUAL PROMPT
In order to be successful, athletes must work hard and constantly push themselves to new limits. What was a time when you challenged yourself to do something difficult?

CHOICES AND CONSEQUENCES

It matters not how strait the gate,
How charged with punishments the scroll.
I am the master of my fate:
    am the captain of my soul.

—from "Invictus" by William Ernest Henley

Choices and Consequences

CONTENTS

CONTENTS

My Independent
Reading List

*Texts not included in these materials.

Learning Strategies

Activating Prior Knowledge
QHT
Marking the Text

My Notes

Learning Targets

- Preview and examine this unit's vocabulary.
- Identify the skills needed to write a literary analysis essay.

Preview

In this activity, you will begin exploring the skills needed to create a literary analysis essay about the novel *Tangerine*.

Making Connections

In prior units, you have read narratives and other fictional stories, as well as articles and informational texts. Learning to write an argument gave you experience in identifying claims and using evidence from texts to support a claim. In this unit, you will read the novel *Tangerine*. After reading the novel, you will write a literary analysis essay in which you will analyze the novel's characters, setting, and actions and cite evidence from the novel to support your analysis.

Essential Questions

Based on your current knowledge, write your answers to these questions.

1. What is the relationship between choices and consequences?

2. What makes a great leader?

INDEPENDENT READING LINK

Reading Plan

During this half of the unit, you will read a novel called *Tangerine* together as a class. This novel explores the relationships between the protagonist, his family members, and the peers that he meets when he transfers to a new school. Research novels, short stories, poetry, and memoirs to read that also focus on relationships between characters. Note the self-selected texts you will read independently in your "My Independent Reading List" space.

Vocabulary Development

Go back to the Contents page and look at the Academic Vocabulary and Literary Terms for the unit. Use a QHT or other vocabulary strategy to determine which terms you know and which you need to learn more about.

Unpacking Embedded Assessment 1

Read the assignment for Embedded Assessment 1: Writing a Literary Analysis Essay.

 Write a multiparagraph literary analysis essay in response to the following prompt (or another provided by your teacher): In Edward Bloor's novel *Tangerine*, how did one character's choices and the consequences of those choices affect the development of the main character?

In your own words, summarize what you will need to know to complete this assessment successfully. With your class, create a graphic organizer to represent the skills and knowledge you will need to complete the tasks identified in the Embedded Assessment.

Reading the Novel *Tangerine*

Learning Targets

- Analyze and discuss the novel *Tangerine* with peers.
- Record text evidence in a journal.
- Use levels of questions to draw connections, predictions, and inferences from the text.

Preview

In this activity, you will ask questions to analyze a novel, and you will note your answers.

1. Preview *Tangerine* by examining the front and back covers of the book, reading the summary, and looking at the title page. Write questions about the story that you hope to answer by the end of the book. Share your questions with your classmates.

2. As you read *Tangerine*, you will take notes in a double-entry journal. Copy or summarize passages from the book on the left side (textual evidence) and write your response to each passage on the right side (commentary). Draw a horizontal line under each entry. For reference, record the page number of each quote.

Responses could include the following:

- **Questions** about things you don't understand
- **Details** about characters or plot events
- **Connections** you make to your life, to real events, or to other texts
- **Predictions** (guesses) about how characters will react to events
- **Inferences** (logical conclusions) about why characters are saying or doing things

Consider this example from the first lines of *Tangerine*.

Learning Strategies

Think-Pair-Share
Skimming/Scanning
Note-taking
Double-Entry Journal
Think Aloud
Questioning the Text

GRAMMAR & USAGE

Citing Literature
When analyzing literature that is written in the first person, do not use the word *I* to refer to the narrator. Instead, use the narrator's name or third-person pronouns, such as *he*, *him*, *she*, and *her*. For example, you might write, "Where is Paul moving? Why is he leaving?"

In addition, when discussing or writing about literature, use the present tense because the characters and events of a story are described in present tense. Example: At the beginning of *Tangerine*, Paul's family is moving to Florida.

Textual Evidence	Page	Commentary
"The house looked strange. It was completely empty now …"	1	**Inference:** I think Paul's family is moving out of their house. **Question:** Where is he moving? **Connection:** My classroom looks like this after the last day of school.

3. As you read and discuss the prologue together as a class, take notes in the blank double-entry journal form that follows. Try to use a variety of responses (question, detail, connection, prediction, inference).

Title of Novel:		
Author:		
Textual Evidence	**Page**	**Commentary**

You will use several double-entry journal pages as you read *Tangerine*. Follow your teacher's directions to create double-entry journal pages in your Reader/Writer Notebook for taking notes on the novel.

4. As you read, consider these questions:

- What is the socioeconomic status of the family?
- Does Paul's mother understand him?
- What is Paul's relationship to his family?

Use your notes to provide evidence in support of your answers to these questions.

Introducing the Strategy: Questioning the Text

A strategy for thinking actively and interpretively about your reading is to ask **questions**. As you read any text, you can ask questions that aid your understanding with different levels of ideas.

- **Literal questions** (Level 1): You can answer questions on the literal level by looking to the text directly.

  Example: What kind of car does Mrs. Fisher drive?

- **Interpretive questions** (Level 2): You cannot find answers to interpretive questions directly in the text; however, textual evidence points to and supports your answers.

  Example: What emotions does Paul feel as he remembers the incident with the mailbox?

- **Universal questions** (Level 3): Universal questions go beyond the text. They require you to think about the larger issues or ideas raised by a text.

  Example: Is it possible that people who are visually impaired can see some things more clearly than people who can see perfectly?

WORD CONNECTIONS

Roots and Affixes

The word **literal** contains the root *liter* from the Latin word *littera*, meaning "letter."

Interpretive contains the root *interpret*, which means "to come to an understanding."

Universal contains the Latin prefix *uni-*, meaning "one," and the root *ver*, meaning "turn."

The suffix *-al* indicates an adjective.

My Notes

5. Write three questions, one of each type, about the prologue to *Tangerine*.

   Literal:

   Interpretive:

   Universal:

6. **Collaborative Discussion:** Remember to follow group norms about discussions, speaking clearly, listening carefully, and allowing each person a turn to question and respond.

   Share your questions with a small group of peers and ask them to respond to each. Take notes. After all group members have shared their questions and responded to one another's three questions, discuss how the questions and responses helped each of you come to a new understanding. Which were the easiest to answer, and which were the most difficult? Which led to the most interesting and informative analysis?

Learning Strategies

Skimming/Scanning
Graphic Organizer
Drafting
Note-taking
Visualizing

VOCABULARY

ACADEMIC

Tone is the overall attitude of a piece of writing. You can determine an author's tone by looking at how the author describes things like characters or setting.

Voice refers to the personality of the speaker. The author writes a voice for the characters. You can recognize a character's voice by studying his or her words, thoughts, and actions.

My Notes

_____
_____
_____
_____
_____
_____
_____
_____
_____
_____
_____
_____
_____
_____
_____
_____
_____
_____

Learning Targets

• Analyze an author's word choice to determine tone and voice.

• Analyze text evidence about choices and consequences, recording commentary in a double-entry journal.

• Write and revise a literary analysis paragraph that uses text evidence and subordinate clauses.

Preview

In this activity, you will reflect on tone and voice in the novel *Tangerine*.

1. **Tone** is the writer's or speaker's attitude expressed through a piece of writing. It can result from an author's word choice and from the way a writer depicts the attitude of a particular character. A tone can be formal or informal, serious or funny, sad or happy, or any other word that describes the "feel" of an outlook or viewpoint. A good way to determine tone is to analyze the connotations of the words a writer uses.

Read the following three quotes. What is the tone of the speaker in each of these three quotes? Use evidence from the text to support your answer.

• Prologue: "Good work, Mom." (Paul)

• Monday, August 21: "Not having a gym, or an auditorium. Two more facts apparently overlooked by your father." (Paul's mother)

• Saturday, August 19: "The young man laughed again ... 'Late summer like this, if you want to stop the muck fire you got to stop the lightning from striking. They ain't figured out how to do that yet.'" (Wayne)

2. A character's **voice** refers to the elements that shape a character's personality and project it to the reader. It is the way a character regards and interacts with the world. In a well-written text, each character has a distinctive voice that sets him or her apart from every other character. Analyzing a character's words, actions, and reactions is a good way to infer voice. Read these quotes. Use text evidence to make an inference about the character based on his or her voice.

• Wednesday, August 23: "But now it's all upside-down, you know? It's all messed up. The rain clouds show up every day, just like they're supposed to, but there aren't any tangerine trees. Just people. And the people have no use for the rain clouds. So the clouds go looking around for all the tangerine trees. They can't find them, they get mad, and they start thundering and lightning and dumping the rain on us." (Paul)

- Wednesday, August 23: "Oh, is that right? You're the one being attacked by disappointed rain clouds. Why don't you lighten up?" (Paul's mother)

- Tuesday, August 29: "She took off again, leaving me thinking. *Why didn't I answer that question? I used to have an answer ready to that question. I used to tell people that I once stared too long at a solar eclipse.*" (Paul)

3. In *Tangerine*, as in real life, people make decisions that carry consequences. Some consequences are obvious right away, while others are not apparent until some time has passed. As you read the novel, use your double-entry journal to keep a record of the choices made by Paul, his parents, and other characters. For some of the choices, you will be able to fill in the consequences and the impact on Paul right away. For other choices, you may not know a consequence or its impact on Paul until you have read more of the novel.

Textual Evidence of a Choice Made by a Character	Page	Commentary on the Consequences of That Choice and the Possible Impact on Paul
Paul's mother calls the fire department about the smoke.	13	Paul's mother and Paul learn about muck fires, and Paul begins to see that his new community has problems.

Continue to take notes in your double-entry journal as you read Part 1 of *Tangerine* by recording textual evidence of choices and making predictions and inferences about possible consequences.

GRAMMAR & USAGE

Direct Quotations

Writers use direct quotations in more than one way. Direct quotations can tell readers who is speaking. In a literary analysis, direct quotations can show that some language has been taken directly from another text or source. Direct quotations always appear inside quotation marks.

Writers can also paraphrase another person's thoughts or speech. This type of writing does not use quotation marks.

As you read the literary analysis on this page, notice the author's use of direct quotations to indicate language that is from another text or source.

4. Mark the text of the following literary analysis paragraph as follows:

- Underline the topic sentence that states the main idea.
- Highlight textual evidence.
- Put an asterisk at the start of any sentence that provides commentary.

Mrs. Fisher's decision to call the fire department affects Paul's initial impression of his new community. Paul notices smoke the first morning he wakes up in the house on Lake Windsor Downs. He writes, "The air had a gray tint to it, and a damp, foul smell like an ashtray. *Smoke*, I thought. *Something around here is on fire.*" When he tells his mother, Mrs. Fisher immediately panics and calls the fire department. After the volunteer fire department representative explains to her that there's nothing she can do to stop the muck fires, she "stares at him in disbelief." Paul realizes that his parents don't know all that much about their new home, and he begins to suspect that everything is not as perfect as they would like him to believe.

Writing to Sources: Informational Text

On a separate page, write a literary analysis paragraph about another choice that a character made in the novel. Be sure to:

- Write a topic sentence that states the main idea.
- Use textual evidence, with quotation marks around direct quotes.
- Provide commentary about the consequences of that choice for Paul.

When you have completed your paragraph, share your topic sentence with a partner or with a group. Invite feedback about your topic sentence and offer your comments on others' sentences. Evaluate the feedback and use it to revise your topic sentence as needed.

LANGUAGE & WRITER'S CRAFT:
Subordinating Conjunctions

A **subordinate clause**, or **dependent clause**, includes both a subject and a verb but cannot stand alone as a sentence because it does not express a complete thought. A subordinate clause is "lower in rank" than an independent clause because the idea in the subordinate clause is less important.

One type of subordinate clause is the **adverbial clause**. An adverbial clause acts like an adverb; it modifies a verb, an adjective, or another adverb. Its purpose is to further define a time, condition, cause, effect, or contrast expressed in the sentence.

An adverbial clause is introduced by a **subordinating conjunction**—a word that shows the relationship between the adverbial clause and the word or words it modifies. Common subordinating conjunctions include:

after	although	if	when	though	because
unless	whenever	since	before	until	while

Examples:

Although Mr. Fisher seems like a concerned father, he is inattentive to Paul.

The Seagulls accept Paul *because he is serious about soccer.*

Notice that when a sentence begins with an adverbial clause, the clause is set off by a comma. When the clause ends the sentence, no comma is necessary.

PRACTICE Find and highlight at least one subordinate clause in the sample literary analysis paragraph from earlier in this activity. Determine whether or not the subordinate clause is an adverbial clause. Then review the literary analysis paragraph you wrote and revise it in your Reader/Writer Notebook, making sure it includes at least one adverbial clause. Experiment with different subordinating conjunctions to see how they change the meaning of your sentence.

WORD CONNECTIONS

Content Connections
The word **subordinate** is made up of the Latin prefix *sub-*, meaning "under" or "below," and the Latin root *ord*, meaning "order" or "rank."

LITERARY
The word **subordinate** has many meanings. A *subordinate* is a person of lower rank. *To subordinate* is to make something less important. Used as an adjective, *subordinate* describes a relationship in which something is less important than or lower than another thing.

VOCABULARY

VOCABULARY

LITERARY

A **flashback** is an interruption in the sequence of events to relate events that occurred in the past.

Flashbacks can be found in literature, television, and film.

Learning Targets

- Draft a literary analysis paragraph about sibling relationships, providing support with text evidence.
- Use a compare-and-contrast structure to organize details.

Preview

In this activity, you will analyze flashback, foreshadowing, and characterization in the novel *Tangerine*.

Flashback

1. *Tangerine* is a text that uses **flashbacks**. Conduct a close reading of Paul's entry for Monday, August 28. How does the author let you know that what you are about to read is a flashback? Make notes in the graphic organizer that follows.

Flashbacks in *Tangerine*	
Signal	**Notes**
1	
2	
3	

My Notes

_____
_____
_____
_____
_____
_____
_____
_____
_____
_____
_____
_____
_____
_____
_____
_____
_____
_____
_____

Foreshadowing

2. Novels often use **foreshadowing** to prepare the audience for action that is to come. Foreshadowing creates an atmosphere of suspense and gives the audience clues about what will happen next in the story.

Identify examples of foreshadowing in *Tangerine* and use them to make inferences. Write your evidence and inferences in the graphic organizer that follows.

LITERARY
Foreshadowing is the use of clues to hint at events that will occur later in the plot.

Authors often use foreshadowing to engage the readers and encourage them to continue reading.

Evidence of foreshadowing in *Tangerine*	Inference about what is being foreshadowed in *Tangerine*

My Notes

_____

☑ Focus on the Sentence

Use your knowledge of flashbacks and foreshadowing to complete the following sentences.

Because foreshadowing creates suspense, _____

_____

While foreshadowing prepares the reader for future actions, flashbacks _____

_____

3. Quickwrite: Both suspense and foreshadowing affect the plot of a story. With your group, discuss how these techniques help the reader think about the conflict. Then write a quickwrite to capture your ideas and those of your group about how suspense and foreshadowing affect plot.

Characterization

4. Characterization is the way an author reveals what the characters are like. Many authors prefer to do this indirectly, through the characters' own words, appearance, thoughts, and actions. Take notes about the ways the author reveals details about the characters of Paul and Mrs. Fisher.

Elements of Characterization	Paul Fisher	Mrs. Fisher
Actions		
Appearance		
Thoughts		
What the Character Says		
What Others Say about the Character		

5. The author has given Paul a certain set of character traits. Write a summary statement about Paul's character and how you think he will confront any conflicts that you predict will occur in the novel.

🌱 Gaining Perspectives

In *Tangerine*, you learned that Paul is legally blind and his mother challenges the principal of Paul's school about safety issues. Imagine you and your partner are students at Paul's school, and you want to advocate to make the school safer for students who have limited sight or are blind. Locate three different types of online sources that describe ways to improve safety for blind people. Compare the sources based on the following categories:

- Effectiveness: How effective would the measures be in helping to increase student safety?
- Cost: How costly would the potential safety measures be to implement?
- Time: How long would it take to implement the changes?

Finally, role-play talking to the principal about your research, making your case and working together to determine a plan to reduce the safety risk for students. When you are done summarize the outcome of the discussion in your Reader/Writer Notebook.

📝 Informational Writing Prompt

Write an explanation of how Paul Fisher is similar to and different from his mother, Mrs. Fisher, based on the details you wrote in the chart earlier in this activity. Tell how the author's characterizations helped create mental images of the characters in your mind as you read. Be sure to:

- Start with a topic sentence of comparison.
- Cite evidence—details, examples, quotations—from the text to support your ideas.
- Include details about the differences and similarities between the two characters and their points of view.
- Revise your explanation's topic sentence based on the added evidence and details.

Oh, Brother!

Learning Strategies

Graphic Organizer
Sharing and Responding

VOCABULARY

LITERARY

A **motif** is a recurring element, image, or idea that has symbolic significance in a work of literature. A novel with the title *Tangerine* might make use of tangerine-related imagery many times and in different ways.

Learning Targets

- Draft a literary analysis paragraph about sibling relationships, providing support with text evidence.
- Compose an informational text using the elements of a compare-and-contrast essay.

Preview

In this activity, you will organize details from your reading to compare and contrast the brothers in the novel *Tangerine*.

1. Family relationships are important in *Tangerine*, especially relationships between brothers and the idea of brotherhood. Find one interesting quote about brothers from the novel. With a partner, discuss how it relates to the **motif** of brotherhood in the novel.

2. After reading or rereading the entries for September 5–6, use the graphic organizer to record and discuss the ways in which the Costello and Fisher brothers relate to each other.

Joey's Relationship with Mike	Mike's Relationship with Joey
Paul's Relationship with Erik	**Erik's Relationship with Paul**

3. With a small group, share your notes and respond to your group members' opinions about the relationships of the Costello and Fisher brothers. Then write one sentence describing each relationship.

Relationship of the Costello brothers:

Relationship of the Fisher brothers:

4. Work with your partner or small group to write a thesis statement comparing the Costello brothers' relationship to the Fisher brothers' relationship. Use a subordinate clause to show which of the two relationships you think is better or more important.

Writing to Sources: Informational Text

With your writing group, write a literary analysis paragraph about one of the sibling relationships (Costello or Fisher brothers). Half the group should write about the Costellos and the other half about the Fishers. Be sure to:

- Use one of the sentences from Step 3 as a topic sentence.
- Provide supporting detail from the novel as textual evidence and write commentary.
- Use transition words and subordinate clauses.

Before you read the two drafts, get sets of four different colored pencils, one set for each member of your group. Choose a color code for each of the following key elements of an effective literary analysis essay and fill in the blanks.

_____ (1st color): topic sentence

_____ (2nd color): textual evidence

_____ (3rd color): commentary

_____ (4th color): transitions

Mark one another's drafts by underlining according to your color key.

Review the markings made on each draft. What do the text markings tell you about your own writing? Are you missing any key elements of the literary analysis paragraph? Use the information to revise and improve your writing.

With your writing group, you have created a thesis statement and two support paragraphs that you could use for a compare-and-contrast literary analysis essay. You still need an introduction and a conclusion to have a complete essay.

5. With your class, brainstorm the key elements of an effective introduction to a literary analysis essay.

6. Next, brainstorm the key elements of an effective conclusion to a literary analysis essay.

7. Write either an introduction or conclusion for your essay while your partner or half of your small group writes the other. Share drafts and respond by marking each other's drafts for the key elements you identified in Step 4.

INDEPENDENT READING LINK

Read and Research

Extend your understanding of the motif of brotherhood in *Tangerine* by doing some research about sibling relationships. Find print and online sources that address why some sets of siblings get along and others do not. You could also research to find another fictional story about siblings who have relationships similar to or different from what is in *Tangerine*. Describe your findings by writing one or two paragraphs in your Independent Reading Log.

8. Compare-and-contrast essays use special transition words to help create internal and external coherence. Revise your draft to add precise transition words that will help your reader follow as you move from one idea to another.

Transitions to use when comparing: *also, alike, both, in the same way, likewise, similarly*

Transitions to use when contrasting: *but, different, however, in contrast, instead, on the other hand, unlike, yet*

9. **Final Draft:** Following your teacher's guidelines, use technology to produce and publish a final draft of your co-constructed essay in collaboration with your partner or small group. As you collaborate, eliminate unnecessary wordiness and repetition. With your class, brainstorm ways that you could publish your essay for an audience and share and respond as a class to the other groups' essays. As you make decisions about publishing, think about your intended audience. Is it your teacher? Classmates? Family? School newspaper readers? Should the final product be handwritten, typed, or online? What should you include, if anything, in the header or footer?

GRAMMAR & USAGE

Punctuating Transitions

When you use a transition at the beginning of a sentence, follow it with a comma. When you use a transition to connect two complete thoughts, precede the transition with a semicolon and follow it with a comma. Notice how these sentences use transitions to connect ideas and indicate a contrast between the Fisher and Costello brothers.

- The Costellos get along well. On the other hand, the Fisher brothers loathe each other.

- The Costello brothers are great friends; in contrast, the Fisher brothers are like enemies.

Learning Strategies

SIFT
Quickwrite
Graphic Organizer
Close Reading

Learning Targets

- Draft a literary analysis paragraph about how the author's word choice contributes to tone and theme in the novel *Tangerine*.
- Revise an informational text to include phrases and appositives.

Preview

In this activity, you will analyze how the author's word choice contributes to tone and theme in the novel *Tangerine*.

1. **Quickwrite:** Part 1 of *Tangerine* ends with Paul experiencing what he calls a "miracle." What is your definition of a miracle? What "miracle" does Paul experience?

Introducing the Strategy: SIFT

SIFT is a strategy for analyzing a fictional text by examining stylistic elements, especially symbols, imagery, and figures of speech, in order to show how these elements work together to reveal tone and theme.

2. Use your glossary to define each term in the first column. In the second column, take notes as you work with your class to SIFT through "Friday, September 15." Working with your group, apply the SIFT strategy to another chapter as your teacher directs. Record your analysis in the third column.

Symbol		
Imagery		
Figurative Language		
Tone		
Theme		

Writing to Sources: Informational Text

After you have shared examples from different chapters with your class, choose one theme that you have identified from Part 1 of *Tangerine*. Write a literary analysis paragraph analyzing how literary elements such as symbols, imagery, figurative language, and tone contributed to that theme. Be sure to:

- Include a topic sentence that identifies a theme.
- Identify specific literary elements.
- Provide textual evidence in the form of quotes.

Write your paragraph in the space that follows, on a separate piece of paper, or in your Reader/ Writer Notebook.

LANGUAGE & WRITER'S CRAFT: Understanding Phrases

You have studied dependent and independent clauses and how to use them to convey complex ideas. Phrases are another important sentence element that can add information and detail.

A **phrase** is a group of words that functions as one part of speech and does not include a subject and verb. Common types of phrases include noun, verb, appositive, and prepositional. Why are all the following examples phrases, not clauses?

smashing into the fence
before the first test
a well-known historian
after the devastation

between ignorance and intelligence
broken into thousands of pieces
her glittering smile

A **prepositional phrase** has a preposition, a noun or pronoun that acts as the object of the preposition, and any modifiers of the object. The preposition shows the relationship between the object and another word in the sentence.

Examples:
There is a crawl space *under the front porch*.
Near the corner store is an empty lot.

An **appositive** is a noun placed near another noun to explain or identify it. An appositive plus its modifiers is an **appositive phrase**. When an appositive phrase gives information not necessary to the basic meaning of the sentence, it is **nonessential**, or **nonrestrictive**, and it is set off by commas.

Examples:
Edward Bloor's first novel, *Tangerine*, is set in Florida (appositive).
Eric, *Paul's older brother*, is a senior in high school (appositive phrase).

PRACTICE Pick two sentences from your SIFT graphic organizer and rewrite them to include a prepositional phrase or an appositive phrase.

3. Choose one sentence from your literary analysis paragraph from earlier in this activity. Revise it to include a prepositional phrase and/or an appositive phrase. Copy your revised sentence here and share it with a partner.

4. As you continue to read the novel *Tangerine*, take notes in your double-entry journal by applying the SIFT strategy. Pay particular attention to recurring symbols, imagery, and themes that are possible motifs.

Same Sport, Different School

Learning Targets

- Draft a literary analysis that cites text evidence to support inferences and predictions about the novel *Tangerine*.
- Compare and contrast two settings in the novel *Tangerine*.

Preview

In this activity, you will use text evidence to support comparisons and contrasts in the novel *Tangerine*.

1. Take out the double-entry journal notes you created for Part 1 in your Reader/Writer Notebook. Select the entry that you think represents the most significant choice in Part 1 and copy it into the first row of the chart that follows. Find at least three people in your class who have recorded different choices. Take notes as they share their entries.

Part 1: Friday, August 18–Friday, September 15

Textual Evidence of a Choice Made by a Character	Page	Commentary on the Consequences of That Choice and the Possible Impact on Paul

LITERARY

Mood is the overall feeling or emotion of a story. A story's mood can be described with an adjective, such as *sinister*, *mournful*, *angry*, or *playful*. Many elements of a story contribute to the mood, including the setting, the characters' words and feelings, and the use of imagery and figurative language.

2. Remember that a novel's setting is the time and place in which characters function and plots unfold. A novel's setting helps shape a story's characters, plot, and **mood**. The muck fires in *Tangerine* are a part of a particular setting. They influence the novel's plot by causing Paul's mother to join the Homeowners' Association. The fires also affect the character development of Paul's mother by causing her to have doubts about their new home. They also affect the mood by creating an overall feeling that Paul's new home isn't safe.

Complete the first two rows of the graphic organizer. Then provide a detail and identify how it affects the plot, character actions, and mood of the story.

Detail about Setting	How does the detail influence a character's action or the plot? (consequence)	How does the detail affect mood?
There are thunderstorms every day at the same time.		
Lake Windsor Middle School has a sinkhole.		

3. As you read the entries for "September 18 and 19," use the graphic organizer that follows to compare and contrast Lake Windsor Middle School and Tangerine Middle School. Write details shared by both schools in the middle space, details specific to Lake Windsor in the left space, and details specific to Tangerine in the right space. Add details about how the setting affects the characters.

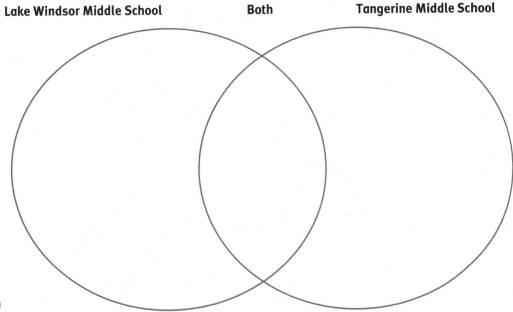

Lake Windsor Middle School   Both   Tangerine Middle School

☑ Focus on the Sentence

Following are three short sentences about the setting and characters you have encountered so far. Use an appositive phrase to expand each sentence:

Lake Windsor Middle School adopts a split-shift schedule.

_____

_____

Charley Burns allowed many unsafe buildings to be built.

_____

_____

Paul Fisher decides to attend Tangerine Middle School.

_____

✏ Writing to Sources: Informational Text

Write a paragraph that explains how the setting of *Tangerine* has influenced the plot so far. You may use your revised sentences from the Focus on the Sentence. Be sure to:

- Create a topic sentence about the setting.
- Cite evidence from the text, such as details and quotations, to support your ideas.
- Use transition words and a variety of sentence structures.

Learning Strategies

Quickwrite
Graphic Organizer
Discussion Groups

My Notes

Learning Targets

• Write observations on the use of literal and figurative language in the novel *Tangerine*.

• Draft a character analysis that cites text evidence from the novel *Tangerine*.

Preview

In this activity, you will describe literal and figurative language and analyze a character in the novel *Tangerine*.

1. The verse that follows uses the imagery of sight and blindness. How is the use of this imagery similar to the use of the imagery in *Tangerine*?

> Amazing grace! how sweet the sound
> That sav'd a wretch like me!
> I once was lost, but now am found,
> Was blind, but now I see.

2. What are the literal meanings of the imagery of sight and blindness? What are possible figurative or symbolic meanings?

Literal:

Figurative:

3. Reread the flashback at the end of Paul's entry for October 5 starting with "I stared hard into the backyard." When is Paul referring to "seeing" in a literal sense, and when do you think he is being figurative?

Literal:

Figurative:

INDEPENDENT READING LINK

Read and Discuss

Meet with a small group to talk about the themes and motifs you have identified and analyzed in your independent reading. Use the notes you have taken in your Independent Reading Log and your Reader/Writer Notebook to help support your ideas during discussion. End the discussion by making generalizations about the motifs you have discussed. Can you connect or find common meaning in any of them?

4. Who Sees? Who Doesn't See?

After reviewing your double-entry journal entries for Part 2 of *Tangerine*, think about the word *see* and its meanings, both literal and figurative, and how it is used as a motif in the novel. Your teacher will either assign a character from the novel *Tangerine* or ask you to choose one. In one lens of the glasses, list or draw the things the character sees or understands; in the other lens, list or draw the things the character does not see or understand (or refuses to see).

Character Name: _____

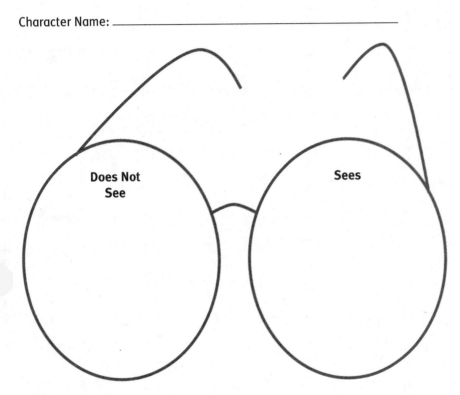

Does Not See

Sees

5. After you have worked on the graphic organizer, meet with others who chose the same character. Compare and discuss what your character sees and doesn't see, adding details or images to your graphic organizer.

6. Next, meet in a group of three or four others, each of whom chose a different character, and compare notes and interpretations about characters with contrasting points of view about the events of the novel. Take notes on one other character besides the one upon which you have focused.

Writing to Sources: Informational Text

Draft a paragraph about your character's ability to "see," based on the details in your graphic organizer. Be sure to:

- Include a topic sentence about what your character does or does not "see."
- Provide supporting details, textual evidence, and commentary.
- Use a variety of sentence structures to signal different relationships between ideas.

LANGUAGE & WRITER'S CRAFT: Active Versus Passive Voice

Verbs change form to show **active voice** or **passive voice**. A verb is in the active voice when the subject of the sentence performs the action. A verb is in the passive voice when the subject receives the action—that is, when the subject has something done to it.

Writers—and readers—generally prefer the active voice because it is more lively, more concise, and easier to understand. Revising your writing to use active voice instead of passive voice will eliminate wordiness and strengthen your writing.

Active voice: The goalie *deflected* the ball.
In this example, the subject (the goalie) is performing the action of deflecting.

Passive voice: The ball was *deflected* by the goalie.
In this example, the subject (the ball) is receiving the action of deflecting.

You can recognize passive voice because the verb phrase includes a form of *to be*, such as *am, is, was, were, are,* or *been*. Another way to recognize sentences with verbs in the passive voice is that they may include a "by ... " phrase after the verb.

PRACTICE Check the paragraph you wrote in response to the writing prompt. If necessary, revise any passive voice verbs so that they will be in active voice to eliminate wordiness and make your writing more concise.

Revise this sentence:

Passive voice:
The game **was won b**y the Tangerine War Eagles.

Active voice:

Conflicts and Consequences

Learning Strategies

Graphic Organizer
Double-Entry Journal
Think-Pair-Share
Drafting
Discussion Groups

Learning Targets

- Draft an analysis of how the conflicts in the novel *Tangerine* shape the novel's plots and subplots.
- Write a paragraph using text evidence to draw connections among the conflicts in the novel *Tangerine*.

Preview

In this activity, you will analyze conflict in the novel *Tangerine*.

1. Take out the double-entry journal notes you created for Part 2 of *Tangerine* in your Reader/Writer Notebook. Select the entry that you think represents the most significant choice in Part 2. Copy it onto the graphic organizer. Find at least two people in your class who selected different choices and take notes as they share.

Part 2: Monday, September 18–Friday, November 10

Textual Evidence of a Choice Made by a Character	Page	Commentary on the Consequences of That Choice and the Possible Impact on Paul

2. A novel is composed of many conflicts and plots. The major conflict involves the protagonist (the main character) and drives the main plot. In the following graphic, state the main conflict of *Tangerine* and list the details of that conflict.

Main Conflict

Individual vs. Self

3. Each of the other types of conflicts in *Tangerine* is represented in a subplot. Find examples in the novel of each type of conflict.

Additional Conflicts

Character vs. Character

Character vs. Nature

Character vs. Society

4. Of the additional conflicts or subplots in this novel, which one of them most directly affects Paul's conflict with himself?

5. Scan Part 3 of *Tangerine* and note the length of the entries for this time period. Why do you think Paul wrote this much at this time? Read the first sentence for "Monday, November 20." Predict what will happen when the science-project group comes to Paul's house.

6. When you present your literary analysis to the class, you will need to use appropriate eye contact, speaking rate, volume, enunciations, a variety of natural gestures, and conventions of language to communicate your ideas effectively to your audience. Your teacher will model this by reading a literary analysis paragraph aloud. Take notes on each of these elements as your teacher presents, and record techniques that you will use when you present.

Eye contact:

Speaking rate:

Volume:

Enunciation:

Gestures:

Conventions of language:

✐ Writing to Sources: Informational Text

Choose one of the subplots in *Tangerine* in which the conflict has not been resolved. Write a literary analysis paragraph describing the conflict of the subplot and explaining how it relates to or reflects the main conflict. Be sure to:

- Use a topic sentence that identifies a conflict and subplot and how it relates to the main conflict.
- Provide supporting details, textual evidence, and commentary.
- Use active voice and a variety of sentence structures.
- Present your literary analysis paragraph to a small group or the class. Be sure to use appropriate eye contact, volume, enunciation, gestures, and conventions of language to present your analysis effectively.

My Notes

Learning Strategies

Note-taking
Choral Reading
Visualizing

My Notes

Learning Targets

- Use the imagery and diction in two poems to help identify their tone and themes.
- Connect the purposes and techniques of different genres.
- Integrate ideas from multiple texts to build knowledge and vocabulary about death and why it appeals to readers and writers.

Preview

In this activity, you will read and compare two poems about death, analyzing the authors' use of imagery and word choice.

Generate Questions

The poem "To an Athlete Dying Young" is referenced in *Tangerine*. Before reading the poem, write some questions about the poem and its use in *Tangerine* that you wish to understand more deeply by the end of this activity.

About the Author

British poet A. E. Housman (1859–1936) spent most of his life as a teacher and a scholar. He is mostly remembered for his poetry, although he published only two volumes of verse during his life. The first collection was called *A Shropshire Lad* (1896), and the second was *Last Poems* (1922). These works are remembered today for their emotional depth.

Setting a Purpose for Reading

- As you read the poem, underline words and phrases that create visual images and place a star next to words about death and dying.
- Circle unknown words and phrases. Try to determine the meaning of the words by using context clues, word parts, or a dictionary.

Poetry

To an Athlete Dying Young

by **A. E. Housman**

KNOWLEDGE QUEST

Knowledge Question:

Why is death a theme that appeals to writers and readers?

In Activity 3.10, you will read two poems about death. While you read and build knowledge about the topic, think about your answer to the Knowledge Question.

The time you won your town the race
We chaired you through the market-place;
Man and boy stood cheering by,
And home we brought you shoulder-high.

5 Today, the road all runners come,
Shoulder-high we bring you home,
And set you at your threshold down,
Townsman of a stiller town.

Smart lad, to slip betimes away
10 From fields where glory does not stay,
And early though the laurel[1] grows
It withers quicker than the rose.

Eyes the shady night has shut
Cannot see the record cut,
15 And silence sounds no worse than cheers
After earth has stopped the ears:

Now you will not swell the rout
Of lads that wore their honours out,
Runners whom renown outran
20 And the name died before the man.

So set, before its echoes fade,
The fleet foot on the sill of shade,
And hold to the low lintel up
The still-defended challenge-cup.

25 And round that early-laurelled head
Will flock to gaze the strengthless dead,
And find unwithered on its curls
The garland briefer than a girl's.

My Notes

Knowledge Quest

- Which images in the poem do you find most striking?
- What stands out about the way death is portrayed?

---

[1] **laurel:** a type of shrub with leaves that are used to make wreaths to honor heroes

Returning to the Text

- Return to the text as you respond to the following questions. Use text evidence to support your responses.
- Write any additional questions you have about the poem in your Reader/Writer Notebook.

1. Who is the "you" the speaker is addressing?

_____

_____

_____

_____

2. KQ What does the speaker mean when he calls the athlete a "townsman of a stiller town"?

_____

_____

_____

_____

3. How does the third stanza contribute to the poem's overall meaning?

_____

_____

_____

_____

4. KQ What is a possible theme of the poem? What makes this theme interesting for readers?

_____

_____

_____

_____

Working from the Text

5. In the "December 1" entry of *Tangerine*, Mr. Donnelly "read some lines from a poem called 'To an Athlete Dying Young.'" Read the poem again carefully. Then go back and reread the "December 1" entry in *Tangerine*. What lines do you think Donnelly read? Which lines would be most appropriate to memorialize Mike's death?

6. With a partner or in small groups, examine the **meter** and **rhyme scheme** of "To an Athlete Dying Young." How would you describe the meter in the first verse? What is the rhyme scheme throughout the poem?

7. Remember that the tone of a text describes its "feel," or the overall attitude it communicates to the reader. What is the tone of the poem? And what effect do meter and rhyme scheme have on the poem? Use text evidence to support your answer.

☑ Check Your Understanding

In the entry for "December 1," the memorial for Mike Costello includes the poem "To an Athlete Dying Young" and the dedication of a laurel oak tree. Why are both appropriate tributes to Mike?

8. In your Reader/Writer Notebook, write a letter to Edward Bloor asking him about a choice he made when writing *Tangerine*. You may choose to ask him why he included the allusion to "To an Athlete Dying Young," or you may choose another thing about the novel to ask him about. In your letter, be sure to include an appropriate greeting and introduce yourself. You can also include your own opinion. Use a friendly but respectful tone, and include a sign-off at the end.

About the Author

Dylan Thomas (1914–1953) published his first book of poetry, *18 Poems*, in 1934 after winning the Poet's Corner Book Prize in London. He spent time recording radio shows and working as a scriptwriter for the British Broadcasting Channel (BBC), participating in over a hundred broadcasts from 1945–1949. He famously pulled many of his poems from notebooks that he kept and wrote in throughout the course of his life. He popularized his work in the United States through reading tours where his boisterousness, energy, and emotional readings ignited listeners' imaginations.

LITERARY

A poem's **meter** refers to its pattern of stressed and unstressed syllables. A stress in a word is a syllable that gets emphasis when read or spoken. Meter is what gives a poem the rhythm and lyrical feel that distinguishes it from prose. A poem's **rhyme scheme** is its pattern of rhyming words. A rhyme scheme is designated by which last words in its lines rhyme with each other. For instance, the following poem has an **ABAB** rhyme scheme:

> Here is a verse **(A)**
> I recite every day. **(B)**
> It helps me rehearse **(A)**
> My lines in the play. **(B)**

📦 INDEPENDENT READING LINK

Read and Connect

Tangerine contains an allusion to the poem "To an Athlete Dying Young." Are there any places in your independent reading where you have encountered an allusion to another work of literature, a real person, or historical event? If not, can you think of a place where the author could have included one? Think about why an author might choose to include an allusion.

Setting a Purpose for Reading

- As you read, underline instances of repetition that carry the main theme of the poem.
- Circle unknown words and phrases. Try to determine the meaning of the words by using context clues, word parts, or a dictionary.

Poetry

Do not go gentle into that good night

KNOWLEDGE QUEST

Knowledge Question:
Why is death a theme that appeals to writers and readers?

My Notes

by **Dylan Thomas**

Do not go gentle into that good night,
Old age should burn and rave at close of day;
Rage, rage against the dying of the light.

Though wise men at their end know dark is right,
5   Because their words had forked no lightning they
Do not go gentle into that good night.

Good men, the last wave by, crying how bright
Their frail deeds might have danced in a green bay,
Rage, rage against the dying of the light.

10   Wild men who caught and sang the sun in flight,
And learn, too late, they grieved it on its way,
Do not go gentle into that good night.

Grave men, near death, who see with blinding sight
Blind eyes could blaze like meteors and be gay,
15   Rage, rage against the dying of the light.

And you, my father, there on the sad height,
Curse, bless, me now with your fierce tears, I pray.
Do not go gentle into that good night.
Rage, rage against the dying of the light.

Knowledge Quest
- What interests you about the speaker's attitude toward death?
- Which line or lines stand out the most to you? Why?

Returning to the Text

- Return to the text as you respond to the following questions. Use text evidence to support your responses.
- Write any additional questions you have about the poem in your Reader/Writer Notebook.

9. What effect does the final stanza have on the poem as a whole?

_____

_____

_____

_____

10. KQ What does the phrase "that good night" mean in the context of the poem? What evidence supports this meaning?

_____

_____

_____

_____

11. What does light symbolize in the poem? How is this symbolism developed?

_____

_____

_____

_____

12. KQ Compare the points of view about death in "Do not go gentle into that good night" and "To an Athlete Dying Young." How do the perspectives of the two speakers differ?

_____

_____

_____

_____

INDEPENDENT READING LINK

You can continue to build your knowledge about death and dying by reading related fiction and poetry at ZINC Reading Labs.

Select the **fiction** and **poetry** filters and type the keyword *death* in the **Search all ZINC articles** field.

ZINC

Knowledge Quest

Use your knowledge of the two poems to discuss with a partner your personal response to the theme of death and why it might appeal to readers and writers. Be sure to:

- Explain your answer to your partner, be specific, and use as many details as possible.
- When your partner responds, ask for clarification by posing follow-up questions as needed.
- After the discussion, write down the ideas you talked about.

The Final Score

Learning Targets

- Draft an outline for a literary analysis topic taken from Part 3 of the novel *Tangerine*.
- Write an analysis of motif and theme in the novel *Tangerine*.

Preview

In this activity, you will organize your approach to writing a literary analysis essay.

1. Take out the double-entry journal notes you created for Part 3 of the novel in your Reader/Writer Notebook. Select the entry that you think represents the most significant choice in Part 3. Copy it onto the graphic organizer that follows. Find someone in your class who selected a different choice and take notes as the student shares.

Part 3: Monday, November 20–Wednesday, December 6

Textual Evidence of a Choice Made by a Character	Page	Commentary on the Consequences of That Choice and the Possible Impact on Paul

2. Review all the notes you made about choices in your double-entry journals and in Activities 3.3, 3.7, and 3.9. Choose one character whose choices had significant consequences in the development of Paul's character. Select three or more of the character's choices and add them to the outline that follows in a logical order. Consider arranging them in one of these three organizational patterns:

   - least important to most important
   - types of choices made (good, bad)
   - chronological order (first to last)

3. Choose and follow an organizational pattern to complete the following outline that explains and evaluates your character's choices.

The Choices _____ **Made**

    I. A choice made by _____ and how it affected Paul:

        A. Describe the choice.

        B. Why this choice was made: _____

        C. How Paul reacted to the choice and its effect on him.

    II. Another choice made by _____ and how it affected Paul:

        A. Describe the choice.

        B. Why this choice was made: _____

        C. How Paul reacted to the choice and its effect on him.

    III. Another choice made by _____ and how it affected Paul:

        A. Describe the choice.

        B. Why this choice was made: _____

        C. How Paul reacted to the choice and its effect on him.

☑ Check Your Understanding

Write an explanation of how Paul shows his growing self-awareness and confidence in the choices he makes.

4. **Exploring Motif:** Consider the different motifs that Edward Bloor uses in *Tangerine*. In your home base group, assign a different motif to each person. Follow your teacher's directions to form an expert group with those who were assigned the same motif as you. Work together to complete one row of the chart that follows by finding examples of your motif in different parts of the novel.

Motif	Textual Evidence from Part 1	Textual Evidence from Part 2	Textual Evidence from Part 3
Sight			
Brothers			
Weather			
Sportsmanship			

5. With your expert group, create a thesis statement about your motif. It should answer the question: How does the motif of _____ help to develop the conflict experienced by the main character of *Tangerine*?

6. Review the notes you took for Activity 3.2 and the modifications you made to those notes during Activity 3.8, "Seeing is Believing." Examine your questions and predictions. Were all of your questions answered? In what ways were your predictions accurate or not accurate? Were you surprised by any new information you got at the end of the book? Include text evidence in your responses.

Independent Reading Checkpoint

Review your independent reading and select three examples of a character's choices. Then write the consequence of each choice and tell how it affected the character.

Writing a Literary Analysis Essay

 ASSIGNMENT

Your assignment is to write a multiparagraph literary analysis essay in response to the following prompt (or another provided by your teacher): In Edward Bloor's novel *Tangerine*, how did one character's choices and the consequences of these choices affect the development of the main character?

Planning and Prewriting: Take time to make a plan for your essay.	■ How will you respond to the prompt in a clear thesis statement? ■ How will you use the notes you have taken to find textual evidence to support your thesis? ■ Will you organize your supporting ideas by importance, type, or time?
Drafting: Write a multiparagraph essay that effectively organizes your ideas.	■ How will you use an outline to help you draft your essay? ■ How will your introduction engage the reader with a hook, summarize the novel, and state your thesis? ■ How will you integrate topic sentences, transitions, details, textual evidence, and commentary in your support paragraphs? ■ How will your conclusion include your thesis as well as an interpretation of the author's purpose and a connection to a larger issue?
Evaluating and Revising the Draft: Create opportunities to review and revise your work.	■ During the process of writing, when can you pause to share and respond with others? ■ What is your plan to include suggestions and revision ideas into your draft? ■ How will you be sure to use precise, academic language, and a variety of sentence structures? ■ How can the Scoring Guide help you evaluate how well your draft meets the requirements of the assignment?
Checking and Editing for Publication: Confirm your final draft is ready for publication.	■ How will you proofread and edit your draft to demonstrate command of the conventions of standard English, capitalization, punctuation, spelling, grammar, and usage? ■ Have you put page numbers in parentheses wherever you quoted directly from the text? ■ What would be an engaging title for your essay? What method will you use to publish your work for your intended audience? ■ How will you effectively present your ideas to the class?

Reflection

After completing this Embedded Assessment, think about how you went about accomplishing this task. Then respond to the following:

- How did the reading and note-taking strategies that you used during this unit help prepare you to write a literary analysis essay?

SCORING GUIDE

Scoring Criteria	Exemplary	Proficient	Emerging	Incomplete
Ideas	The essay • has a focused, insightful thesis that addresses the prompt fully and precisely • uses well-selected textual evidence • provides precise and insightful commentary showing the relationship between the evidence and the thesis.	The essay • has a focused thesis that addresses the prompt • uses textual evidence that is relevant and sufficient • provides relevant and clear commentary.	The essay • has a thesis that may address some part of the prompt • uses some textual evidence to support the thesis • provides little relevant commentary.	The essay • does not have a thesis appropriate for a multiparagraph essay • is missing textual evidence or the evidence does not support the thesis • is missing commentary or the commentary is not related to the overall concept.
Structure	The essay • presents a strong introduction with a hook and clear thesis • is coherent with well-developed body paragraphs that use effective transitions • presents an insightful and compelling conclusion that follows directly from the ideas of the thesis.	The essay • presents a focused introduction with a clear thesis • contains body paragraphs that develop ideas of the thesis and establish cohesion with transitions • has a conclusion that follows from the ideas of the thesis.	The essay • presents an introduction without a strong thesis • contains body paragraphs that do little to develop the thesis • has a minimal conclusion that may not relate to the thesis.	The essay • may be lacking an introduction or thesis • may be missing body paragraphs or the paragraphs are not developed • may not have a conclusion or the conclusion may be only a summary statement.
Use of Language	The essay • shows a sophisticated variety of sentence types used appropriately • uses formal style and precise academic language • contains so few errors in grammar, spelling, capitalization, and punctuation that they do not detract from excellence.	The essay • uses a variety of well-chosen sentence types • uses formal and academic language appropriately • contains only a few errors in spelling and grammar.	The essay • shows little variety in sentence types • shows difficulty with the conventions of formal language and academic vocabulary • contains some errors in grammar and spelling that interfere with meaning.	The essay • shows serious flaws in the construction of purposeful sentences to convey ideas • has language that is confused or confusing • contains errors in grammar, spelling, and conventions that interfere with meaning.

Unpacking Embedded Assessment 2

Learning Targets
- Reflect on the first half of the unit and adjust responses to the Essential Questions.
- Develop a plan to successfully complete Embedded Assessment 2.

Preview
In this activity, you will begin exploring the form and conventions of a biographical multimedia presentation.

Making Connections
In the first part of this unit, you read the novel *Tangerine* and analyzed its characters, setting, and mood. You also learned to predict future actions based on the author's use of foreshadowing. Describe one of the activities in the first half of the unit that helped prepare you to do well on Embedded Assessment 1. What did you do and learn in the activity, and how did it prepare you for success?

Developing Vocabulary
Look at your Reader/Writer Notebook and review the new vocabulary you learned as you studied the novel and its analysis. Which words do you know completely, and which do you need to learn more about?

Essential Questions
Now that you have read the novel *Tangerine* and analyzed the choices made by characters and the resulting consequences, how would you change your answer to the first Essential Question: "What is the relationship between choices and consequences?"

Unpacking Embedded Assessment 2
Read the assignment for Embedded Assessment 2: Creating a Biographical Presentation.

 Your assignment is to work with a research group to create a biographical multimedia presentation of a great leader whose choices had positive consequences for society.

In your own words, summarize what you will need to know to complete this assessment successfully. With your class, create a graphic organizer to represent the skills and knowledge you will need to complete the tasks identified in the Embedded Assessment.

INDEPENDENT READING LINK
Reading Plan
For this half of the unit, find an appropriate biography, autobiography, or work of historical fiction about a leader who has had a positive impact on society. As you read, think like a writer by noting the use of vivid details and specific words to describe real characters, settings, and events; rely on transitions to move the plot forward and indicate a change of time and place; and use dialogue to bring the story to life. Use your Reader/Writer Notebook to track any questions, comments, or reactions you might have to your reading. Your teacher may ask questions about your text, and making notes in your Reader/Writer Notebook will help you answer them.

My Notes

Learning Targets

- Analyze the presentation of biographical and historical information in a film.
- Conduct research to answer questions about the consequences of a leader's choices on society.

Preview

In this activity, you will watch excerpts from the film *Invictus*, analyze imagery from the excerpts, and make predictions.

1. As you preview the first minute of the film *Invictus*, use the My Notes space on this page to take notes on the images you see. Which images stand out? What inferences and predictions can you make?

2. Read the following summary of the film excerpted from the DVD's back cover and discuss how the imagery of the film clip helped prepare the viewer.

"He was imprisoned 27 years for his heroic fight against apartheid. So what does Nelson Mandela do after he is elected President of South Africa? He rejects revenge, forgives his oppressors and finds hope of national unity in an unlikely place: the rugby field."

Setting a Purpose for Viewing

- In your home base group, review each of the three sections of the *Invictus* chart that follows. Assign one section of the chart to each group member. Record notes in your assigned section while viewing the film.

- Write down unknown words and phrases. Try to determine the meaning of the words by using context clues, word parts, or a dictionary.

In this scene from *Invictus*, Nelson Mandela (played by Morgan Freeman) meets François Pienaar (Matt Damon), the president of the Springboks.

Invictus

Clip 1: A New South Africa	Clip 2: Bodyguards and Rugby	Clip 3: A Symbol of Apartheid

Section 1: Questions about Nelson Mandela and other characters in the film

Details from Clip 1:	Details from Clip 2:	Details from Clip 3:

Section 2: Questions about events and incidents from the film

Details from Clip 1:	Details from Clip 2:	Details from Clip 3:

Section 3: Questions about South Africa and specific settings from the film

Details from Clip 1:	Details from Clip 2:	Details from Clip 3:

☑ **Focus on the Sentence**

Write three types of sentences about the film clips you watched.

Statement:

_____

_____

Question:

_____

_____

Exclamation:

_____

_____

Working from the Film

3. After you have viewed the clips, discuss your notes with your expert group and then return to your home base group. Choose the best examples from each clip relating to your section to present your insights to the group. As each group member presents, take notes.

Research and Independent Reading

For Embedded Assessment 2, you will need to create and deliver a biographical presentation of a great leader of your choice. Choose the leader you want to present and begin doing independent reading and research on his or her life.

As you complete the next several activities, add to your research and consider additional questions, topics, or visuals to explore. Be prepared, as you research and learn about your subject, to revise your initial research questions and come up with more focused or insightful ones.

A Long Walk to Peace

Learning Targets

- Cite evidence from texts to support an analysis of the features of biography and autobiography.
- Analyze how two texts about the same topic present information by providing different evidence or interpreting the facts differently.
- Integrate ideas from multiple texts to build knowledge and vocabulary about studying history from different perspectives.

Preview

In this activity, you will compare a biography of Nelson Mandela with an excerpt from Mandela's autobiography.

Setting a Purpose for Reading

- As you read the biography, underline one notable event in Mandela's life in each paragraph.
- Circle unknown words and phrases. Try to determine the meaning of the words by using context clues, word parts, or a dictionary.

Biography

The Nobel Peace Prize 1993, Biography of Nelson Mandela

from **Nobel Lectures**

1   Nelson Rolihlahla Mandela was born in Transkei, South Africa on July 18, 1918. His father was Chief Henry Mandela of the Tembu Tribe. Mandela himself was educated at University College of Fort Hare and the University of Witwatersrand and qualified in law in 1942. He joined the African National Congress in 1944 and was engaged in resistance against the ruling National Party's apartheid policies after 1948. He went on trial for treason in 1956–1961 and was **acquitted** in 1961.

2   After the banning of the ANC in 1960, Nelson Mandela argued for the setting up of a military wing within the ANC. In June 1961, the ANC executive considered his proposal on the use of violent tactics and agreed that those members who wished to involve themselves in Mandela's campaign would not be stopped from doing so by the ANC. This led to the formation of *Umkhonto we Sizwe*. Mandela was arrested in 1962 and sentenced to five years' imprisonment with hard labour. In 1963, when many fellow leaders of the ANC

KNOWLEDGE QUEST

Knowledge Question:
What can we learn about history by studying it from multiple perspectives?
In Activity 3.14, you will read two texts about an influential global leader, Nelson Mandela. While you read and build knowledge about the topic, think about your answer to the Knowledge Question.

acquitted: declared innocent

My Notes

and the *Umkhonto we Sizwe* were arrested, Mandela was brought to stand trial with them for plotting to overthrow the government by violence. His statement from the **dock** received considerable international publicity. On June 12, 1964, eight of the accused, including Mandela, were sentenced to life imprisonment. From 1964 to 1982, he was incarcerated at Robben Island Prison, off Cape Town; thereafter, he was at Pollsmoor Prison, nearby on the mainland.

3 During his years in prison, Nelson Mandela's reputation grew steadily. He was widely accepted as the most significant black leader in South Africa and became a potent symbol of resistance as the anti-apartheid movement gathered strength. He consistently refused to compromise his political position to obtain his freedom.

4 Nelson Mandela was released on February 11, 1990. After his release, he plunged himself wholeheartedly into his life's work, striving to attain the goals he and others had set out almost four decades earlier. In 1991, at the first national conference of the ANC held inside South Africa after the organization had been banned in 1960, Mandela was elected President of the ANC while his lifelong friend and colleague, Oliver Tambo, became the organisation's National Chairperson.

The front page of *City Press*, a South African newspaper, on February 11, 1990

⌀ Knowledge Quest

- What details about Mandela's life stood out to you the most in the excerpt?
- Which events as described in the excerpt were most interesting to you?

dock: courtroom

Returning to the Text

- Return to the text as you respond to the following questions. Use text evidence to support your responses.
- Write any additional questions you have about the poem in your Reader/Writer Notebook.

1. According to the text, what was the purpose of *Umkhonto we Sizwe*? What role did Mandela play in its formation?

_____

_____

_____

_____

2. KQ Based on the context, what does the word *resistance* mean in the first paragraph?

_____

_____

_____

3. KQ What can we learn from studying the perspectives of both the ruling party and the anti-apartheid movement?

_____

_____

_____

_____

4. Write a brief summary of the events that led up to Mandela's life sentence.

_____

_____

_____

_____

5. What effect did Mandela's reputation in prison most likely have on later events?

_____

_____

_____

_____

WORD CONNECTIONS

Roots & Affixes

The word **autobiography** consists of three Greek roots: *auto*, meaning "self," *bio*, meaning "life," and *graph*, meaning "write." These roots also appear in other words, such as *autograph*, *biology*, *automobile*, and *geography*. The suffix -*y* indicates that the word is a noun.

Working from the Text

6. If you read only paragraph 1 of this biography of Nelson Mandela, what overall impression would you form of him? Why?

7. What experiences in Mandela's life, as described in paragraphs 1 and 2, likely contributed to his reputation in prison?

8. Use your text markings and notes to add to your KWHL chart as follows:

   • Add new questions to your "W" column.
   • Add new information to your "L" column.
   • In the "H" column, describe how this source was helpful in understanding what kind of leader Nelson Mandela was.

Nelson Mandela			
K: What I Know	**W: What I Want to Know**	**H: How I Will Find Out**	**L: What I Learned**
		Nobel Prize Biography	
		Autobiographical Excerpt	

Setting a Purpose for Reading

- As you read the autobiography, underline language that refers to freedom and hunger.
- Circle unknown words and phrases. Try to determine the meaning of the words by using context clues, word parts, or a dictionary.

About the Author

Nelson Mandela (1918–2013) was an anti-apartheid activist, philanthropist, recipient of the Nobel Peace Prize, and the first black president of South Africa. He started writing his autobiography, *Long Walk to Freedom*, while imprisoned on Robben Island in 1976, where he wrote in secret through the night and then shared handwritten pages with fellow prisoners for comment. The manuscript was smuggled out of prison later that year, but it was not until the early 1990s, when Mandela, finally freed from prison, finished the book in collaboration with ghostwriter Richard Stengel. The book was first published in 1994.

Autobiography

Long Walk to Freedom

by **Nelson Mandela**

1   I was not born with a hunger to be free. I was born free—free in every way that I could know. Free to run in the fields near my mother's hut, free to swim in the clear stream that ran through my village, free to roast mealies under the stars and ride the broad backs of slow-moving bulls. As long as I obeyed my father and abided by the customs of my tribe, I was not troubled by the laws of man or God.

2   It was only when I began to learn that my boyhood freedom was an illusion, when I discovered as a young man that my freedom had already been taken from me, that I began to hunger for it. At first, as a student, I wanted freedom only for myself, the **transitory** freedoms of being able to stay out at night, read what I pleased, and go where I chose. Later, as a young man in Johannesburg, I yearned for the basic and honorable freedoms of achieving my potential, of earning my keep, of marrying and having a family—the freedom not to be obstructed in a lawful life.

3   But then I slowly saw that not only was I not free, but my brothers and sisters were not free. I saw that it was not just my freedom that was curtailed, but the freedom of everyone who looked like I did. That is when I joined the African National Congress, and that is when the hunger for my own freedom

GRAMMAR & USAGE

Correlative Conjunctions

A **correlative conjunction** is a pair of conjunctions that work together to connect parts of sentences. In English, the primary correlative conjunctions are the following:

both ... and
either ... or
neither ... nor
not ... but
not only ... but (also)

For example, in paragraph 3, Mandela uses a correlative conjunction in the sentence "But then I slowly saw that *not only* was I not free, *but* my brothers and sisters were not free."

 KNOWLEDGE QUEST

Knowledge Question:
What can we learn about history by studying it from multiple perspectives?

transitory: temporary

Nelson Mandela and his wife Winnie Madikizela-Mandela raise their fists in front of a cheering crowd after Mandela's release from prison on February 11, 1990.

became the greater hunger for the freedom of my people. It was this desire for the freedom of my people to live their lives with dignity and self-respect that **animated** my life, that transformed a frightened young man into a bold one, that drove a law-abiding attorney to become a criminal, that turned a family-loving husband into a man without a home, that forced a life-loving man to live like a monk. I am no more virtuous or self-sacrificing than the next man, but I found that I could not even enjoy the poor and limited freedoms I was allowed when I knew my people were not free. Freedom is indivisible; the chains on any one of my people were the chains on all of them, the chains on all of my people were the chains on me.

4   It was during those long and lonely years that my hunger for the freedom of my own people became a hunger for the freedom of all people, white and black. I knew as well as I knew anything that the oppressor must be liberated just as surely as the oppressed. A man who takes away another man's freedom is a prisoner of hatred, he is locked behind the bars of prejudice and narrow-mindedness. I am not truly free if I am taking away someone else's freedom, just as surely as I am not free when my freedom is taken from me. The oppressed and the oppressor alike are robbed of their humanity.

5   When I walked out of prison, that was my mission, to liberate the oppressed and the oppressor both. Some say that has now been achieved. But I know that that is not the case. The truth is that we are not yet free; we have merely achieved the freedom to be free, the right not to be oppressed. We have not taken the final step of our journey, but the first step on a longer and even more difficult road. For to be free is not merely to cast off one's chains, but to live in a way that respects and enhances the freedom of others. The true test of our devotion to freedom is just beginning.

6   I have walked that long walk to freedom. I have tried not to falter; I have made missteps along the way. But I have discovered the secret that after climbing a great hill, one only finds that there are many more hills to climb. I have taken a moment here to rest, to steal a view of the glorious vista that surrounds me, to look back on the distance I have come. But I can rest only for a moment, for with freedom comes responsibilities, and I dare not linger, for my long walk is not yet ended.

⊘ Knowledge Quest

- What words of Mandela's jump out at you?
- How do you feel after reading about Nelson Mandela's life from his own perspective?

animated: gave energy to

Returning to the Text

- Evaluate the autobiography to answer text-dependent questions.
- Generate any additional questions you have about the autobiography and write them in your Reader/Writer Notebook.

9. What three stages of thinking about freedom does Mandela describe in paragraphs 1–3 of his autobiography?

_____

_____

_____

_____

10. KQ What words in paragraph 3 help you determine the meaning of the word *curtailed*?

_____

_____

_____

_____

11. What figurative language does Mandela use in paragraph 4?

_____

_____

_____

_____

12. Paraphrase the part of Mandela's autobiography in which he describes what true freedom is.

_____

_____

_____

_____

13. KQ Compare the details of the Mandela biography with those of Mandela's autobiography. How does each interpret his mission once out of prison?

_____

_____

_____

_____

INDEPENDENT READING LINK

You can continue to build your knowledge about learning history from different perspectives by reading other texts at ZINC Reading Labs. Search for keywords such as *historical or cultural history*.

 ZINC

 Knowledge Quest

Use your knowledge of "Biography of Nelson Mandela" and Long Walk to Freedom to consider the way that we learn about history. Write an opinion essay that responds to the question: Why is it important to learn history from multiple perspectives? Be sure to:

- Include a clear statement about your opinion.
- Explain how the details in each text provide specific kinds of information.
- Cite evidence from the texts to support your ideas.

INDEPENDENT READING LINK

Read and Connect

Identify the genre of the text you are reading independently and consider its benefits and limitations. Then find another source online about the same person or time period, but choose a source that is a different genre from your independent reading. Create a graphic organizer like the one that follows to compare and contrast the genres and the information they present.

Working from the Text

14. Choose one of the examples of vivid imagery that you marked in the text. Visualize it in your mind, and then sketch it in the margins. Then discuss how the imagery helped you understand Nelson Mandela's tone, voice, or personality.

15. Use your text markings and notes to add to your KWHL chart as follows:
    - Add new questions to your "W" column.
    - Add new information to your "L" column.
    - In the "H" column, describe how helpful this source was in helping you understand what kind of leader Nelson Mandela was.

16. Based on the two different versions of Nelson Mandela's life that you have read, analyze how biographical and autobiographical sources emphasize different evidence and interpret facts differently. Also think about the benefits and limits of each. Make one observation in each section of the chart that follows and then add to or modify your response during class discussion.

Genre	Biography	Autobiography
How Evidence Is Emphasized		
How Facts Are Interpreted		
Benefits of the Genre		
Limits of the Genre		

17. **Brainstorm:** Besides print texts of biography and autobiography, what other kinds of sources could you use to answer your questions about Nelson Mandela? Where would you find them?

LANGUAGE & WRITER'S CRAFT: Adjective Phrases

An **adjective** is a word that is used to **modify**, or describe, a noun or pronoun.

Examples:

I petted the dog.

I petted the furry dog.

Notice that the adjective *furry* modifies the noun *dog*.

An **adjective phrase** is a group of words that works together to modify a noun or pronoun.

Examples:

Those prices are *way too high*.

The charity helps children *born with heart defects*.

In the first example, the adjective phrase modifies the noun *prices*. In the second, it modifies the noun *children*.

A **prepositional phrase** includes a **preposition**, a noun or pronoun that is the object of the preposition, and usually some modifiers of the object. When a prepositional phrase modifies a noun or pronoun, it is a type of adjective phrase.

Examples:

The seats *at the new stadium* are green.

Liza is studying the birds *of the Northeast*.

In the first sentence, the prepositional phrase functions as an adjective because it modifies the noun *seats*. In the second sentence, the prepositional phrase modifies the noun *birds*, telling *which birds*. Both of these prepositional phrases are adjective phrases.

Remember that the verb of a sentence must agree with its subject. Agreement can become tricky when an adjective phrase comes between the subject and the verb. The verb should always agree with the subject.

Correct: Every **student** in Mr. Ramos's classes **is** expected to try hard.

Incorrect: Every student in Mr. Ramos's classes are expected to try hard.

PRACTICE Write two sentences that describe Nelson Mandela. Use an adjective phrase in each sentence. Make one of your adjective phrases a prepositional phrase used as an adjective. Make certain to incorporate correct subject-verb agreement.

18. Compose two sentences with adjective phrases. Be sure to use correct subject-verb agreement. Write your sentences in the My Notes space.

19. Revisit paragraph 3 of the excerpt from Mandela's autobiography. Look for adjective phrases. Mandela uses them to create a clearer, more detailed vision of the idea of freedom. Copy the sentences containing adjective phrases into the My Notes space.

Planning for Research and Citing Sources

Learning Targets

- Answer research questions by gathering and evaluating information from multiple sources, generating additional questions, and developing an annotated bibliography.
- Orally present claims, relevant facts, and details.

Preview

In this activity, you will gather, compose, and orally present research about the life of Nelson Mandela.

Learning Strategies

Previewing
KWHL Chart
Note-taking
Graphic Organizer
Metacognitive Markers
Choral Reading

My Notes

1. In a later activity, you will be comparing text to film versions of *Invictus*. Look at the list of background topics that follow. Mark each as follows:

   - Put a question mark (?) next to subjects that you have never heard of.
   - Put an asterisk (*) next to subjects that you know something about.
   - Put an exclamation point (!) next to subjects that you find interesting.

   Nelson Mandela
   Apartheid in South Africa
   African National Congress
   Afrikaners/Afrikaans
   South Africa Sport Boycott
   1995 Rugby World Cup
   Rugby
   Springboks

2. Follow your teacher's instructions to form a research group of two to three students and choose a topic or topics. On paper, create an individual KWHL chart and complete the first two columns by recording prior knowledge and generating research questions. Use the flowchart in Activity 2.3 to help you generate your questions.

3. Collaborate with your research group to identify at least one different research question for each group member. In the "H" column of your KWHL chart, list search terms that you might use and types of sources that you might find online to answer your question(s).

4. Use the Internet Source Evaluation Chart that follows to evaluate three different sources that might answer your question(s). A "yes" answer to many of the questions indicates that your source has a high degree of reliability and is a good source.

5. Choose the best source, based on the results of your evaluation. Copy the web address (URL) here:

Internet Source Evaluation Chart

- Use a search engine to locate a website for your topic or research question.
- In column 1, answer each question with a "yes," "no," or N/A (not applicable).
- Do the same in columns 2 and 3 for two more websites. Write the URLs of the websites you researched in the My Notes space and label each as 1, 2, or 3.

Criteria	Question	1	2	3
Accuracy	Is the site free from grammatical and typographical errors?			
	Do the links and graphics operate properly?			
	Was the information verified by a third party?			
Validity or Objectivity	Does the information appear to be well researched?			
	Is there a bibliography or list of sources?			
	Is there a statement about the purpose of the site?			
	Is there a place to note and communicate errors on the site?			
	Does the site appear to be free from bias or a single position?			
Authority	Are the author's name and qualifications clearly identified?			
	Does the URL address match the site's name?			
	Does the site identify itself as a .gov site in its address?			
	Does the author appear to be well qualified to write on the subject?			
	Does this site identify itself as an .edu site in its address?			
Currency and Uniqueness	Does the date the site was last updated appear?			
	Has the site been updated recently?			
	Are any parts of the site "under construction"?			
	Are the majority of the articles on the site a part of that site (as opposed to links to other sites)?			
Coverage	Does the site seem to cover the topic fully?			
	Are there other, related topics discussed on the site?			
	Is there a resources section with links to other sites?			

6. Create a note card to record your findings from the website you chose. On the side of the note card without lines, write the complete bibliographical citation. Use the Internet, a word processing program, or a print reference to review the Modern Language Association (MLA) format for a citation. You may also want to try out a program that allows your group to record and share information using a computer.

Sample citation information:

"Nelson Mandela—Biography." Nobelprize.org, 1993. Web. 14 Feb. 2012. ‹http://www.nobelprize.org/nobel_prizes/peace/laureates/1993/mandela-bio.html›

7. An annotated bibliography provides both the citation information and a brief explanation or summary of the source as well. On the back (lined) side of your notecard, write an annotation. Include the following:

- A brief summary of the content of the site
- An evaluation of the site's accuracy, validity, usefulness, and so on
- How this site helped you answer your research question

Sample annotation:

This site provides a brief biography of Nelson Mandela in order to give an overview of the events that led to his selection as a Nobel Peace Prize winner. While the site has validity and authority, it does not cover Mandela's life in very much detail. It answers the question "Why did he go to jail?" by explaining that he was accused of plotting to overthrow the government during his protest of apartheid.

8. Share your findings with your research partner or group. Prepare a brief summary of your findings to present to a larger group. When you present, be sure to:

- Present your claim and the evidence from your research in an organized way, including facts, details, and examples.
- Use appropriate eye contact, adequate volume, clear pronunciation, and appropriate register.

As you listen to your peers, take notes in the "L" column of your KWHL chart.

My Notes

WORD CONNECTIONS

Cognates
The English and Spanish languages contain words derived from ancient Greek and Latin. As a result, they have many words with similar spellings and pronunciations. Both feature words using the root *biblio*, which comes from ancient Greek and means "book." The Spanish word for *bibliography*, or list of books, is *bibliografia*. But the commonalities are not consistent. For example, the Spanish word for *library* is *biblioteca*. The English word comes not from Greek but from the Latin word for book, *liber*.

My Notes

9. Participate in a whole-class discussion about your group's research presentations.

- Prepare for the discussion by reviewing your KWHL chart. Make note of the information that you learned that was most useful in understanding Nelson Mandela's life.
- Follow rules for discussion such as by taking turns and establishing a group goal for the discussion. One possible goal could be to identify the most effective presentation method for biographical information.
- Ask thought-provoking questions and provide carefully considered observations in response to others' questions.
- Listen for new information and presentation ideas and add them to your Reader/Writing Notebook.

☑ Check Your Understanding

What makes an effective research presentation? What elements were present in the summaries you heard today? What elements would have made them more interesting and engaging?

Research and Independent Reading

Review the information you have researched so far on the leader you have chosen for Embedded Assessment 2. Write a letter to the person you are researching, expressing an opinion about an issue that was important to that person. Be sure to use at least three facts that you have learned from your research.

INDEPENDENT READING LINK

Read and Recommend

Apply what you have learned about bibliography annotations by writing an annotation of the text you are reading independently. After the annotation, include a statement about whether you would recommend the source for use in a research presentation. Explain why you think the source is reliable, credible, and a good choice for research on the topic. Draw upon specific details and information from your Independent Reading Log and Reader/Writer Notebook.

Visual Impact

Learning Targets

- Analyze ideas and details in informational material and song lyrics to gain an understanding of the topic of Nelson Mandela and apartheid.
- Create visuals that represent research about apartheid and Nelson Mandela.

Preview

In this activity, you will read and interpret graphics, a time line, and song lyrics about apartheid.

My Notes

1. **Quickwrite:** Respond to the image of Nelson Mandela by discussing your observations and making inferences. Then write a caption for the photo.

Caption:

2. The pie charts that follow represent voting and unemployment statistics in South Africa under apartheid. What conclusions can you draw about the political and economic rights of black people in South Africa during apartheid? Write your responses in the My Notes section.

Voter Turnout in South Africa

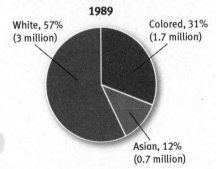

1989

White, 57%
(3 million)

Colored, 31%
(1.7 million)

Asian, 12%
(0.7 million)

Unemployed South Africans

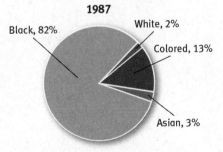

1987

Black, 82%

White, 2%

Colored, 13%

Asian, 3%

My Notes

3. Discuss: The poster has both images and text. What do you observe about the images? What information does the text add? Write at least one question that you have about the poster.

4. Based on the graph that follows, how did American companies respond to the South African government's apartheid policies? What questions do you have about the information in the graph?

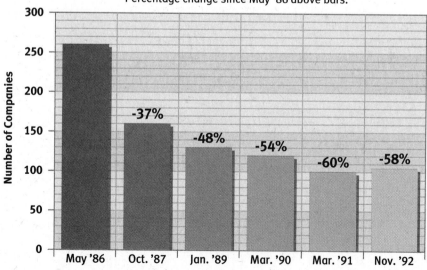

Changes in the Number of U.S. Companies Doing Business in South Africa

Percentage change since May '86 above bars.

5. Use the information from the table that follows to create your own bar graph or pie chart comparing the lives of blacks and whites in South Africa under apartheid. You may draw your chart or use technology if you have access to a computer. Remember to place a title on your chart and label it appropriately.

A 1978 Snapshot of South Africa under Apartheid		
	Blacks	Whites
Population	19 million	4.5 million
Ownership of Land	13 percent	87 percent
Share of National Income	<20 percent	75 percent
Ratio of Average Earnings	1	14
Minimum Taxable Income	360 rands	750 rands
Annual Expenditure on Education per Pupil	$45	$696
Teacher/Pupil Ratio	1/60	1/22

6. Present your completed bar graph or pie chart to a classmate. As part of your presentation, show your classmate where you got the information in your graphic. After your classmate presents his or her graphic to you, talk about the advantages and the limitations of bar graphs and pie charts in presenting data.

Setting a Purpose for Reading

- As you read the informational text, put a star next to features that indicate an organizational structure.
- Circle unknown words and phrases. Try to determine the meaning of the words by using context clues, word parts, or a dictionary.

Informational Text

Landmarks of Nelson Mandela's Life

from **BBC News**

Early Days

1918 – Rolihlahla Dalibhunga Mandela is born into a tribal clan in a small village in South Africa's Eastern Cape. He is later given his English name, Nelson, by a teacher at his school.

1919 – His father is **dispossessed** on the orders of a white magistrate, losing most of his cattle, land and income.

Campaign Begins

1943 – Joins the African National Congress (ANC), initially as an activist.

1944 – With close friends Oliver Tambo and Walter Sislu, Mr. Mandela forms the Youth League of the ANC. Marries his first wife, Evelyn Mase. They were divorced in 1957 after having three children.

1955 – The Freedom Charter is adopted at the Congress of the People, calling for equal rights and equal share of wealth with the country's white population.

1956 – Mr. Mandela, along with 155 other political activists, is accused of conspiring to overthrow the South African state by violent means and is charged with high treason. But the charges are dropped after a four-year trial.

1958 – Marries Winnie Madikizela.

1960 – Police open fire on men, women, and children in Sharpeville protesting the new Pass Laws which limited the movement of blacks, killing 69 of them. The ANC is banned, and Mandela forms an underground military wing.

dispossessed: stripped of property

Life Sentence

1964 – Captured by police after more than a year on the run, he is convicted of sabotage and treason in June and sentenced to life imprisonment, initially on Robben Island. His wife Winnie spearheads a campaign for his release.

1968 and 1969 – His mother dies and his eldest son is killed in a car crash. Mandela is not allowed to attend the funerals.

1980 – His friend Mr. Tambo, who is in exile, launches an international campaign for his release.

1986 – The international community tightens sanctions against South Africa. It is estimated that, between 1988 and 1990, the economic embargoes cost the country's treasury more than $4bn in revenue.

Changing Times

1990 – Bowing to the pressure, President FW de Klerk lifts the ban on the ANC and Mr. Mandela is released from prison. The ANC and the white National Party soon begin talks on forming a multi-racial democracy for South Africa.

1993 – Mr. Mandela and Mr. de Klerk are awarded the Nobel Peace Prize for their efforts to transform South Africa against a backdrop of bloodshed.

1994 – In the first multi-racial democratic elections in South Africa's history, Mr. Mandela is elected president. The ANC won 252 of the 400 seats in the national assembly.

1995 – South Africa wins the Rugby Union World Cup, and Mr. Mandela is publicly presented with a team jersey by the team captain, seen as a highly symbolic gesture of unity between blacks and whites.

☑ Focus on the Sentence

Expand the following sentences by answering the question words:

They tightened sanctions.

Who: _____

When: _____

Why: _____

Expanded sentence: _____

_____

They received the Nobel Peace Prize.

Who: _____

When: _____

Why: _____

Expanded sentence: _____

WORD CONNECTIONS

Content Connections
Sanctions are restrictions or penalties that one nation or a group of nations imposes on another to enforce certain behaviors. **Embargoes** are official bans on the trade of goods and services from a particular nation or region. Like sanctions, embargoes are put in place by other nations in order to get a country or region to change its political or economic policies.

My Notes

_____

_____

_____

_____

_____

_____

_____

_____

_____

_____

_____

_____

_____

_____

_____

_____

_____

_____

Working from the Text

7. Using your annotations, analyze the method that the author used to organize categories and subcategories of information. How did this organizational structure help you understand the text?

8. Using the information you learned from the time line of Mandela's life, work with a partner or small group to create an illustrated time line that includes at least five key events from the time line. For each event, include a date, a caption, and a visual image.

9. Present your time line to another group and get their feedback about how your images enhanced the presentation. Record their comments in the My Notes space.

☑ Check Your Understanding

Reflect on the use of images in a presentation by responding to the questions in the diagram.

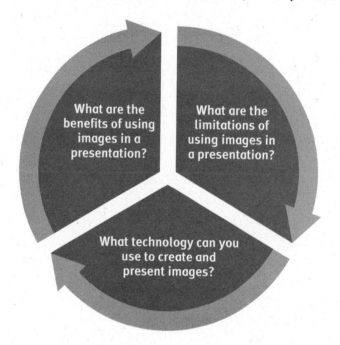

About the Musicians

The Specials are a British ska band that topped the United Kingdom (UK) music charts in the early 1980s with their number one hit "Ghost Town." Their mix of political and social commentary mixed with upbeat music hit the airwaves at a time when punk music was fading from the world stage but social unrest in the UK was growing. After the song "Nelson Mandela" hit the UK charts at number six, songwriter Jerry Dammers formed the group Artists Against Apartheid and became an anti-apartheid activist, taking part in a cultural embargo on South Africa in protest of apartheid.

Song

Nelson Mandela

by **The Specials**

Free Nelson Mandela
Free, Free, Free, Nelson Mandela
Free Nelson Mandela
Twenty-one years in captivity
5 His shoes too small to fit his feet
His body abused but his mind is still free
Are you so blind that you cannot see

I say Free Nelson Mandela
I'm begging you
10 Free Nelson Mandela

He pleaded the causes of the ANC
Only one man in a large army
Are you so blind that you cannot see
Are you so deaf that you cannot hear his plea

15 Free Nelson Mandela
I'm begging you Free Nelson Mandela

Twenty-one years in captivity
Are you so blind that you cannot see
Are you so deaf that you cannot hear
20 Are you so dumb that you cannot speak

I say Free Nelson Mandela
I'm begging you
Oh free Nelson Mandela, free

Nelson Mandela I'm begging you
25 begging you Please free Nelson Mandela
free Nelson Mandela
I'm telling you, you've got to free Nelson Mandela

Making Observations
- Which part of the song captures your attention?
- What emotions does the author have throughout the song?

Returning to the Text

- Return to the text as you respond to the following questions. Use text evidence to support your responses.
- Write any additional questions you have about the song lyrics in your Reader/Writer Notebook.

10. What effect does the repetition of the word *begging* have on the song? How would replacing it with the word *asking* change the tone of the song?

_____

_____

_____

_____

11. What facts from Nelson Mandela's life are included in the lyrics of the song?

_____

_____

_____

_____

12. From what you read in the historical accounts of Nelson Mandela's life, what causes does the line "He pleaded the causes of the ANC" refer to?

_____

_____

_____

_____

Working from the Text

13. Consider the way that the song represents the issue of Nelson Mandela's imprisonment. Think about the purpose of the song and the information the songwriters chose to include. Look through the time line of Nelson Mandela's life and make a list of events that you think provide important information that the song left out.

14. In a small group, create a verse of your own version of the song "Nelson Mandela," pulling from any of the events in his life. Combine your verse with that of other groups to form a new song.

Comparing Text and Film

Learning Targets

- Use text evidence to compare the theme of a poem to events in the life of a great leader.
- Use text evidence to compare a film text and a nonfiction text on a similar subject.

Preview

In this activity, you will compare a poem, a film, and an informational text on a similar subject.

Setting a Purpose for Reading

- As you read the poem, underline descriptive words and phrases that Henley applies to difficulties he has faced.
- Circle unknown words and phrases. Try to determine the meaning of the words by using context clues, word parts, or a dictionary.

About the Author

William Ernest Henley (1849–1903) was a British poet. As a child, Henley contracted tuberculosis of the bone and had to have his foot and part of his leg amputated. He spent much of his time in hospitals and wrote *Invictus*[1] while recovering from a second surgery.

This bust of Henley was created by the French sculptor Auguste Rodin, whose work Henley championed in England.

Learning Strategies

Choral Reading
Marking the Text
Graphic Organizer
Diffusing

My Notes

Poetry

Invictus

by **William Ernest Henley**

Out of the night that covers me,
Black as the Pit from pole to pole,
I thank whatever gods may be
For my unconquerable soul.

5   In the **fell** clutch of circumstance
I have not winced nor cried aloud.
Under the **bludgeonings** of chance
My head is bloody, but unbowed.

fell: deadly
bludgeonings: beatings

---

[1] **invictus:** Latin, meaning "unconquered, unconquerable, undefeated"

Beyond this place of **wrath** and tears
10 Looms but the Horror of the shade,
And yet the menace of the years
Finds, and shall find, me unafraid.

It matters not how strait the gate,
How charged with punishments the scroll.
15 I am the master of my fate:
I am the captain of my soul.

wrath: anger

Making Observations

- What are your first thoughts about the poem?
- What details and ideas stand out to you?
- What images catch your attention?

Returning to the Text

- Evaluate the poem to answer text-dependent questions.
- Generate any additional questions you have about the text and write them in your Reader/Writer Notebook.

1. How does each stanza of "Invictus" set up a contrast?

_____

_____

_____

_____

2. What central idea or theme does the speaker develop by referring to his soul in stanzas 1 and 4?

_____

_____

_____

_____

Working from the Text

3. Work with your group to write a one-sentence summary of each stanza in the margins. Identify and discuss the theme of the poem.

4. **Discuss:** Based on what you have read about Nelson Mandela's personal history, why might this poem have been important to him? What connections can you make between his life and the ideas in the poem?

My Notes

Setting a Purpose for Reading

- As you read the text, underline words and phrases that identify the emotions of both Mandela and his visitor, François Pienaar.
- Circle unknown words and phrases. Try to determine the meaning of the words by using context clues, word parts, or a dictionary.

About the Author

John Carlin (1956–) is an English author who writes about sports and politics. During his early years, he lived in Argentina but returned to England for much of his school years. Carlin has worked as a journalist for numerous newspapers in various parts of the world, including South Africa. He has also written the scripts for documentary films and other television broadcasts about Nelson Mandela and South Africa.

Nonfiction

Playing the Enemy:
Nelson Mandela and the Game
That Made a Nation (Part 1)

by **John Carlin**

The President and the Captain

1   Dressed in a dark suit and tie, Pienaar entered through a small door at the buildings' west wing, ducked through a metal detector, and presented himself before two policemen waiting for him at a desk behind a green-tinted window of thick bulletproof glass. Both being Afrikaners,[1] they immediately started engaging him animatedly on rugby. The policemen dropped him off at a small waiting room, bare save for a table and some leather chairs, into which stepped Mandela's personal assistant, a tall imposing black lady called Mary Mxadana who asked him to take a seat and wait a moment. He sat in the room alone for five minutes, his palms sweating. "I was incredibly tense as the moment arrived when I would meet him," he recalled. "I was really in awe of him. I kept thinking, 'What do I say? What do I ask him?'"

***

---

[1] **Afrikaner:** a South African of European descent

My Notes

2   Pienaar looked around the large wood-paneled office, vaguely registering a blend of décor old South African and new; ox-wagon watercolors side by side with shields of leather hide and wooden African sculptures. Mandela broke in. "Do you take milk, François?"

3   In less than five minutes Pienaar's mood had been transformed. "It's more than just being comfortable in his presence," Pienaar recalled. "You have a feeling when you are with him that you are safe."

***

4   Pienaar would not have guessed it at the time, but winning him over—and through him, enlisting the rest of the Springbok team—was an important objective for Mandela. For what Mandela had **reckoned**, in that half instinctive, half calculating way of his, was that the World Cup might prove helpful in the great challenge of national unification that still lay ahead.

5   Mandela never made his purpose **overt** in that first meeting with Pienaar, but he did edge closer to the main theme when he switched the conversation to his memories of the Barcelona Olympic Games, which he had attended in 1992 and recalled with great enthusiasm. "He talked about the power that sport had to move people and how he had seen this not long after his release in the Barcelona Olympics, which he especially remembered for one particular moment when he said he stood up and he felt the whole stadium reverberating," said Pienaar, in whose mind Mandela was seeking to plant the first seeds of a political idea.

6   "François Pienaar was the captain of rugby and if I wanted to use rugby, I had to work with him," Mandela said. "I concentrated in our meeting on complimenting him for the role which he was playing and which he could play. And I briefed him on what I was doing about sports and why I was doing so. And I found him a highly intelligent person." The time had come, as Mandela explained to his guest, to abandon the old perception of the Springbok rugby team as "enemies" and see them as compatriots and friends. His message was, "Let us use sport for the purpose of nation-building and promoting all the ideas which we think will lead to peace and stability in our country."

Making Observations
- Whom do we meet in the text?
- What details and images stand out to you?

reckoned: figured
overt: clear

Returning to the Text

- Evaluate the nonfiction text to answer text-dependent questions.
- Generate any additional questions you have about the nonfiction text and write them in your Reader/Writer Notebook.

5. What text in paragraph 1 indicates Pienaar's attitude toward his meeting with Nelson Mandela?

_____

_____

_____

_____

6. Why did Mandela want to meet with Pienaar, the captain of the rugby team? Use text evidence to support your explanation.

_____

_____

_____

_____

7. What inference can you make from paragraph 6 about Nelson Mandela's ability to understand and work with other people?

_____

_____

_____

_____

Working from the Text

8. In the graphic organizer that follows, add key details from the text that you can use to make predictions about how the scene will look on film. After viewing the film clip, make comments in the third column evaluating the accuracy of your predictions. In some cases, the film portrays the facts just as Carlin's book recorded them. In others, you will notice that the film alters the facts.

Details from the Text That Help Me Visualize the Film	How I Predict the Film Will Show Character and Emotion	Comments After Viewing the Film Clip
Nelson Mandela		
François Pienaar		

9. Discussion: Compare and contrast the film and text versions. How were they similar and different? Why do you think some of the facts were altered in the film version?

Setting a Purpose for Reading

- As you read the nonfiction text, underline words and phrases that help convey Nelson Mandela's perspective.
- Circle unknown words and phrases. Try to determine the meaning of the words by using context clues, word parts, or a dictionary.

Nonfiction

Playing the Enemy: Nelson Mandela and the Game That Made a Nation (Part 2)

Robben Island

1   [The Springbok players] found themselves on a ferry bound for Robben Island. It had been Morné du Plessis's idea. Du Plessis [the Springbok team manager] had begun to see just how enormous the impact of this "One Team, One Country" business was, not only in terms of the good it would do the country, but the good it would do the team.

2   "There was a cause-and-effect connection between the Mandela factor and our performance in the field," Du Plessis said. "It was a cause and effect on a thousand fronts. In players overcoming the pain barrier, in a superior desire to win, in luck going your way because you make your own luck, in all kinds of tiny details that go together or separately mark the difference between winning and losing. It all came perfectly together. Our willingness to be the nation's team and Mandela's desire to make the team the national team."

3   Robben Island was still being used as a prison and all the prisoners there were either Black or Coloured. Part of the day's events involved meeting them, but first the players took turns viewing the cell where Mandela had spent eighteen of his twenty-seven years in captivity. The players entered the cell one or two at a time; it couldn't hold any more than that. Having just met Mandela, they knew he was a tall man like most of them if not as broad. It required no great mental leap to picture the challenges, physical and psychological, of being confined in a box so small for so long.

***

My Notes

4   After Mandela's cell the Springbok players went outside to the yard where Mandela had once been obliged to break stones. Waiting for them was a group of prisoners.

5   "They were so happy to see us," Pienaar said. "Despite being confined here they were obviously so proud of our team. I spoke to them about our sense that we were representing the whole country now, them included, and then they sang us a song. James Small—I'll never forget this—stood in a corner, tears streaming out. James lived very close to the sword and I think he must have felt, 'I could have been here.' Yes, he felt his life could so easily have gone down another path. But," Pienaar added, recalling the bruising fights he would get into when he was younger, the time he thought he had killed a man, "... but mine too, eh? I could have ended up there too."

6   Small remembered the episode. "The prisoners not only sang for us, they gave us a huge cheer and I ... I just burst into tears," he said, his eyes reddening again at the recollection. "That was where the sense really took hold in me that I belonged to the new South Africa, and where I really got a sense of the responsibility of my position as a Springbok. There I was, hearing the applause for me, and at the same time thinking about Mandela's cell and how he spent twenty-seven years in prison and came out with love and friendship. All that washed over me, that huge realization, and the tears just rolled down my face."

Making Observations

- What questions do you have after reading the text?
- What did you notice that someone else might miss?
- What emotions do you feel after reading the text?

How does this image from the film *Invictus* demonstrate the way Nelson Mandela used rugby to unite South Africans?

Returning to the Text

- Evaluate the nonfiction text to answer text-dependent questions.
- Generate any additional questions you have about the nonfiction text and write them in your Reader/Writer Notebook.

10. Why does the author include the quotation from Du Plessis in paragraph 2?

_____

_____

_____

_____

11. In paragraph 6, what effect does meeting with the prisoners have on team members? Use a quote from the text to support your response.

_____

_____

_____

_____

12. How did James Small feel about "One Team, One Country"?

_____

_____

_____

_____

Working from the Text

13. After viewing the film clip, work with a partner or small group to record differences between the text and film. Make inferences about why you think the changes were made.

How the Text Was Changed in the Film	Effect of the Change on the Audience

☑ Check Your Understanding

Did the film version of the scene capture the emotional spirit of the text version? Explain your opinion using evidence from both the film and the book.

Viewing the Film *Invictus*

14. Imagine trying to effectively capture the spirit of a sporting event on film. What would the challenges be? How might a filmmaker deal with these challenges? Can you think of any films that have done this well?

    As you watch the final clip from *Invictus*, take notes on the effects of the filmmaker's choices regarding images and dialogue. While analyzing the film's images, take note of the following film techniques:

    • Camera angles: Is it a wide shot or a close up?
    • Lighting: What stands out in the scene? Where are the shadows?
    • Focus: What details can you see?
    • Sound: What do you hear? Is there background noise or music?

    Think about what you can see and hear in each shot and which details stand out. You may choose to divide the work with a partner and share notes after viewing the film clip.

Film techniques:	Effect on the audience:
Dialogue:	Effect on the audience:

Setting a Purpose for Reading

- As you read the nonfiction text, underline words and phrases that appeared in the film *Invictus*.
- Circle unknown words and phrases. Try to determine the meaning of the words by using context clues, word parts, or a dictionary.

Nonfiction

Playing the Enemy:
Nelson Mandela and the Game That Made a Nation (Part 3)

The Rugby World Cup

1   "When the game ended," Morné du Plessis said, "I turned and started running towards the tunnel and there was Edward Griffiths, who had invented the 'One Team, One Country' slogan, and he said to me, 'Things are never going to be the same again.' And I agreed instantly, because I knew right there that the best was behind, that life could offer nothing better. I said to him 'We've seen it all today.'"

2   But Du Plessis was wrong. There was more. There was Mandela going down onto the **pitch**, with his jersey on, with his cap on his head to hand over the cup to his friend François. And there was the crowd again—"Nelson! Nelson! Nelson!"—enraptured, as Mandela appeared at the touchline, smiling from ear to ear, waving to the crowd, as he prepared to walk toward a little podium that had been placed on the field where he would hand the world cup trophy to François Pienaar.

***

3   The gods at that moment were Mandela and Pienaar, the old man in green, crowned king of all South Africa, handing the cup to Pienaar, the young man in green, **anointed** that day as the spiritual head of born-again Afrikanerdom.

4   As the captain held the cup, Mandela put his left hand on his right shoulder, fixed him with a fond gaze, shook his right hand and said, "François, thank you very much for what you have done for our country."

5   Pienaar, meeting Mandela's eyes, replied, "No, Mr. President. Thank you for what you have done for our country."

6   Had he been preparing for this moment all his life, he could not have struck a truer chord. As Desmond Tutu said, "That response was made in

WORD CONNECTIONS

Etymology
A **trophy** is a cup or other object given to winners of a contest. The word has its roots in ancient times, when warriors would take the weapons of those whom they had conquered as a prize of battle. The word comes to us from the French *trophée*, which referred to the display of such weapons.

My Notes

pitch: playing field
anointed: chosen to lead

3.17

My Notes

At the 1995 Rugby World Cup, President Nelson Mandela congratulates Springbok skipper François Pienaar after handing him the William Webb Ellis trophy at Ellis Park in Johannesburg, South Africa. How does this moment in South African history symbolize a greater future for the country?

heaven. We human beings do our best, but those words at that moment, well ... you couldn't have scripted it."

7   Maybe a Hollywood scriptwriter would have had them giving each other a hug. It was an impulse Pienaar confessed later that he only barely restrained. Instead the two just looked at each other and laughed. Morné du Plessis, standing close by, looked at Mandela and the Afrikaner **prodigal** together, he saw Pienaar raise the cup high above his shoulders as Mandela, laughing, pumped his fists in the air, and he struggled to believe what his eyes were seeing. "I've never seen such complete joy," Du Plessis said. "He is looking at François and just, sort of, keeps laughing ... and François is looking at Mandela and ... the bond between them!"

8   It was all too much for the tough-minded Slabbert, hard-nosed veteran of a thousand political battles. "When François said that into the microphone, with Mandela there listening, laughing, and waving to the crowd and raising his cap to them, well," said Slabbert, "*everybody* was weeping. There wasn't a dry eye in the house."

9   There wasn't a dry eye in the country.

Making Observations
- What emotions did you feel as you read this last excerpt?
- What details did you notice as you read?

prodigal: whose people had wronged Mandela's people

268   SpringBoard® English Language Arts Grade 7

Returning to the Text

- Evaluate the nonfiction text to answer text-dependent questions.
- Generate any additional questions you have about the nonfiction text and write them in your Reader/Writer Notebook.

15. What text evidence supports the idea that rugby had the national effect that Mandela was counting on?

_____

_____

_____

_____

16. What is meant by the expression "[t]here wasn't a dry eye in the house" in paragraph 8?

_____

_____

_____

_____

Working from the Text

17. Paragraph 7 suggests that a Hollywood scriptwriter would change the final scene. Why do you think they did not? What responsibilities do you think an author has when portraying a true event?

18. Present your response to your small group, being sure to use eye contact, speaking rate, volume, enunciation, a variety of natural gestures, and conventions of language to communicate your critique effectively.

Learning Targets
- Explore how pronouns work.
- Use pronouns clearly and effectively when writing.

Preview
In this activity, you will examine the clear and effective use of pronouns.

Understanding Pronouns and Antecedents

Clarity is very important to writing. Readers can easily misunderstand what you mean if your writing is unclear. They may also stop paying attention to your ideas if your writing is confusing or boring. Using pronouns correctly can add variety to your sentences and help make your writing clear.

Pronouns are words that, like nouns, refer to persons, places, ideas, and things. *He, she,* and *it* are all pronouns that are very common in English. In a sentence, a pronoun can take the place of or refer to a noun. That noun is the pronoun's **antecedent**. Here is an example sentence from paragraph 4 of *Playing the Enemy: Nelson Mandela and the Game That Made a Nation*, by John Carlin.

> Pienaar would not have guessed it at the time, but winning <u>him</u> over—and through <u>him</u>, enlisting the rest of the Springbok team—was an important objective for Mandela.

In this example, *Pienaar* is replaced by the pronoun *him* twice in the sentence. *Him* is the pronoun, and *Pienaar* is the antecedent.

1. Read this sentence from the same text. Mark the pronouns being used and circle their antecedents.

   Mandela never made his purpose overt in that first meeting with Pienaar, but he did edge closer to the main theme when he switched the conversation to his memories of the Barcelona Olympic Games.

2. Understanding antecedents becomes more important over the course of a paragraph. Read these sentences from the beginning of *Playing the Enemy* and identify the antecedent of each underlined pronoun.

   Dressed in a dark suit and tie, Pienaar entered through a small door at the buildings' west wing, ducked through a metal detector, and presented himself to two policemen waiting for [1] <u>him</u> at a desk behind a green-tinted window of thick bulletproof glass. Both being Afrikaners, [2] <u>they</u> immediately started engaging [3] <u>him</u> animatedly on rugby. The policemen dropped [4] <u>him</u> off at a small waiting room, bare save for a table and some leather chairs, into which stepped Mandela's personal assistant, a tall imposing black lady called Mary Mxadana who asked [5] <u>him</u> to take a seat and wait a moment. [6] <u>He</u> sat in the room alone for five minutes, [7] <u>his</u> palms sweating. "I was incredibly tense as the moment arrived when I would meet [8] <u>him</u>," he recalled. "I was really in awe of [9] <u>him</u>. I kept thinking, 'What do I say? What do I ask [10] <u>him</u>?'"

[1] Pienaar	[6]
[2]	[7]
[3]	[8]
[4]	[9]
[5]	[10]

Using Clear References in Your Writing

3. Read the following sentences and mark each pronoun. Explain what is confusing about the sentence.

a. Nick read about Mandela and Pienaar and his plan to harness the power of sports for good.

b. Sports affect many people strongly, and they can offer new opportunities for understanding.

c. Although Pienaar is unsure what to expect at the meeting with Mandela, he makes him feel safe.

4. Quickwrite: What can make pronoun use confusing in these kinds of sentences?

Pronoun-Antecedent Agreement

A pronoun must agree in number with its antecedent. If the pronoun refers to a singular noun, a singular pronoun should be used consistently in the remainder of the sentence. Here's an example from *Playing the Enemy*:

> Mandela never made his purpose overt in that first meeting with Pienaar, but he did edge closer to the main theme when he switched the conversation to his memories of the Barcelona Olympic Games, which he had attended in 1992 and recalled with great enthusiasm.

The pronouns *his, he, he, his,* and *he* all refer to Mandela. Because the noun being replaced is singular, each pronoun must also be singular.

5. In this sentence, find the error in pronoun-antecedent agreement. Mark the error and write a corrected version of the sentence.

The time had come to abandon old, counterproductive ideas, mainly because it had been holding people back.

Revising

Read this paragraph from a student's response to *Playing the Enemy*. Work with a partner to check whether the pronouns are clear and correct. Revise any sentences that could be clearer, that have errors in pronoun-antecedent agreement, or that could flow more naturally with the use of pronouns.

[1] When a person reads about Nelson Mandela, they can see how he was considerate when interacting with diverse groups of people. [2] He was always respectful of his or her intelligence and point of view. [3] He was considerate about bringing up and introducing them to new ideas. [4] He took time with Pienaar to determine that Pienaar was "a highly intelligent person" before introducing Pienaar to the idea of using rugby "for the purpose of nation-building." [5] He didn't know how he would actually react to the idea, but his understanding of people's perspectives allowed him to gauge their response.

☑ Check Your Understanding

Imagine you are doing a peer review of a partner's draft and you come across the following sentences:

The players had their practice cancelled and were concerned that they would be unable to prepare for the upcoming championship. They were going to take place in three days, and time was running out. The team didn't know what they could do with so little time to adjust its plans.

In your own words, give your partner clear directions for revising this paragraph and using pronouns correctly in the future. Then add a question to your Editor's Checklist that will remind you to check pronouns in your own writing.

Practice

Return to the text-dependent question responses that you wrote in Activity 3.17 and check your use of pronouns and antecedents. Work with a partner to:

- Underline each pronoun.
- Circle the antecedent to which the underlined pronoun refers.
- Fix any incorrect pronoun-antecedent agreement and revise to correct unclear references.

Follow the Leader

Learning Targets

- Analyze a speech for evidence of outstanding leadership qualities.
- Analyze information to identify a subject for a biographical presentation.
- Generate research questions on a chosen subject.

Preview

In this activity, you will consider what a speech by Nelson Mandela reveals about his personal qualities.

Setting a Purpose for Reading

- As you read the speech, underline words and phrases that express the author's point of view, including his emotions, values, or personality traits.
- Circle unknown words and phrases. Try to determine the meaning of the words by using context clues, word parts, or a dictionary.

Speech

from Nelson Mandela's Nobel Prize Acceptance Speech

1   We do not believe that this Nobel Peace Prize is intended as a **commendation** for matters that have happened and passed.

2   We hear the voices which say that it is an appeal from all those, throughout the universe, who sought an end to the system of apartheid.

3   We understand their call, that we devote what remains of our lives to the use of our country's unique and painful experience to demonstrate, in practice, that the normal condition for human existence is democracy, justice, peace, non-racism, non-sexism, prosperity for everybody, a healthy environment and equality and solidarity among the peoples.

4   Moved by that appeal and inspired by the eminence you have thrust upon us, we undertake that we too will do what we can to contribute to the renewal of our world so that none should, in future, be described as the "wretched of the earth".

5   Let it never be said by future generations that indifference, cynicism or selfishness made us fail to live up to the ideals of humanism which the Nobel Peace Prize encapsulates.

6   Let the strivings of us all, prove Martin Luther King Jr. to have been correct, when he said that humanity can no longer be tragically bound to the starless midnight of racism and war.

7   Let the efforts of us all, prove that he was not a mere dreamer when he spoke of the beauty of genuine brotherhood and peace being more precious han diamonds or silver or gold.

8   Let a new age dawn!

My Notes

commendation: form of praise

3.18

Making Observations
- What emotions do you feel while reading the speech?
- What emotions do you feel while reading the speech?
- What details do you notice that you think others may miss when skimming the speech?

Returning to the Text
- Evaluate the speech to answer text-dependent questions.
- Generate any additional questions you have about the speech and write them in your Reader/Writer Notebook.

1. What does Mandela believe about human nature? In which part of the excerpt does he most clearly state that belief?

2. What kinds of imagery does Mandela use in the last three paragraphs of his speech? Why do you think he included it?

Working from the Text

3. **Quickwrite:** What are some of the character traits that great leaders have in common? Who are some historical or modern figures that you consider to be great leaders?

4. **Discussion:** What made Nelson Mandela a great leader?

5. As you explore speeches by other great leaders, complete the following graphic organizer to evaluate the character revealed by their words. Think of their potential as a possible subject for your biographical presentation.

Name of Speaker and Quote from Speech	Character Traits Revealed by Speaker's Words	Why I Might Be Interested in Researching This Speaker

Name of Speaker and Quote from Speech	Character Traits Revealed by Speaker's Words	Why I Might Be Interested in Researching This Speaker

6. Meet with your research group or partner and compare notes to generate a list of potential subjects for your biographical presentation and draft an initial set of research questions. As you consider subjects from your independent reading and begin asking questions, draw on the information you have learned in this unit about Nelson Mandela's leadership. Then select a leader whose choices also had positive consequences for society.

LANGUAGE & WRITER'S CRAFT: Misplaced Modifiers

As you prepare to complete Embedded Assessment 1, think about how you will use language for your presentation and on your visuals. Careful writers create sentences that are vivid and powerful. They are also careful not to create confusion with misplaced modifiers.

A **misplaced modifier** is a word, phrase, or clause that is separated from the word it modifies. This separation can cause confusion for the reader, and it often creates silly sentences.

Example: She saw a moose *on the way to the store.*

In this sentence, the prepositional phrase *on the way to the store* seems to modify the word *moose* and makes it sound as though the moose is on its way to the store. To fix the sentence, the writer needs to move the prepositional phrase closer to the word it really modifies—*She.* The sentence should read:

On the way to the store, she saw a moose.

PRACTICE Identify the two sentences that include misplaced modifiers and then revise them in your Reader/Writer Notebook so that the sentences are clearer.

In 1990, after 27 years in prison, President F. W. de Klerk ordered the release of Nelson Mandela. Mandela then worked to end the racist apartheid system in their country with de Klerk. Their efforts earned the two men the Nobel Peace Prize. Four years after leaving prison, Mandela became the first black president of South Africa.

Independent Reading Checkpoint

Use your independent reading notes to list three facts you have learned about Nelson Mandela and three facts you have learned about the subject of your independent reading text.

Creating a Biographical Presentation

 ASSIGNMENT

Work with a research group to create and deliver a biographical multimedia presentation of a great leader whose choices have had positive consequences for society.

Planning and Prewriting: Take time to collaborate on a plan for your presentation.	▪ Who are some possible subjects, that is, great leaders who have contributed to positive change? ▪ What research strategies (such as KWHL) will help your group generate research questions? ▪ What visuals will you need to find or create? ▪ Are there any texts with different genres or formats that you will need to create in order to communicate your topic and purpose?
Researching: Gather information from a variety of reliable sources.	▪ How will you gather a variety of useful sources, and what criteria will you use to determine reliability? ▪ How will you create note cards to record each source's bibliographic information as well as the information that answers your research questions? ▪ How will you revise your search and generate new research questions based on what you learn?
Drafting and Creating: Create a multimedia project and annotated bibliography.	▪ How will you create an annotated list with a citation, summary, and evaluation of each source? How will you synthesize information from these sources? ▪ How will you use multimedia to present your subject's history, character, choices, actions, and words to justify your selection of that person as a great leader? ▪ How can the Scoring Guide help you evaluate how well your project meets the requirements of the assignment?
Rehearsing and Presenting: Refine your communication skills as a speaker and listener.	▪ How and when will you present your project to another group for feedback and suggestions? ▪ How and when will you present your multimedia project to the class? ▪ How will you take notes on your observations, reflections, and questions during the other class presentations?

Reflection

After completing this Embedded Assessment, think about how you went about accomplishing this task and respond to the following:

- What were the challenges of creating a collaborative multimedia presentation? How did you and your group confront these challenges?

SCORING GUIDE

Scoring Criteria	Exemplary	Proficient	Emerging	Incomplete
Ideas	The presentation • clearly describes in detail the subject's character and personal history and includes specific examples of the choices, actions, and words that made him or her a great leader • shows extensive evidence of research conducted • maintains focus on the main points of the summary and effectively communicates to the intended audience.	The presentation • describes the subject's character and personal history and includes examples of the choices, actions, and/or words that made him or her a great leader • contains evidence of research conducted • focuses on the main points and clearly communicates to the intended audience.	The presentation • contains little information and neglects to make clear what distinguishes the subject as a great leader • contains minimal evidence of research conducted.	The presentation • provides no clear sense of what distinguishes the subject as a great leader • contains no evidence of research conducted.
Structure	The presentation • uses well-chosen and relevant visuals with informational captions and includes photos, tables, and/or charts created and interpreted by students • shows collaborative group work to present the project, using all members effectively • contains a precise annotated bibliography, a well-written summary of relevant source information, and a description of how each source was evaluated and assisted the research.	The presentation • uses a variety of relevant visuals created or interpreted by the students • shows collaborative group work to present the project with equal division of work • contains an annotated bibliography of sources with few errors, a summary of source information, and a description of how each source was evaluated and assisted the research.	The presentation • contains few visuals or visuals that are not clear in their purpose • shows that the group did not work collaboratively to present the project • may be missing sources or have incorrect citations (multiple errors in conventions and/or spelling), a minimal summary of the information contained in the source, and/or an inadequate description of how each source assisted the research.	The presentation • may be lacking visuals • shows little or no collaboration among group members • is missing sources or has numerous errors in citations, minimal or no summary of the information contained in sources, and/or no description of how each source assisted the research.

SCORING GUIDE

Scoring Criteria	Exemplary	Proficient	Emerging	Incomplete
Use of Language	Each presenter • uses appropriate eye contact, adequate volume, and clear pronunciation • displays a sophisticated variety of sentence types used appropriately • uses formal style and precise academic language • displays few errors in grammar, spelling, capitalization, and punctuation that do not detract from excellence.	Each presenter • connects with the audience through adequate volume, eye contact, and pronunciation • uses a variety of well-chosen sentence types • uses formal and academic language appropriately • displays only a few errors in spelling and grammar.	Each presenter • fails to maintain connection to audience with effective eye contact, volume, and/or speech clarity • shows little variety in sentence types • shows difficulty with the conventions of formal language and academic vocabulary • includes some errors in grammar and spelling.	Each presenter • shows serious flaws in the ability to construct purposeful sentences to convey ideas • uses language that is confused or confusing • includes errors in grammar, spelling, and conventions that interfere with meaning.

VISUAL PROMPT
What techniques do performers use to communicate with their audience? Which of these techniques do we use in our day-to-day lives?

HOW WE CHOOSE TO ACT

We wear the mask that grins and lies,
It hides our cheeks and shades our eyes—
This debt we pay to human guile;
With torn and bleeding hearts we smile

CONTENTS

My Independent Reading List

Previewing the Unit

Learning Strategies

Activating Prior Knowledge
Think-Pair-Share
QHT
Close Reading

Learning Targets

- Develop a plan to successfully complete Embedded Assessment 1.
- Self-select a text for independent reading and develop an independent reading plan.

Preview

In this activity, you will look ahead at the Embedded Assessment and plan your learning.

Making Connections

In this unit, you will study oral presentations and performance. You will be making creative choices about how to write and present a monologue. You will also present a scene from Shakespeare and will make choices about how to address your audience as a performer.

Essential Questions

Based on your current knowledge, how would you answer these questions?

1. How do writers and speakers use language for effect?

2. How do performers communicate meaning to an audience?

Developing Vocabulary

Look through the Table of Contents and use a QHT chart to sort the Academic Vocabulary and Literary Terms.

VOCABULARY

LITERARY
A **persona** is the voice or character speaking or narrating a story.

The phrase *public persona* is used to describe how an individual presents him- or herself to other people.

Unpacking Embedded Assessment 1

Do a close reading of Embedded Assessment 1. Underline or highlight key skills and knowledge you will need to be successful with the assignment.

 Your assignment is to write and present a monologue about a topic that sparks a strong emotion (e.g., amusement, regret, disappointment, excitement, joy, sadness, contentment, or anger). You may choose to speak as yourself, or you may adopt a **persona**.

You will work with your class to paraphrase the expectations and create a graphic organizer to use as a visual reminder of the required concepts and skills. After each activity, use this graphic to guide reflection about what you have learned and what you still need to learn to be successful on the Embedded Assessment.

 INDEPENDENT READING LINK

Reading Plan
During this half of the unit, you will read and create monologues. For independent reading, choose a work of fiction written from a first-person point of view. Preview possible choices by reading a few pages to make sure the text is interesting to you. Use your Reader/Writer Notebook to create a reading plan and respond to any questions, comments, or reactions you might have to your reading. Also, you can jot notes in your Independent Reading Log.

Creating an Independent Reading Plan

The unit focuses on literary text analysis, using language for effect, and presentation skills. Throughout the unit, you will be asked to transform chunks of your selected Independent Reading text into monologue format, and you will practice delivering your text orally in front of your peers. After choosing a text, add it to your Independent Reading List and make a plan for when you will read and how many pages you will read each day.

Using Language for Effect

Learning Strategies

Summarizing
Questioning the Text
Rereading
Marking the Text
Note-taking
Drafting

Learning Targets

- Analyze the use of vocabulary, diction, punctuation, and poetic musical devices in poetry.
- Analyze and orally present an interpretation of a poem.
- Compare and contrast two poems.

Preview

In this activity, you will analyze how different poets use language.

Setting a Purpose for Reading

- As you read the poem, underline words and phrases that help you create mental images. Write a slash in places where there seems to be a natural break.
- Circle unknown words and phrases. Try to determine the meaning of the words by using context clues, word parts, or a dictionary.

About the Author

For much of his life, Robert Frost (1874–1963) lived on a farm in New Hampshire and wrote poems about farm life and the New England landscape. Like "The Road Not Taken," this poem takes place in a natural setting, with no other people around. Frost wrote "Stopping by Woods on a Snowy Evening" in 1922, and he described it as his favorite work, calling it his "best bid for remembrance."

Poetry

Stopping by Woods on a Snowy Evening

by **Robert Frost**

Whose woods these are I think I know,
His house is in the village though;
He will not see me stopping here
To watch his woods fill up with snow.

My Notes

5 My little horse must think it queer
To stop without a farmhouse near
Between the woods and frozen lake
The darkest evening of the year.

He gives his harness bells a shake
10 To ask if there is some mistake.
The only other sound's the sweep
Of easy wind and downy flake.

The woods are lovely, dark and deep,
But I have promises to keep,
15 And miles to go before I sleep,
And miles to go before I sleep.

Making Observations
- What do you notice about the setting of the poem?
- What images catch your attention?
- What emotions do you feel as you read?

Returning to the Text

- Return to the text as you respond to the following questions. Use text evidence to support your responses.
- Write any additional questions you have about the poem in your Reader/Writer Notebook.

1. What does *queer* mean in line 5? Describe the process by which you arrived at your answer.

_____

_____

_____

_____

2. Write a description of how the speaker gives the reader more information in each stanza, creating a complete explanation of the speaker's situation by the poem's conclusion.

_____

_____

_____

_____

Working from the Text

Poetry is meant to be read aloud. Poets are masters of language who delight in the sense and the music of language. When reading poetry, always be aware of how it can be read aloud. An oral interpretation is a speaker's interpretation of the sense and sound of the language of poetry.

When reading for the sense of a poem, pay attention to the following:

- vocabulary
- diction
- punctuation
- poetic musical devices

In order to read for the sound of a poem, pay attention to rhyme, **alliteration**, **assonance**, and **consonance**. Poets use these devices to create a musical effect with language, which is why these devices are called *poetic musical devices*.

LITERARY

Alliteration is the repetition of a consonant sound at the beginning of a word.

Assonance is the repetition of identical or similar vowel sounds in neighboring words.

Consonance is the repetition of consonant sounds.

VOCABULARY

Roots and Affixes

Diction contains the Latin root *dict*, meaning "say, declare, proclaim." The root appears in *dictionary, predict, contradict,* and *dictator.* The Latin suffix *-ion* means "being the result of."

My Notes

3. Read "Stopping by Woods on a Snowy Evening" multiple times to prepare for an oral interpretation. Remember that an oral interpretation is a read aloud of a literary work with expression. Work with a partner to mark the poem for volume, rate, pitch, and inflection. Then practice reading the poem aloud multiple times with your partner. Use the following annotations to mark the poem for reading aloud.

- **Volume** is the loudness of a speaker's voice. Use a <u>double underline</u> for louder and a <u>single underline</u> for softer.
- **Rate** is the speed at which a speaker delivers words. Use a right arrow (→) above words to indicate faster and a left arrow (←) to indicate slower.
- **Pitch** is the highness or lowness of a speaker's voice. Use an up arrow to indicate a higher pitch (↑ = high) and a down arrow to indicate a lower pitch (↓ = low).
- **Inflection** is the emphasis a speaker places on words through change in volume or pitch. Highlight words to emphasize.

Before you read the poem aloud, circle any unfamiliar words, and look them up in a dictionary to determine the meaning, pronunciation, and syllabication. You may wish to use an online dictionary that allows you to listen to the pronunciation. Then record the pronunciation on your poem.

☑ Check Your Understanding

Each stanza in the poem "Stopping by Woods on a Snowy Evening" is connected by rhyme. Using four different colors, highlight the words that rhyme with each other. Is there a pattern to the rhymes used? If so, what is it?

Setting a Purpose for Reading

- As you read each poem, underline words and phrases that help you to create a mental image. In My Notes, write down instances of alliteration, assonance, and/or consonance.
- Circle unknown words and phrases. Try to determine the meaning of the words by using context clues, word parts, or a dictionary.

About the Author

E. E. (Edward Estlin) Cummings (1894–1962) was born in Cambridge, Massachusetts, and attended Harvard University. He is known for experimenting with form, spelling, and punctuation in his poetry, and he kept the unique style that he developed through this experimentation throughout his career. At the time of his death in 1962, Cummings was one of the most widely read American poets, and his popularity endures to this day.

Poetry

maggie and milly and molly and may

by **E. E. Cummings**

maggie and and molly and may
went down to the beach(to play one day)

and maggie discovered a shell that sang
so sweetly she couldn't remember her troubles,and

5 milly befriended a stranded star
whose rays five **languid** fingers were;

and molly was chased by a horrible thing
which raced sideways while blowing bubbles:and

may came home with a smooth round stone
10 as small as a world and as large as alone.

For whatever we lose(like a you or a me)
it's always ourselves we find in the sea

Children Playing by a Rockpool, by Dorothea Sharp

Making Observations
- What is one thing the characters in the poem have in common?
- Which character has the most interesting experience?

languid: limp, drooping

My Notes

About the Author

Langston Hughes (1902–1967) began his writing career early. By eighth grade, he was named class poet. Langston Hughes went on to become a prominent figure in the Harlem Renaissance. His poems, plays, and stories frequently focused on the African American experience, particularly on the struggles and feelings of individuals.

Poetry

Mother to Son

by **Langston Hughes**

Well, son, I'll tell you:
Life for me ain't been no crystal stair.
It's had tacks in it,
And splinters,
5 And boards torn up,
And places with no carpet on the floor
Bare.
But all the time
I'se been a-climbin' on,
10 And reachin' landin's,
And turnin' corners,
And sometimes goin' in the dark
Where there ain't been no light.
So boy, don't you turn back.
15 Don't you set down on the steps
'Cause you finds it's kinder hard.
Don't you fall now—
For I'se still goin', honey,
I'se still climbin',
20 And life for me ain't been no
crystal stair.

Making Observations
• Who is the speaker in the poem?
• What traits do you notice in that character?
• What has that character's life been like?

About the Author

Mexican writer José Juan Tablada (1871–1945), who introduced haiku to the Spanish language, is considered the father of modern Mexican poetry. During a visit to Japan, he was introduced to haiku, a traditional poetry form that is usually made up of three lines with a total of 17 syllables. Writing in Spanish, Tablada did not try to imitate Japanese culture in his haiku but created poems that reflected Mexican culture.

Poetry

Haiku

by **José Juan Tablada,** *translated by* **Samuel Beckett**

The brilliant moon
working through its web
keeps the spider awake.

Sea the black night,
the cloud a shell,
the moon a pearl.

Tender willow,
almost gold, almost amber,
almost light …

Although he never stirs from home
the tortoise, like a load of furniture,
jolts down the path.

The garden is thick with dry leaves:
on the trees I never saw
so many green, in spring …

Making Observations

• What were some images that you pictured while reading?
• What emotions did you feel while reading these haiku?

My Notes

About the Author

Rosemary Catacalos lives in San Antonio, Texas, where her family has lived for more than a century. In 2013, she was named the Poet Laureate (official poet) of Texas. Her poems frequently evoke her Greek and Mexican heritage, as well as Texan history and geography. The poem "Homesteaders" is from her 1984 collection *Again for the First Time*.

Poetry

Homesteaders

For the Edwards Aquifer

by **Rosemary Catacalos**

They came for the water,
came to its sleeping place
here in the bed of an old sea,
the dream of the water.
5 They sank hand and tool into
soil where the bubble of springs
gave off hope, fresh and long,
the song of the water.
Babies and crops ripened
10 where they settled,
where they married their sweat
in the ancient wedding,
the blessing of the water.
They made houses of limestone
15 and adobe, locked together blocks
descended from shells and coral,
houses of the bones of the water,
shelter of the water.
And they swallowed the life
20 of the lime in the water,
sucked its mineral up
into their own bones
which grew strong as the water,

WORD CONNECTIONS

Roots and Affixes

The word *aquifer* contains the Latin roots *aqua*, meaning *"water,"* and *fer, meaning "bring."* An aquifer is a layer of rock through which water can move. Aquifers can provide drinking water and water for irrigation.

the gift of the water.
25 All along the counties they lay,
mouth to mouth with the water,
fattened in the smile of the water,
the light of the water,
water flushed pure through the
30 spine and ribs of the birth of life,
the old ocean,
the stone,
the home of the water.

My Notes

Making Observations
- What images stand out to you?
- What words did you notice when you were reading the poem?

The Edwards Aquifer is an important source of water for South Central Texas.

Returning to the Text

- Revisit the poems as you respond to the following questions. Use text evidence to support your responses.
- Write any additional questions you have about the poems in your Reader/Writer Notebook.

"maggie and milly and molly and may"

4. What effect does Cummings create with his unusual capitalization and punctuation?

_____

_____

_____

_____

5. The last line of the poem says, "it's always ourselves we find in the sea." How does each couplet of the poem prepare the reader for the poem's final two lines?

_____

_____

_____

_____

6. What tone does the rhyming in "maggie and milly and molly and may" create for nearly all of the poem? How does that tone relate to the subject matter of the poem?

_____

_____

_____

_____

"Mother to Son"

7. What effect does Hughes create with his use of punctuation in "Mother to Son"?

_____

_____

_____

_____

8. How does the poem's speaker try to help the listener?

_____

_____

_____

9. How does the poem's overall text support the tone created by lines 1–2 and lines 20–21?

_____

_____

_____

"Haiku"

10. How does the author use words to develop sensory images in these haiku?

_____

_____

_____

11. How does José Juan Tablada use punctuation for effect in the third haiku?

_____

_____

_____

_____

"Homesteaders"

12. Water is the primary image in the poem "Homesteaders." How does Catacalos connect that image to the everyday lives of the people in her poem?

_____

_____

_____

13. What effect does Catacalos's repetition of the phrase "of the water" create throughout "Homesteaders?"

_____

_____

_____

_____

My Notes

Working from the Text

Your teacher will assign your group one of the poems to study and read aloud. In your group, analyze the poem you have been assigned for its use of vocabulary, diction, punctuation, and musical devices. Mark the text to prepare an oral interpretation and practice reading the poem out loud. Make sure to take detailed notes during the discussion; you will be responsible for reading and teaching this poem to a new group.

14. In your jigsaw group, listen as others present their oral interpretations. Take notes (focusing on the writer's use of language) and ask questions for clarification when you need more information or a different explanation. When it is your turn to speak, present your poem and oral interpretation. Be sure to make eye contact and speak with appropriate volume and rate.

☑ Check Your Understanding

Select a poem (or set of poems) you listened to and explain how listening to the oral interpretation affected your understanding of the ideas and emotions in the poem. Be sure to use **precise** language to explain your response.

✍ Writing to Sources: Informational Text

Select two poems and compare and contrast the writers' use of language (vocabulary, diction, punctuation) and of poetic musical devices. What effect do the poets achieve through their language choices? Be sure to:

- Start with a topic sentence that explains the effect of the poems' language and poetic musical devices.
- Use examples of specific language from each of the poems.
- Use the specific literary terminology you have learned in this activity.

VOCABULARY

ACADEMIC

When you are **precise**, you are accurate and careful about details. This *precision* creates *preciseness,* or clarity of thought. Using language accurately and choosing exact words is important in describing ideas; it is also important in mathematics and science.

Analyzing a Comedic Monologue

Learning Targets

- Analyze the ideas, structure, and word choice in a comedic monologue.
- Create a written response to a comedic monologue.
- Write a comedic monologue with effective ideas, structure, and language.

Preview

In this activity, you will analyze a comedic monologue and then write your own.

Learning Strategies

Word Maps
Note-taking
Quickwrite
Discussion Groups
Graphic Organizer
Drafting

The Oral Tradition

Sharing information and stories begins with oral communication. The oral tradition of telling and listening to stories is an ancient art form that has a modern expression in drama. Actors, though, are not the only people who communicate orally. The art of expressing yourself orally is probably one of the most important communication skills you can master.

1. **Quickwrite:** Think about speeches or dialogue by characters you may have seen on television. What made them catch your attention? What was interesting or memorable about them?

Performance is a way of honing your ability to communicate with others by making physical and vocal choices in order to convey a certain idea, feeling, or tone. Tone, which you studied in the last unit, is a writer's or speaker's attitude toward a subject.

As you discovered in the previous activity, oral interpretation involves understanding a literary text and then using your voice (through volume, rate, and inflection) to best convey its meaning. Another type of oral performance is a **monologue**. A monologue is an extended speech, written from the first-person point of view, in which a performer presents his or her—or a character's—thoughts on a subject.

Monologues have a certain **structure**: a beginning that hooks the reader, a middle that sequences and develops ideas, and an end that offers a conclusion. Content is tailored to the purpose and audience. Because monologues are written to be performed, they sometimes contain stage directions (italicized instructions for physical and/or oral delivery in parentheses) and line or paragraph numbers. Monologues can be humorous or dramatic, as you will see.

2. Create a word map in your Reader/Writer Notebook for *monologue*. Record and share what you already know and what you learn during class. As your understanding deepens throughout the unit, continue to take notes and organize information and examples related to this form of writing.

LITERARY

A **monologue** is a speech or written expression of thoughts by a character and is always written from the first-person point of view.

ACADEMIC

Structure refers to the arrangement of the parts of something. In this usage, *structure* is a noun. In its verb form, to *structure* something is to build or construct or arrange in a definite pattern or organization.

WORD CONNECTIONS

Roots and Affixes
Monologue comes from the Greek words *mono*, meaning "one," and *logos*, meaning "words, speech, or reason."

This combination of words conveys the idea that a monologue is a speech by one person. The prefix *mono-* is also found in words such as *monorail*, *monogamy*, and *monochromatic*.

My Notes

_____

_____

_____

_____

_____

_____

_____

_____

_____

_____

_____

_____

_____

_____

_____

_____

_____

_____

_____

_____

_____

_____

_____

_____

_____

_____

_____

_____

_____

_____

_____

_____

_____

_____

_____

_____

_____

Viewing a Comedic Monologue

3. **Quickwrite:** When you think of Halloween, what images, memories, and/or feelings come to mind? Can you remember your worst or best Halloween? If so, what made it so awful or so fun?

4. Your teacher will show you a video clip of a comedic performance. As you watch the scene, think about the audience and purpose. Write as much as you can about both.

   Audience:

   Purpose:

5. As you discuss the audience and purpose in class, write down the statement of audience and purpose that your class develops.

   Audience:

   Purpose:

6. As you view the clip for the second time, think about what makes a monologue comedic and how oral delivery and physical action help the viewer to understand the comic performance. Use the Embedded Assessment 1 Scoring Guide to analyze and evaluate your assigned area—ideas, structure, or use of language—and write your comments in the following graphic organizer. Determine how effective the monologue is for your assigned area, given the intended audience and purpose.

A. Ideas: See descriptors on Scoring Guide.
Explanation:

B. Structure: See descriptors on Scoring Guide.
Explanation:

C. Use of Language: See descriptors on Scoring Guide.
Explanation:

7. Name the intended audience and purpose for this monologue.

8. Share your evaluation of the monologue you viewed with your expert group, listen to others' evaluations, and agree upon one rating and explanation to share with the class.

LANGUAGE & WRITER'S CRAFT: Dangling and Misplaced Modifiers

A **modifier** is a word, phrase, or clause that describes, clarifies, or gives more detail about another word or word group in the sentence. In this example, the opening phrase modifies, or describes, the noun *Halloween*.

Example: *With its festive air, costumes, and candy,* Halloween is an exciting time.

A **dangling modifier** occurs when the modifier has nothing to describe, clarify, or add detail to.

Example: *Eagerly awaiting Halloween,* my costume hung in my closet.

To fix a dangling modifier, you should revise the sentence to make it clear what the modifier is describing. In this revised sentence, the modifier clearly describes the pronoun *I*.

Example: *Eagerly awaiting Halloween,* I hung my costume in my closet.

A **misplaced modifier** is one that is placed too far away from the word or word group it modifies. Misplaced modifiers can cause confusion and result in some silly sentences. In the following sentence, it seems like the writer's parents, not the costume, are actually from the store.

Example: After many years of my begging, my parents *from the store* bought me a costume.

To correct a misplaced modifier, move the modifier close to the word or word group it modifies. The preceding example should be revised as follows so that the modifier clearly describes the costume, not the parents.

Example: After many years of my begging, my parents bought me a costume *from the store*.

PRACTICE Review your monologue evaluation, paying close attention to how modifiers are used. Revise sentences that contain misplaced or dangling modifiers.

☑ Check Your Understanding

Consider how a comedic performance relies on all three elements (ideas, structure, and language) to create humor. Then revisit your monologue word map and add another layer of information and examples about successful monologues.

▣ Narrative Writing Prompt

Draft an original narrative monologue about a real or imagined comic holiday experience. Be sure to:

- Use narrative techniques and craft to tell the story and create interest.
- Follow the monologue structure, logically sequencing the events.
- Use specific language to communicate a humorous tone.
- Guide the oral interpretation by noting where specific movements, facial expressions, or voice inflections should be used.

Analyzing and Presenting a Dramatic Monologue

Learning Strategies

Marking the Text
Discussion Groups
Brainstorming
Rehearsal
Choral Reading
Role-Playing
Drafting

Learning Targets

- Analyze and compare the text and performance of a dramatic monologue.
- Create stage directions and present an effective oral interpretation.

Preview

In this activity, you will analyze a dramatic monologue and then present an oral interpretation of the monologue.

Preparing for an Oral Presentation

First, your teacher will do an oral interpretation of one of the monologues included in this activity.

1. As you listen to and watch the oral interpretation of the monologue, think about the voice, facial expressions, and gestures that you see. How do they help convey the tone and sense of the monologue?

2. While listening a second time, turn to the page with the text of the monologue and mark the text by highlighting punctuation. Also place an asterisk (*) next to interesting use of language that helps you understand the persona of the speaker and the intended audience.

Setting a Purpose for Reading

- As you read your assigned monologue, mark words that help you understand the persona of the speaker.
- Circle unknown words and phrases. Try to determine the meaning of the words by using context clues, word parts, or a dictionary.

My Notes

My Notes

About the Author

Mary Hall Surface was born in Bowling Green, Kentucky in 1958. She is an accomplished playwright, producer, and director who focuses on theater for young people and family audiences. Her plays have been performed around the world. She has been nominated nine times for the prestigious Helen Hayes Award, winning as Outstanding Director of a Musical in 2002.

Monologue

The Paper Avalanche

by **Mary Hall Surface**

Makena: [Talking to her friend, Erin.] Erin, it's horrible! I feel personally responsible for the death of thousands of trees! All I did was join one nature organization. I wanted to save the animals. It only cost fifteen dollars and the wolf stuffed toy you got for joining was so cute. How

5 could I resist? But now, I get big fat envelopes twice a week from every environmental organization on the planet. They all want me and they lure me in with these cute animal pictures on return address labels. I might fall for it if they'd spell my name right, but they usually don't. How could all these people who are supposed to care about the Earth waste all this paper

10 on an eleven-year-old kid? Wait a minute. I got it. I'll write an article for the newspaper. "Stop the paper avalanche! Take kids off wildlife mailing lists." I'll mail

15 it. Better idea! I'll e-mail it! Not another piece of paper will be sacrificed in this cause. Oh Erin do you think it'll work?

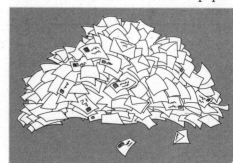

Monologue

Dreams

by **Mary Hall Surface**

Terry/Teri: [Talking to his/her friend, Corey.] Look at that. His feet are twitching. And watch his mouth. Even his whiskers move. He's dreaming. I know he is. He'll start whimpering soon, with little soft barks. Then his legs will start moving. Like he's chasing something. (*To the dog.*) What

5   are you dreaming about, Scout? That white squirrel you saw in Granny's backyard? (*To his friend.*) You should have seen him. Scout saw that squirrel and turned into a pointer right before my eyes. (*To the dog.*) You dreaming about running around the park after your yellow ball? Huh? (*To his friend.*) Bet he's dreaming of his dog-lives past, when he hunted badgers

10 for German royalty or herded sheep in Mongolia! I wish my dreams were as fun as his. My dreams aren't half this fun. When I'm asleep … or awake. What do you dream about, Corey?

Monologue

Study Tips

by **Mary Hall Surface**

Christoff: [Talking to his friend, Anton.] So. Here's the new technique for studying. It's great! They taught us all about it in advisory. First you breathe deeply. (*He does.*) Then blo-o-o-o-w it out. Breathing keeps you calm. Relaxed. (*He does another big breath*). Blo-o-o-o-w. Now, I visualize
5   myself taking the test, assigning a positive thought to each movement. I pull out my chair, I say "I will succeed." I sit down, I say "I am prepared." I lift my pencil. I say … I say … "Get me out of here! How's a kid supposed to know all this information after only six weeks of school? I couldn't *find* history class for the first week because all the halls look exactly alike! I
10 couldn't use my book till last week because I forgot the combination to my locker. And now you want me to take a fifty-question multiple-
15 choice test?" I visualize myself getting grounded till Christmas because I'm going to fail my first middle school exam. That is not a pretty
20 picture. Man, I need a new technique. Anton, how do you study?

About the Author

Jenny Lyn Bader is a New York City–based playwright and author who specializes in short theatrical works. She is the author of the plays *Mona Lisa Speaks*, *In Flight*, and *None of the Above*. She has had 11 works published in the acclaimed Smith and Kraus's *Best Ten-Minute Plays* series. Her monologue "The Children's Crusade" is frequently performed by young people in classrooms and on stage.

Monologue

The Children's Crusade

by **Jenny Lyn Bader**

CHRIS: James VI was crowned King of Scotland when he was one year old. Louis XIV was five when he became King of France. So I ... should be able to take the bus by myself. According to history? All your rules make no sense. The videos you won't let me watch because they're too

5 violent? Kids were once a major part of official violence! An army of kids marched across Europe in the thirteenth century. The Children's Crusade. Sure, it didn't turn out too well for most of them, but ... it was a whole war. For kids! Joan of Arc—visited by visions when she was twelve, then became a soldier. I'm as old as she was, and you don't even let me watch

10 wars when they're on TV! I'm not saying I want to start a war. I'm saying I have all these words I'm not allowed to say, books I'm not allowed to read, movies I'm not allowed to see, while at another time I might have been in charge of—Macedonia! Look at K'ang-Hsi, emperor of China at seven ... Tutankhamen, "King Tut," pharaoh of Egypt at nine. Right now I'm

15 older than either of them, and you still won't let me take the bus. I know you think I'd miss my stop, but all I need is a chance to prove [*Interrupts self.*]—and yeah, I know you gave me one when you said you'd-let-me-take-the-bus-by-myself-next-time-if-I-just-got-off-at-the-right-stop, and I realize I messed that up. But my book got so good around Seventy-Ninth

20 Street ... it was about the Roman Empire, which Constantine VII ruled the eastern part of when he was just five? Sure it looked bad when I missed our stop, and the ... three ... stops after that. But it wasn't a fair test. Because you were there. And you need to trust that if I were alone, I'd stop reading and be able to handle the local bus! But you think I'm ... This ... idea that

25 I'm a "child"—it's such a recently invented, technical category—can't you see that? How you always say I should play with the Altmans' kid, Danny ... How I'd like him so much, since we're both twelve. Danny Altman collects worms! You think I'd like playing with someone I don't know, with completely different interests, simply because we're both twelve? Do I tell

30 you to play with my gym teacher, Mr. Phelps, because you're both thirty-seven? No. I'd choose friends for you more thoughtfully. For a long time, this "child" thing didn't matter. No one cared. Because at one time, children would be given kingdoms, over which ... We ... would rule.

My Notes

_____

_____

_____

_____

_____

_____

_____

_____

_____

_____

ACTIVITY 4.4
continued

Working from the Text

3. Examine Mary Hall Surface's "The Paper Avalanche." Describe the tone of the passage as it begins, identify the point at which that tone changes, and describe that change. Use text evidence in your response.

4. Identify and examine the stage directions in Mary Hall Surface's "Dreams." What information do they contain that would be useful to someone performing the monologue? Use text evidence in your response.

5. In "Study Tips," Mary Hall Surface uses an unusual spelling of the word blo-o-o-o-w. What does this signal to someone performing the monologue? Use text evidence in your response.

6. "The Children's Crusade," by Jenny Lyn Bader, contains the lengthy hyphenated phrase "you'd-let-me-take-the-bus-by-myself-next-time-if-I-just-got-off-at-the-right-stop." What does this unusual punctuation signal to someone performing the monologue, and what does it tell the performer about the character's approach to the situation? Use text evidence in your response.

7. With your discussion group, read and analyze your assigned monologue to determine the audience and purpose. Write a description of the persona in the monologue.

8. How is the persona of the speaker revealed through the speech?

9. In preparation for a group discussion of the monologue, examine the monologue to determine which words you should emphasize in your oral interpretation. Make sure you consider how the punctuation affects the meaning and tone. Look up the pronunciation and syllabication of words as needed.

10. Circle words and phrases that give clues to the persona of the speaker. Label those circles with adjectives describing that persona ("kind," "angry," "successful," "intelligent," and so on).

11. Mark the text to indicate effective **volume**, **rate** (speed), **pitch** (high or low), **inflection** (emphasis on specific words for effect), and **tone** (speaker's attitude toward the subject) throughout the monologue. Remember: these elements should shift if the ideas or speaker shifts.

12. Also mark the text to indicate appropriate **eye contact**, **facial expressions**, and **movement**. These elements should support your **tone**.

13. **Pantomime** and props help the audience determine meaning during a presentation; both support the oral and physical delivery. Brainstorm creative yet simple ideas and record your ideas next to specific sections in the monologue.

14. Hold a group discussion about the monologue. Take turns presenting your ideas, drawing on your notes in the text. Listen carefully to what other group members think about the persona of the speaker and how the monologue should be presented. Ask questions to clarify your understanding and offer comments that build on others' ideas. Consider their perspectives and adjust your own ideas as necessary.

15. Then define the roles of group members by dividing the lines of the monologue equally between group members in preparation for your oral interpretation. Incorporate a choral reading to emphasize certain lines.

LITERARY

Pantomime is a form of acting without words, using motions, gestures, and expressions to convey emotions or situations. It is a way of communicating without speaking.

VOCABULARY

My Notes

Introducing the Strategy: Choral Reading

With choral reading, a group reads a word, phrase, or line aloud while others listen. Members of the group may read the text aloud together or independently by rotating lines as part of presenting an interpretation of a text. Using this strategy, readers create different voices and emphasize words and lines to reflect interpretations. Choral reading is a strategy that helps a reader practice reading a text to develop fluency with the words.

16. Notice the stage directions in your monologue (the text in italics). How will your group follow these directions to deliver the monologue? What additional stage directions will you use? Write them beside your lines.

17. Rehearse your presentation with your group. Remember: when you are delivering a monologue from someone else's perspective, you are adopting a persona, which means you should imagine that you are that person. As you rehearse:

   * Read your lines several times to become familiar with them so you can deliver the lines fluently.
   * Practice delivering your lines multiple times, using a different volume, rate, pitch, inflection, and tone to see what works best, and then choose and mark what you will use for your presentation.
   * Practice using eye contact, facial expressions, and movement appropriate for your lines.

During Presentations

18. When it is your turn, deliver your oral interpretation of the monologue. Remember to deliver your lines with expression.

19. As you listen to others' presentations, make notes about the ideas, structure, and use of language that helped you understand their interpretations.

After Presentations

20. Reflect on the preparation process and your presentation:

   a. Are you satisfied with your presentation? Explain.

   b. What helped you plan and prepare your presentation? Did anything interfere with your planning and preparation? Explain.

   c. How did your presentation skills improve? What do you still need to work on?

   d. What are your goals for next time?

21. Revisit your *monologue* word map and add another layer of information and examples relating to successful dramatic monologues.

Gaining Perspectives

In several of the monologues that you read, the speakers are worried about a situation. They seem to be experiencing stress and frustration. Too much stress can make a person physically ill. It can weaken the immune system. Imagine you are friends with the speaker in one of the monologues. What advice would you give him or her? What kind of communication skills could you to use help him or her reduce stress? How would you explain the risks of being too stressed? What communication skills might help the speaker work through the situation he or she is in? Share your ideas with a partner. Together, role play the conversation you would have. When you are done, summarize the outcome of the discussion in your Reader/Writer Notebook.

LANGUAGE & WRITER'S CRAFT: Varying Syntax for Effect

Syntax refers to how words and phrases are arranged to create well-formed sentences. Writers should use varying sentence structures to signal different relationships among ideas and keep their audience interested. Using too many of the same kind of sentence can make ideas seem choppy, uninteresting, or confusing.

A **simple sentence** is made up of just one **independent clause**—a clause that has a subject and a verb and expresses a complete thought. Simple sentences can be used to slow the pace of the writing or to emphasize certain ideas. A simple sentence may be very short or not so short.

> **Examples:** I feel personally responsible for the death of thousands of trees!
> I got it.

A **compound sentence** has two independent clauses and no dependent clauses. Connecting two independent clauses in one sentence can help show the relationship between the ideas or can make the writing flow better. The two clauses should be connected with a comma plus a coordinating conjunction (*and, or,* etc.) or with a semicolon.

> **Example:** Sure, it didn't turn out too well for most of them, but ... it was a whole war.

A **complex sentence** has one independent clause and at least one **dependent clause**—a word group that has a subject and a verb but does not express a complete thought on its own. Complex sentences are good for showing relationships between ideas. In the following example, the dependent clause is "because I'm going to fail my first middle school exam."

> **Example:** I visualize myself getting grounded til Christmas because I'm going to fail my first middle school exam.

Sentence fragments are incomplete sentences punctuated as though they were complete sentences. Skilled writers sometimes use sentence fragments intentionally to reinforce ideas or convey emotion.

INDEPENDENT READING LINK

Read and Connect
Select a passage from your independent reading book that contains a similarity to something you have experienced in your own life. Analyze how that passage and your experience could be transformed into a monologue that you could perform as an oral interpretation. Document your ideas in your Reader/Writer Notebook.

My Notes

Example: I'll mail it. *Better idea!* I'll e-mail it!

Another writing tool that can be used for effect is **parallel structure**—the use of the same pattern of words for ideas that have the same level of importance. Parallel structure helps create rhythm, clarity, and emphasis.

Example: I have all these words I'm not allowed to say, books I'm not allowed to read, movies I'm not allowed to see...

One other way writers can better express their meaning is by avoiding **redundancy.** Redundancy occurs when a writer uses more words than necessary in a sentence—words that could be eliminated without the sentence losing its meaning.

Redundant: The students in the English class will review the notes they took during English class and write their papers based on the notes they took.

The preceding example would be less wordy if it were rewritten as follows: *The students in English class will use their notes to write their papers.*

PRACTICE In your Reader/Writer Notebook, rewrite the following sentences to make them more concise by choosing precise words and eliminating redundancy.

- The summer I remember most clearly stands out the most because of how fun I remember it being.
- I spent most of my time out back with friends from my block and the next block building a clubhouse behind my family's garage almost every day.

Then review your answers for Step 20. Identify places where you can use the sentence structures discussed previously. Look for places where you have wording that is redundant.

✏️ Narrative Writing Prompt

Most people have vivid memories associated with their elementary and middle school experience. Draft a monologue about a dramatic school experience. Be sure to:

- Use diction, syntax, and punctuation to create a persona and a dramatic effect.
- Vary the length and complexity of your sentence structure (syntax) for effect.
- Watch out for dangling and misplaced modifiers.
- Carefully sequence the narrative that you are retelling.
- Include specific details to develop your narrative.

Analyzing and Responding to Narrative Poetry

Learning Targets

- Describe the structures and features of narrative poetry.
- Explain a writer's use of language and literary elements in a narrative poem.

Preview

In this activity, you will analyze and describe the structures, language, and literary elements in a narrative poem.

1. Name five things you know about narratives (Unit 1).

2. Name three things you know about poetry.

3. Make one prediction about what a narrative poem is.

Prose versus Poetry

Prose is writing that is not in poetic form, such as essays, stories, articles, and letters. Ideas are written in sentences and organized by paragraphs. Language (i.e., diction, syntax, and rhetorical devices) is used for effect.

Verse is poetry. Ideas are usually written in lines, and lines are organized by *stanzas* (a group of lines, usually similar in length and pattern). Poetry contains language that appeals to the reader's emotions or imagination, and it can take several forms. For example, in *free verse* poetry, the writer uses lines that do not have a regular *rhyme scheme* (i.e., a pattern for rhyming, such as ending lines with similar sounding words).

Narrative poetry tells a story in verse. Narrative poems usually contain the same elements as short stories, such as setting, characters, conflict, and plot. Like a short story, a narrative poem has a beginning, middle, and end. Writing narrative poetry is similar to writing narrative prose in that you consider the purpose of your poem (your story), your audience, and the language you want to use to communicate your story and paint a mental image for the reader.

4. Poets use **poetic devices**, including figurative language, to express ideas and create meaning. In your group, create, present, and post Word Wall cards for your assigned figurative language and poetic device. As other groups present, complete the Interpretation column.

My Notes

LITERARY VOCABULARY

Verse is a synonym for *poetry*, and **prose** could be considered an antonym of *poetry*.
Poetic devices are poetic techniques used for effect. These devices include personification, metaphor, simile, and more.

Literary Element	Definition	Example from a Published Poet	Interpretation
Metaphor	a figure of speech that makes a comparison between two unlike things in which one thing becomes another		
Personification	a kind of metaphor that gives human characteristics or qualities to objects or abstract ideas		
Simile	a figure of speech that makes a comparison between two unlike things using the words *like* or *as*		
Symbol	any object, person, place, or action that has both a literal and a figurative meaning and represents a larger concept or idea		
Hyperbole	extreme exaggeration used for dramatic or humorous effect		
Imagery	word pictures created by descriptive, sensory, or figurative language		

Poetic Musical Device	Definition	Example from a Published Poet	Interpretation
Refrain	a regularly repeated word, phrase, line, or group of lines in a poem or song, usually at the end of a stanza or between stanzas		
Rhythm	the pattern of stressed and unstressed syllables in a poem		
Onomatopoeia	the use of words that imitate the sounds of what they describe, such as *buzz, bang,* or *crash*		

Setting a Purpose for Reading

- As you read the poem, underline words and phrases that create a mood. Mark words or phrases that you find new or appealing.
- Circle unknown words and phrases. Try to determine the meaning of the words by using context clues, word parts, or a dictionary.

My Notes

About the Author

Edgar Allan Poe (1809–1849) was a writer who is best known for his chilling and suspenseful tales of horror. "The Raven" (1845) gave Poe his first major success as a writer. Poe's purpose for writing this poem was simple. He wanted to show his readers a mind filled with "fantastic terrors."

Poetry

The Raven

by **Edgar Allan Poe**

Once upon a midnight dreary, while I pondered, weak and weary,
Over many a quaint and curious volume of forgotten lore—
While I nodded, nearly napping, suddenly there came a tapping,
As of someone gently rapping, rapping at my chamber door—
5 "'Tis some visitor," I muttered, "tapping at my chamber door—
    Only this and nothing more."

Ah, distinctly I remember it was in the bleak December;
And each separate dying ember **wrought** its ghost upon the floor.
Eagerly I wished the morrow;—vainly I had sought to borrow
10 From my books surcease of sorrow—sorrow for the lost Lenore—
For the rare and radiant maiden whom the angels name Lenore—
    Nameless here for evermore.

And the silken, sad, uncertain rustling of each purple curtain
Thrilled me—filled me with fantastic terrors never felt before;
15 So that now, to still the beating of my heart, I stood repeating,
"'Tis some visitor entreating entrance at my chamber door—
Some late visitor entreating entrance at my chamber door;—
    This it is and nothing more."

Presently my soul grew stronger; hesitating then no longer,
20 "Sir," said I, "or Madam, truly your forgiveness I **implore**;
But the fact is I was napping, and so gently you came rapping,
And so faintly you came tapping, tapping at my chamber door,
That I scarce was sure I heard you"—here I opened wide the door;—
    Darkness there and nothing more.

wrought: formed
implore: beg

25 Deep into that darkness peering, long I stood there wondering, fearing,
Doubting, dreaming dreams no mortal ever dared to dream before;
But the silence was unbroken, and the stillness gave no token,
And the only word there spoken was the whispered word, "Lenore?"
This I whispered, and an echo murmured back the word, "Lenore!"—
30 　　Merely this and nothing more.

Back into the chamber turning, all my soul within me burning,
Soon again I heard a tapping somewhat louder than before.
"Surely," said I, "surely that is something at my window lattice;
Let me see, then, what thereat is, and this mystery explore—
35 Let my heart be still a moment and this mystery explore;—
　　'Tis the wind and nothing more!"

Open here I flung the shutter, when, with many a flirt and flutter,
In there stepped a stately Raven of the saintly days of yore;
Not the least **obeisance** made he; not a minute stopped or stayed he;
40 But, with mien of lord or lady, perched above my chamber door—
Perched upon a bust of Pallas[1] just above my chamber door—
　　Perched, and sat, and nothing more.

Then this ebony bird beguiling my sad fancy into smiling,
By the grave and stern decorum of the **countenance** it wore,
45 "Though thy crest be shorn and shaven, thou," I said, "art sure no **craven**,
Ghastly grim and ancient Raven wandering from the Nightly shore—
Tell me what thy lordly name is on the Night's Plutonian[2] shore!"
　　Quoth the Raven "Nevermore."

Much I marvelled this ungainly fowl to hear discourse so plainly,
50 Though its answer little meaning—little relevancy bore;
For we cannot help agreeing that no living human being
Ever yet was blest with seeing bird above his chamber door—
Bird or beast upon the sculptured bust above his chamber door,
　　With such name as "Nevermore."

55 But the Raven, sitting lonely on the placid bust, spoke only
That one word, as if his soul in that one word he did outpour.
Nothing further then he uttered—not a feather then he fluttered—
Till I scarcely more than muttered "Other friends have flown before—
On the morrow he will leave me, as my hopes have flown before."
60 　　Then the bird said "Nevermore."

---

[1] **bust of Pallas:** a statue of Pallas Athena, Greek goddess of wisdom
[2] **Plutonian:** of Pluto or the dark underworld

obeisance: respectful gesture
countenance: face
craven: coward

My Notes

Startled at the stillness broken by reply so aptly spoken,
"Doubtless," said I, "what it utters is its only stock and store
Caught from some unhappy master whom unmerciful Disaster
Followed fast and followed faster till his songs one burden bore—
65   Till the dirges of his Hope that melancholy burden bore
     Of 'Never—nevermore.'"

But the Raven still beguiling my sad fancy into smiling,
Straight I wheeled a cushioned seat in front of bird, and bust and door;
Then, upon the velvet sinking, I betook myself to linking
70   Fancy unto fancy, thinking what this ominous bird of yore—
  What this grim, ungainly, ghastly, gaunt and ominous bird of yore
     Meant in croaking "Nevermore."

This I sat engaged in guessing, but no syllable expressing
To the fowl whose fiery eyes now burned into my bosom's core;
75   This and more I sat **divining**, with my head at ease reclining
On the cushion's velvet lining that the lamp-light gloated o'er,
But whose velvet violet lining with the lamp-light gloating o'er,
     She shall press, ah, nevermore!

Then, methought, the air grew denser, perfumed from an unseen censer[3]
80   Swung by Seraphim[4] whose foot-falls tinkled on the tufted floor.
"Wretch," I cried, "thy God hath lent thee—by these angels he hath sent thee
Respite—respite and nepenthe,[5] from thy memories of Lenore;
Quaff, oh quaff this kind nepenthe and forget this lost Lenore!"
     Quoth the Raven "Nevermore."

85   "Prophet!" said I, "thing of evil!—prophet still, if bird or devil!—
Whether Tempter sent, or whether tempest tossed thee here ashore,
Desolate yet all undaunted, on this desert land enchanted—
On this home by Horror haunted—tell me truly, I implore—

Is there—is there balm in Gilead?[6]—tell me—tell me, I implore!"
90   Quoth the Raven "Nevermore."

---

divining: discovering

[3] **censer:** a container for burning incense
[4] **Seraphim:** angels
[5] **nepenthe:** a remedy to make one forget grief
[6] **balm in Gilead:** a soothing ointment; Gilead is in Israel

"Prophet!" said I, "thing of evil—prophet still, if bird or devil!
By that Heaven that bends above us—by that God we both adore—
Tell this soul with sorrow laden if, within the distant Aidenn,[7]
It shall clasp a sainted maiden whom the angels name Lenore—
95 Clasp a rare and radiant maiden whom the angels name Lenore."
      Quoth the Raven "Nevermore."

"Be that word our sign in parting, bird or fiend!" I shrieked, upstarting—
"Get thee back into the tempest and the Night's Plutonian shore!
Leave no black plume as a token of that lie thy soul hath spoken!
100 Leave my loneliness unbroken!—quit the bust above my door!
Take thy beak from out my heart, and take thy form from off my door!"
      Quoth the Raven "Nevermore."

And the Raven, never flitting, still is sitting, still is sitting
On the pallid bust of Pallas just above my chamber door;
105 And his eyes have all the seeming of a demon's that is dreaming,
And the lamp-light o'er him streaming throws his shadow on the floor;
And my soul from out that shadow that lies floating on the floor
      Shall be lifted—nevermore!

Making Observations

- What emotions do you feel while reading this poem?
- What images do you find most striking?
- What do you notice about the language of this poem?

My Notes

---

[7] **Aidenn:** Muslim paradise, Eden

Returning to the Text

- Return to the text as you respond to the following questions. Use text evidence to support your responses.
- Write any additional questions you have about the poem in your Reader/Writer Notebook.

5. How does the speaker describe his mood in lines 7–12 of the poem? What can you infer about the cause of his mood?

_____

_____

_____

_____

6. What synonyms could you use in place of *rare* and *radiant* in line 11 of the poem? What connotations do "rare" and "radiant" have that other synonyms do not? Why might Poe have chosen these words?

_____

_____

_____

_____

7. What is the speaker's attitude toward the raven when it first enters the room? Use text evidence to support your answer.

_____

_____

_____

_____

8. How does the speaker interpret "Nevermore" the first time the raven says it? Use text evidence to support your answer.

_____

_____

_____

_____

9. What do lines 58–59 suggest about the speaker's recent life? What inference does this support about the speaker's mood?

_____

_____

_____

_____

10. Highlight the adjectives in lines 19–54. How do Poe's word choices add to the atmosphere and mood of the poem?

_____

_____

_____

11. What is the speaker saying in lines 85–86?

_____

_____

_____

12. What words in lines 79–84 indicate that the narrator is becoming more and more upset or agitated?

_____

_____

_____

_____

13. How does the speaker interpret "Nevermore" in line 95? How is this different from the way he first interpreted "Nevermore"?

_____

_____

_____

_____

Working from the Text

14. In one or two sentences, summarize the story of "The Raven," being sure to maintain meaning and logical order.

15. What is the dominant image of this poem? How does Poe use language and imagery to create a dark and eerie tone?

VOCABULARY

LITERARY

With **internal rhyme**, a word within the line rhymes with a word at the end of the line. For example, in the line, "Once upon a midnight dreary, while I pondered weak and weary," the words *dreary* and *weary* have internal rhyme.

16. You already know about end rhyme, the most common form of rhyme. In "The Raven," Poe also makes use of **internal rhyme**. What examples of internal rhyme do you see in the first two stanzas?

17. How does the poem's structure or organization contribute to its meaning? Use evidence from the poem.

18. How does Poe use other poetic devices to develop the poem? Provide specific examples.

19. Read back through the poem and find one example each of metaphor, hyperbole, personification, and symbolism. Record each example in your Reader/Writer Notebook, including the language, its line number, and your interpretation of the effect the language creates.

	Example	Interpretation
Metaphor		
Hyperbole		
Personification		
Symbolism		

☑ Focus on the Sentence

Use the words listed to write complete sentences about "The Raven."

when/repetition

_____

_____

because/internal rhyme

_____

_____

_____

✍ Writing to Sources: Informational Text

Based on your analysis of the poem, write a paragraph that explains the purpose and effect of "The Raven." Be sure to:

- Use the summary you wrote.
- Include your understanding of the central image.
- Discuss one or two poetic devices Poe uses for effect.
- Use evidence from the poem.

Language Checkpoint: Using Prepositions

Learning Targets

- Identify prepositions and prepositional phrases that are commonly used in English.
- Understand the function of prepositions and prepositional phrases and how they influence subject-verb agreement.
- Edit sentences for proper use of prepositions and prepositional phrases.

Preview

In this activity, you will learn how prepositions and prepositional phrases are used in writing to establish relationships between different things. Then you will practice editing your own writing, as well as that of your peers, to make sure you use prepositions and prepositional phrases correctly.

Identifying Prepositions

A preposition is one of the most common types of words used in the English language. Common prepositions include *above, below, to, before, after, with, for, on, in, under, at, by,* and *from*. A preposition's job is to indicate the relationship between different things. (*Where* are they? *How* are they? *When* are they?) Prepositions help writers add detail and communicate clearly.

1. Circle the prepositions in the following lines from "The Raven." There may be more than one in a line. Then write what relationship the preposition shows.

   Example: I remember it was in the bleak December. (*When* was it?)

   a. And so faintly you came tapping, tapping at my chamber door,

   b. Nameless here for evermore.

   c. Startled at the stillness broken by reply so aptly spoken, at and by

Identifying Prepositional Phrases

A prepositional phrase consists of a preposition, the object of the preposition, and any modifiers of the object.

Here are some examples of prepositional phrases (in **bold**):

   My cousin went **to the haunted house**.

   He arrived **at home** just **in time** to close the windows and dim the lights.

2. Circle the prepositional phrases in the following lines from "The Raven."

   a. but, with mien of lord or lady, perched above my chamber door

   b. Ghastly grim and ancient Raven wandering from the Nightly shore

Practice with Prepositions

3. In the sentences that follow, fill in each blank with a common preposition that could start the prepositional phrase. There may be more than one correct option from the list. Then highlight the prepositional phrase you create.

a. The raven flew _____ the house during the storm.

b. The medicine was combined _____ water so that it could be drunk.

c. The fish remained _____ the water to avoid the raven circling _____ the lake.

d. The lights _____ the pier went out before the storm even hit the shore.

Prepositions and Subject-Verb Agreement

Proper writing has clear subject-verb agreement. Singular nouns need singular verbs, and plural nouns need plural verbs. For example: *The raven squawks* or *The ravens squawk*.

Prepositional phrases that come between a subject and its verb usually do not change the subject-verb agreement. For example: *A flock of ravens circles the neighborhood*. In this sentence, "a flock" is the subject, and it is singular. "Circles" is the verb, and it is also singular. "Of ravens" is the prepositional phrase, so even though "ravens" is plural, it does not change the verb.

4. Complete the following sentences by writing the correct form of the verb on the line.

a. The men in the story (goes/go) _____ crazy with fear.

b. The storms off the coast (is coming/are coming) _____ ashore.

c. His house in the mountains (is/are) _____ very, very spooky.

d. The terrifying black raven near their homes (scares/scare) _____ them all.

Common Prepositions
above
below
before
after
under
over
to
with
for
on
off
in
at
by

Editing

Read the following paragraph about "The Raven." Many of the sentences have prepositional phrases, and some of them have errors. Some problems relate to the preposition used, and others relate to subject-verb agreement. Highlight the prepositional phrases, find the errors, and provide corrections.

"The Raven" by Edgar Allan Poe is a spooky poem about a man, the speaker of the poem, who is being tormented by terror. The descriptions in the poem are very creepy. Things in the man's house is described with words like "bleak," "silence," and "grave." Poe writes that each of the dying embers in the fire are like a ghost. The raven that perches in the man's door seems stern, ghastly, grim, and ominous. Readers of this terrifying, classic poem is sure to walk away with a spooky feeling.

☑ Check Your Understanding

Add an item to your Editor's Checklist to help you avoid making errors when you use prepositional phrases.

Practice

Return to the piece of writing you completed at the end of Activity 4.5. Reread your draft, keeping a close eye on your use of prepositions and prepositional phrases. Make sure you are using the appropriate prepositions. Also check for correct subject-verb agreement when a prepositional phrase comes between subject and verb.

Learning Targets

- Analyze a narrative poem's structure, language, and effect.
- Transform a narrative into a monologue and deliver it as an effective oral presentation.

Preview

In this activity, you will read a **parody** of a classic story and think about how the author transformed the tale.

Setting a Purpose for Reading

- As you read the poem, underline words and phrases that create a comic effect.
- Circle unknown words and phrases. Try to determine the meaning of the words by using context clues, word parts, or a dictionary.

About the Author

Roald Dahl (1916–1990) is best known for his mischievous children's stories, such as *James and the Giant Peach* and *Charlie and the Chocolate Factory*. His stories usually unfold with unexpected events and endings, and they often depict a kind child who triumphs over an adult villain. Dahl also wrote screenplays and works for adults.

Learning Strategies

Marking the Text
Note-taking
Drafting
Discussion Groups
Sharing and Responding
Brainstorming
Rehearsal

LITERARY

A **parody** is a literary or artistic work that imitates the characteristic style of an author or a work for comic effect or ridicule. A parody can be a written work, a song, or a film.

VOCABULARY

My Notes

Poetry

Little Red Riding Hood and the Wolf

by **Roald Dahl**

As soon as Wolf began to feel
That he would like a decent meal,
He went and knocked on Grandma's door.
When Grandma opened it, she saw

5   The sharp white teeth, the horrid grin,
And Wolfie said, "May I come in?"
Poor Grandmamma was terrified,
"He's going to eat me up!" she cried.
And she was absolutely right.

10   He ate her up in one big bite.
But Grandmamma was small and tough,
And Wolfie wailed, "That's not enough!

My Notes

I haven't yet begun to feel
That I have had a decent meal!"

15 He ran around the kitchen yelping,
"I've *got* to have a second helping!"
Then added with a frightful **leer**,
"I'm therefore going to wait right here
Till Little Miss Red Riding Hood

20 Comes home from walking in the wood."
He quickly put on Grandma's clothes,
(Of course he hadn't eaten those).
He dressed himself in coat and hat.
He put on shoes, and after that

25 He even brushed and curled his hair,
Then sat himself in Grandma's chair.
In came the little girl in red.
She stopped. She stared. And then she said,
"What great big ears you have, Grandma."

30 "All the better to hear you with," the Wolf replied.
"What great big eyes you have, Grandma,"
said Little Red Riding Hood.
"All the better to see you with," the Wolf replied.
He sat there watching her and smiled.

35 He thought, I'm going to eat this child.
Compared with her old Grandmamma
She's going to taste like caviar.
Then Little Red Riding Hood said, "But Grandma,
what a lovely great big furry coat you have on."

40 "That's wrong!" cried Wolf. "Have you forgot
To tell me what BIG TEETH I've got?
Ah well, no matter what you say,
I'm going to eat you anyway."
The small girl smiles. One eyelid flickers.

45 She whips a pistol from her knickers.
She aims it at the creature's head
And *bang bang bang*, she shoots him dead.
A few weeks later, in the wood,
I came across Miss Riding Hood.

50 But what a change! No cloak of red,
No silly hood upon her head.
She said, "Hello, and do please note
My lovely furry wolfskin coat."

leer: sly look

Making Observations
- What emotions did you feel as you read this poem?
- What details from this poem stand out to you?

Returning to the Text
- Return to the text as you respond to the following questions. Use text evidence to support your responses.
- Write any additional questions you have about the poem in your Reader/Writer Notebook.

1. What descriptive details does Dahl use in the poem "Little Red Riding Hood and the Wolf" that create a comic effect?

_____

_____

_____

_____

2. What words in the text of the poem tell you what the wolf is like? What do you expect Little Red Riding Hood to be like?

_____

_____

_____

_____

3. What effect do the rhyme scheme and meter in lines 29–33 have on the poem?

_____

_____

_____

_____

4. What is Little Red Riding Hood like in this version of the story? How can you tell?

_____

_____

_____

_____

☑ Check Your Understanding
As you read the poem, think about how you could deliver it as a monologue. Which parts could you emphasize for comic effect? Which parts could you emphasize for dramatic effect? Highlight these sections in the poem.

Working from the Text

5. With your discussion group, reread the poem. Mark the text by highlighting and labeling each element of language listed in the graphic organizer that follows. Be prepared to explain how Dahl uses language for effect throughout the narrative poem.

Element of Language	Effect
Sensory Language	
Poetic Devices, Including Figurative Language	
Variety of Syntax	
Dialogue and Diction	

6. Think about the ideas and organization Dahl uses.

   • How does Dahl use the narrative technique of dialogue to develop the comic effect of the story? Find examples in the text.

   • How does Dahl develop and contrast the points of view of different characters?

- Think about the traditional version of the story of Little Red Riding Hood. How does Dahl organize his narrative so that it imitates the original?

- How does Dahl organize his narrative so that it is different from the original?

📝 Narrative Writing Prompt

With a partner, transform the story into a monologue that represents just one particular character's point of view (the Wolf, Grandma, Red Riding Hood). Be sure to:

- Use monologue structure, genre characteristics, and features.
- Use Roald Dahl's language and tone to guide your transformation.

Performing Your Monologue

7. Once you have written your monologue, prepare to perform it as an oral interpretation.

   - Mark the text to indicate effective volume, rate (speed), pitch (high or low), inflection (emphasis on specific words for effect), and tone (speaker's attitude toward the subject) throughout the monologue. Remember: these elements should shift if the ideas or speaker shifts.

   - Mark the text to indicate appropriate eye contact, facial expressions, and movement. These elements should support your tone.

   - Brainstorm creative yet simple ideas for pantomime and props, recording your ideas next to appropriate sections in the monologue.

   - Divide the lines equally and rehearse your presentation with your partner. Remember: when you are delivering a monologue from someone else's point of view, you are adopting a persona. Become that person!

   - Rehearse.
     - Practice adapting your speech for a comedic task rather than a formal and serious one.
     - Practice delivering your lines fluently.
     - Practice delivering your lines with an effective volume, rate, pitch, inflection, and tone.
     - Practice using eye contact, facial expressions, and movement appropriate for your lines.

   - With your partner, deliver your presentation of the monologue.

   - As part of the audience, listen to other students' presentations. Use the Scoring Guide Criteria to compare and contrast the most effective elements of a presentation.

After Presentation

8. Reflect on the process and product.

a. Explain how satisfied you are with your presentation.

b. What helped you plan and prepare your presentation? Did anything interfere with your planning and preparation? Explain.

c. How did your presentation skills improve? What do you still need to work on?

d. What are your goals for next time?

Sharing Feedback

9. Use the following sentence frames to give feedback to your classmates' presentations.

I like how you _____.

The best part of your presentation was when _____.

I was really impressed when you _____.

If I had reviewed your presentation first, I would have _____.

I did not quite understand it when _____.

One thing you could do to improve would be to _____.

10. Revisit your monologue word map and add another layer of information and examples relating to successful monologues. For the personal monologue you will create for Embedded Assessment 1, add information and examples relating to heroes and/or villains that you have encountered in your life. Be sure to identify a specific emotion associated with each idea.

INDEPENDENT READING LINK

Read and Connect

Transform a chunk of text from your independent reading book into a monologue. Use your Reader/Writer Notebook to record your monologue. Include notes about elements that would help you deliver your monologue, including pitch, inflection, and tone.

Using Language to Develop Theme

- Analyze a narrative poem for effective writing.
- Compare and contrast a poem and an informational passage on the same topic.
- Write a monologue from the point of view of a character from a narrative poem.
- Integrate ideas from multiple texts to build knowledge and vocabulary about highwaymen.

Preview

In this activity, you will read and compare an informational text and a poem about highwaymen.

Setting a Purpose for Reading

- As you read the text, mark the key ideas and supporting details about highwaymen.
- Circle unknown words and phrases. Try to determine the meaning of the words by using context clues, word parts, or a dictionary.

Informational Text

The Highwaymen of Hounslow Heath

1   Once part of the extensive Forest of Middlesex, and now largely buried beneath the runways of London Airport, Hounslow Heath was for more than 200 years the most dangerous place in Britain. Between the 17th and early 19th centuries, the Heath occupied perhaps 25 square miles. No one was really certain where its boundaries lay, and no one cared, for it was a tract of country to be crossed as quickly as possible. Though Hounslow itself was not large, it was after London the most important of coaching centres. Across the Heath ran the Bath Road and the Exeter Road, along which travelled wealthy visitors to West Country resorts and courtiers travelling to Windsor. All provided rich pickings for highwaymen lurking in copses bordering the lonely ways.

2   The first of the legendary highwaymen were Royalist officers who "took to the road" when they were outlawed under the Commonwealth. These were men familiar with the relatively newfangled pistols, which gave them an advantage over their victims, usually only armed with swords.

Learning Strategies

Summarizing
Marking the Text
Rereading
Close Reading
RAFT
Drafting

 **KNOWLEDGE QUEST**

Knowledge Question:

Why did popular culture celebrate highwaymen as heroes?

In Activity 4.7, you will read an informational text about highwaymen in the 17th through early 19th centuries and a narrative poem about a highwayman. While you read and build knowledge about highwaymen, think about your answer to the Knowledge Question.

WORD CONNECTIONS

Etymology

The word **newfangled** comes from *new* and the obsolete word *fangol*, "inclined to take." The original word was used to describe people who were drawn to new things or ideas. Over time it came to be used for the new things themselves, with the meaning "recently invented, of the newest style."

My Notes

3   Perhaps because they concentrated on the wealthy, the highwaymen became popular heroes. No one, except the victims, grieved when the dukes of Northumberland and St Albans were held up on the Heath at the end of the 17th century. And when one **audacious** villain pasted notices on the doors of rich Londoners telling them they should not venture forth with less than a watch and 10 guineas, the whole town was convulsed with laughter.

Famous Highwaymen on the Heath

4   While many of the highwaymen were thugs pure and simple, it cannot be denied that some of them had a certain flair. There was Twysden, Bishop of Raphoe, who was shot and killed while carrying out a robbery on the Heath—though it was later given out that he had died of "an inflammation." Others returned money to needy victims and released women and children unmolested, including the children of the Prince of Wales, held up at Hounslow in 1741. There are even accounts of robberies in which the victim is referred to as "a man" and the robber as "a gentleman."

5   To be robbed by a famous highwayman was regarded as something of an honor. When James Maclaine accidentally wounded Horace Walpole while attempting to rob him, the **antiquarian** bore no grudge and wrote to tell him so. In June 1750, Maclaine also held up Lord Eglington, taking 50 guineas and his lordship's blunderbuss[1]. Dick Turpin is credited with having stayed in most old pubs in the Hounslow area, but in fact he mostly confined his activities to Essex, North London, and Yorkshire. The most gallant of the Heath's highwaymen was probably the French-born Claude Duval, who danced with a beautiful victim on the Heath and let her wealthy husband go for £100.

The Highwayman by Eyles, Derek Charles (1902–74).

audacious: bold, daring
antiquarian: collector

[1] **blunderbuss:** an old-fashioned gun with a short barrel and a wide muzzle

Working from the Text

1. Briefly summarize the main ideas of the text.

2. In an era when the term *gentleman* indicated a member of the upper class, highwaymen were sometimes called "gentlemen of the roads." Write a paragraph explaining how they came to be seen as more than common thieves and how realistic this view was. Support your ideas with information from the text.

Setting a Purpose for Reading

- As you read the poem, place brackets around words that describe the highwayman.
- Circle unknown words and phrases. Try to determine the meaning of the words by using context clues, word parts, or a dictionary.

About the Author

English poet Alfred Noyes (1880–1958) wrote more than five volumes of poetry, many of them long narrative poems or epic poems. He is best known for "The Highwayman" and *Drake*, a 200-page epic. Noyes published his first volume of poetry at age 21. His poetry was clearly influenced by Romantic poets such as Wordsworth and Tennyson. Noyes spent time in the United States as a professor of literature at Princeton University from 1914 to 1923, and he also lived in Canada and the United States during World War II. He returned to Great Britain in 1949.

KNOWLEDGE QUEST

Knowledge Question:

Why did popular culture celebrate highwaymen as heroes?

Poetry

The Highwayman

by **Alfred Noyes**

Part One

The wind was a torrent of darkness upon the gusty trees,   a
The moon was a ghostly galleon² tossed upon cloudy seas,   a
The road was a ribbon of moonlight looping the purple moor,   b
And the highwayman came riding—   c
5   Riding—riding—   c
The highwayman came riding, up to the old inn door.   b

He'd a French cocked hat on his forehead, a bunch of lace at his chin;
A coat of the **claret** velvet, and breeches of fine doe-skin.
They fitted with never a wrinkle. His boots were up to the thigh.
10 And he rode with a jeweled twinkle,
        His pistol butts a-twinkle,
His rapier³ hilt a-twinkle, under the jeweled sky.

Over the cobbles he clattered and clashed in the dark inn-yard.
He tapped with his whip on the shutters, but all was locked and barred.
15 He whistled a tune to the window, and who should be waiting there
But the landlord's black-eyed daughter,
        Bess, the landlord's daughter,
Plaiting a dark red love-knot into her long black hair.

And dark in the dark old inn-yard a stable-wicket creaked
20 Where Tim the ostler listened. His face was white and peaked.
His eyes were hollows of madness, his hair like mouldy hay,
But he loved the landlord's daughter,
        The landlord's red-lipped daughter.
Dumb as a dog he listened, and he heard the robber say—

25 "One kiss, my bonny sweetheart, I'm after a prize tonight,
But I shall be back with the yellow gold before the morning light.
Yet if they press me sharply, and harry⁴ me through the day,
Then look for me by moonlight,
        Watch for me by moonlight,

claret: deep red

² **galleon:** a sailing ship used from the 15th to 17th centuries
³ **rapier:** a thin sword with a very sharp tip
³ **harry:** to carry out attacks on someone

30 I'll come to thee by moonlight, though hell should bar the way."

He rose upright in the stirrups. He scarce could reach her hand,

But she loosened her hair in the casement. His face burnt like a brand

As the black cascade of perfume came tumbling over his breast;

And he kissed its waves in the moonlight,

35   (O, sweet, black waves in the moonlight!)

Then he tugged at his rein in the moonlight, and galloped away to the west.

Part Two

He did not come in the dawning. He did not come at noon;

And out of the tawny sunset, before the rise of the moon,

When the road was a gypsy's ribbon, looping the purple moor,

40 A red-coat troop came marching—

      Marching—marching—

King George's men came marching, up to the old inn-door.

They said no word to the landlord. They drank his ale instead.

But they gagged his daughter, and bound her, to the foot of her narrow bed.

45 Two of them knelt at her casement, with muskets at their side!

There was death at every window;

      And hell at one dark window;

For Bess could see, through her casement, the road that he would ride.

They had tied her up to attention, with many a sniggering jest,

50 They had bound a musket beside her, with the barrel beneath her breast!

"Now, keep good watch!" and they kissed her. She heard the doomed man say—

Look for me by moonlight;

      Watch for me by moonlight;

I'll come to thee by moonlight, though hell should bar the way!

55 She twisted her hands behind her; but all the knots held good!

She writhed her hands till her fingers were wet with sweat or blood!

They stretched and strained in the darkness, and the hours crawled by like years,

Till, now, on the stroke of midnight,

      Cold, on the stroke of midnight,

60 The tip of one finger touched it! The trigger at least was hers!

The tip of one finger touched it. She strove no more for the rest.

Up, she stood up to attention, with the muzzle beneath her breast.

She would not risk their hearing, she would not strive again;

For the road lay bare in the moonlight;

65   Blank and bare in the moonlight;
And the blood in her veins, in the moonlight, throbbed to her love's refrain.
Tlot-tlot; tlot-tlot! Had they heard it? The horsehoofs, ringing clear;
Tlot-tlot, tlot-tlot, in the distance? Were they deaf that they did not hear?
Down the ribbon of moonlight, over the brow of the hill,
70 The highwayman came riding—
      Riding—riding—
The red-coats looked to their priming[5]! She stood up, straight and still.

Tlot-tlot, in the frosty silence! *Tlot-tlot,* in the echoing night!
Nearer he came and nearer. Her face was like a light.
75 Her eyes grew wide for a moment; she drew one last deep breath,
Then her finger moved in the moonlight,
      Her musket shattered the moonlight,
Shattered her breast in the moonlight and warned him—with her death.

He turned. He spurred to the west; he did not know who stood
80 Bowed, with her head o'er the musket, drenched with her own blood!
Not till the dawn he heard it, and his face grew grey to hear
How Bess, the landlord's daughter,
      The landlord's black-eyed daughter,
Had watched for her love in the moonlight, and died in the darkness there.

85 Back, he spurred like a madman, shouting a curse to the sky,
With the white road smoking behind him and his rapier brandished high.
Blood-red were his spurs in the golden noon; wine-red was his velvet coat;
When they shot him down on the highway,
      Down like a dog on the highway,
90 And he lay in his blood on the highway, with a bunch of lace at his throat.

And still of a winter's night, they say, when the wind is in the trees,
When the moon is a ghostly galleon tossed upon cloudy seas,
When the road is a ribbon of moonlight over the purple moor,
A highwayman comes riding—
95   *Riding—riding—*
A highwayman comes riding, up to the old inn-door.

Over the cobbles he clatters and clangs in the dark inn-yard.
He taps with his whip on the shutters, but all is locked and barred.
He whistles a tune to the window, and who should be waiting there
100 *But the landlord's black-eyed daughter,*

---

[5] **priming:** preparing a gun for firing

Bess, the landlord's daughter,
Plaiting a dark red love-knot into her long black hair.

⊘ Knowledge Quest
- What are your first thoughts about the poem?
- What feelings about the highwayman do you have as you read the poem?

Returning to the Text
- Return to the text as you respond to the following questions. Use text evidence to support your responses.
- Write any additional questions you have about the poem in your Reader/Writer Notebook.

3. KQ Why would highwaymen be portrayed as heroes when they were, in fact, robbers?

_____

_____

_____

_____

4. KQ What does the poet mean by the phrase "a torrent of darkness"?

_____

_____

_____

5. Lines 7–12 give a detailed description of the highwayman's clothes. Does this description compare to the idea of the noble highwayman discussed in the informational text? How does it compare to the historical reality of highwaymen? Use text examples to support your answer.

_____

_____

_____

_____

6. Did the soldiers just happen to come to the inn, or did they somehow have information about the highwayman's movements? Support your answer with evidence from the text.

_____

_____

_____

_____

7. Identify and interpret examples of alliteration and onomatopoeia in "The Highwayman," explaining how each example impacts the poem.

_____

_____

_____

_____

8. Stanzas 16 and 17 are almost the same as stanzas 1 and 3. How are they alike and different? What does this communicate to the reader?

_____

_____

_____

_____

 INDEPENDENT READING LINK

You can continue to build your knowledge about highwaymen by reading other articles at ZINC Reading Labs. Search for keywords such as *highwayman* or *heroes*.

 ZINC

 Knowledge Quest

Use your knowledge of the informational text and the poem to consider the history of highwaymen and the way popular culture depicted them. Write a paragraph that responds to the question: Why did popular culture celebrate highwaymen as heroes? Be sure to:

• Include a clear statement of your opinion.
• Provide reasons and explanations to support your opinion.
• Cite evidence from the text to support your ideas.

Working from the Text

9. How does the information from the text "The Highwaymen of Hounslow Heath" help you understand the poem "The Highwayman"?

10. By the time Alfred Noyes wrote "The Highwayman," these thieves no longer existed. Does the poet use a realistic or a romanticized version of this figure from English history? Compare and contrast the historical character with the fictional character.

☑ Focus on the Sentence

Reread lines 37–51 of the poem "The Highwayman." Choose one character from the poem and write four different types of sentences from the point of view of that character.

Statement: _____

_____

Question: _____

_____

clamation: _____

_____

Command: _____

_____

Introducing the Strategy: RAFT

RAFT is a strategy that is primarily used to create new texts by manipulating elements of a text during prewriting and drafting. This strategy helps you create or substitute various roles, audiences, formats, and topics as a way to focus your thinking about a new text.

Role: What is your perspective?	Audience: Who is the target audience for this text?	Format: What is the best format to capture your ideas?	Topic: What is the topic?
1. Bess, the landlord's daughter 2. the highwayman 3. Tim the ostler 4. a redcoat	• your father, the landlord • the general public • yourself • your commanding officer	• monologue	• to describe what you saw, heard, felt, and did as events unfolded, and why you acted as you did

Narrative Writing Prompt

Your teacher will assign you a role. Use the RAFT strategy to create a monologue from the point of view of one of the characters from "The Highwayman." Imagine what he or she might say about the events of the story as it is. You do not have to write a rhyming poem.
Be sure to:

- Review the elements of monologues to decide what to include.
- Use diction, syntax, and punctuation to create a persona and a dramatic effect.
- Vary the length and complexity of your sentence structure (syntax) for effect.
- Carefully sequence the narrative you are retelling.

 Independent Reading Checkpoint

Pick one character from your independent reading and write a text from that character's point of view. Choose a genre or format that is appropriate.

Creating and Presenting a Monologue

 ASSIGNMENT

Your assignment is to write and present a monologue about a topic that sparks a strong emotion (e.g., amusement, regret, disappointment, excitement, joy, sadness, contentment, or anger). You may choose to speak as yourself, or you may adopt a persona.

Planning and Prewriting: Take time to make a plan for your monologue.	■ How will you use your notes from your Reader/Writer Notebook and the activities in this unit to generate ideas? ■ How can you use prewriting strategies (such as RAFT or a web) to organize your ideas? ■ What tone would be appropriate, and should it shift or remain constant?
Drafting and Revising: Write and revise your monologue in the proper structure and format.	■ How will you use your understanding of narrative techniques to be sure that your monologue has a strong beginning, middle, and end? ■ How will you use diction, syntax, and devices effectively for your purpose, audience, and tone? ■ How can you effectively share and respond in your discussion group, and how will you use the feedback?
Rehearsing: Plan and rehearse the performance with your partner and others.	■ How will you mark your monologue to indicate key aspects of your oral and physical delivery? ■ How can you enhance your monologue with a costume and/or prop? ■ How can the Scoring Guide help you evaluate how well your own and your peers' presentations meet the requirements of the assignment?
Presenting and Listening: Present your monologue and take notes on your classmates' performances.	■ How will you use pantomime, eye contact, facial expressions, and movement to engage your audience? ■ How will you evaluate and compare/contrast presentations using the Scoring Guide criteria?

Reflection

After completing this Embedded Assessment, think about how you went about accomplishing this task and respond to the following:

- How have your writing and speaking skills improved during this unit?
- You observed many other monologues. If you were to do this assessment again, what would you do differently?

SCORING GUIDE

Scoring Criteria	Exemplary	Proficient	Emerging	Incomplete
Ideas	The presenter • uses narrative techniques skillfully and smoothly weaves details into the story to create interest and develop a believable persona • uses clever props, facial expressions, and movement to create meaning for the audience • shows excellent oral delivery with volume, rate, pitch, and inflection that add to the interpretation.	The presenter • uses narrative techniques and details to create interest and develop a persona • uses appropriate props, delivery techniques, facial expressions, and/or movement to aid audience understanding and engagement • delivers fluently with appropriate volume, rate, pitch, and inflection.	The presenter • follows only some narrative techniques and provides few details to develop a persona • uses some props and/or movement to aid audience understanding • delivers with little expression or change in volume, rate, pitch, and inflection.	The presenter • follows few narrative techniques and provides few or no details to develop a persona • uses no props and/or movement to aid audience understanding • delivers with little expression or change in volume, rate, pitch, and inflection.
Structure	The monologue • engages and orients the audience with a creative hook that sets the tone and establishes context and point of view • follows a careful sequence and provides a clever ending • uses transitions smoothly to convey sequence and signal shifts.	The monologue • engages and orients the audience with a hook that establishes context and point of view • follows a logical sequence and provides a conclusive ending • uses a variety of transitions to convey sequence and signal shifts.	The monologue • attempts to create a hook but does not clearly establish a context or point of view • does not follow a logical sequence and/or provide a conclusive end • includes few transitions.	The monologue • begins without a hook to establish a context and point of view for the audience • is disorganized and difficult to follow • includes no transitions.
Use of Language	The monologue • uses specific language to communicate tone • creates imagery with figurative language and sensory details • uses multiple sentence types • cleverly uses literary devices and punctuation for meaning, reader interest, and style.	The monologue • creates tone with language used for effect • creates imagery with figurative language and sensory details • uses a variety of sentence types • uses literary devices and punctuation for meaning, reader interest, and style.	The monologue • attempts to create tone, but it is not clear • uses some figurative language and sensory details • uses few sentence types • uses few literary devices or punctuation to aid meaning, reader interest, and style.	The monologue • does not use effective language to create tone • uses little figurative language or sensory details • uses few sentence types • uses few or no literary devices or punctuation to aid meaning, reader interest, and style.

Unpacking Embedded Assessment 2

Learning Targets

- Analyze the skills needed to be successful on Embedded Assessment 2.
- Identify the components of a successful performance.

Preview

In this activity, you will begin to explore oral presentations.

Making Connections

In the first part of this unit, you performed several monologues and oral interpretations. Along the way, you learned various techniques and devices that authors employ when they use language for effect. In this part of the unit, you will focus on analyzing a Shakespearean play, *Twelfth Night*, as you prepare for a performance of a dramatic dialogue.

Essential Questions

1. Now that you have studied how writers and poets use language and have completed several oral interpretations yourself, reflect on your current understanding of the first Essential Question: How do writers and speakers use language for effect? How has your understanding of language changed over the course of this unit?

2. What did you learn in the first half of the unit that might cause you to adjust your answer to the second Essential Question: How do performers communicate meaning to an audience?

Developing Vocabulary

Use the QHT strategy to re-sort the vocabulary you have studied in the first part of this unit. Compare this sort with your original sort. How has your understanding changed? Select a word from the chart and write about your understanding of it.

Unpacking Embedded Assessment 2

Closely read the assignment for Embedded Assessment 2.

Your assignment is to work collaboratively with a partner to plan, rehearse, and perform a dialogue from William Shakespeare's *Twelfth Night*.

Write down five things you believe you will need to know in order to complete this assignment successfully. Then work with your class to paraphrase the expectations in the Scoring Guide and create a graphic organizer to use as a visual reminder of the required concepts (what you need to know) and skills (what you need to do). Copy the graphic organizer for future reference.

After each activity in this part of the unit, use the graphic you have created to guide reflection about what you have learned and what you still need to learn in order to be successful on the Embedded Assessment.

My Notes

INDEPENDENT READING LINK

Reading Plan

To support your learning in the second half of the unit, choose a drama or selection of monologues to read. Ask your teacher or librarian for suggestions. Use your Reader/ Writer Notebook to create a reading plan and respond to any questions, comments, or reactions you might have to your reading.

WORD CONNECTIONS

Cognates

The noun **mask** means "something worn to cover the face" or "a pretense to hide true feelings or character." The verb *mask* means "cover with a mask" or "hide, conceal." The adjective *masked* means "wearing a mask; hidden." These English words come from the same root as the Spanish words *una máscara, enmascarar,* and *enmascarado.*

My Notes

guile: deception
myriad: numerous, countless

Learning Targets

• Analyze the elements of a poem.
• Analyze how symbols and imagery convey tone.

Preview

In this activity, you will read a poem and think about symbols and imagery. Then you will use symbols and imagery to create a visual interpretation of a text.

Setting a Purpose for Reading

• As you read the poem, put an exclamation point next to words and phrases that have strong emotions. Underline any words or phrases that are repeated in the poem.
• Circle unknown words and phrases. Try to determine the meaning of the words by using context clues, word parts, or a dictionary.

About the Author

The son of former slaves, Paul Laurence Dunbar (1872–1906) had his poetry published in the *Dayton Herald* at age 14. Dunbar was unable to attend college for financial reasons, and he took a job as an elevator operator. He self-published his first book, *Oak and Ivy*, and sold it for a dollar to people riding his elevator. He eventually became the first African American writer to earn his living solely by writing poetry and fiction. He was also the first to gain a national audience of mostly white readers.

Poetry

We Wear the Mask

by **Paul Laurence Dunbar**

> We wear the mask that grins and lies,
> It hides our cheeks and shades our eyes—
> This debt we pay to human **guile**;
> With torn and bleeding hearts we smile,
> 5 And mouth with **myriad** subtleties.
>
> Why should the world be over-wise,
> In counting all our tears and sighs?
> Nay, let them only see us, while
> We wear the mask.

10 We smile, but, O great Christ, our cries
      To thee from tortured souls arise.
      We sing, but oh the clay is vile
      Beneath our feet, and long the mile;
      But let the world dream otherwise,
15 We wear the mask!

Making Observations
- Which words jump out to you?
- What images stick with you?

Returning to the Text

- Return to the text as you respond to the following questions. Use text evidence to support your responses.
- Write any additional questions you have about the poem in your Reader/Writer Notebook.

1. Reread the About the Author text and then reread the poem. How does the poet's personal history help you understand the message of the poem further?

_____

_____

_____

_____

2. Identify an example of alliteration in "We Wear the Mask." Then explain the effect it has on the poem.

_____

_____

_____

_____

3. How does stanza 2 relate to stanza 1? How does stanza 3 relate to stanza 2? What effect do these relationships have on the meaning of the poem as a whole?

_____

_____

_____

_____

4. Summarize "We Wear the Mask."

_____

_____

_____

_____

☑ Focus on the Sentence

Write complete, correct sentences using the words given.

though/suffering

_____

_____

because/mask

_____

Working from the Text

5. Return to the poem and take notes in the margin as you work with your class to apply the SIFT strategy. Identify symbols, imagery, figurative language, tone, and theme.

6. Select a line from one of the readings in the unit or from your independent reading. Create a mask with symbols and imagery to convey the tone of the quote. Include colors and other details that you associate with the emotion or attitude of your chosen quote.

7. Memorize the quote. While wearing your mask, present the quote to your peers. As you observe and listen to other students, try to guess the tone of each mask.

8. Reflect: Could you identify the tone of each mask? Did the mask change how you interpreted the different quotes?

Improvisation

Learning Targets

- Analyze plot elements and character in a text.
- Create mental images to deepen understanding of a text or character.

Preview

In this activity, you will explore character through improvisation and role-playing.

VOCABULARY

ACADEMIC

When you **improvise**, you perform with little or no preparation and usually without a script.

Improvisation means that you are inventing as you perform.

1. The plot of *Twelfth Night* centers on a character who masks her true identity and pretends to be something that she is not. Think of other examples from real life, literature, or film, and brainstorm reasons why someone would disguise his or her true identity.

2. In *Twelfth Night*, Viola is a young woman who disguises herself as a man. Predict why she might have done this and what difficulties might arise from her decision.

My Notes

3. Read one of the plot summaries that follow Step 4 and work with a partner to **improvise**, role-playing the scene. Practice your improvisation several times before presenting it to a group of your peers. Be sure to:

- Say the characters' real names frequently in your presentation: "Hey, *Viola*, do you think ..." "Sure, *Olivia*, but ..."
- Include specific details from the plot summary.
- Use pantomime and gestures to enhance your performance.

4. After each of your peers' performances, ask questions to clarify what happened in the scene and which characters were involved. Take notes under each plot summary to describe the performance and record memorable details.

Twelfth Night Plot Summaries for Role-Play

A. Viola and **the captain** are washed up onshore after a shipwreck. Viola is worried about her twin brother (Sebastian), who was lost at sea. The captain tells her that they have landed in Illyria, a land ruled by Duke Orsino. Viola decides to dress up as a man to go work for Orsino.

Performance Notes:

B. Duke Orsino is talking to his servant **Cesario** (who is really a young woman named Viola in disguise). Orsino tells Cesario about his love for a woman (Olivia) who will not date him. Orsino wants Cesario to convince Olivia to go out with him. Cesario doesn't want to but agrees anyway.

Performance Notes:

C. Olivia meets **Cesario** (who is really a young woman named Viola in disguise). Cesario is trying to convince Olivia to date his boss, Duke Orsino. Unfortunately, Olivia has no interest in Duke Orsino and actually starts flirting with Cesario, which makes Cesario uncomfortable.

Performance Notes:

D. Duke Orsino complains to **Cesario**, his servant, about Olivia—the woman he loves. (Cesario is really a young woman named Viola who is in love with Duke Orsino.) Cesario tries to convince Orsino to try other women, but Orsino says no woman can truly love. Cesario disagrees.

Performance Notes:

My Notes

E. Olivia decides she is in love with **Cesario** (who is really a young woman named Viola—in disguise). Cesario tries to hint that he is not really the man Olivia thinks he is and tries to convince Olivia to give her boss (Duke Orsino) a chance. Olivia keeps flirting with Cesario.

Performance Notes:

F. Sebastian meets **Olivia** in the streets of Illyria. Olivia immediately declares her love for Sebastian, thinking that he is Cesario (Sebastian's twin sister Viola in disguise). Sebastian is confused but feels pretty lucky that this beautiful, rich woman wants him, so he marries her.

Performance Notes:

Creating Visual Representations

5. Use what you learned from the role-plays to create a visual representation of *Twelfth Night*. You may want to explore the key events in a plot diagram (see Unit 1) or create a graphic organizer that represents the characters' relationships to one another. Use technology to find online sources of both images and text. Use your notes and the plot summaries as guides. Arrange your visual representation in a publishing program. Cite your sources. Decide whether you will print your representation or display it digitally.

As you view the visual representations created by your class, discuss which ones are the most effective at helping you understand the plot and characters. What makes them effective?

☑ Focus on the Sentence

Pick one character from *Twelfth Night* and write two statements and two questions about the character. Draw details from your classmates' plot summary improvisations.

Statement 1: _____

_____

Statement 2: _____

_____

Question 1: _____

_____

Question 2: _____

_____

Analyzing and Delivering a Shakespearean Monologue

Learning Targets

- Demonstrate knowledge of literary genres by comparing and contrasting the written text of a drama with the performance of it.
- Deliver a choral reading of a Shakespearean monologue with appropriate register, vocabulary, tone, and voice.
- Integrate ideas from multiple texts to build knowledge and vocabulary about William Shakespeare.

Preview

In this activity, you will read a monologue and then analyze a performance of the same monologue.

Setting a Purpose for Reading

- As you read the informational text, mark facts about William Shakespeare's life.
- Circle unknown words and phrases. Try to determine the meaning of the words by using context clues, word parts, or a dictionary.

About the Author

Little is known about the early life of William Shakespeare (1564–1616) except that he was born and grew up in Stratford-upon-Avon, England. Shakespeare moved to London to become an actor, playwright, and poet. He wrote 37 plays (comedies, tragedies, and histories) and 154 sonnets (poems). Shakespeare is considered one of the world's greatest dramatists, and his plays continue to be performed in theaters around the world.

My Notes

Informational Text

William Shakespeare

by **The Shakespeare Globe Trust**

1   William Shakespeare is world famous. We know quite a lot about him but there is still much that remains a mystery. We don't know his date of birth. We don't know the date of his marriage. We even have very little idea of what he looked like. So what DO we know about William Shakespeare, the man?

⊘ Knowledge Quest

Knowledge Question:

What can we learn about William Shakespeare from his life and work?

In Activity 4.11, you will read an informational text about William Shakespeare and a monologue from one of his most popular plays. While you read and build knowledge about William Shakespeare, think about your answer to the Knowledge Question.

When and where was Shakespeare born?

2   William Shakespeare was born in 1564 in Stratford-upon-Avon, a market town in a farming area of the Midlands. About 1000 people lived there. Shakespeare was baptised on 26th April 1564, but we don't know his exact date of birth.

What was Shakespeare's family like?

3   William was born to prosperous parents. His mother, Mary, was the daughter of a local farmer. His father, John, was a glove-maker and wool trader with a large family house. When William was four years old, his father was elected Bailiff of Stratford – effectively the mayor.

4   But his early life wasn't easy. Although William was the third of eight children, he grew up as the oldest. His two older sisters both died very young. And William was lucky to survive. When he was just a baby, in 1564, **plague** killed about 200 people in Stratford – 1 in 5 of the population. Fortunately, William survived.

Where did Shakespeare go to school?

5   From the age of seven, boys like William went to **grammar school**. There was one in Stratford and it is still there today. But schooling was different then. The boys learned to read, speak and write in Latin. They also had to memorise and perform stories from history – useful skills for an actor and writer. Shakespeare probably left school aged fifteen.

When did Shakespeare marry?

6   In late 1582, we don't know the exact date, Shakespeare married Anne Hathaway – a local farmer's daughter. William was only 18 years old. Most men at this time married in their mid- to late-20s. So why did William marry so young? The answer came six months later, when William's daughter, Susanna, was baptised.

What do we know of Shakespeare's family life?

7   The answer is ... practically nothing. We know William and Anne had two more children, Hamnet and Judith, twins, born in 1585. Anne and the three children probably lived with William's parents at first. Later, they moved to New Place, a large house in Stratford. But it was a strange family life. Shakespeare spent most of his time 100 miles away, in London.

What did Shakespeare do in London?

8   From about 1590 to 1613, Shakespeare lived mainly in London and by 1592 was a well-known actor there. He was also a playwright. His play, Henry VI, was performed at the Rose theatre in 1592. He went on to write, or cowrite, about 40 plays. Shakespeare was also a poet and in 1609 published a book of 154 sonnets.

plague: a highly contagious disease

grammar school: school to learn Latin

In 2017, actors and actresses performed the Shakespearean play *Twelfth Night* in the Globe Theatre in London. This is an image from the theatrical performers' photo-call.

9 And Shakespeare was a businessman too. He was a sharer (part-owner) of a theatre company called The Lord Chamberlain's Men. And from 1599, he was part-owner of the Globe Theatre.

10 So, for about twenty years, he made money from acting, writing and running a theatre company.

William Shakespeare became part owner of the Globe Theatre, which was destroyed when a theatrical cannon misfired during a performance. It was rebuilt the next year.

When did Shakespeare die?

11 After 1613, Shakespeare spent more time at Stratford. Then, in January 1616, he made a will and died on 23rd April 1616. He is buried in Holy Trinity church in Stratford-upon-Avon.

Shakespeare's Signature

12 We have six surviving versions of Shakespeare's signature. They are all different. He wrote:

- Willm Shakp
- Wm Shakspe
- Willm Shakspere
- William Shaksper
- Willm Shakspere
- William Shakespere
- and William Shakespeare.

The last version, taken from his will in 1616 is the version we use today.

⊘ Knowledge Quest

- What questions do you have about William Shakespeare?
- Which part of the text stands out to you? Why?

Returning to the Text

- Return to the text as you respond to the following questions. Use text evidence to support your responses.
- Write any additional questions you have about the informational text in your Reader/Writer Notebook.

1. KQ How do you think people learned about these events in William Shakespeare's life?

2. What reason does the text give to support the idea that William Shakespeare's family life was strange?

3. What details can you infer about what William Shakespeare's life must have been like from the images of the Globe Theatre?

4. KQ What does the word surviving mean in the context of the text in paragraph 12?

Setting a Purpose for Reading

- As you read the monologue, underline words and phrases that indicate how the speaker feels.
- Circle unknown words and phrases. Try to determine the meaning of the words by using context clues, word parts, or a dictionary.

KNOWLEDGE QUEST

Knowledge Question:
What can we learn about William Shakespeare from his life and work?

My Notes

Drama

Monologue from

Twelfth Night

by **William Shakespeare**

Duke Orsino:

If music be the food of love, play on;
Give me excess of it, that, **surfeiting**,
The appetite may sicken, and so die.
That strain again, it had a dying fall:

5 O, it came o'er my ear like the sweet sound,
That breathes upon a bank of violets,
Stealing and giving odor! Enough; no more:
'Tis not so sweet now as it was before.
O spirit of love, how quick and fresh art thou,

10 That, notwithstanding thy capacity
Receiveth as the sea, nought enters there,
Of what validity and pitch soe'er,
But falls into abatement and low price,
Even in a minute: so full of shapes is fancy

15 That it alone is high fantastical.

Knowledge Quest

- What emotions do you feel while reading this monologue?
- What imagery could you picture in your mind?

Returning to the Text

- Return to the text as you respond to the following questions. Use text evidence to support your responses.
- Write any additional questions you have about the monologue in your Reader/Writer Notebook.

5. Paraphrase the monologue in modern English.

_____

_____

_____

surfeiting: overindulging

6. In which lines does the tone shift in the monologue?

_____

_____

_____

7. KQ Use context to determine the meaning of *fancy* at the end of line 14. How can this description also be applied to the play itself?

_____

_____

_____

8. KQ What does this monologue, combined with the information from the previous text, reveal about William Shakespeare?

_____

_____

_____

_____

9. How do each of the stanzas relate to each other and build on the monologue's meaning?

_____

_____

_____

_____

_____

⊘ Knowledge Quest

Use your knowledge from "William Shakespeare" and the monologue from *Twelfth Night* to discuss with a partner what you have learned about William Shakespeare. Be sure to:

- Explain your answer to your partner, be specific and use as many details from the two texts as possible.

- When your partner responds, ask for clarification by posing follow-up questions as needed.

After the discussion, add what you learned to a class list and display it.

INDEPENDENT READING LINK

You can continue to build your knowledge about William Shakespeare by reading other articles at ZINC Reading Labs. Search for the keyword *Shakespeare*.

 ZINC

Working from the Text

10. Play the following drama game with a small group or with a partner: Choose a simple question, such as "What are you doing?" and a response such as "Nothing important." Sitting in a circle, have one student ask the question in a happy tone of voice and the student to the left respond in a happy tone. Then have the responder repeat the question in a different tone. Keep moving clockwise around the circle until you run out of different emotions.

11. Describe the tone you would expect in a monologue by a man who is in love with a woman who refuses to see him.

12. Work with a partner or small group to summarize how the speaker feels about love.

13. Listen to an actor performing the monologue, taking notes on the actor's vocal delivery. This includes the speaker's tone, pitch, volume, rate (or speed) of speech, pauses, and emphasis.

14. Compare your observations of the audio version with your analysis of the written monologue. How does the actor's performance affect your understanding of the meaning of the monologue? Use specific examples from your response to item 6.

15. Plan and rehearse a choral reading of the monologue. Include some of the following vocal and visual delivery techniques to enhance the monologue:

    - Read some lines as a group, some with a partner, and some alone.
    - Use pantomime and gestures to enhance visual delivery.
    - Deliver lines fluently with appropriate vocal delivery.

16. While observing several choral readings, take notes on the different interpretations.

Vocal Delivery: Tone, Pitch, Volume, Rate, Pauses, Emphasis	Visual Delivery: Gestures, Movement, Facial Expressions

17. Look at your notes from the graphic organizer and think about which vocal and visual delivery techniques were most effective. Why were they effective? Which ones might you use in an oral presentation?

☑ Check Your Understanding

Think back to the monologues presented in the first part of the unit and the choral reading of the scene from Shakespeare. How were they different, and how were they alike? What visual and vocal techniques did you observe, and how were they effective in communicating meaning to an audience?

Acting for Understanding

Paraphrasing
Marking the Text
Oral Reading
Rereading
Discussion Groups
Rehearsal

Learning Targets

- Use evidence from the text to support understanding.
- Paraphrase a text in a way that maintains meaning and order.

Preview

In this activity, you will read a **dialogue** and think about how the characters interact.

Setting a Purpose for Reading

- As you read the dialogue, underline lines that tell you what the characters have seen or heard and put a star next to lines that hint at what might happen next.
- Circle unknown words and phrases. Try to determine the meaning of the words by using context clues, word parts, or a dictionary.

VOCABULARY

LITERARY
A **dialogue** is a conversation between two characters in a play. The word *dialogue* can also be used to describe conversations between two characters in other types of media, such as television, film, or novels.

Drama

from

Twelfth Night,

Act 1, Scene 2

by **William Shakespeare**

My Notes

Viola: What country, friends, is this?

Captain: This is Illyria, lady.

Viola: And what should I do in Illyria?

My brother he is in Elysium.

5 Perchance he is not drown'd: what think you, sailors?

Captain: To comfort you with chance,

Assure yourself, after our ship did split,

I saw your brother bind himself

To a strong mast that lived upon the sea.

10 **Viola:** For saying so, there's gold:

Know'st thou this country?
Captain: Ay, madam, well; for I was bred and born

Not three hours' travel from this very place.
Viola: Who governs here?

15 **Captain:** A noble duke, in nature as in name.

My Notes

Viola: What is the name?

Captain: Orsino.

Viola: Orsino! I have heard my father name him:

He was a bachelor then.

20 **Captain:** And so is now, or was so very late;

For but a month ago I went from hence,

And then 'twas fresh in murmur

That he did seek the love of fair Olivia.

Viola: I prithee, and I'll pay thee bounteously,

25 Conceal me what I am, and be my aid

For such disguise as haply shall become

The form of my intent. I'll serve this duke.

Captain: Be you his servant, and your mute I'll be:

When my tongue blabs, then let mine eyes not see.

30 **Viola:** I thank thee: lead me on.

Making Observations
- What details do you notice in this dialogue?
- What characters do we meet in the scene?

☑ Focus on the Sentence

Read the short sentences that follow. Then expand the sentences by providing more details as prompted by the questions.

He may have survived the wreck.

Who? _____

How? _____

Expanded Sentence: _____

_____

Viola wants to work for Duke Orsino.

Where? _____

How? _____

Expanded Sentence: _____

_____

Returning to the Text

- Return to the text as you respond to the following questions. Use text evidence to support your responses.

- Write any additional questions you have about the drama in your Reader/Writer Notebook.

1. *Elysium* in Greek mythology refers to a heavenly afterlife. What does Viola think happened to her brother?

_____

_____

_____

_____

2. What do you think the captain means by "'twas fresh in murmur" that Orsino loves Olivia?

_____

_____

_____

_____

3. What does Viola mean when she says, "Conceal me what I am"? What does this tell you about what might happen next in the play?

_____

_____

_____

_____

Working from the Text

4. Interpret the dialogue and paraphrase each sentence in modern English.

5. After paraphrasing the dialogue, conduct an oral reading with a small group, reading your paraphrases first and then the original text.

6. With a partner, go back and annotate each of your character's lines with notes for vocal and visual delivery.

7. Perform the dialogue with at least three different people who prepared the other character's lines.

☑ Check Your Understanding

In a paragraph, reflect on the effectiveness of your own and other students' delivery of the dialogue. What aspects of the performances helped communicate meaning to the audience?

My Notes

Learning Targets
- Analyze the relationship between character and plot.
- Analyze how playwrights develop characters in drama.

Preview
In this activity, you will read a dialogue, rehearse it, and perform it with a partner.

Setting a Purpose for Reading
- As you read the dialogue, underline words and phrases that provide information about characters and mark details that reveal a conflict with a star.
- Circle unknown words and phrases. Try to determine the meaning of the words by using context clues, word parts, or a dictionary.

Drama

from # Twelfth Night,
Act 1, Scene 4

by **William Shakespeare**

Viola (*disguised as the servant Cesario, speaking to herself*):
If the duke continue these favours towards you,
Cesario, you are like to be much advanced: he hath
known you but three days, and already you are no stranger.
5 Here comes the count. (*Enter DUKE ORSINO*)

Duke Orsino: Who saw Cesario, ho?

Viola: On your attendance, my lord; here.

Duke Orsino: Cesario, Thou know'st no less but all; I have unclasp'd
To thee the book even of my secret soul:
10 Therefore, good youth, address thy **gait** unto her;
Be not denied access, stand at her doors,
And tell them, there thy fixed foot shall grow
Till thou have audience.

Viola: Sure, my noble lord,
15 If she be so abandon'd to her sorrow
As it is spoke, she never will admit me.

Duke Orsino: Be **clamorous** and leap all civil bounds
Rather than make unprofited return.

Viola: Say I do speak with her, my lord, what then?

gait: step
clamorous: loud, pushy

20 **Duke Orsino:** O, then unfold the passion of my love,
Surprise her with discourse of my dear faith:
It shall become thee well to act my woes;
She will attend it better in thy youth
Than in a nuncio's of more grave aspect.

25 **Viola:** I think not so, my lord.

Duke Orsino: Dear lad, believe it;
For they shall yet belie thy happy years,
That say thou art a man: Diana's lip
Is not more smooth and rubious; thy small pipe

30 Is as the maiden's organ, shrill and sound,
And all is semblative a woman's part.
I know thy constellation is right apt for this affair.

Viola: I'll do my best
To woo your lady:

35 (*Aside*) yet, a barful strife!
Whoe'er I woo, myself would be his wife.

My Notes

Drama

from # Twelfth Night,

Act 1, Scene 5

by **William Shakespeare**

Olivia (*to herself*): Give me my veil. Come, throw it o'er my face.

Viola: Are you the lady of the house?

Olivia: If I do not **usurp** myself, I am.

Viola: Most certain, if you are she, you do usurp
5 yourself; for what is yours to bestow is not yours
to reserve. I will on with my speech in your praise,
and then show you the heart of my message.

Olivia: Come to what is important in't: I forgive you the praise.

Viola: Alas, I took great pains to study it, and 'tis poetical.

10 **Olivia:** It is the more like to be **feigned**: I pray you,
if you have reason, be brief. Speak your office.

Viola: Good madam, let me see your face.

Olivia: We will draw the curtain and show you the picture.
Look you, sir, is't not well done? (*Unveiling*)

15 **Viola:** Lady, you are the cruell'st she alive,
If you will lead these graces to the grave
And leave the world no copy.

Olivia: Were you sent hither to praise me?

Viola: I see you what you are, you are too proud;
20 But, my lord and master loves you.

Olivia: Your lord does know my mind; I cannot love him:
He might have took his answer long ago.
I cannot love him: let him send no more;
Unless, perchance, you come to me again.

25 **Viola:** Farewell, fair cruelty. (*Exits*)

Olivia: Thy tongue, thy face, thy limbs, actions and spirit,
Do give thee five-fold blazon. How now!
Even so quickly may one catch the plague?
Methinks I feel this youth's perfections
30 With an invisible and subtle stealth
To creep in at mine eyes. Well, let it be.

usurp: take over
feigned: insincere

Making Observations

- What surprises you most about these scenes?
- What emotions do the characters display?

Returning to the Text

- Return to the text as you respond to the following questions. Use text evidence to support your responses.
- Write any additional questions you have about the drama in your Reader/Writer Notebook.

Scene 4

1. How does Orsino's physical description of Cesario reveal that Viola's disguise is not completely successful? Provide specific examples.

   _____

   _____

   _____

   _____

2. What does Orsino mean when he says, "And tell them, there thy fixed foot shall grow / Till thou have audience"?

   _____

   _____

   _____

   _____

3. Why does Viola try to talk Orsino out of having her tell Olivia of his love? How do you know?

   _____

   _____

   _____

   _____

Scene 5

4. How do you know that Olivia doesn't want to show her face to strangers?

   _____

   _____

   _____

   _____

5. What lines in the text tell you what Viola thinks of Olivia?

_____

_____

_____

_____

6. Examine Olivia's last lines in this dialogue. What is she saying here? How does this develop her character and the plot?

_____

_____

_____

_____

Working from the Text

7. With a partner, choose one of the dialogues and then select your roles.

8. Meet with a group of students who are performing the same dialogue. Work together to diffuse the text and paraphrase the lines.

9. Divide your group in two so that you are working only with students who have the same role. Work together to annotate your scene for vocal and visual delivery.

10. Work with your group to create a visual representation of your character. Draw a stick figure or outline and annotate the image with words and other images to convey the traits of the character. You may also include words or images to indicate how the character's choices affect other characters in the play. Add significant quotes from your dialogue and any information that you have from the role-playing in Activity 4.12.

Visual Representation of My Character:

11. Meet with your original partner to rehearse your dialogue together. Perform your dialogue for at least one other group who rehearsed a different dialogue.

☑ Focus on the Sentence

Read the short sentences that follow. Then expand the sentences by providing more details as prompted by the questions.

He tells Viola.

Who? _____

What? _____

Why? _____

Expanded Sentence: _____

_____

She loves Viola.

Who? _____

Why? _____

Expanded Sentence: _____

_____

📝 Writing to Sources: Informational Text

Explain how you made choices about vocal and visual delivery to interpret your character in a performance. Be sure to:

- Identify specific character traits that your character possesses.
- Provide textual evidence of characterization: dialogue, thoughts, appearance, emotions, and actions.
- Explain how you portrayed the character in your performance.

Stage Directions

Learning Strategies

Marking the Text
Rereading
Discusasion Groups
Rehearsal
Graphic Organizer

Learning Targets

- Using a stage diagram, plan and rehearse a scene with stage movement and character interaction based on your analysis of the text.
- Analyze a dramatic scene.

Preview

In this activity, you will read and analyze a dialogue and think about how the characters interact and move.

My Notes

Setting a Purpose for Reading

- As you read the dialogue, note in the margin ideas you have about how the characters might interact with each other on stage.
- Circle unknown words and phrases. Try to determine the meaning of the words by using context clues, word parts, or a dictionary.

Drama

from # Twelfth Night,
Act 4, Scenes 1–2

by **William Shakespeare**

Olivia: Be not offended, dear Cesario. I prithee, gentle friend,
Go with me to my house. Do not deny.

Sebastian: What relish is in this? how runs the stream?
Or I am mad, or else this is a dream:
5 Let fancy still my sense in Lethe steep;
If it be thus to dream, still let me sleep!

Olivia: Nay, come, I prithee; would thou'ldst be ruled by me!

Sebastian: Madam, I will.

Olivia: O, say so, and so be!

***

10 **Sebastian:** This is the air; that is the glorious sun;
This pearl she gave me, I do feel't and see't;
And though 'tis wonder that enwraps me thus,
Yet 'tis not madness.
For though my soul disputes well with my sense,
15 That this may be some error, but no madness,
Yet doth this accident and flood of fortune
So far exceed all instance, all discourse,

That I am ready to distrust mine eyes
And wrangle with my reason that persuades me

20 To any other trust but that I am mad
Or else the lady's mad; there's something in't
That is deceivable. But here the lady comes.

Olivia: Blame not this haste of mine. If you mean well,
Now go with me and with this holy man

25 Into the chantry by: there, before him,
And underneath that **consecrated** roof,
Plight me the full assurance of your faith;
That my most jealous and too doubtful soul
May live at peace. He shall conceal it

30 Whiles you are willing it shall come to note,
What time we will our celebration keep
According to my birth. What do you say?

Sebastian: I'll follow this good man, and go with you;
And, having sworn truth, ever will be true.

35 **Olivia:** Then lead the way, good father; and heavens so shine,
That they may fairly note this act of mine!

Making Observations
- What happens in these scenes?
- What details or ideas stand out to you?

consecrated: holy
plight: promise

Returning to the Text

- Return to the text as you respond to the following questions. Use text evidence to support your responses.
- Write any additional questions you have about the drama in your Reader/Writer Notebook.

1. What are the possible explanations Sebastian comes up with for Olivia's love for him? Cite examples from the text.

_____

_____

_____

_____

2. What happens in this scene? Cite evidence from the text. How does this affect the overall development of the plot?

_____

_____

_____

_____

VOCABULARY

ACADEMIC

Diagram has many different meanings. It can be a verb and a noun; in this case, it is used to describe a kind of pictorial representation.

As a verb, it means "to draw a pictorial representation."

WORD CONNECTIONS

Etymology

The stage directions **upstage** and **downstage** come from theater history. In most modern theaters, the stage is level, but the seats are "raked," or set on an incline, so that the audience can see the stage. Early theaters took the opposite approach. The audience was on level ground but the stage itself was raked, sloping upward from front to back. When actors moved upstage, they literally walked up a slope on the stage. An actor at a higher point on the stage could draw the audience's attention away from the actors downstage. This led to the figurative meaning of *upstage*, "to divert attention, outshine someone else."

Working from the Text

3. Review the image of the stage **diagram**. Note that stage directions are always from the actors' perspective. You learned in Activity 4.4 that stage directions are the instructions to actors in a drama script. In a small group, practice using and following stage directions by taking turns playing director and calling out directions to the actors, such as "Viola, move downstage left" or "Orsino, enter stage right."

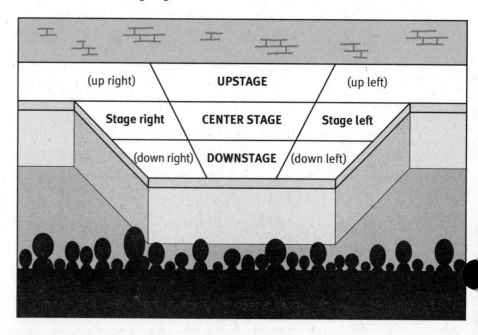

Staging Graphic Organizer:

Up Right	Upstage	Up Left
Stage Right	**Center Stage**	**Stage Left**
Down Right	**Downstage**	**Down Left**

Audience

4. Using the image of the stage diagram as a guide, work with a small group to annotate the scene with stage directions. Note that there are actually two scenes, so decide how the characters will enter and exit each scene. Sketch a plan on the graphic organizer, using arrows to indicate movement.

5. Rehearse the scene, revising the stage directions as needed. Remember to do the following:

   • Always face the audience; when two characters are having a conversation, they should stand at an angle toward the audience.

   • Use physical interactions between the characters, such as linking arms or shaking hands.

   • Respond with appropriate facial expressions and gestures while the other character is speaking.

6. Perform your scene for at least two other groups.

Sharing Feedback

As you observe your classmates' presentations, think about some suggestions you can provide. Include both positive and constructive feedback so that you can help your classmates improve. To help you frame your ideas, consider using the following sentence frames:

Positive Feedback	Constructive Feedback
"I like how you …"	"One thing that you can improve is …"
"One thing I would like to borrow from your presentation is …"	"One area that might need more information is …"
"Your staging really shows …"	"Another way you might do it is …"
"You selected great movement when …"	"You might try …"

For each presentation, provide at least one piece of positive feedback and one piece of constructive feedback.

☑ Check Your Understanding

Write a brief description of what you need to do to prepare for presenting a scene. Include the things you have learned to do to enhance a performance, such as analyzing a character, considering elements of visual and vocal delivery, and planning the staging (props, etc.).

Exploring: Theatrical Elements

Learning Targets

- Analyze the use of vocal delivery techniques.
- Analyze the use of theatrical elements in photographs and illustrations of a performance.

Preview

In this activity, you will listen to a performance of a scene and think about the actors' choices for vocal delivery. Then you will view and analyze images of staged versions of the play and think about how you would use theatrical elements to stage a scene.

Setting a Purpose for Reading

- As you read and listen to the scene, mark with a plus sign any lines where the actors increase their volume, rate, or tone. Underline details that reveal information about the characters.
- Circle unknown words and phrases. Try to determine the meaning of the words by using context clues, word parts, or a dictionary.

Drama

from

Twelfth Night,

Act 5, Scene 1

by **William Shakespeare**

Duke Orsino: Here comes the countess: now heaven walks on earth.

Olivia: What would my lord, but that he may not have,
Wherein Olivia may seem serviceable?
Cesario, you do not keep promise with me.

5 **Viola:** Madam!

Duke Orsino: Gracious Olivia—

Olivia: What do you say, Cesario? Good my lord—

Viola: My lord would speak; my duty hushes me.

Olivia: If it be aught to the old tune, my lord,
10 It is as fat and fulsome to mine ear
As howling after music.

Duke Orsino: Still so cruel?

Olivia: Still so constant, lord.

Duke Orsino: What, to perverseness? you uncivil lady,
15 What shall I do?

Olivia: Even what it please my lord, that shall become him.

My Notes

Duke Orsino: Why should I not, had I the heart to do it,
Kill what I love?
Come, boy, with me; my thoughts are ripe in mischief:
20 I'll sacrifice the lamb that I do love,
To spite a raven's heart within a dove.

Viola: And I, most jocund, apt and willingly,
To do you rest, a thousand deaths would die.

Olivia: Where goes Cesario?

25 **Viola:** After him I love
More than I love these eyes, more than my life,
More, by all mores, than e'er I shall love wife.

Olivia: Ay me, detested! how am I beguiled!

Viola: Who does beguile you? who does do you wrong?

30 **Olivia:** Hast thou forgot thyself? is it so long?
Call forth the holy father.

Duke Orsino: Come, away!

Olivia: Whither, my lord? Cesario, husband, stay.

Duke Orsino: Husband!

35 **Olivia:** Ay, husband: can he that deny?

Duke Orsino: Her husband, sirrah!

Viola: No, my lord, not I.

Olivia: Fear not, Cesario; take thy fortunes up:
A contract of eternal bond of love.

40 **Duke Orsino:** O thou **dissembling** cub!
Farewell, and take her; but direct thy feet
Where thou and I henceforth may never meet.

Viola: My lord, I do protest—

Olivia: O, do not swear!
45 Hold little faith, though thou hast too much fear. (*Enter Sebastian*)

Sebastian: Pardon me, sweet one, even for the vows
We made each other but so late ago.

Duke Orsino: One face, one voice, one habit, and two persons,
A natural perspective, that is and is not!
50 How have you made division of yourself?
An apple, cleft in two, is not more twin
Than these two creatures.

Olivia: Most wonderful!

Sebastian: Do I stand there? I never had a brother;

55 I had a sister,

dissembling: false, cheating

Whom the blind waves and surges have devour'd.
Of charity, what kin are you to me?
What countryman? what name? what parentage?

Viola: Of Messaline: Sebastian was my father;
60 Such a Sebastian was my brother too,
So went he suited to his watery tomb.

Sebastian: Were you a woman, as the rest goes even,
I should my tears let fall upon your cheek,
And say 'Thrice-welcome, drowned Viola!'

65 **Viola:** My father had a mole upon his brow.

Sebastian: And so had mine.

Viola: And died that day when Viola from her birth
Had number'd thirteen years.

Sebastian: O, that record is lively in my soul!
70 He finished indeed his mortal act
That day that made my sister thirteen years.

Viola: If nothing lets to make us happy both
But this my masculine usurp'd attire,
I'll bring you to a captain in this town,
75 Where lie my maiden weeds; by whose gentle help
I was preserved to serve this noble count.

Sebastian (*To Olivia*): So comes it, lady, you have been mistook:
You would have been contracted to a maid;
Nor are you therein, by my life, deceived,
80 You are betroth'd both to a maid and man.

Duke Orsino: Be not amazed; right noble is his blood.
If this be so, as yet the glass seems true,
I shall have share in this most happy wreck. (*To Viola*)
Boy, thou hast said to me a thousand times
85 Thou never shouldst love woman like to me.

Viola: And all those sayings will I overswear.

Duke Orsino: Give me thy hand;
And let me see thee in thy woman's weeds.

Viola: The captain that did bring me first on shore
90 Hath my maid's garments.

Duke Orsino: Your master quits you;
And since you call'd me master for so long,
Here is my hand: you shall from this time be
Your master's mistress. Cesario, come;

95 For so you shall be, while you are a man;
But when in other habits you are seen,
Orsino's mistress and his fancy's queen.

Making Observations
- What lines are the most emotional or interesting?
- What do you appreciate most about the characters?

Returning to the Text
- Return to the text as you respond to the following questions. Use text evidence to support your responses.
- Write any additional questions you have about the drama in your Reader/Writer Notebook.

1. We have seen the three characters in this triangle express their love: Olivia for Viola/Cesario, Viola for Orsino, and Orsino for Olivia. In this scene, we see how each one interacts with the non-beloved member of the triangle. What is this interaction like? Use examples from the text to illustrate your ideas.

_____

_____

_____

_____

2. How does Viola respond to Orsino's threats to kill her just to get back at Olivia? Cite examples from the text.

_____

_____

_____

_____

3. Throughout the play, mistaken identities have created confusion. What is their effect in this scene? Use examples from the text for support.

_____

_____

_____

_____

4. What lines in the text show that Olivia thinks Viola/Cesario is afraid?

_____

_____

_____

_____

5. Upon seeing someone who looks like Cesario, Orsino says, "One face, one voice, one habit, and two persons ... An apple, cleft in two, is not more twin / Than these two creatures." In this excerpt, what does *cleft* mean?

_____

_____

_____

_____

6. Give examples from the text to show how Sebastian and Viola react to finally seeing each other. Based on what you know, are they equally surprised? Explain your answer.

_____

_____

_____

_____

7. What lines in the text explain why it takes Sebastian so long to accept Viola's identity?

_____

_____

_____

_____

8. How does an instance of mistaken identity solve one of the biggest problems facing the characters? Cite evidence from the text in your answer.

_____

_____

_____

_____

9. What conclusion does the play seem to make about identity and disguise?

_____

_____

_____

_____

Working from the Text

10. Choose one line from the scene and think about how the actor in the performance chose to deliver the line. How could you change the interpretation of the character's thoughts or feelings by delivering the lines in a different way?

11. In addition to vocal delivery and stage directions, actors and directors use theatrical elements to add to their interpretation of a play. Look at the following images of different productions of *Twelfth Night* and take notes in the graphic organizer about the theatrical elements you see. What is the effect of these elements?

1903 production of *Twelfth Night*, starring Viola Allen as Viola

Anne Hathaway as Viola and Raul Esparza as Duke Orsino in the June 2009 Shakespeare in the Park performance in New York City

Twelfth Night performed in western France during the 60th edition of the Anjou Festival

Portrait of British actress Barbara Jefford in costume as Viola at the Old Vic Theatre in London on April 1, 1958

Theatrical Elements	Effect on the Play
Costumes	
Set Design/Setting	
Props	

12. Annotate the scene with ideas for how you could use theatrical elements if you were performing this scene in class. Consider the following:

   - What kinds of costumes could you create out of clothing that you already own?
   - What could you draw or collect to create a setting?
   - What props could you create or assemble?
   - What songs do you know of that capture the emotions in your scene?

13. With a partner, select one of the dialogues from the previous activities. Begin your performance plan by brainstorming and annotating the scene for theatrical elements.

☑ Check Your Understanding

What role do costumes play in *Twelfth Night*? How do the characters' costumes affect the plot? How do the actors' costumes affect the plot? Discuss your ideas with a partner. Then share them with the class.

⊕ Independent Reading Checkpoint

Throughout the second half of this unit, you have selected plays and monologues to read independently. Select a character from your independent reading and describe how the playwright developed the character through dialogue and staging.

Performing a Shakespearean Dialogue

ASSIGNMENT

Your assignment is to work collaboratively with a partner to plan, rehearse, and perform a dialogue from William Shakespeare's *Twelfth Night*.

Planning: Select and annotate one of the dialogues from *Twelfth Night*.	▪ What is the meaning of each of your character's lines? ▪ How will you use vocal delivery to express your character's thoughts and feelings? ▪ How will you use visual delivery and staging to interpret the scene and interact with your partner's character? ▪ How will you and your partner make notes and plan your performance?
Rehearsing: Memorize your lines and rehearse the performance with your partner and others.	▪ What are the "cues" in your partner's lines that will remind you of what to say? ▪ While your partner is speaking, how should your character react? ▪ How can you speak to your partner's character while both of you face the audience? ▪ How can you make the scene more understandable and interesting for your audience with facial expressions, vocal inflection, and gestures? ▪ How can you enhance your scene with at least one of the following theatrical elements: set design, masks, costumes, props, or music? ▪ How can the Scoring Guide help you evaluate how well your planned performance will meet the requirements of the assignment?
Performing and Listening: Perform your scene for an audience of your peers and take notes on your classmates' performances.	▪ Who are the characters involved? ▪ What is the dialogue about? ▪ How did the performers help you understand and appreciate the scene?
Reflecting in Writing: Write a paragraph explaining the strengths and challenges of your performance.	▪ What would you do differently in a future performance? ▪ How did performing a dialogue help you understand Shakespearean language? ▪ What were the best performances you saw, and what made them effective?

Reflection

After completing this Embedded Assessment, think about how you went about accomplishing this task and respond to the following:

- How did you feel about performing and speaking in front of others before this unit?
- How did this experience prepare you to be a confident oral presenter?

SCORING GUIDE

Scoring Criteria	Exemplary	Proficient	Emerging	Incomplete
Ideas	The performance • delivers an insightful interpretation, and meaning is cleverly communicated through tone, pauses, volume, facial expressions, movements, and gestures • includes several theatrical elements that expand meaning for the audience.	The performance • delivers an effective interpretation, and meaning is communicated through tone, pauses, volume, facial expressions, movements, and gestures • includes one or more theatrical elements.	The performance • delivers an acceptable interpretation, but meaning is not clearly communicated through tone, pauses, volume, facial expressions, movements, or gestures • includes a theatrical element, but it does not enhance the presentation.	The performance • delivers an unclear interpretation, and meaning is confused through inappropriate or inadequate tone, pauses, volume, facial expressions, movements, or gestures • includes no theatrical elements.
Structure	The performance • includes detailed scene annotations with performance notes and a creative plan for the performance • notes show excellent evidence of listening to and evaluating peer performances • reflection demonstrates insightful commentary on strengths, challenges, growth, and evaluation of performances.	The performance • includes an annotated scene with performance notes and a plan for the performance • notes show adequate evidence of listening to and evaluating peer performances • reflection demonstrates adequate commentary on strengths, challenges, growth, and evaluation of performances.	The performance • includes some scene annotations with some performance notes and elements of a plan for the performance • notes show some evidence of listening to and evaluating peer performances • reflection demonstrates little commentary on strengths, challenges, growth, and evaluation of performances.	The performance • includes few annotations and/or little planning for the performance • notes are missing or show little evidence of listening to and evaluating peer performances • reflection is missing or includes little or no commentary on strengths, challenges, growth, and evaluation of performances.
Use of Language	The performance • uses language that delivers a faithful and dramatic representation through visual and vocal delivery • effectively communicates meaning for the audience through gestures, inflection, volume, and pitch.	The performance • uses language that delivers a faithful representation with effective visual and vocal delivery • adequately communicates meaning for the audience.	The performance • includes mispronunciations, mumbled words, and/or language that does not correctly represent the scene • does not adequately communicate meaning for the audience.	The performance • does not include significant parts of the scene and/or shows unclear vocal delivery • does not communicate meaning for the audience.

Resources

Independent Reading

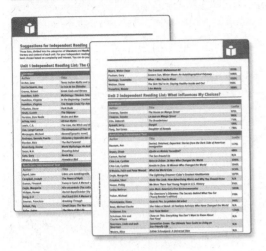

Learning Strategies

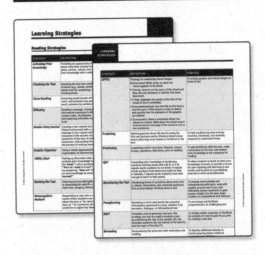

Graphic Organizers

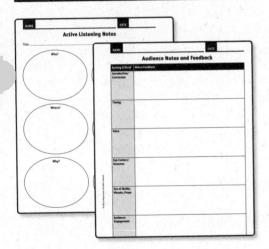

English-Spanish Glossary

Index of Skills

Index of Authors and Titles

Suggestions for Independent Reading

These lists, divided into the categories of **Literature** and **Nonfiction/Informational Text**, include titles related to the themes and content of each unit. For your independent reading, you can select from this wide array of titles, which have been chosen based on complexity and interest. You can do your own research and select titles that intrigue you.

Unit 1 Independent Reading List: The Choices We Make

Literature		
Author	**Title**	**Lexile**
Archer, Jane	*Texas Indian Myths and Legends*	N/A
Garcia-Sineriz, Ana	*La isla de los filósofos*	N/A
Graves, Robert	*Greek Gods and Heroes*	990L
Hamilton, Edith	*Mythology: Timeless Tales of Gods and Heroes*	1040L
Hamilton, Virginia	*In the Beginning: Creation Stories From Around the World*	700L
Hamilton, Virginia	*The People Could Fly: American Black Folktales*	660L
Hijuelos, Oscar	*Dark Dude*	980L
Hinds, Gareth	*The Odyssey*	840L
Hurston, Zora Neale	*Mules and Men*	1020L
Jeffrey, Gary	*African Myths*	N/A
Lewis, C.S.	*The Lion, the Witch and the Wardrobe*	940L
Lise, Lunge-Larson	*The Adventures of Thor the Thunder God*	N/A
Morpugno, Michael	*Beowolf* [graphic novel]	N/A
Restrepo, Germán Puerta	*Historias y leyendas del cielo*	1040L
Riordan, Rick	*The Red Pyramid*	650L
Rosenberg, Donna	*World Mythology: An Anthology of Great Myths and Epics*	1030L
Snzai, N.H.	*Shooting Kabul*	800L
Soto, Gary	*Novio Boy*	N/A
Whelan, Gloria	*Homeless Bird*	800L

Nonfiction/Informational Text		
Author	**Title**	**Lexile**
Agard, John	*Libro: una autobiografía.*	920L
Campbell, Joseph	*The Power of Myth*	NP
Dumas, Firoozeh	*Funny in Farsi: A Memoir of Growing Up Iranian in America*	1030L
Engle, Margarita	*Aire encantado: Dos culturas, dos alas: Una memoria*	N/A
Hickam, Homer	*Rocket Boys/October Sky*	900L
Jiang, Ji-Li	*Red Scarf Girl: A Memoir of the Cultural Revolution*	780L
Jimenez, Francisco	*Breaking Through*	750L
Kehret, Peg	*Small Steps: The Year I Got Polio*	890L
Keller, Helen	*The Story of My Life*	1150L

Nonfiction/Informational Text		
Author	Title	Lexile
Myers, Walter Dean	The Greatest: Muhammad Ali	1030L
Paulsen, Gary	Eastern Sun, Winter Moon: An Autobiographical Odyssey	1080L
Santiago, Esmeralda	When I Was Puerto Rican	1020L
Webber, Diane	The Skin You're In: Staying Healthy Inside and Out	900L
Yousafzai, Malala	I Am Malala	1000L

Unit 2 Independent Reading List: What Influences My Choices?

Literature		
Author	Title	Lexile
Ellis, Deborah	The Breadwinner	710L
Gonzales, Christina Diaz	The Red Umbrella	590L
Gonzales, Christina Diaz	La Sombrilla Roja	N/A
Spinelli, Jerry	Stargirl	590L
Yang, Dori Jones	Daughter of Xanadu	780L

Nonfiction/Informational Text		
Author	Title	Lexile
Bausum, Ann	Denied, Detained, Deported: Stories from the Dark Side of American Immigration	1170L
Brown, Dinah	¿Quién es Malala Yousafzai?	680L
Carson, Rachel	The Sea Around Us	N/A
Chin-Lee, Cynthia	Akira to Zoltan: 26 Men Who Changed the World	1060L
Chin-Lee, Cynthia	Amelia to Zora: 26 Women Who Changed the World	1040L
D'Aluisio, Faith and Peter Menzel	What the World Eats	1150L
Engle, Margarita	The Lightning Dreamer: Cuba's Greatest Abolitionists	1070L
Graydon, Shari	Made You Look: How Advertising Works and Why You Should Know	N/A
Hoose, Phillip	We Were There Too! Young People in U.S. History	950L
Lasky, Kathryn	John Muir: America's First Environmentalist	1050L
Pollan, Michael	The Omnivore's Dilemma: The Secrets Behind What You Eat (Young Reader's edition)	930L
Poniatowska, Elena	Ocatvio Paz. La palabra del arbol	940L
Ross, Michael Elsohn	She Takes a Stand: 16 Fearless Activists Who Have Changed the World	N/A
Schlosser, Eric	Fast Food Nation	1240L
Scholsser, Eric and Charles Wilson	Chew on This: Everything You Don't Want to Know About Fast Food	N/A
Sivertsen, Linda and Josh Sivertsen	Generation Green: The Ultimate Teen Guide to Living an Eco-Friendly Life	N/A
Waters, Alice	Edible Schoolyard: A Universal Idea	N/A

Unit 3 Independent Reading List: Choices and Consequences

Literature

Author	Title	Lexile
Alvarez, Julia	*Return to Sender*	890L
Coerr, Eleanor	*Sadako and the Thousand Paper Cranes*	690L
Gangsei, Jan	*Zero Day*	680L
Green, John	*Bajo la misma estrella*	N/A
Green, John	*The Fault in Our Stars*	850L
Na, An	*A Step from Heaven*	670L
Nye, Naomi Shihab	*19 Varieties of Gazelle: Poems of the Middle East*	970L
Palomas, Alejandro	*Un hijo*	N/A
Papademetriou, Lisa	*The Wizard, the Witch, and Two Girls from New Jersey*	690L
Peacock, Carol Antionette	*Red Thread Sisters*	700L
Perkins, Mitali	*Bamboo People*	680L
Sanchez, Alex	*Bait*	630L

Nonfiction/Informational Text

Author	Title	Lexile
Collier, Peter	*Choosing Courage: Inspiring True Stories of What It Means to Be a Hero*	1150L
Dakers, Diane	*Nelson Mandela: South Africa's Anti-Apartheid Revolutionary*	1100L
Douglas, Gabrielle	*Grace, Gold, and Glory: My Leap of Faith*	N/A
Douglass, Frederick	*The Narrative of the Life of Frederick Douglass*	1040L
Gandhi, Mohandas	*Autobiography: The Story of My Experiments with Truth*	1010L
Gregory, Josh	*Cesar Chavez*	930L
Herman, Gail	*Who Was Jackie Robinson?*	670L
Keller, Helen	*The Story of My Life*	1150L
King Jr., Martin Luther	*The Autobiography of Martin Luther King, Jr.*	N/A
Leighton, Ralph and Richard Feynman	*Surely You're Joking, Mr. Feynman!*	N/A
Mandela, Nelson	*Long Walk to Freedom*	1120L
McGrayne, Sharon Bertsch	*Nobel Prize Women in Science*	N/A
O'Connor, Sandra Day and H. Alan Day	*Lazy B: Growing up on a Cattle Ranch in the American Southwest*	N/A
Obama, Barack	*Dreams from My Father: A Story of Race and Inheritance*	N/A
Ottaviani, Jim	*Feynman (Graphic Novel)*	620L
Petry, Ann	*Harriet Tubman: Conductor on the Underground Railroad*	1000L
Playfoot, Janet N.	*My Life for the Poor: Mother Teresa of Calcutta*	N/A
Tavares, Matt	*Llegar a ser pedro*	870L
Vansant, Wayne	*Gettysburg: The History of America's Most Famous Battle and Turning Point*	N/A

Unit 4 Independent Reading List: How We Choose to Act

Literature

Author	Title	Lexile
Wong, Janet S.	*Suitcase of Seaweed*	N/A
Zusak, Markus	*The Book Thief*	730L

Nonfiction/Informational Text

Author	Title	Lexile
Belli, Mary Lou and Dinah Lenney	*Acting for Young Actors: Ultimate Teen Guide*	N/A
Cofer, Judith Ortiz	*Bailando en silencio*	1160L
Guerrero, Diane	*In the Country We Love: My Family Divided*	780L
Santiago, Esmerelda	*When I Was Puerto Rican*	1020L
Somervill, Barbara A.	*Actor (Cool Arts Careers)*	860L
Stanley, Diane and Peter Vennema	*Bard of Avon: The Story of William Shakespeare*	1030L
Turnbull, Stephanie	*Acting Skills*	890L

Independent Reading Log

Directions: This log is a place to record your progress and thinking about your independent reading during each unit. Add your log pages to your Reader/Writer Notebook or keep them as a separate place to record your reading insights.

Unit _____

Independent Reading Title _____

Author(s) _____ Text Type _____

Pages read: from _____ to _____

_____
_____
_____
_____
_____

Independent Reading Title _____

Author(s) _____ Text Type _____

Pages read: from _____ to _____

_____
_____
_____
_____
_____

Independent Reading Title _____

Author(s) _____ Text Type _____

Pages read: from _____ to _____

_____
_____
_____
_____
_____
_____
_____

Unit _____

Independent Reading Title _____

Author(s) _____ Text Type _____

Pages read: from _____ to _____

_____

_____

_____

_____

_____

Independent Reading Title _____

Author(s) _____ Text Type _____

Pages read: from _____ to _____

_____

_____

_____

_____

_____

Independent Reading Title _____

Author(s) _____ Text Type _____

Pages read: from _____ to _____

_____

_____

_____

_____

_____

Independent Reading Title _____

Author(s) _____ Text Type _____

Pages read: from _____ to _____

_____

_____

_____

_____

_____

Learning Strategies

Reading Strategies

STRATEGY	DEFINITION	PURPOSE
Activating Prior Knowledge	Providing an opportunity for students to think about what they already know about a concept, place, person, culture, and so on, and share their knowledge with a wider audience	To prepare students to encounter new concepts, places, persons, cultures, and so on, prior to reading a text; an Anticipation Guide and a Quickwrite can be used to activate and assess prior knowledge
Chunking the Text	Breaking the text into smaller, manageable units of sense (e.g., words, sentences, paragraphs, whole text) by numbering, separating phrases, drawing boxes	To reduce the intimidation factor when encountering long words, sentences, or whole texts; to increase comprehension of difficult or challenging text
Close Reading	Accessing small chunks of text to read, reread, mark, and annotate key passages, word-for-word, sentence-by-sentence, and line-by-line	To develop comprehensive understanding by engaging in one or more focused readings of a text
Diffusing	Reading a passage, noting unfamiliar words, discovering meaning of unfamiliar words using context clues, dictionaries, and/or thesauruses, and replacing unfamiliar words with familiar ones	To facilitate a close reading of text, the use of resources, an understanding of synonyms, and increased comprehension of text
Double-Entry Journal	Creating a two-column journal (also called Dialectical Journal) with a student-selected passage in one column and the student's response in the second column (e.g., asking questions of the text, forming personal responses, interpreting the text, reflecting on the process of making meaning of the text)	To assist in note-taking and organizing key textual elements and responses noted during reading in order to generate textual support that can be incorporated into a piece of writing at a later time
Graphic Organizer	Using a visual representation for the organization of information from the text	To facilitate increased comprehension and discussion
KWHL Chart	Setting up discussion that allows students to activate prior knowledge by answering, "What do I **know**?"; sets a purpose by answering, "What do I **want** to know?"; helps preview a task by answering, "**How** will I learn it?"; and reflects on new knowledge by answering, "What have I **learned**?"	To organize thinking, access prior knowledge, and reflect on learning to increase comprehension and engagement
Marking the Text	Selecting text by highlighting, underlining, and/or annotating for specific components, such as main idea, imagery, literary devices, and so on	To focus reading for specific purposes, such as author's craft, and to organize information from selections; to facilitate reexamination of a text
Metacognitive Markers	Responding to text with a system of cueing marks where students use a ? for questions about the text; a ! for reactions related to the text; an * for comments about the text; and an underline to signal key ideas	To track responses to texts and use those responses as a point of departure for talking or writing about texts

STRATEGY	DEFINITION	PURPOSE
OPTIC	Strategy for evaluating visual images. **O** (Overview): Write notes on what the visual appears to be about. **P** (Parts): Zoom in on the parts of the visual and describe any elements or details that seem important. **T** (Title): Highlight the words of the title of the visual (if one is available). **I** (Interrelationships): Use the title as the theory and the parts of the visual as clues to detect and specify how the elements of the graphic are related. **C** (Conclusion); Draw a conclusion about the visual as a whole. What does the visual mean? Summarize the message of the visual in one or two sentences.	To analyze graphic and visual images as forms of text
Predicting	Making guesses about the text by using the title and pictures and/or thinking ahead about events that may occur based on evidence in the text	To help students become actively involved, interested, and mentally prepared to understand ideas
Previewing	Examining a text's structure, features, layout, format, questions, directions, prior to reading	To gain familiarity with the text, make connections to the text, and extend prior knowledge to set a purpose for reading
QHT	Expanding prior knowledge of vocabulary words by marking words with a **Q**, **H**, or **T** (Q signals words students do not know; H signals words students have heard and might be able to identify; T signals words students know well enough to teach to their peers)	To allow students to build on their prior knowledge of words, to provide a forum for peer teaching and learning of new words, and to serve as a prereading exercise to aid in comprehension
Questioning the Text	Developing levels of questions about text; that is, literal, interpretive, and universal questions that prompt deeper thinking about a text	To engage more actively and independently with texts, read with greater purpose and focus, and ultimately answer questions to gain greater insight into the text; helps students to comprehend and interpret
Paraphrasing	Restating in one's own words the essential information expressed in a text, whether it be narration, dialogue, or informational text	To encourage and facilitate comprehension of challenging text
RAFT	Primarily used to generate new text, this strategy can also be used to analyze a text by examining the role of the speaker (R), the intended audience (A), the format of the text (F), and the topic of the text (T).	To initiate reader response; to facilitate an analysis of a text to gain focus prior to creating a new text
Rereading	Encountering the same text with more than one reading	To identify additional details; to clarify meaning and/or reinforce comprehension of texts

STRATEGY	DEFINITION	PURPOSE
SIFT	Analyzing a fictional text by examining stylistic elements, especially symbol, imagery, and figures of speech in order to show how all work together to reveal tone and theme	To focus and facilitate an analysis of a fictional text by examining the title and text for symbolism, identifying images and sensory details, analyzing figurative language and identifying how all these elements reveal tone and theme
Skimming/Scanning	Skimming by rapid or superficial reading of a text to form an overall impression or to obtain a general understanding of the material; scanning focuses on key words, phrases, or specific details and provides speedy recognition of information	To quickly form an overall impression prior to an in-depth study of a text; to answer specific questions or quickly locate targeted information or detail in a text
SMELL	Analyzing a persuasive speech or essay by asking five essential questions: • **S**ender-receiver relationship—What is the sender-receiver relationship? Who are the images and language meant to attract? Describe the speaker of the text. • **M**essage—What is the message? Summarize the statement made in the text. • **E**motional Strategies—What is the desired effect? • **L**ogical Strategies—What logic is operating? How does it (or its absence) affect the message? Consider the logic of the images as well as the words. • **L**anguage—What does the language of the text describe? How does it affect the meaning and effectiveness of the writing? Consider the language of the images as well as the words.	To analyze a persuasive speech or essay by focusing on five essential questions
SOAPSTone	Analyzing text by discussing and identifying **S**peaker, **O**ccasion, **A**udience, **P**urpose, **S**ubject, and **Tone**	To facilitate the analysis of specific elements of nonfiction, literary, and informational texts, and show the relationship among the elements to an understanding of the whole
Summarizing	Giving a brief statement of the main points or essential information expressed in a text, whether it be narration, dialogue, or informational text	To facilitate comprehension and recall of a text
Think Aloud	Talking through a difficult passage or task by using a form of metacognition whereby the reader expresses how he/she has made sense of the text	To reflect on how readers make meaning of challenging texts and to facilitate discussion

STRATEGY	DEFINITION	PURPOSE
TP-CASTT	Analyzing a poetic text by identifying and discussing **T**itle, **P**araphrase, **C**onnotation, **A**ttitude, **S**hift, **T**heme, and **T**itle again	To facilitate the analysis of specific elements of a literary text, especially poetry. To show how the elements work together to create meaning
Visualizing	Forming a picture (mentally and/or literally) while reading a text	To increase reading comprehension and promote active engagement with text
Word Maps	Using a clearly defined graphic organizer such as concept circles or word webs to identify and reinforce word meanings	To provide a visual tool for identifying and remembering multiple aspects of words and word meanings

Writing Strategies

STRATEGY	DEFINITION	PURPOSE
Adding	Making conscious choices to enhance a text by adding additional words, phrases, sentences, or ideas	To refine and clarify the writer's thoughts during revision and/or drafting
Brainstorming	Using a flexible but deliberate process of listing multiple ideas in a short period of time without excluding any idea from the preliminary list	To generate ideas, concepts, or key words that provide a focus and/or establish organization as part of the prewriting or revision process
Deleting	Providing clarity and cohesiveness for a text by eliminating words, phrases, sentences, or ideas	To refine and clarify the writer's thoughts during revision and/or drafting
Drafting	Composing a text in its initial form	To incorporate brainstormed or initial ideas into a written format
Freewriting	Writing freely without constraints in order to capture thinking and convey the writer's purpose	To refine and clarify the writer's thoughts, spark new ideas, and/or generate content during revision and/or drafting
Generating Questions	Clarifying and developing ideas by asking questions of the draft. May be part of self-editing or peer editing	To clarify and develop ideas in a draft; used during drafting and as part of writer response
Graphic Organizer	Organizing ideas and information visually (e.g., Venn diagrams, flowcharts, cluster maps)	To provide a visual system for organizing multiple ideas, details, and/or textual support to be included in a piece of writing
Looping	After freewriting, one section of a text is circled to promote elaboration or the generation of new ideas for that section. This process is repeated to further develop ideas from the newly generated segments.	To refine and clarify the writer's thoughts, spark new ideas, and/or generate new content during revision and/or drafting

STRATEGY	DEFINITION	PURPOSE
Mapping	Creating a graphic organizer that serves as a visual representation of the organizational plan for a written text	To generate ideas, concepts, or key words that provide a focus and/or establish organization during the prewriting, drafting, or revision process
Marking the Draft	Interacting with the draft version of a piece of writing by highlighting, underlining, color-coding, and annotating to indicate revision ideas	To encourage focused, reflective thinking about revising drafts
Note-taking	Making notes about ideas in response to text or discussions; one form is the double-entry journal in which textual evidence is recorded on the left side and personal commentary about the meaning of the evidence on the other side	To assist in organizing key textual elements and responses noted during reading in order to generate textual support that can be incorporated into a piece of writing at a later time. Note-taking is also a reading and listening strategy.
Outlining	Using a system of numerals and letters in order to identify topics and supporting details and ensure an appropriate balance of ideas	To generate ideas, concepts, or key words that provide a focus and/or establish organization prior to writing an initial draft and/or during the revision process
Quickwrite	Writing for a short, specific amount of time in response to a prompt provided	To generate multiple ideas in a quick fashion that could be turned into longer pieces of writing at a later time (may be considered as part of the drafting process)
RAFT	Generating a new text and/or transforming a text by identifying and manipulating its component parts of Role, Audience, Format, and Topic	To generate a new text by identifying the main elements of a text during the prewriting and drafting stages of the writing process
Rearranging	Selecting components of a text and moving them to another place within the text and/or modifying the order in which the author's ideas are presented	To refine and clarify the writer's thoughts during revision and/or drafting
Self-Editing/Peer Editing	Working individually or with a partner to examine a text closely in order to identify areas that might need to be corrected for grammar, punctuation, spelling	To provide a systematic process for editing a written text to ensure correctness of identified components such as conventions of standard English
Sharing and Responding	Communicating with another person or a small group of peers who respond to a piece of writing as focused readers (not necessarily as evaluators)	To make suggestions for improvement to the work of others and/or to receive appropriate and relevant feedback on the writer's own work, used during the drafting and revision process
Sketching	Drawing or sketching ideas or ordering of ideas (includes storyboarding, visualizing)	To generate and/or clarify ideas by visualizing them (may be part of prewriting)
Substituting/ Replacing	Replacing original words or phrases in a text with new words or phrases that achieve the desired effect	To refine and clarify the writer's thoughts during revision and/or drafting

STRATEGY	DEFINITION	PURPOSE
TWIST	Arriving at a thesis statement that incorporates the following literary elements: Tone, Word choice (diction), Imagery, Style, and Theme	To craft an interpretive thesis in response to a prompt about a text
Webbing	Developing a graphic organizer that consists of a series of circles connected with lines to indicate relationships among ideas	To generate ideas, concepts, or key words that provide a focus and/or establish organization prior to writing an initial draft and/or during the revision process
Writer's Checklist	Using a co-constructed checklist (that could be written on a bookmark and/or displayed on the wall) in order to look for specific features of a writing text and check for accuracy	To focus on key areas of the writing process so that the writer can effectively revise a draft and correct mistakes
Writing Groups	A type of discussion group devoted to sharing and responding to student work	To facilitate a collaborative approach to generating ideas for and revising writing

Speaking and Listening Strategies

STRATEGY	DEFINITION	PURPOSE
Choral Reading	Reading text lines aloud in student groups and/ or individually to present an interpretation	To develop fluency; differentiate between the reading of statements and questions; practice phrasing, pacing, and reading dialogue; show how a character's emotions are captured through vocal stress and intonation
Note-taking	Creating a record of information while listening to a speaker or reading a text	To facilitate active listening or close reading; to record and organize ideas that assist in processing information
Oral Reading	Reading aloud one's own text or the texts of others (e.g., echo reading, choral reading, paired readings)	To share one's own work or the work of others; build fluency and increase confidence in presenting to a group
Rehearsal	Encouraging multiple practices of a piece of text prior to a performance	To provide students with an opportunity to clarify the meaning of a text prior to a performance as they refine the use of dramatic conventions (e.g., gestures, vocal interpretations, facial expressions)
Role-Playing	Assuming the role or persona of a character	To develop the voice, emotions, and mannerisms of a character to facilitate improved comprehension of a text

Collaborative Strategies

STRATEGY	DEFINITION	PURPOSE
Discussion Groups	Engaging in an interactive, small-group discussion, often with an assigned role; to consider a topic, text, or question	To gain new understanding of or insight into a text from multiple perspectives
Think-Pair-Share	Pairing with a peer to share ideas before sharing ideas and discussion with a larger group	To construct meaning about a topic or question; to test thinking in relation to the ideas of others; to prepare for a discussion with a larger group

Graphic Organizer Directory

Contents

Active Listening Feedback

Presenter's name: _____

Content

What is the presenter's purpose? _____

What is the presenter's main point? _____

Do you agree with the presenter? Why or why not? _____

_____

_____

Form

Did the presenter use a clear, loud voice? ☐ yes ☐ no

Did the presenter make eye contact? ☐ yes ☐ no

One thing I really liked about the presentation:

_____

_____

_____

One question I still have:

_____

_____

_____

Other comments or notes:

Active Listening Notes

Title: _____

Who?

What?

Where?

When?

Why?

How?

Audience Notes and Feedback

Scoring Criteria	Notes/Feedback
Introduction/ Conclusion	
Timing	
Voice	
Eye Contact/ Gestures	
Use of Media, Visuals, Props	
Audience Engagement	

Cause and Effect

Title: _____

Cause: What happened?	Effect: An effect of this is

Cause: What happened?	Effect: An effect of this is

Cause: What happened?	Effect: An effect of this is

Cause: What happened?	Effect: An effect of this is

Character Map

Character name: _____

What does the character look like?

How does the character act and feel?

What do other characters say or think about the character?

Collaborative Dialogue

Topic: _____

Use the space below to record ideas.

"Wh-" Prompts
Who?   What?   Where?   When?   Why?

Speaker 1

Speaker 2

Conclusion Builder

Evidence

Evidence

Evidence

Based on this evidence, I can conclude

Conflict Map

Title: _____

What is the main conflict in this story?

What causes this conflict?

How is the conflict resolved?

What are some other ways the conflict could have been resolved?

Conversation for Quickwrite

1. Turn to a partner and restate the prompt in your own words.

2. Brainstorm key words to use in your quickwrite response.

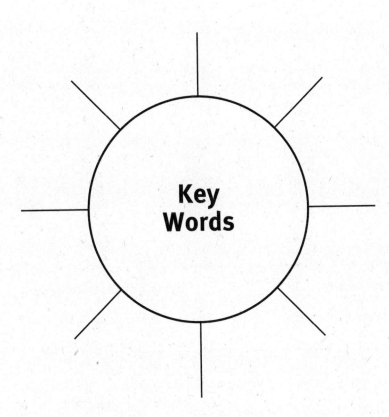

3. Take turns explaining your ideas to your partner. Try using some of the key words you brainstormed.

4. On your own, write a response to the quickwrite.

Definition and Reflection

Academic Vocabulary Word
Definition in own words
Illustration (literal or symbolic)

My experiences with this concept:

- I haven't really thought about this concept.

_____

- I have only thought about this concept in English Language Arts class.

_____

- I have applied this concept in other classes.

_____

- I have applied this concept outside of school.

_____

My level of understanding:

- I am still trying to understand this concept.

_____

- I am familiar with this concept, but I am not comfortable applying it.

_____

- I am very comfortable with this concept and I know how to apply it.

_____

- I could teach this concept to another classmate.

_____

Discourse Starters

Questioning and Discussing a Text

One question I have is _____.

Could this mean _____?

Why do you think the author _____?

I understand _____, but I wonder _____.

I notice that _____.

I think this (word/sentence/paragraph) means _____.

I think _____ because the text says _____.

In paragraph _____, the author says _____.

According to the text, _____.

One way to interpret _____ is _____.

Summarizing

The main events that take place are _____.

The major points of the text are _____.

The main idea of _____ is _____.

One central idea of this text is _____.

Another central idea is _____.

All in all, the message is _____.

The author's main purpose is to _____.

Basically, the author is saying that _____.

Comparing and Contrasting

_____ and _____ are similar because _____.

_____ and _____ are similar in that they both _____.

_____ is _____. Similarly, _____ is _____.

One thing _____ and _____ have in common is _____.

_____ and _____ are different because _____.

_____ and _____ are different in that _____.

_____ is _____. On the other hand, _____ is _____.

One difference between _____ and _____ is _____.

Clarifying

I'm not sure I understand the instructions.

Could you repeat that please?

I have a question about _____.

I am having trouble with _____.

Will you explain that again?

Could you clarify _____?

Would you mind helping me with _____?

Which (page/paragraph/section) are we reading?

How do you spell/pronounce _____?

Discourse Starters

Agreeing and Disagreeing

I agree with the idea that _____ because _____.

I share your point of view because _____.

You made a good point when you said _____.

I agree with (a person) that _____.

Although I agree that _____, I also think _____.

I understand where you're coming from, but _____.

I disagree with the idea that _____ because _____.

I see it a different way because _____.

You have a point, but the evidence suggests _____.

Arguing and Persuading with Evidence

I believe that _____ because _____.

It is clear that _____ because _____.

One reason I think _____ is _____.

Based on evidence in the text, I think _____.

Evidence such as _____ suggests that _____.

An example to support my position is _____.

This is evident because _____.

What evidence supports the idea that _____?

Can you explain why you think _____?

Evaluating

This is effective because _____.

The evidence _____ is strong because _____.

This is convincing because _____.

I see why the author _____, but I think _____.

This is not very effective because _____.

The evidence _____ is weak because _____.

This would have been better if _____.

What do you think about the writer's choice to _____?

Why do you think _____ (is/isn't) effective?

Giving Feedback and Suggesting

The part where you _____ is strong because _____.

What impressed me the most is how you _____.

This is a good start. Maybe you should add _____.

I like how you _____, but I would try _____.

You might consider changing _____.

I would suggest revising _____ so that _____.

One suggestion would be to _____.

Why did you choose _____?

A better choice might be _____.

This would be clearer if _____.

Editor's Checklist

Over the course of the year with SpringBoard, customize this Editor's Checklist as your knowledge of language conventions grows. The three examples below show you how to write a good checklist item.

	Are all the sentences complete?
	Do the subject and verb of each sentence agree?
	Do all the sentences have correct punctuation?

Writer's Checklist

Ideas

	Does your first paragraph hook the reader?
	Is the purpose of your writing clear (to inform, to make an argument, etc.)?
	Is the genre of writing appropriate for your purpose?
	Is your main idea clear and easy to summarize?
	Does your text contain details and information that support your main idea?
	Are the ideas in the text well organized?
	Do you connect your ideas by using transitions?
	Do you use parallel structure to keep your ideas clear?
	Does each paragraph have a conclusion that transitions to the next paragraph?
	Does your writing end with a strong conclusion that restates the original purpose of the tex

Language

	Do you keep a consistent point of view throughout?
	Do you use the present tense when writing about a text?
	Are any shifts in verb tense easy to follow and necessary?
	Have you removed unnecessary or confusing words?
	Do you use vivid verbs and descriptive adjectives when appropriate?
	Do you use different styles of language (like figurative or sensory) when appropriate?
	Do you use a variety of sentence types?
	Do you vary the way you begin your sentences?
	Did you split up run-on sentences?
	Are your pronoun references clear?

Evaluating Online Sources

The URL
• What is its domain?
   • .com = a for-profit organization
   • .gov, .mil, .us (or other country code) = a government site
   • .edu = affiliated with an educational institution
   • .org = a nonprofit organization
• Is this URL someone's personal page?
• Do you recognize who is publishing this page?	

Sponsor: • Does the website give information about the organization or group that sponsors it? • Does it have a link (often called "About Us") that leads you to that information? • What do you learn?	
Timeliness: • When was the page last updated (usually this is posted at the top or bottom of the page)? • Is the topic something that changes frequently, like current events or technology?	
Purpose: • What is the purpose of the page? • What is its target audience? • Does it present information, opinion, or both? • Is it primarily objective or subjective? • How do you know?	
Author: • What credentials does the author have? • Is this person or group considered an authority on the topic?	
Links • Does the page provide links? • Do they work? • Are they helpful? • Are they objective or subjective?	

Idea and Argument Evaluator

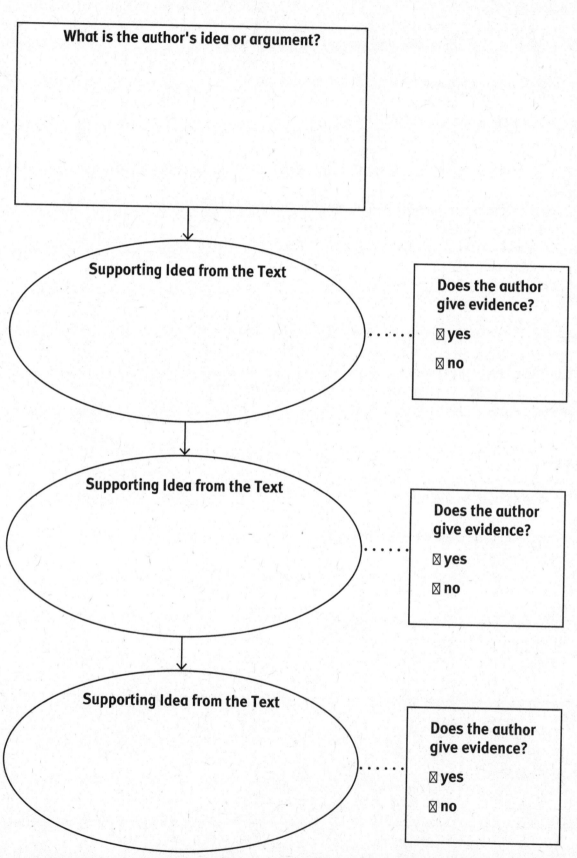

What is the author's idea or argument?

Supporting Idea from the Text

Does the author give evidence?

☒ yes

☒ no

Supporting Idea from the Text

Does the author give evidence?

☒ yes

☒ no

Supporting Idea from the Text

Does the author give evidence?

☒ yes

☒ no

Idea Connector

Directions: Write two simple sentences about the same topic. Next, write transition words around the Idea Connector. Then, choose an appropriate word to connect ideas in the two sentences. Write your combined sentence in the space below.

Sentence One

Sentence Two

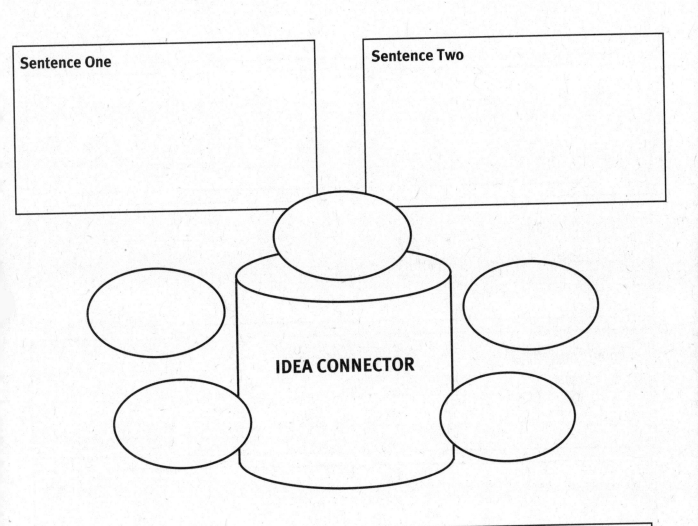

IDEA CONNECTOR

Combined Sentence

Key Idea and Details Chart

Title/Topic _____

Key Idea _____
_____
_____

Supporting detail 1 _____
_____
_____

Supporting detail 2 _____
_____
_____

Supporting detail 3 _____
_____
_____

Supporting detail 4 _____
_____
_____

Restate topic sentence: _____
_____

Concluding sentence: _____
_____

Narrative Analysis and Writing

Response

Response

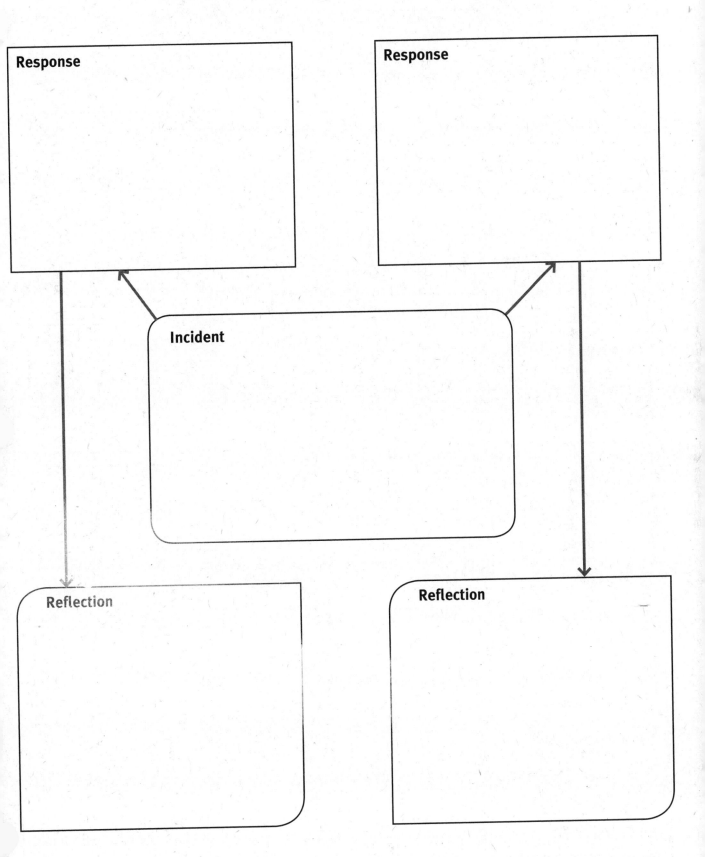

Incident

Reflection

Reflection

Notes for Reading Independently
Fiction

Title: _____

Author: _____

Something interesting I noticed:

A question I have:

Summary:

Illustration:

Connections to my life/other texts I've read:

How challenging this text was:

Easy   1   2   3   4   5   6   7   8   9   10   *Challenging*

Notes for Reading Independently
Nonfiction

Title: _____

Author: _____

Main idea:

Facts I learned:

Summary:

Questions I still have:

Connections to my life/other texts I've read:

How challenging this text was:

Easy   1   2   3   4   5   6   7   8   9   10   *Challenging*

Opinion Builder

Reason

Reason

Based on these reasons, my opinion is

Reason

Reason

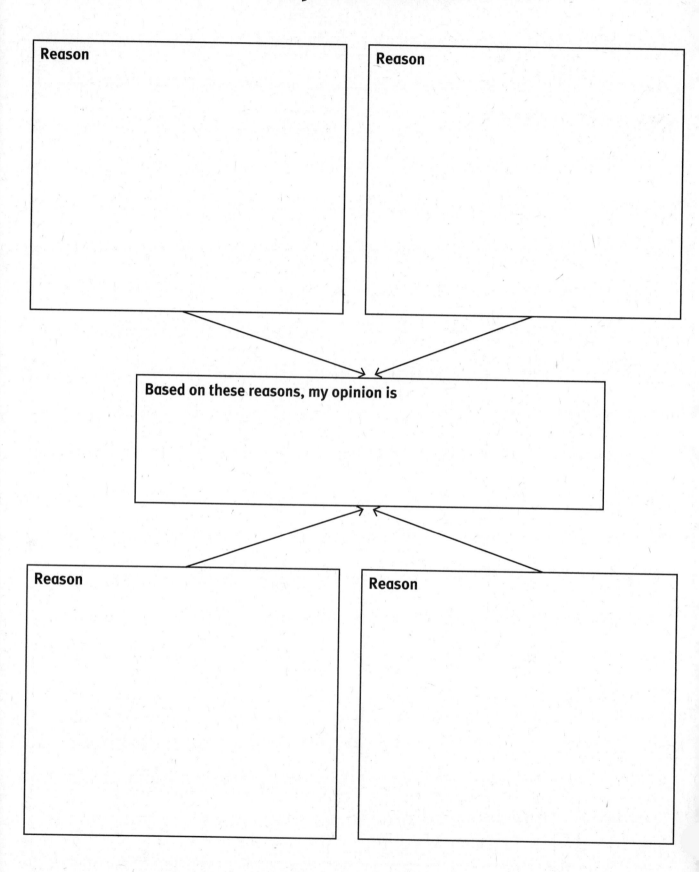

Paragraph Frame for Conclusions

Conclusion Words and Phrases

shows that

based on

suggests that

leads to

indicates that

influences

The _____ *(story, poem, play, passage, etc.)* shows that *(helps us to conclude that)* _____

_____

_____

There are several reasons why. First, _____

_____

_____

_____

_____

A second reason is _____

_____

_____

_____

_____

Finally, _____

_____

_____

_____

In conclusion, _____

_____

_____

_____

Paragraph Frame for Sequencing

Sequence Words and Phrases

at the beginning

in the first place

as a result

later

eventually

in the end

lastly

In the _____ (story, poem, play, passage, etc.)

there are three important _____

(events, steps, directions, etc.)

First, _____

_____

_____

_____

_____

Second, _____

_____

_____

_____

_____

Third, _____

_____

_____

_____

_____

Finally, _____

_____

_____

_____

_____

Paraphrasing and Summarizing Map

What does the text say?	How can I say it in my own words?

How can I use my own words to summarize the text?

Peer Editing

Writer's name: _____

Did the writer answer the prompt? ☐ yes ☐ no

Did the writer use appropriate details or evidence to develop their writing? ☐ yes ☐ no

Is the writing organized in a way that makes sense? ☐ yes ☐ no

Did the writer use a variety of sentence types to make the writing more interesting? ☐ yes ☐ no

Are there any spelling or punctuation mistakes? ☐ yes ☐ no

Are there any grammar errors? ☐ yes ☐ no

Two things I really liked about the writer's story:

1. _____
   _____
   _____

2. _____
   _____
   _____

One thing I think the writer could do to improve the writing:

1. _____
   _____
   _____

Other comments or notes:

Persuasive/Argument Writing Map

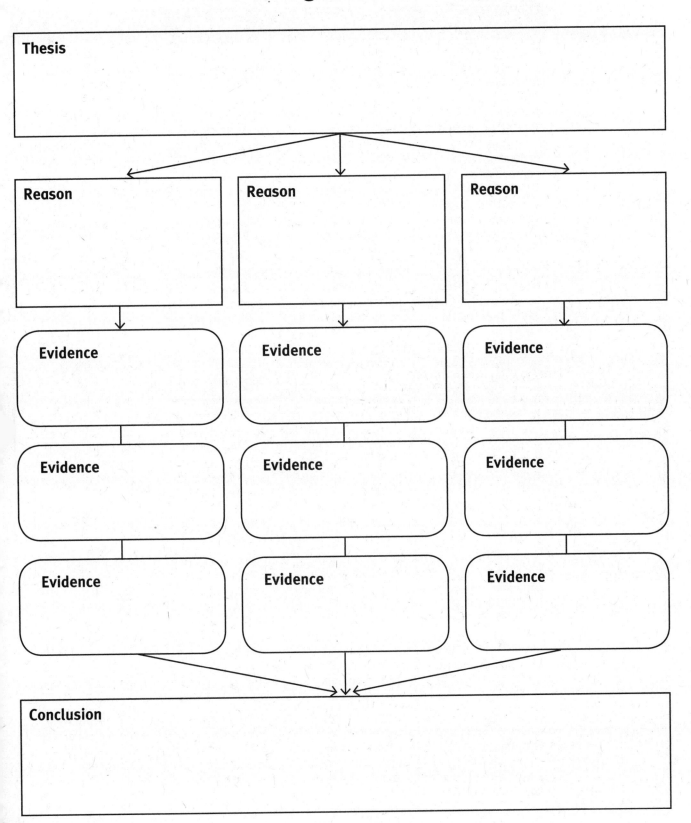

Thesis

Reason

Reason

Reason

Evidence

Evidence

Evidence

Evidence

Evidence

Evidence

Evidence

Evidence

Evidence

Conclusion

Presenting Scoring Guide

Scoring Criteria	Exemplary	Proficient	Emerging	Incomplete
Introduction / Conclusion	The presentation • provides a clear, engaging, and appropriate introduction to the topic or performance • provides a clear, engaging, and appropriate conclusion that closes, summarizes, draws connections to broader themes, or supports the ideas presented.	The presentation • provides a clear and appropriate introduction to the topic or performance • provides a clear and appropriate conclusion that closes, summarizes, draws connections to broader themes, or supports the ideas presented.	The presentation • provides an adequate introduction to the topic or performance • provides an adequate conclusion that closes, summarizes, draws connections to broader themes, or supports the ideas presented.	The presentation • does not provide an introduction to the topic or performance • does not provide a conclusion that closes, summarizes, draws connections to broader themes, or supports the ideas presented.
Timing	The presentation • thoroughly delivers its intended message within the allotted time • is thoughtfully and appropriately paced throughout.	The presentation • mostly delivers its intended message within the allotted time • is appropriately paced most of the time.	The presentation • delivers some of its intended message within the allotted time • is sometimes not paced appropriately.	The presentation • does not deliver its intended message within the allotted time • is not paced appropriately.
Voice (Volume, Enunciation, Rate)	The presentation • is delivered with adequate volume enabling audience members to fully comprehend what is said • is delivered with clear enunciation.	The presentation • is delivered with adequate volume enabling audience members to mostly comprehend what is said • is delivered with mostly clear enunciation.	The presentation • is delivered with somewhat adequate volume enabling audience members to comprehend some of what is said • is delivered with somewhat clear enunciation.	The presentation • is not delivered with adequate volume, so that audience members are unable to comprehend what is said • is delivered with unclear enunciation.
Eye Contact / Gestures	The presentation • is delivered with appropriate eye contact that helps engage audience members • makes use of natural gestures and/or body language to convey meaning.	The presentation • is delivered with some appropriate eye contact that helps engage audience members • makes use of gestures and/or body language to convey meaning.	The presentation • is delivered with occasional eye contact that sometimes engages audience members • makes some use of gestures and/or body language to convey meaning.	The presentation • is not delivered with eye contact to engage audience members • makes little or no use of gestures and/or body language to convey meaning.
Use of Media, Visuals, Props	The presentation • makes use of highly engaging visuals, multimedia, and/or props that enhance delivery.	The presentation • makes use of visuals, multimedia, and/or props that enhance delivery.	The presentation • makes use of some visuals, multimedia, and/or props that somewhat enhance delivery.	The presentation • makes use of few or no visuals, multimedia, and/or props that enhance delivery.
Audience Engagement	The presentation • includes thoughtful and appropriate interactions with and responses to audience members.	The presentation • includes appropriate interactions with and responses to audience members.	The presentation • includes a few interactions with and responses to audience members.	The presentation • does not include interactions with and responses to audience members.

NAME

DATE

RAFT

Role	Who or what are you as a writer?
Audience	As a writer, to whom are you writing?
Format	As a writer, what format would be appropriate for your audience (essay, letter, speech, poem, etc.)?
Topic	As a writer, what is the subject of your writing? What points do you want to make?

Roots and Affixes Brainstorm

Directions: Write the root or affix in the circle. Brainstorm or use a dictionary to find the meaning of the root or affix and add it to the circle. Then, find words that use that root or affix. Write one word in each box. Write a sentence for each word.

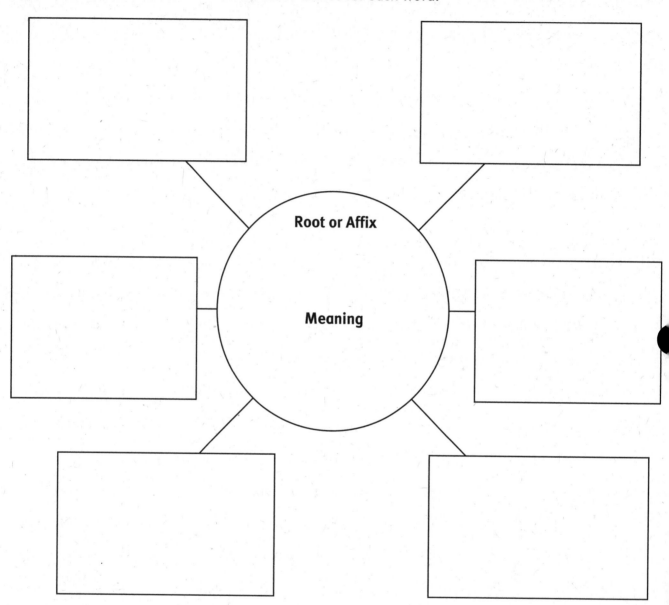

Root or Affix

Meaning

Round Table Discussion

Directions: Write the topic in the center box. One student begins by stating his or her ideas while the student to the left takes notes. Then the next student speaks while the student to his or her left takes notes, and so on.

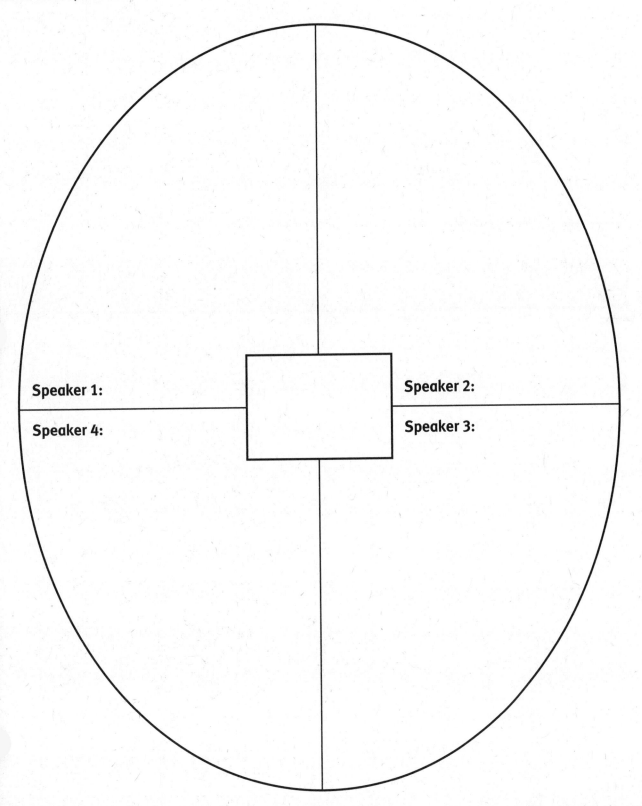

Speaker 1:

Speaker 2:

Speaker 4:

Speaker 3:

Sequence of Events Time Line

Title: _____

What happened first?

Next?

Beginning ——————————— Middle ——————————— End

Then?

Finally?

SMELL

Sender-Receiver Relationship—Who are the senders and receivers of the message, and what is their relationship (consider what different audiences the text may be addressing)?

Message—What is a literal summary of the content? What is the meaning/significance of this information?

Emotional Strategies—What emotional appeals (*pathos*) are included? What seems to be their desired effect?

Logical Strategies—What logical arguments/appeals (*logos*) are included? What is their effect?

Language—What specific language is used to support the message? How does it affect the text's effectiveness? Consider both images and actual words.

SOAPSTone

SOAPSTone	Analysis	Textual Support
Subject What does the reader know about the writer?		
Occasion What are the circumstances surrounding this text?		
Audience Who is the target audience?		
Purpose Why did the author write this text?		
Subject What is the topic?		
Tone What is the author's tone, or attitude?		

Text Structure Stairs

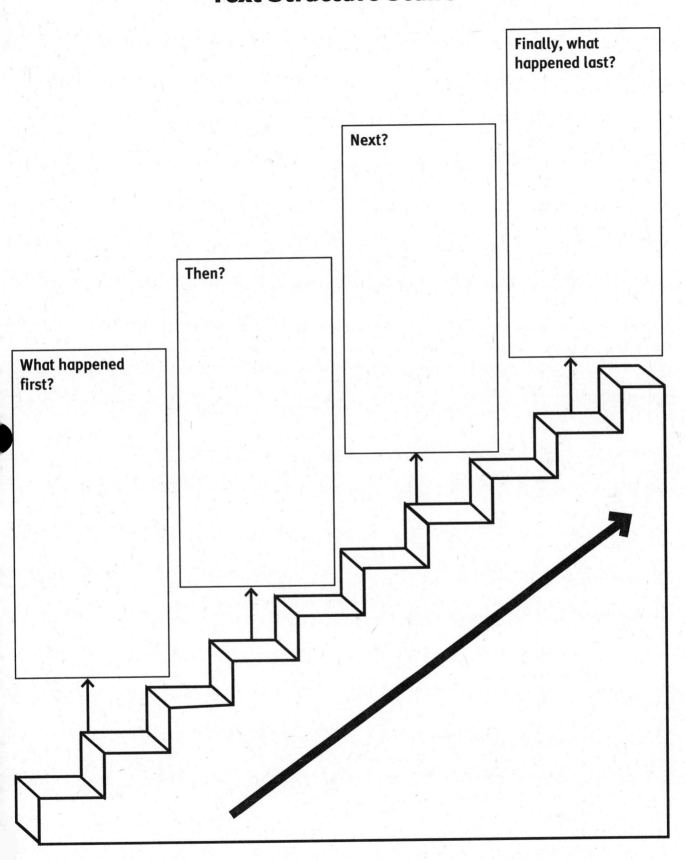

What happened first?

Then?

Next?

Finally, what happened last?

TP-CASTT Analysis

Poem Title:

Author:

Title: Make a Prediction. What do you think the title means before you read the poem?

Paraphrase: Translate the poem in your own words. What is the poem about? Rephrase difficult sections word for word.

Connotation: Look beyond the literal meaning of key words and images to their associations.

Attitude: What is the speaker's attitude? What is the author's attitude? How does the author feel about the speaker, about other characters, about the subject?

Shifts: Where do the shifts in tone, setting, voice, etc., occur? Look for time and place, keywords, punctuation, stanza divisions, changes in length or rhyme, and sentence structure. What is the purpose of each shift? How do they contribute to effect and meaning?

Title: Reexamine the title. What do you think it means now in the context of the poem?

Theme: Think of the literal and metaphorical layers of the poem. Then determine the overall theme. The theme must be written in a complete sentence.

TP-CASTT

Poem Title:

Author:

Title		
Paraphrase		
Connotation		
Attitude		
Shifts		
Title		
Theme		

Unknown Word Solver

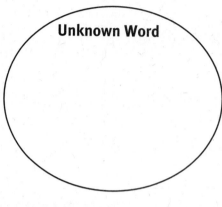

Can you find any context clues? List them.

Unknown Word

Do you recognize any word parts?

Prefix:

Root Word:

Suffix:

Do you know another meaning of this word that does not make sense in this context?

Does it look or sound like a word in another language?

What is the dictionary definition?

How can you define the word in your own words?

Venn Diagram for Writing a Comparison

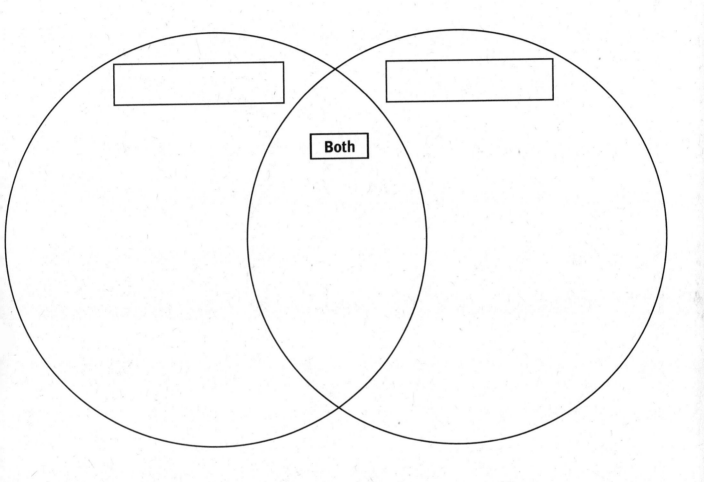

Both

They are similar in that _____	They are different in that _____
_____	_____
_____	_____
_____	_____
_____	_____
_____	_____
_____	_____

Verbal & Visual Word Association

Definition in Your Own Words	Important Elements

Academic Vocabulary Word

Visual Representation	Personal Association

Web Organizer

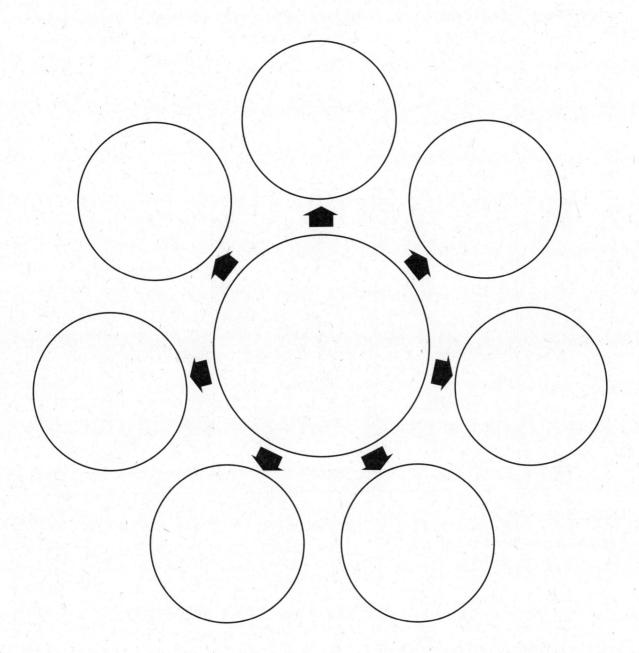

Word Choice Analyzer

Word or phrase from the text	Definition of word or phrase	How can I restate the definition in my own words?	What effect did the author produce by choosing these words?

Explain Your Analysis

The author uses the word or phrase _____ , which means

_____

Another way to say this is _____

_____

I think the author chose these words to _____

_____

_____

One way I can modify this sentence to add detail is to _____

_____

Word Map

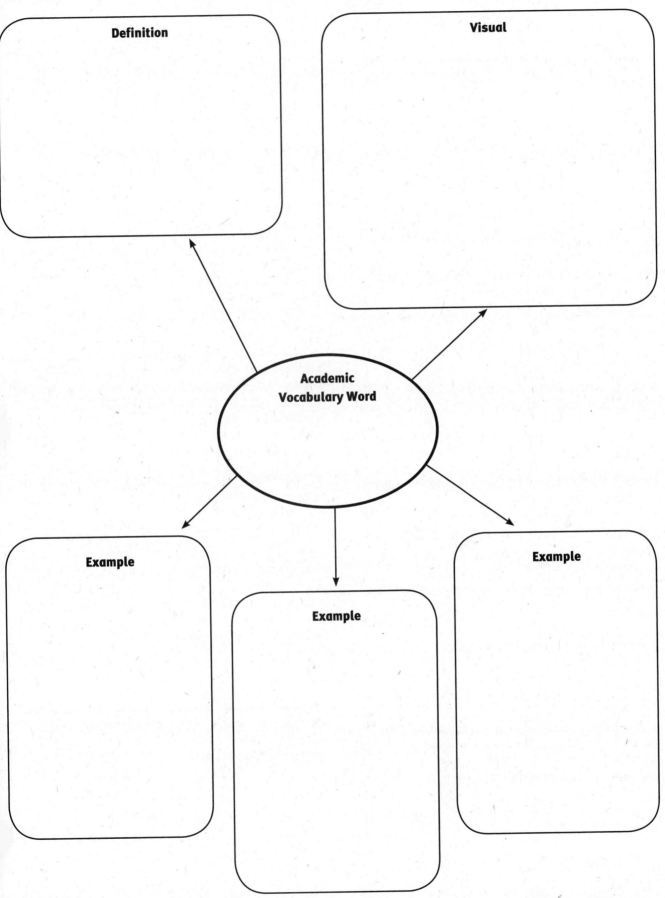

Definition

Visual

Academic
Vocabulary Word

Example

Example

Example

Glossary/Glosario

A

advertising: the use of print, graphics, or videos to persuade people to buy a product or use a service
publicidad: uso de impresos, gráfica o videos para persuadir a las personas a comprar un producto o usar un servicio

allegory: a story in which the characters, objects, or actions have a meaning beyond the surface of the story
alegoría: cuento en el que los personajes, objetos o acciones tienen un significado que va más allá de la superficie de la historia

alliteration: the repetition of consonant sounds at the beginnings of words that are close together
aliteración: repetición de sonidos consonánticos al comienzo de palabras que están cercanas

allusion: a reference to a well-known person, place, event, literary work, or work of art
alusión: referencia a una persona, lugar, obra literaria u obra de arte muy conocidos

analogy: a comparison of the similarity of two things; for example, comparing a *part to a whole* or the *whole to a part*
analogía: comparación de la semejanza de dos cosas; por ejemplo, comparar una *parte con un todo* o el *todo con una parte*

analyze (literary): study the details of a work to identify essential features or meaning
analizar (literario): estudiar los detalles de una obra para identificar características o significados esenciales

anecdote: a brief, entertaining account of an incident or event
anécdota: breve relato entretenido de un incidente o suceso

annotate: write notes to explain or present ideas that help you analyze and understand a text
anotar: tomar notas para explicar o presentar las ideas que te ayuden a analizar y a entender un texto

antonyms: words with opposite meanings
antónimos: palabras con significados opuestos

archetype: a character, symbol, story pattern, or other element that is common to human experience across cultures and that occurs frequently in literature, myth, and folklore
arquetipo: personaje, símbolo, patrón de un cuento u otro elemento que es común a la experiencia humana a través de diversas culturas y que aparece con frecuencia en literatura, mitos y folclor

argument: facts or reasoning offered to support a position as being true
argumento: hechos o razonamiento entregados para apoyar una posición como verdadera

artifact: an object made by a human being, typically an item that has cultural or historical significance
artefacto: objeto hecho por un ser humano, habitualmente un objeto que tiene significación cultural o histórica

atmosphere: the feeling created by a literary work or passage
atmósfera: sentimiento creado por una obra o pasaje literario

audience: the intended readers of specific types of texts or the viewers of a program or performance
público: lectores objetivo de tipos específicos de textos o espectadores de un programa o actuación

B

balanced sentence: a sentence that presents ideas of equal weight in similar grammatical form to emphasize the similarity or difference between the ideas
oración balanceada: oración que presenta ideas de igual peso en forma gramatical similar para enfatizar la semejanza o diferencia entre las ideas

bibliography: a list of source materials used to prepare a research paper or presentation
bibliografía: lista de las fuentes utilizadas para preparar una investigación o una presentación

body paragraph: a paragraph that contains a topic sentence, supporting details and commentary, and a concluding sentence and that is usually part of a longer text
párrafo representativo: párrafo que contiene una oración principal, detalles de apoyo y comentarios, y una oración concluyente que normalmente forma parte de un texto más extenso

C

caricature: a visual or verbal representation in which characteristics or traits are distorted for emphasis
caricatura: representación visual o verbal en la que las características o rasgos son distorsionados para dar énfasis

cause: an initial action; an event that makes something else happen
causa: acción inicial; suceso que hace que otra cosa ocurra

character: a person or animal that takes part in the action of a literary work
personaje: persona o animal que participa en la acción de una obra literaria

characterization: the methods a writer uses to develop characters; for example, through description, actions, and dialogue
caracterización: métodos que usa un escritor para desarrollar personajes; por ejemplo, a través de descripción, acciones y diálogo

citation: giving credit to the authors of source information
cita: dar crédito a los autores de información usada como fuente

claim: a writer's statement of a position or opinion about a topic
afirmación: declaración de un escritor acerca de una posición u opinión sobre un tema

cliché: an overused expression or idea
cliché: expresión o idea usada en exceso

climax: the turning point or the high point of a story
clímax: punto de inflexión o momento culminante de un cuento

coherence: the clear and orderly presentation of ideas in a paragraph or essay
coherencia: presentación clara y ordenada de las ideas en un párrafo o ensayo

collaborate: work together with other members of a group
colaborar: trabajar en conjunto con otros miembros de un grupo

comedy: an entertainment that is amusing or humorous
comedia: espectáculo que es divertido o cómico

commentary: explanation of the way the facts, details, and/or examples in a paragraph or essay support the topic sentence
comentario: explicación de la manera en que los hechos, detalles y ejemplos de un párrafo o ensayo apoyan la oración principal

commercialism: an emphasis on gaining profits through advertising or sponsorship
mercantilismo: énfasis en obtener utilidades por medio de la publicidad o el auspicio

communication: the process of giving or exchanging information. **Verbal communication** involves the written or spoken word. **Nonverbal communication** involves movement, gestures, or facial expressions.
comunicación: proceso de dar o intercambiar información. La **comunicación verbal** involucra palabras escritas o habladas. La **comunicación no verbal** involucra movimientos, gestos o expresiones faciales.

compare: to identify similarities in two or more items; *see also* contrast
comparar: identificar semejanzas entre dos o más elementos; *ver también*, contrastar

concluding sentence: a final sentence that pulls together the ideas in a paragraph by restating the main idea or by summarizing or commenting on the ideas in the paragraph
oración concluyente: oración final que reúne las ideas de un párrafo, reformulando la idea principal o resumiendo o comentando las ideas del párrafo

conclusion: the ending of a paragraph or essay, which brings it to a close and leaves an impression with the reader
conclusión: fin de un párrafo o ensayo, que lo lleva a su término y deja una impresión en el lector

conflict: a struggle between opposing forces. In an **external conflict**, a character struggles with an outside force, such as another character or something in nature. In an **internal conflict**, the character struggles with his or her own needs, desires, or emotions.
conflicto: lucha entre fuerzas opuestas. En un **conflicto externo**, un personaje lucha contra una fuerza externa, como por ejemplo otro personaje o algo de la naturaleza. En un **conflicto interno**, el personaje lucha contra sus propias necesidades, deseos o emociones.

connotation: the suggested or implied meaning or emotion associated with a word—beyond its literal definition
connotación: significado o emoción sugerida o implícita que se asocia con una palabra—más allá de su definición literal

consumer: a buyer; a person who acquires goods and services
consumidor: comprador, persona que adquiere bienes y servicios

consumerism: the buying and consuming of goods and products; the belief that it is good to buy and consume goods and services
consumismo: compra y consumo de bienes y productos; creencia de que es bueno comprar y consumir bienes y servicios

context clue: information in words and phrases surrounding an unfamiliar word that hint at the meaning of the unfamiliar word.

clave de contexto: información en las palabras y frases que rodean una palabra no conocida y que dan una pista acerca del significado de esa palabra.

contrast: to identify differences in two or more items; *see also* compare

contrastar: identificar diferencias entre dos o más elementos; *ver también,* comparar

controversy: a public debate or dispute concerning a matter of opinion

controversia: debate público o disputa sobre una cuestión sujeta a opinión

copy: the actual text in an advertisement

texto publicitario: información actual en un anuncio publicitario

counter-argument: reasoning or facts given in opposition to an argument

contraargumento: razonamiento o hechos dados en oposición a un argumento

credible: to be trusted or believed

creíble: ser confiable o creíble

criteria: the facts, rules, or standards on which judgments are based.

criterios: hechos, reglas o estándares sobre las cuales están basadas las opiniones.

D

debate: *n.* a discussion involving opposing points of view; *v.* to present the sides of an argument by discussing opposing points

debate: *s.* discusión que involucra puntos de vista opuestos; *v.* presentar los lados de un argumento discutiendo puntos opuestos

definition: the process of making clear the meaning or nature of something

definición: proceso de aclarar el significado o naturaleza de algo

denotation: the exact, literal meaning of a word

denotación: significado exacto y literal de una palabra

detail: in writing, evidence (facts, statistics, examples) that supports the topic sentence

detalle: en la escritura, evidencia (hechos, estadística, ejemplos) que apoya la oracón principal

dialogue: conversation between characters

diálogo: conversación entre personajes

diction: a writer's or speaker's choice of words

dicción: selección de palabras por parte del escritor u orador

dissolve: the slow fading away of one image in a film as another fades in to take its place

desvanecimiento: desaparición lenta de una imagen en una película a medida que otra aparece progresivamente para tomar su lugar

drama: a genre of literature that is intended to be performed before an audience; a play

drama: género literario destinado a ser representado ante un público; obra teatral

dystopia: an imagined place or state in which the condition of life is imperfect or bad

distopía: lugar o estado imaginario en el que las condiciones de vida son imperfectas o malas

E

editorial: a short essay in which a publication, or someone speaking for a publication, expresses an opinion or takes a stand on an issue

editorial: ensayo corto en el que una publicación, o alguien que representa una publicación, expresa una opinión o toma partido acerca de un tema

effect: the result of an event or action

efecto: resultado de un suceso o acción

epic: a long narrative poem about the deeds of heroes or gods

épica: poema narrativo largo acerca de las proezas de héroes o dioses

epilogue: a section at the end of a book or play that extends or comments on the ending

epílogo: sección al final de un libro u obra teatral, que extiende o comenta el final

essay: a short literary composition on a single subject

ensayo: composición literaria corta acerca de un único tema

ethos: a rhetorical appeal that focuses on the character or qualifications of the speaker

ethos: recurso retórico centrado en el carácter o las capacidades del orador

euphemism: an inoffensive expression that is used in place of one that is considered harsh or blunt

eufemismo: expresión inofensiva usada en lugar de una considerada cruel o ruda

evaluate: to examine and judge carefully to determine the value of something, such as an idea, a comment, or a source
evaluar: estudiar y juzgar cuidadosamente para determinar el valor de algo, tal como una idea, un comentario, o una fuente

evidence: the information that supports or proves an idea or claim; forms of evidence include facts, statistics (numerical facts), expert opinions, examples, and anecdotes; see also anecdotal, empirical, and logical evidence
evidencia: información que apoya o prueba una idea o afirmación; algunas formas de evidencia incluyen hechos, estadísticas (datos numéricos), opiniones de expertos, ejemplos y anécdotas; ver también evidencia anecdótica, empírica y lógica

explanatory essay: an essay that makes an assertion and explains it with details, reasons, textual evidence, and commentary
ensayo explicativo: ensayo que hace una afirmación y la explica con detalles, razones, evidencia textual y comentarios

explanatory paragraph: a paragraph that makes an assertion and supports it with details and commentary
párrafo explicativo: párrafo que hace una afirmación y la apoya con detalles y comentarios

exposition: events that give a reader background information needed to understand a story
exposición: sucesos que entregan al lector los antecedentes necesarios para comprender un cuento

F

fable: a brief story that teaches a lesson or moral, usually through animal characters that take on human qualities
fábula: cuento breve que enseña una lección o moraleja, normalmente por medio de personajes animales que asumen cualidades humanas

fact: a statement that can be proven
hecho: enunciado que puede demostrarse

fairy tale: a story that involves fantasy elements such as witches, goblins, and elves. These stories often involve princes and princesses and today are generally told to entertain children.
cuento de hadas: cuento que involucra elementos fantásticos como brujas, duendes y elfos. A menudo, estos cuentos involucran a príncipes y princesas y hoy se cuentan generalmente para entretener a los niños.

falling action: events after the climax of a story but before the resolution
acción descendente: sucesos posteriores al clímax de un cuento, pero antes de la resolución

fantasy: a story based on things that could not happen in real life
fantasía: cuento basado en cosas que no podrían ocurrir en la vida real

fiction: writing that consists of imagined events
ficción: escritura que consiste en acontecimientos imaginados

figurative language: imaginative language that is not meant to be interpreted literally
lenguaje figurativo: lenguaje imaginativo que no pretende ser interpretado literalmente

flashback: a sudden and vivid memory of an event in the past; also, an interruption in the sequence of events in the plot of a story to relate events that occurred in the past
narración retrospectiva: recuerdo repentino y vívido de un suceso del pasado; además, interrupción en la secuencia de los sucesos del argumento de un cuento para relatar sucesos ocurridos en el pasado

fluency: the ability to use language clearly and easily
fluidez: capacidad de usar el lenguaje fácilmente y de manera clara

folk literature: the traditional literature of a culture, consisting of a variety of myths and folk tales
literatura folclórica: literatura tradicional de una cultura, consistente en una variedad de mitos y cuentos folclóricos

folk tale: an anonymous traditional story passed on orally from one generation to another
cuento folclórico: cuento tradicional anónimo pasada oralmente de generación en generación

folklore: the stories, traditions, sayings, and customs of a culture or a society
folclor: historias, tradiciones, dichos y costumbres de una cultura o sociedad

foreshadowing: clues or hints signaling events that will occur later in the plot
presagio: claves o pistas que señalan sucesos que ocurrirán mas adelante en el argumento

formal style: a style of writing or speaking that is appropriate for formal communication such as in academics or business
estilo formal: estilo de escribir o hablar adecuado para la comunicación formal como la académica o comercial

free verse: a kind of poetry that does not follow any regular pattern, rhythm, or rhyme
verso libre: tipo de poesía que no sigue ningún patrón, ritmo o rima regular

G

genre: a category or type of literature, such as short story, folk tale, poem, novel, play
género: categoría o tipo de literatura, como el cuento corto, cuento folclórico, poema, novela, obra teatral

global revision: the process of deeply revising a text to improve organization, development of ideas, focus, and voice
revisión global: proceso de revisar en profundidad un texto para mejorar su organización, desarrollo de ideas, enfoque y voz

graphic novel: a narrative told through visuals and captions
novela gráfica: narrativa que se cuenta por medio de efectos visuales y leyendas

H

headline: a short piece of text at the top of an article, usually in larger type, designed to be the first words the audience reads
titular: trozo corto de texto en la parte superior de un artículo, habitualmente en letra más grande, diseñado para ser las primeras palabras que el público lear

humor: the quality of being comical or amusing
humor: cualidad de ser cómico o divertido

hook: *n.* a compelling idea or statement designed to get readers' attention in an introduction
gancho: *n.* idea o afirmación atractiva diseñada para captar la atención del lector en una introducción

hyperbole: extreme exaggeration used for emphasis, often used for comic effect
hypérbole: exageración extrema usada para dar énfasis, habitualmente usada para dar efecto cómico

I

iamb: a metrical foot that consists of an unstressed syllable followed by a stressed syllable
yambo: pie métrico que consta de una sílaba átona seguida de una sílaba tónica

iambic pentameter: a rhythmic pattern of five feet (or units) of one unstressed syllable followed by a stressed syllable
pentámetro yámbico: patrón rítmico de cinco pies (o unidades) de una sílaba átona seguida de una sílaba tónica

idiom: a figure of speech that cannot be defined literally
expresión idiomatica: figura del discurso que no puede definirse literalmente

image: a picture, drawing, photograph, illustration, chart, or other graphic that is designed to affect the audience in some purposeful way
imagen: pintura, dibujo, fotografía, ilustración, cuadro u otra gráfica diseñada para producir algún efecto intencional sobre el público

imagery: descriptive or figurative language used to create word pictures; imagery is created by details that appeal to one or more of the five senses
imaginería: lenguaje descriptivo o figurativo utilizado para crear imágenes verbales; la imaginería es creada por detalles que apelan a uno o más de los cinco sentidos

improvise: to respond or perform on the spur of the moment
improvisar: reaccionar o representar impulsivamente

incident: a distinct piece of action as in an episode in a story or a play. More than one incident may make up an event.
incidente: trozo de acción distintivo como un episodio de un cuento o de una obra teatral. Más de un incidente puede conformar un suceso.

inference: a logical guess or conclusion based on observation, prior experience, or textual evidence
inferencia: conjetura o conclusión lógica basada en la observación, experiencias anteriores o evidencia textual

inflection: the emphasis a speaker places on words through change in pitch or volume
inflexión: énfasis que pone un orador en las palabras por medio del cambio de tono o volumen

interpretation: a writer's or artist's representation of the meaning of a story or idea
interpretación: representación que hace un escritor o artista del significado de un cuento o idea

interview: a meeting between two people in which one, usually a reporter, asks the other questions to get that person's views on a subject
entrevista: reunión entre dos personas, en la que una, normalmente un reportero, hace preguntas a la otra para conocer sus opiniones acerca de un tema

introduction: the opening paragraph of an essay, which must get the reader's attention and indicate the topic
introducción: párrafo inicial de un ensayo, que debe captar la atención del lector e indicar el tema

L

legend: a traditional story believed to be based on actual people and events. Legends, which typically celebrate heroic individuals or significant achievements, tend to express the values of a culture.
leyenda: cuento tradicional que se considera basado en personas y sucesos reales. Las leyendas, que típicamente celebran a individuos heroicos o logros importantes, tienden a expresar los valores de una cultura.

limerick: a light, humorous, nonsensical verse of few lines, usually with a rhyme scheme of a-a-b-b-a
quintilla: verso liviano, humorístico, disparatado y de pocas líneas, normalmente con un esquema a-a-b-b-a

listening: the process of receiving a message and making meaning of it from verbal and nonverbal cues
escuchar: proceso de recibir el mensaje y comprender su significado a partir de claves verbales y no verbales

literary analysis: the process of examining closely and commenting on the elements of a literary work
análisis literario: proceso de examinar atentamente y comentar los elementos de una obra literaria

local revision: revising a text on a word or sentence level
revisión local: revisar un texto a nivel de palabras o de oraciones

logo: a unique design symbol used to identify a company visually
logotipo: símbolo único de diseño, utilizado para identificar visualmente una empresa

logos: a rhetorical appeal to reason or logic through statistics, facts, and reasonable examples
logos: apelación retórica a la razón o la lógica por medio de estadísticas, hechos y ejemplos razonables

M

media: the various means of mass communication, such as radio, television, newspapers, and magazines
medios de comunicación: los diversos medios de comunicación masiva, como radio, televisión, periódicos y revistas

media channel: a type of media, such as television or newspaper
canal mediático: tipo de medios de comunicación, como televisión o periódicos

metaphor: a comparison between two unlike things in which one thing becomes another
metáfora: comparación entre dos cosas diferentes en la que una cosa se convierte en otra

monologue: a speech or written expression of thoughts by a character
monólogo: discurso o expresión escrita de pensamientos por parte de un personaje

mood: the overall emotional quality of a work, which is created by the author's language and tone and the subject matter
carácter: la calidad emocional general de una obra, que es creada por el lenguaje y tono del autor y por el tema

motif: a recurring element, image, or idea in a work of literature
motivo: elemento, imagen o idea recurrente en una obra literaria

multimedia: the use of several media (for example, print, film, audio, and video) to communicate ideas
multimedia: uso de varios medios de comunicación (por ejemplo: impresos, cine, audio y video) para comunicar ideas

multiple intelligences: the variety of learning styles that everyone has in varying degrees. In each individual, different intelligences predominate.
inteligencias múltiples: diversidad de estilos de aprendizaje que todos tienen en diversos grados. En cada individuo predominan diferentes inteligencias.

myth: a traditional story that explains the actions of gods or heroes or the origins of the elements of nature
mito: cuento tradicional que explica las acciones de dioses o héroes o los orígenes de los elementos de la naturaleza

N

narrative: a type of writing that tells a story or describes a sequence of events in an incident

narrativa: tipo de escritura que cuenta un cuento o describe una secuencia de sucesos de un incidente

narrative poem: a story told in verse

poema narrativo: historia contada en verso

news article: an article in a news publication that objectively presents both sides of an issue

artículo noticioso: artículo de una publicación noticiosa que presenta objetivamente ambos lados de un asunto

nonfiction: writing that is based on facts and actual events

no ficción: escritura que se basa en hechos o acontecimientos reales

nonprint text: a text, such as film or graphics, that communicates ideas without print

texto no impreso: texto, como una película o gráfica, que comunica ideas sin imprimir

nonverbal communication: gestures, facial expressions, and inflection that form unspoken communication

comunicación no verbal: gestos, expresiones faciales e inflexión que forman la comunicación no hablada

novel: a type of literary genre that tells a fictional story

novela: tipo de género literario que cuenta una historia ficticia

O

objective: supported by facts and not influenced by personal opinion

objetivo: apoyado por hechos y no influenciado por la opinión personal

objective camera view: in film, when the camera takes a neutral point of view

visión objetiva de la cámara: en el cine, cuando la cámara toma un punto de vista neutro

omniscient: a third-person point of view in which the narrator is all-knowing

omnisciente: punto de vista de una tercera persona, en la que el narador lo sabe todo

onomatopoeia: the use of words that imitate the sounds of what they describe

onomatopeya: el uso de palabras que imitan los sonidos de lo que describen

one-liner: a short joke or witticism expressed in a single sentence

agudeza: chiste u comentario ingenioso que se expresa en una sola oración.

opinion: a perspective that can be debated

opinión: perspectiva que es debatible

oral interpretation: reading aloud a literary text with expression

interpretación oral: leer en voz alta un texto literario con expresión

oxymoron: a figure of speech in which the words seem to contradict each other; for example, "jumbo shrimp"

oxímoron: figura del discurso en la que las palabras parecen contradecirse mutuamente; por ejemplo, "audaz cobardía"

P

pantomime: a form of acting without words, in which motions, gestures, and expressions convey emotions or situations

pantomima: forma de actuación sin palabras, en la que los movimientos, gestos y expresiones transmiten emociones o situationes

paraphrase: to restate in one's own words

parafrasear: reformular en nuestras propias palabras

parody: a humorous imitation of a literary work

parodia: imitación humorística de una obra literaria

pathos: a rhetorical appeal to the reader's or listener's senses or emotions through connotative language and imagery

pathos: apelación retórica a los sentidos o emociones del lector u oyente por medio de un lenguaje connotativo y figurado

performance: presenting or staging a play

actuación: presentar o poner en escena una obra teatral

persona: the voice or character speaking or narrating a story

persona: voz o personaje que habla o narra una historia

personal letter: a written communication between friends, relatives, or acquaintances that shares news, thoughts, or feelings

carta personal: comunicación escrita entre amigos, parientes o conocidos, que comparte noticias, pensamientos o sentimientos

personal narrative: a piece of writing that describes an incident and includes a personal response to and reflection on the incident
narrativa personal: texto escrito que describe un incidente e incluye una reacción personal ante el incidente y una reflexión acerca de él

personification: a kind of metaphor that gives objects or abstract ideas human characteristics
personificación: tipo de metáfora que da características humanas a los objetos o ideas abstractas

perspective: the way a specific character views a situation or other characters
perspectiva: manera en que un personaje específico visualiza una situación o a otros personajes

persuasion: the act or skill of causing someone to do or believe something
persuasión: acto o destreza de hacer que alguien haga o crea algo

persuasive essay: an essay that attempts to convince the reader to take an action or believe an idea
ensayo persuasivo: ensayo que intenta convencer al lector de que realice una acción o crea una idea

phrasing: dividing a speech into smaller parts, adding pauses for emphasis
frasear: dividir un discurso en partes más pequeñas, añadiendo pausas para dar énfasis

pitch: the highness or lowness of a sound, particularly the voice in speaking
tono: altura de un sonido, especialmente de la voz al hablar

plagiarism: taking and using as your own the words and ideas of another
plagio: tomar y usar como propias las palabras e ideas de otro

plot: the sequence of related events that make up a story or novel
trama: secuencia de sucesos relacionados, que conforman un cuento o novela

point of view: the perspective from which a story is told. In **first-person** point of view, the teller is a character in the story telling what he or she sees or knows. In **third-person** point of view, the narrator is someone outside of the story.
punto de vista: perspectiva desde la cual se cuenta una historia. En el punto de vista de la **primera persona**, el relator es un personaje del cuento que narra lo que ve o sabe. En el punto de vista de la **tercera persona**, el narrador es alguien que está fuera del cuento.

prediction: a logical guess or assumption about something that has not yet happened
predicción: conjetura lógica o suposición acerca de algo que aún no ha ocurrido

presentation: delivery of a formal reading, talk, or performance
presentación: entrega de una lectura, charla o representación formal

prose: the ordinary form of written language, using sentences and paragraphs; writing that is not poetry, drama, or song
prosa: forma común del lenguaje escrito, usando oraciones y párrafos; escritura que no es poesía, drama ni canción

pun: the humorous use of a word or words to suggest another word with the same sound or a different meaning
retruécano: uso humorístico de una o varias palabras para sugerir otra palabra que tiene el mismo sonido o un significado diferente

purpose: the reason for writing; what the writer hopes to accomplish
propósito: razón para escribir; lo que el escritor espera lograr

Q

quatrain: a four-line stanza in poetry
cuarteta: en poesía, estrofa de cuatro versos

R

rate: the speed at which a speaker delivers words
rapidez: velocidad a la que el orador pronuncia las palabras

reasons: the points that explain why the author is making a certain claim
razones: los puntos que explican por qué un autor propone cierta afirmacón

reflection: a kind of thinking and writing that seriously explores the significance of an experience, idea, or observation
reflexión: tipo de pensamiento y escritura que explora seriamente la importancia de una experiencia, idea u observación

reflective essay: an essay in which the writer explores the significance of an experience or observation
ensayo reflexivo: ensayo en que el autor explora la importancia de una experiencia u observación

refrain: a regularly repeated word, phrase, line, or group of lines in a poem or song

estribillo: palabra, frase, verso o grupo de versos de un poema o canción que se repite con regularidad

relevant: closely connected to the matter at hand (for example, evidence supporting a claim)

relevante: relacionado estrechamente con el asunto en cuestión (por ejemplo, la evidencia que apoya una afirmación)

repetition: the use of the same words or structure over again

repetición: uso de las mismas palabras o estructura una y otra vez

research: (*v.*) to locate information from a variety of sources; (*n.*) the information found from investigating a variety of sources

investigar: (*v.*) proceso de buscar información en una variedad de fuentes; *también*, **investigación** (*n.*) información que se halla al investigar una variedad de fuentes

resolution: the outcome of the conflict of a story, when loose ends are wrapped up

resolución: resultado del conflicto de un cuento, cuando se atan los cabos sueltos

revision: a process of evaluating a written piece to improve coherence and use of language; *see also* local revision, global revision

revisión: proceso de evaluar un texto escrito para mejorar la coherencia y el uso del lenguaje; *ver también*, revisión local, revisión global

rhetorical appeals: the use of emotional, ethical, and logical arguments to persuade in writing or speaking

recursos retóricos: uso de argumentos emotivos, éticos y lógicos para persuadir al escribir o hablar

rhetorical question: a question asked to emphasize a point or create an effect; no answer is expected

pregunta retórica: pregunta que se hace para enfatizar un punto o crear un efecto; no se espera una respuesta

rhyme: the repetition of sounds at the ends of words

rima: repetición de sonidos al final de las palabras

rhyme scheme: a consistent pattern of end rhyme throughout a poem

esquema de la rima: patrón consistente de una rima final a lo largo de un poema

rhythm: the pattern of stressed and unstressed syllables in spoken or written language, especially in poetry

ritmo: patrón de sílabas acentuadas y no acentuadas en lenguaje hablado o escrito, especialmente en poesía

rising action: major events that develop the plot of a story and lead to the climax

acción ascendente: sucesos importantes que desarrollan la trama de un cuento y conducen al clímax

S

science fiction: a genre in which the imaginary elements of the story could be scientifically possible

ciencia ficción: género en que los elementos imaginarios del cuento podrían ser científicamente posibles

sensory language: words or information that appeal to the five senses

lenguaje sensorial: palabras o información que apelan a los cinco sentidos

sequence: the order in which events happen

secuencia: orden en que ocurren los sucesos

setting: the time and the place in which a narrative occurs

ambiente: tiempo y lugar en que ocurre un relato

short story: a work of fiction that presents a sequence of events, or plot, that deals with a conflict

cuento corto: obra de ficción que presenta una secuencia de sucesos, o trama, que tratan de un conflicto

simile: a comparison between two unlike things, using the words *like* or *as*

símil: comparación entre dos cosas diferentes usando las palabras como o *tan*

slogan: a catchphrase that evokes a particular feeling about a company and its product

eslogan: frase o consigna publicitaria que evoca un sentimiento en particular acerca de una empresa y su producto

source: a place from which information comes or is obtained

fuente: lugar de donde surge o se obtiene la información

speaker: the voice that communicates with the reader of a poem

hablante: la voz que se comunica con el lector de un poema

speaking: the process of sharing information, ideas, and emotions using verbal and nonverbal means communication

hablar: proceso de compartir información, ideas y emociones usando medios de comunicación verbales y no verbales

stanza: a group of lines, usually similar in length and pattern, that form a unit within a poem

estrofa: grupo de versos, normalmente similares en longitud y patrón, que forman una unidad dentro de un poema

stereotype: a fixed, oversimplified image of a person, group, or idea; something conforming to that image
estereotipo: imagen fija y demasiado simplificada de una persona, grupo o idea; algo que cumple esa imagen

subjective: influenced by personal opinions or ideas
subjectivo: influenciado por opiniones o ideas personales

subjective camera view: in film, when the camera seems to show the events through a character's eyes
visión subjetiva de la cámara: en el cine, cuando la cámara parece mostrar los sucesos a través de los ojos de un personaje

subplot: a secondary plot that occurs along with a main plot
trama secundaria: argumento secundario que ocurre conjuntamente con un argumento principal

sufficient: adequate for the purpose of supporting a claim or reason
suficiente: adecuado para cumplir con el propósito de apoyar una afirmación o razón

summarize: to briefly restate the main ideas of a piece of writing
resumir: reformular brevemente las ideas principales de un texto escrito

supporting details: in writing, evidence (facts, statistics, examples) that supports the topic sentence
detalles de apoyo: en la escritura, evidencia (hechos, estadísticas ejemplos) que apoya la oracon principal

symbol: an object, a person, or a place that stands for something else
símbolo: objeto, persona o lugar que representa otra cosa

symbolism: the use of symbols
simbolismo: el uso de símbolos

synonyms: words with similar meanings
sinónimos: palabras con significados semejantes

synthesize: to combine elements from different sources to create, express, or support a new idea
sintetizar: combinar elementos de diferentes fuentes para crear, expresar o apoyar una idea nueva

T

tableau: a purposeful arrangement of characters frozen as if in a painting or a photograph
cuadro: disposición intencional de personajes que permanecen inmóviles como en una pintura o foto

talking points: important points or concepts to be included in a presentation
puntos centrales: puntos o conceptos importantes a incluirse en una presentación

tall tale: a highly exaggerated and often humorous story about folk heroes in local settings
cuento increíble: cuento muy exagerado y normalmente humorístico acerca de héroes folclóricos en ambientes locales

target audience: the specific group of people that advertisers aim to persuade to buy
público objetivo: grupo específico de personas a quienes los publicistas desean persuadir de comprar

tempo: the speed or rate of speaking
ritmo: velocidad o rapidez al hablar

textual evidence: quotations, summaries, or paraphrases from text passages to support a position
evidencia textual: citas, resúmenes o paráfrasis de pasajes de texto para apoyar una position

theme: the central idea, message, or purpose of a literary work
tema: idea, mensaje o propósito central de una obra literaria

thesis statement: a sentence, in the introduction of an essay, that states the writer's position or opinion on the topic of the essay
enunciado de tesis: oración, en la introducción de un ensayo, que plantea el punto de vista u opinión del autor acerca del tema del ensayo

tone: a writer's or speaker's attitude toward a subject
tono: actitud de un escritor u orador hacia un tema

topic sentence: a sentence that states the main idea of a paragraph; in an essay, it also makes a point that supports the thesis statement
oración principal: oración que plantea la idea principal de un párrafo; en un ensayo, también plantea un punto que apoya el enunciado de tesis

transitions: words or phrases that connect ideas, details, or events in writing
transiciones: palabras o frases que conectan ideas, detalles o sucesos de un escrito

TV news story: a report on a news program about a specific event
documental de televisión: reportaje en un programa noticioso acerca de un suceso específico

U

utopia: an ideal or perfect place
utopía: lugar ideal o perfecto

V

verse: a unit of poetry, such as a line or a stanza
verso: unidad de la poesía, como un verso o una estrofa

voice: a writer's distinctive use of language
voz: uso distintivo del lenguaje por parte de un escritor

voice-over: the voice of an unseen character in film expressing his or her thoughts
voz en off: voz de un personaje de una película, que no se ve pero que expresa sus pensamientos

volume: the degree of loudness of a speaker's voice or other sound
volumen: grado de intensidad sonora de la voz de un orador o de otro sonido

W

wordplay: a witty or clever verbal exchange or a play on words
juego de palabras: intercambio verbal ingenioso u ocurrente o un juego con palabras

Index of Skills

Literary Skills

Action, 40, 41, 54, 210, 375

Advertising, 94, 95–96, 97, 98, 104, 106, 107–112, 118, 120

Alliteration, 285, 286, 336, 344

Allusion, 221

Analyzing faulty reasoning, 121

Annotating the text, 248, 366, 378, 379, 380

Argumentative text, 94, 136–137, 143, 164, 165

Article, 309

Assonance, 285, 286

Atmosphere, 199, 317

Audience, 103, 109, 115, 118, 142, 152, 157, 164, 165, 304, 309

Author's purpose, 49, 142, 151, 163, 229, 296, 304, 309

Autobiography, 6, 17, 118, 238, 239–240, 241, 243

Biography, 6, 235–236, 238, 241, 243

Cause-and-effect relationship, 107, 110, 129, 164, 307

Character, 54, 72, 87, 89, 211, 216, 225–228, 233, 287, 288, 309, 327, 337, 346, 348, 358

  actions, 40, 41, 54, 210, 375

  motivations and behaviors of, 66, 71, 76, 84, 216, 242, 243, 262, 274, 346, 348, 368, 375

  point of view of, 201, 213, 326, 327, 337, 338

Characterization, 22, 34, 35, 45, 66, 67, 69, 71, 73, 83, 194, 200–201, 210, 231, 316, 325, 326, 360, 371, 378

  actions, 41, 64, 70, 84, 194, 200, 210, 365

  appearance, 200, 365, 375

  emotions, 64, 210, 260, 262, 317, 346, 354, 365, 374, 375, 379

  thoughts, 65, 66, 194, 200, 359, 364, 365, 379

  words, 70, 194, 200, 210, 274–275, 375

Claim, 143, 149, 153, 170, 173, 179

Conflict, 54, 55, 66, 70, 87, 199, 201, 216, 217, 228, 309, 360

Consonance, 285, 286

Controlling idea, 66, 97, 112

Correspondence, 309

Creation stories/myths, 78–83, 85, 86

Details, 9, 22, 23, 24, 34, 35, 36, 42, 45, 46–47, 48, 65, 67, 69, 70, 75, 89, 96, 102, 103, 141, 149, 163, 172, 200, 210, 212, 213, 231, 236, 240, 241, 258, 261, 262, 268, 274, 325, 329, 335, 340, 353, 358, 363, 367, 371

Dialogue, 22, 40, 64, 65, 66, 70, 231, 326, 357, 358, 359, 363, 364, 366, 379

Diction (word choice), 12, 13, 16, 34, 36, 46, 64, 65, 83, 141, 151, 163, 179, 220, 256, 285, 294, 309, 316, 317, 325, 326, 335

Direct address, 157, 158, 165

Drama, 295, 308, 338, 354, 357–358, 360–362, 366–367, 371–373

Effect, 13, 38, 107, 110, 111, 112, 118, 141, 150, 163, 165–166, 167, 170, 173, 282, 292, 293, 294, 308, 309, 310, 318, 319, 325, 326, 336, 338, 341, 344, 376, 378

Effectiveness, 41, 49, 50, 88, 89, 94, 110, 111, 112, 113, 157, 164, 174, 179, 204, 217, 248, 256, 269, 327, 339, 348, 356, 359, 379

Essay, 27, 39, 110, 131, 134, 135, 136–137, 138–140, 141, 143, 149, 154, 168–169, 171–172, 177–178, 204, 229, 309

Essential questions, 4, 53, 94, 124, 135, 190, 231, 282, 341

Examples, 113, 114, 134, 154, 155, 156, 163, 201, 226, 228, 306, 318, 326, 328, 335, 374

Fable, 54, 73–75

Fairy tale, 54

Figurative language, 13, 35, 36, 46–47, 48, 52, 55, 89, 206, 207, 210, 241, 269, 309, 310, 326, 340, 345

Figurative meaning, 13, 16, 55, 76, 77, 212, 213, 310

Flashback, 198, 199, 212

Folklore, 54, 80

Foreshadowing, 199

Genre, 6, 242, 243

  types of, 6, 7, 17

Haiku, 289, 293

Historical facts, 232, 239, 242, 243, 256, 262, 269, 337

Humor, 141, 296, 297, 298, 310, 325, 326

Hyperbole, 13, 121, 310, 318

Imagery, 46, 52, 63, 70, 82, 206, 207, 210, 212, 232, 242, 258, 261, 274, 284, 289, 291, 293, 296, 310, 315, 317, 319, 340, 343, 345

Incident, response, reflection, 17, 23, 24, 34, 35, 46

Inferring, 65, 76, 83, 103, 232, 265, 316, 353

Informational text, 78–79, 95–96, 97, 100–102, 103, 110, 116–117, 129, 131, 143, 252–253, 329–330, 335, 336, 349–352, 353

Internal rhyme, 318

Interpreting images, 47, 232, 249, 250, 264, 268

Key ideas, 79, 97, 134, 141, 259, 326, 329, 331, 337

Legend, 54

Letter, 309

Literal meanings, 55, 212, 213

Literary terms, 2, 6, 9, 13, 46, 54, 55, 92, 94, 110, 157, 188, 190, 197, 198, 199, 202, 210, 221, 280, 282, 285, 294, 295, 305, 309, 318, 323, 357

Loaded language, 138, 141, 166, 167

Logical fallacies, 166–167

Memoir, 6, 29–33

Mental images, 201, 309

Metaphor, 13, 34, 310, 318

Meter, 221, 325

Monologue, 282, 295, 300–303, 304, 305, 306, 307, 325, 327, 338, 354, 355, 356

Mood, 210, 311, 316, 317

Motif, 202, 204, 208, 212, 213, 226, 227, 228

Myth, 54–55, 56–63, 67–69, 71, 78–83, 85, 86

Narrative, 17, 53, 309, 326, 327, 339

  personal, 6, 17, 18–21, 23, 29–33, 39, 40, 42–44, 49

  poetry, 309, 323–324, 326, 327

News article, 125–127, 150, 151

Nonfiction, 260–261, 263, 265, 269

Novel, 195, 197, 199, 201, 202, 209, 210, 213, 216, 225, 229, 231

Occasion, 142, 152

Onomatopoeia, 311, 336

Opinion, 38, 110, 121, 132, 143, 164, 211, 242, 248, 336

Oral tradition, 54, 295

Reading Skills

Writing Skills

Index of Authors and Titles

Image Credits